# *Liberating the*
# Bruised

Rev. Dr. Joe Allbright

# Liberating the Bruised

PRINTED IN THE UNITED STATES OF AMERICA
BY SMOOTH SAILING PRESS

Smooth Sailing Press
9306 Max Conrad Drive / Suite C / Spring, Texas 77379
(281) 251-0830
www.smoothsailingpress.com

First Printing May 1997
Second Printing 2005
Third Printing 2011

ISBN: 978-1-933660-47-9

Scripture quotations marked NSSB are taken from **The New Scofield Study Bible**, New York: Oxford University Press, 1967

SMOOTH SAILING
PRESS
www.smoothsailingpress.com

**Our Lord Jesus Christ** *"...bore our sin in His own body on the tree, that we, having died in our sins, might live for righteousness..."*
(II Peter 2:24)

**Lord Jesus**, *"...You are my rock and my fortress; therefore, for Your name's sake, lead me and guide me. Pull me out of the net which they have secretly laid for me, for You are my strength. Into Your hand I commit my spirit; You have redeemed me, O LORD God of truth."*
(Psalm 31:3)

# ACKNOWLEDGMENTS

From the bottom of my heart I thank you, my precious sister-in-the-Lord, Sandy Griffin, for editing and proof-reading *"Liberating the Bruised"*. I'm so thankful for your dedication and sacrifice of your time to enhance this book for the sake of helping hurting souls. I remain so very grateful to you and our dear brother-in-the-Lord, Rev. Buddy Griffin, for your loving encouragement and prayer support as I sought to fulfill God's will in writing this book. May the Lord bless you abundantly!

To all the anonymous, untold thousands who have supported me over the years with their love, prayers, and sacrificial love offerings, thank you from the bottom of my heart! God bless you abundantly!

To Rita, my precious wife and co-laborer in God's Kingdom, I thank you so much for your diligent work on the computer to produce the printed material. I am so grateful for your faithful love and support since our marriage in 1957. A huge thanks! I love you! May the Lord bless you abundantly!

And, last but surely not least, to my children, Michele, Joe Jr. and Michael, their spouses and children who are all so very precious to me, thank you from the depth of my heart for all your love and support that I have so faithfully received from you in spite of your sacrifices due to my ministry. I love you! God bless you abundantly!

Thank you all again from the bottom of my heart! God bless each one of you for joining hearts with me in making the wonderful truths of our Lord—our ultimate, Wonderful Counselor—available to help liberate the bruised!

# FOREWORD

# THERE IS VICTORY FOR GOD'S CHILDREN

In I Corinthians 13, we see that God's "love hopeth all things." His love within my heart is full of hope. My hope is that the contents of this book from cover to cover will give you a very beneficial view of how counselees with different types of problems can be helped. I pray that God will use the case studies of my precious counselees to more deeply implant hope and the truth that God is truly sufficient, no matter how difficult or complex the case. Whether the problem involves the need for salvation, or a saved soul's deeply-rooted hurts, along with ancestral demons, lifestyle demons, or fragmented personalities, I hope these counselees will bring to light that there is…without doubt, victory through Jesus Christ. I hope they will give hope to the hopeless and empty out unbelief and instill belief in God and His truths. I pray that you will see that our Lord Jesus wants His people free, and that it is the Christian's responsibility and right to appropriate our victory in Him.

My heart's prayer is that this book will make you hungrier to faithfully feed on God's Word in order to gain His knowledge and wisdom as you walk upon His pathways for your life. My hope is that this book will help open your eyes more widely to the truths in God's Word concerning the spiritual battle in which we are engaged against the enemy, Satan the father of lies, and that you can stand strong against him in the Lord and the power of His might. My desire is that you will consistently refuse to succumb to defeat, believing and trusting that God has already made deliverance, peace, and joy available. I pray that you will choose to continually stay **snuggled up** to Him and get to know Him well…behold Him in His awesome love, mercy, grace, and power.

As I remember scores and scores of desperate, anxious people willing to wait seven months or more to gain help from ministries like mine, I hope that this book will help multiply that aid for them. Over and over again I have heard so many souls tell me that they long so for their pastor and church to become equipped to offer this type of counseling. This is my hope also.

My prayer is that this book will help encourage you as pastors and as church members to stand strong and fulfill God's calling in your individual yet corporate lives as God's Church. I pray that you will join together in unity and choose not to shirk your mission on earth and to battle diligently against the Devil and his demonic forces for the sake of others until Jesus comes. I pray that the biblical truths that I have shared, along with those Christian men whom I have quoted who are strong in doctrine will be imbedded deeply in your hearts and will be used for God's glory. My hope is that you as pastors and flock will refuse to be intimidated by people who have not yet come to believe God's truths in these matters, and will care enough to share His truths with the unbelieving ones and those who have not yet heard.

I pray that you will choose to not succumb to Satan's temptation to fearfully maintain silence on the subject of the demonic, but will choose to speak confidently, teaching God's truths that will help train up the untaught and set the captives free. The Lord addressed this very need when He said:

*...When he saw the multitudes, he was moved with compassion on them, because they were faint, and were scattered abroad, as sheep having no shepherd. Then saith he unto his disciples, the harvest truly is plenteous, but the laborers are few. Pray ye, therefore, the Lord of the harvest, that he will send forth laborers into his harvest. And when he had called unto him his twelve disciples, he gave them power against unclean spirits, to cast them out... (Matt. 9:36-10:1; NSSB)*

*Take heed, therefore, unto yourselves, and to all the flock, over which the Holy Spirit hath made you overseers, to feed the church of God, which he hath purchased with his own blood. For I know this, that after my departing shall grievous wolves enter in among you, not sparing the flock. (Acts 20:28-29; NSSB)*

It is my heart's desire, hope, and prayer that this book will be a tool to help equip the saints in spiritual warfare in these last days, and to encourage them to snuggle up to the Lord and His Word—to not only witness to the lost but also to labor in **Liberating the Bruised**. My hope is that my appeal is heard and heeded, as I've been faithful to preach God's Word. My earnest prayer is that when our earthly walks are done, we will hear Jesus say, "...Well done, thou good and faithful servant..." (Matt. 25:21).

*Rev. Dr. Joe Allbright*

# PREFACE

I would like for you to know a little about my background before you read this book. For out of my past pain and suffering, the Lord brought forth my empathy and compassion for hurting, troubled souls, thus, my reason for obeying the Lord when He instructed me to write **Liberating the Bruised**.

I was born in a small, frame house on the old Love Lady Road, five miles outside a small east Texas town named Crockett. I was born to a share-cropper and his wife who already had one child, a two-year-old son. My dad died nine days before my first birthday. Being a share-cropper, his death brought not only the loss of a dad and provider, but also the loss of our home. My mother, brother, and I were kicked from **pillar to post** for about a year. Then, my mother chose to give my brother and me away because she was unable to work as a live-in maid and keep us at the same time.

The day before I was two years old, I was given to a man and woman who lived in Houston, in a part of town called the Heights. When I was eight years old--a week after Christmas--this man died, and his wife had to go to work. When I was nine, "Mama Bea," as I called her, worked as a practical nurse, going from home to home and caring for rich ladies and their new babies for two-week stays. The first week, she would spend twenty-four hours a day with them. The second week, she would spend about fourteen hours a day. The third week, she would start over again with a new job. As a result, I stayed alone a great deal from the age of nine until the age of ten. I went to bed almost every night with a little dog named Tiny in one hand and a thirty-two revolver in the other. With the covers pulled over my head--I hoped a stranger wouldn't pull them down in the night. I lived my life in total worry and fear.

My mother came back into my life when I was ten, bringing with her my brother, whom I had seen about six times during the eight years I had lived with Mama Bea. She and my brother crowded into the little two-bedroom home with Mama Bea and me, and none of us got along very well. When I was eleven, my mother met and married our new milkman, who delivered milk to our home twice a week. He had been married and divorced three times. He didn't have any children and didn't want any children, yet he married a lady with two--and we didn't get along well either.

The four of us lived with Mama Bea until I was thirteen years old, and then we moved into our own home. That living arrangement lasted only about a year and a half. At that time my step-dad was called back into the Air Force, and he and my mother were eventually stationed in London, England. I was sent back to live with Mama Bea, while my brother was sent to live with a man we called Uncle Steve, who was a homosexual. Shortly thereafter, Mama Bea became ill and had to have major surgery, a situation which forced me to leave school at fifteen years of age--at the end of my ninth grade year--to get a job to support us. My brother helped me to find work at Texas Pipe Bending Company, where he also worked. From that day forward, I was never out of the workaday world.

I was saved when I was ten years old, through Baptist Temple's bus ministry in Houston's Heights. I was led to the Lord by their pastor, Dr. T. C. Jester, on a Saturday afternoon, October 12, 1946, and was baptized October 13, 1946. I spent the next fifteen years attending Baptist Temple.

At the age of twenty, at Baptist Temple, I met my one-and- only wife, Rita, and married her when I was twenty-one. She and I held teaching positions there for a number of years. What Rita didn't know about me when we married was that I was very insecure, and that God had called me to preach when I was eighteen years old. When I had gone down the aisle during the invitation that Sunday morning, the preacher had asked me why I had come forward. I was so insecure that I lied, and told him I had come to rededicate my life. I kept that call from Rita. That lie started a fifteen-year, secret run from God's will, with the last five years finding me a drunk.

During that time I entered the life insurance business, becoming very successful and making a lot of money. Still suffering from the rejection of my mother's leaving me, however, I always fought a tormenting loneliness, accompanied with questions of, "Did I even belong?" and "Should I have even been born?" I felt like I just didn't fit into this world. Due to the overwhelming feelings of inferiority, insecurity, and inadequacy, those fifteen years was characterized by my needing to be in control of my life, to excel, and to be financially successful and secure. Ultimately, the pressures of trying to excel and be socially accepted became overwhelming. The demands of the life insurance business put me in such a pressure-cooker that drinking became my sedative. Even though my drinking began on a social note, alcohol became my drug of choice, which allowed me to hide from the pain and yet live with a boldness that was drug-produced.

In the midst of those fifteen years, the Lord gave Rita and me three wonderful children. Rita and I are so grateful that all of our children and their wonderful mates are saved and love the Lord very much. We are also grateful for our precious grandchildren! We have been married since October 11, 1957, and we thank the Lord for the wonderful work He has done in our individual lives and marriage.

Because Rita was such a good wife and mother, my children didn't know that I drank alcohol, much less that I was an alcoholic, until I gave my testimony about it for the first time. I came in drunk from work after they were in bed and I, of course, was sober when I left for work in the mornings. I did care enough about my family that I didn't drink at the house. When I suffered hangovers in the mornings, Rita simply explained to the children that their daddy wasn't feeling well and asked them to be very quiet. During those days, the only way I actually hurt my children was by my long hours of work keeping me from spending quality time with them in their early years. Rita had to be both mom and dad to them. By the time Michele was twelve, I had quit drinking. So I am grateful to the Lord that while my children were still young, I was able to ask their forgiveness for neglecting them in some areas. I was blessed in being able to express my love for them in word and deed long before they **left the nest**.

When I was drinking Rita was hurt very deeply, but she chose not to seek to get back at me by turning my children against me. She chose to obey God and neither tried to change me nor to become a bitter woman over the situation. She took her heartache to the only One she knew could help her and change me--the Lord Jesus--and left the convicting and changing up to Him.

At last I allowed God to get through to me, and I finally surrendered to preach on April 9, 1969, at Oak Ridge Baptist Church just outside Conroe, Texas. I later earned four degrees, the last being from Trinity Theological Seminary--Doctor of Ministry in Counseling. I was in the pastorate for more than seven years. Then God placed me in a preaching and counseling ministry, where I have been since 1976. During this time, Rita and I have made biblical counseling available at no charge to hundreds and hundreds of sin-sick, broken-hearted, and hurting people. God's grace and His wonderful and generous people have made this ministry possible.

In addition to my preaching ministry, God has led us to specialize in three major areas of counseling, which I will explain in more detail later. The first area of our specialty concerns healing the inner-man by pulling down and eliminating demonic strongholds and claiming back ground lost to sin--ground lost through our own sin, as well as through the sins of others against us. This process deals from our childhood to the present. The second area involves dealing with fragmented personalities, or what psychology calls M.P.D. (Multiple Personality Disorders). The third area regards dealing with the demonic realm which manipulates and controls the lives of precious people.

As I began writing this book and thinking back to the time when I finally surrendered to God's call on my life at age thirty-three, I remembered the scripture He had used to call me, the one which so grabbed my heart and life. That scripture is found in Luke 4:18, 19 where the Lord Jesus said:

> *"The spirit of the Lord is upon me, because He hath anointed me to preach the gospel to the poor; He hath sent me to heal the brokenhearted, to preach deliverance to the captives and recovering of sight to the blind, to set at liberty them that are bruised, to preach the acceptable year of the Lord."*

I dedicate this book to all the hurting people to whom Rita and I have ministered since 1969. I have written it with the intent that it further the ministry of **Liberating the Bruised**.

# INTRODUCTION

There is a greatly neglected area in the world of counseling today. It is the need to tell people the whole, undiluted truth in order to expose what is really wrong in their lives and to explain what is needed to make corrections. I believe the truth is a priceless tool in working with people. We see this transformation explained in the Word of God in John 8:32 and 36: "And ye shall know the truth, and the truth shall make you free...if the Son therefore shall make you free, ye shall be free indeed." [1] Truth of every kind always--to some degree--sets us free, while untruth always puts us in bondage. Many people believe lies more quickly than they believe truth, especially if the truth is harder to visualize or **denotes** unpleasant or frightening subject matter. Many deny the truth despite knowing in their hearts that it is the truth.

Today I see a huge area of bondage in people's lives, caused by their blindness to and disbelief in God's great love and His plan of salvation that He provides through Jesus Christ. I also see a second area of bondage caused by failure to understand and believe that the Devil is real, and that he intensely hates God and mankind. Sadly enough, ignorance and unbelief have kept the people of the world largely unaware of the Devil, his demons, and their methods. Their choosing to remain ignorant of demonology (belief in demons) and spiritual powers has given Satan opportunity to put them in further bondage and to control their lives.

Ignorance and unbelief by God's people regarding Satan and his methods have made it even easier for the Devil to carry out his work as the great deceiver. The Devil has spent thousands of years striving to keep the world and the people of God blinded to himself, his ways, and his demons. Many churches in this century--in denying these truths about Satan and his methods--in essence take sides with Satan. Therefore, an attitude of teachability regarding all truth is essential if we are to be protected from the kind of false knowledge which has misled, destroyed, and killed many in both past and present generations.

One method that Satan uses to deceive God's people is to nullify the importance of Christians repenting of their sins and claiming back the ground that these sins have given to the Devil. If Satan accomplishes this deception, he knows these sins will be passed down to other generations as inherited iniquity. In the Ten Commandments the Lord promised that He would visit the iniquity of the fathers to the third and fourth generations of their descendants. This promise is found in Exodus 20:5, 6 where the Lord says:

> *...For I, the Lord your God, am a jealous God, visiting the iniquity of the fathers upon the children to the third and fourth generations of those who hate me, but showing mercy to thousands of those who love me and keep my commandments. (Also Ex. 24:7; Num. 14:18; and Deut. 5:9; NSSB)*

Later I will have much more to say about the passing down of the iniquity of the fathers.

One of the most amazing developments in today's world is the overwhelming resurgence of interest in Satan and occultic activities. For a number of years, we did not see such interest. It almost seemed as though Satan were dead or that he just didn't exist. Also, during our generation, a movement sprang forth proclaiming "God is dead." It is increasingly apparent that both of these thoughts are untrue. God is definitely alive, and the Christian must conclude from studying God's Word and observing obvious demonic influences--both past and present--that Satan is very much alive. He is openly and brazenly involved in today's world, continuing to inflict the iniquity of past generations on the present, and to destroy and maim lives.

Many scientists, philosophers, educators, and others scoff at the thought of a real and personal Devil, but many well-educated people all over the world meet on a regular basis to worship Satan through some form of witchcraft or New Age cult. A number of years ago in San Francisco, Anton Szandor LaVey became the pastor and founding father of the First Satanic Church, which even carried a tax exempt status with the Internal Revenue Service. Some of the church members--who are fully dedicated to the worship of the Devil--have committed brutal crimes of sacrificial murder, while others have committed vile acts of sexual immorality.

For many years witchcraft, séances and fortune-telling were mostly found amidst the ignorant and superstitious, or those involved in childhood games. However, we can now read about these things (and sometimes even see them recommended) in highly-acclaimed journals, books, and newspapers. Local newspapers typically carry horoscopes, and prime-time television programs and newscasts report occultic events taking place in various communities.

The majority of Christians, either through blindness or lack of knowledge, do not participate in active warfare against Satan and his army of wicked spirits. Many Christians shrink away from this reality; consequently, there is a great absence of teaching in our churches as to how to protect us and others from this ever-present, ever-real threat of Satan and his demons. Denial of his existence and power is a method Satan uses to help him render God's Church powerless. For the Christian who prayerfully searches the scriptures with a teachable mind, the Word of God shines the much-needed light of truth upon the scope and nature of Satan's powers.

Many Christians, including preachers, claim that if Christ is preached, it is not necessary to direct our attention to the existence of the Devil, much less the demons. Largely due to the silence of preachers and the Church pertaining to the vital truth of what Satan and his demons can do to Christians, lessons in spiritual warfare go untaught. Because of this lack of teaching, a massive number of God's children have become prey for the Devil and his hordes. Today's Church, sadly but truthfully, is unprepared for the closing days of God's Church Age.

The Holy Word of God, in John 4:24, teaches that God is a Spirit and that He directs a great number of angels called **ministering spirits** (Hebrews 1:14) who worship God in heaven and carry out His assignments upon earth. At the same time, the Devil, our invisible enemy, directs a well-tuned and organized host of evil or demonic spirits. This group is a formidable foe aligned against God and His Church (Ephesians 6:11-12).

Many God-fearing pastors and professional counselors, who are sound in the doctrines of God's Word and who work with troubled Christians, testify to the reality of demons and to the certainty that Christians can be demonized. For the counselor, studying God's Word is vital, but it must be joined with continual prayer in seeking God's wisdom as to how to counsel. This combination of prayer and Bible study allows the Holy Spirit--who indwells all Christians--to teach those Christians on the front lines of the war against Satan. This also allows those who counsel hurting people to gain discernment and wisdom from God and gain first-hand knowledge of the enemy.

Dr. Merrill F. Unger, in his book, **What Demons Can Do To Saints**,[2] Dr. C. Fred Dickason, in his book **Demon Possession and the Christian**,[3] and Jessie Penn-Lewis, in her book **War on the Saints**,[4] all allude to the fact that the believer knows in his spirit the truth of the divine Word of God. They say that through experience the believer acquires a personal knowledge of the inspiration of scripture and of the truth of its testimony concerning the existence of supernatural beings, their diabolical works, and the ways in which they deceive and mislead the children of men.

In today's world of the ever-accelerating activity of Satan and his demons, the question that must be asked and answered is: "How far can demons go in working confusion in the lives of God's people?" The answer to this question is pressing and urgent, because of the wide-spread ignorance of and confessed uncertainty about this subject. These difficult times and the current experiences of God's people demands clarification of the precise part Satan and his demons play in the lives of believers. This clarification, in turn, requires a study of the connection between Satan and his demons and God's creatures.

Even though a study of Satan and the demonic world cannot be conclusive, there is one truth that stands out: It is that humanity, especially redeemed humanity, has Satan and his demons as its ferocious enemy. This foe is dedicated to alienating man from his Creator and to keeping man from knowing and appropriating Christ's saving and delivering grace. Satan is untiring and merciless in his hatred of God and His children. What makes the Devil such a dreadful foe is his position as the god of this world. God has allowed him a certain degree of authority over creation. Fallen angels or demons help Satan carry out his work. Satan's forces most assuredly confront all of fallen humanity, both the redeemed and the unredeemed.

**Liberating the Bruised** is an examination of the information that I have gathered during my many years in the preaching and counseling ministry along with a plea to "come let us reason together" about this information. It is a serious look at demonology--belief in demons--how it began and how it fits into biblical counseling and church ministry in the Church Age. It returns to foundational truths in both the Old and New Testaments, and also takes a fresh look at demonology today. I pray that this study will well serve the purpose of removing the overwhelming blindness and ignorance regarding the subject of Satan and his demonic forces. I pray that it will well serve to unveil the truth about the occult and its demonic assault on the world and God's people.

This author hopes that this crucial study will shed light on how to liberate the bruised through the understanding and application of biblical truths in counseling and that it will show the reality of the demonization of God's people in the Old and New Testaments as well as in our present day. I pray that this study will serve to sound the alarm about ancestral demons and the part they play in God's visiting the iniquity of the fathers upon the children to the third and fourth generations. Finally, I pray that it will serve to declare the fact that deliverance and victory over Satan and his demons is a reality for God's children.

God has led me to divide the book into four parts. Part one deals with **God's Foundational Truths on Demonology**. This thorough background is particularly essential for those with limited knowledge in this area. Part two covers **God's Gift of Reconciliation** and includes the fall and restoration of man and restoring true worship. It also unveils the clouded issues concerning body, soul, and spirit. Part three focuses on **God's Truths for Counseling Today's Bruised**, and includes practical suggestions about counseling and about dealing with demons, ancestral demons and fragmented personalities. Part four is about **God's Children, Liberated!** It consists of excerpts from some of my counseling sessions. I pray that you will benefit greatly as you read **Liberating the Bruised**.

**NOTES**

1.  C. I. Scofield, D.D., <u>The New Scofield Study Bible</u>, p. 1137 (All future references this edition will be referred to within the text with the scripture reference followed by NSSB.
2.  Merrill F. Unger, <u>What Demons Can Do To Saints</u>, p. 59, 60.
3.  C. Fred Dickason, <u>Demon Possession and the Christian</u>, p. 158, 159.
4.  Jessie Penn-Lewis, <u>War On The Saints</u>, p. 3.

# TABLE OF CONTENTS

# PART I
# GOD'S FOUNDATIONAL TRUTHS ON DEMONOLOGY

# PART II
## GOD'S GIFT OF RECONCILIATION

# PART III
# GOD'S TRUTHS FOR COUNSELING TODAY'S BRUISED

# PART IV
## GOD'S CHILDREN LIBERATED!

# PART I

# GOD'S FOUNDATIONAL TRUTHS
# ON
# DEMONOLOGY

# CHAPTER ONE
# THE ORIGIN OF DEMONOLOGY

## BIBLICAL ACCOUNTS OF ITS BEGINNING

A brief biblical study of the origin of the Devil, Satan, or Lucifer (to use a few of his names) is necessary to understand the origin of demonology. It will help to know where he came from, who he is, what he is doing, and where he is now.

The Holy Scriptures are the rightful source of information concerning Satan. The Bible directly mentions Satan more than two hundred times. He is found entering the realm of human history in Genesis 3, tempting Adam and Eve, with their yielding to the temptation resulting in their fall. In Matthew 4, Satan is seen tempting the God-Man, Jesus. Satan's coming final incarceration and eternal judgment are found in Revelation. I believe that the Christian has in the Bible the full true story of the fall, the works, and the destiny of Satan.

> *Son of man, take up a lamentation upon the king of Tyre, and say unto him, thus saith the Lord God: Thou sealest up the sum, full of wisdom, and perfect in beauty. Thou has been in Eden, the garden of God; every precious stone was thy covering, the sardius, topaz, and the diamond, the beryl, the onyx, and the jasper, the sapphire, the emerald, and the carbuncle, and gold; the workmanship of thy timbrels and of thy flutes was prepared in thee in the day that thou wast created. Thou art the anointed cherub that covereth, and I have set thee so; thou wast upon the holy mountain of God; thou hast walked up and down in the midst of the stones of fire. Thou wast perfect in thy ways from the day that thou wast created, till iniquity was found in thee. By the multitudes of thy merchandise they have filled the midst of thee with violence, and thou hast sinned; therefore I will cast thee as profane out of the mountain of God, and I will destroy thee, O covering cherub, from the midst of the stones of fire. Thine heart was lifted up because of thy beauty, thou hast corrupted thy wisdom by reason of thy brightness; I will cast thee to the ground, I will lay thee before kings, that they may behold thee. Thou hast defiled thy sanctuaries by the multitudes of thine iniquities, by the iniquity of thy merchandise; therefore will I bring forth a fire from the midst of thee; it shall devour thee, and I will bring thee to ashes upon the earth in the sight of all them that behold thee. All they that know thee among the people shall be appalled at thee; thou shalt be a terror, and never shalt thou be any more (Ezekiel 28:12-19; NSSB).*

Lester Sumrall in his book, **Demon Possession** says that Satan was created an archangel, one of the highest orders of God's creation. As I do, he believes that this description in Ezekiel can only be applied to a super being, not a man who ruled Tyre.[1] It is obvious that many of the responsibilities in the administration of the affairs of God had been entrusted to Lucifer (his name before the fall). In the Bible, there are different ranks of God's angels, and Lucifer had many of the host of heaven under his authority.

The word **cherubim** is the plural of **cherub** and they seem to be of the highest order or class. They were created by God with indescribable power and beauty. Their job seems to be proclaimers and protectors of God's presence and holiness. Only three cherubim are known to have had personal names given them. They are **Lucifer** (who fell), **Michael**, and **Gabriel**. At the gate of the Garden of Eden we find the first cherubim mentioned. They were posted to guard the way of the tree of life, keeping man out after the fall (Genesis 3:24). The next time they appear is in connection with the Tabernacle, the Ark, and the Mercy Seat. (Exodus 25:17-22). They were also designated **the cherubim of glory** (Hebrews 9:5), probably connected with the glory of God.

Dr. Jack R. Taylor in his book, **Victory Over the Devil** indicates he believes that Lucifer was not an inferior angel, but was one of God's archangels of the highest order and was probably over the highest order, the cherubim.[2] This belief is based on what is said in Ezekiel 28:14, "Thou art the anointed cherub that covereth."

The prophet Isaiah describes Lucifer's actual fall from his place of honor and glory as one of the archangels:

> *How art thou fallen from heaven, O Lucifer, son of the morning! How art thou cut down to the ground, who didst weaken the nations! For thou hast said in thine heart, I will ascend into heaven, I will exalt my throne above the stars of God; I will sit also upon the mount of the congregation, in the sides of the north, I will ascend above the heights of the clouds, I will be like the Most High (Isaiah 14:12-14; NSSB).*

Lucifer, in his unfallen state, possessed a will which was in total accord with the will of God. Had Lucifer possessed no will, he could not have later executed his own will and wishes, rebelling against God's will. Five references to his prideful will are found in the above quoted scripture in Isaiah. First, "I will ascend into heaven" (Isaiah 14:13); secondly, "I will exalt my throne above the stars of God"; thirdly, "I will sit also upon the mount of the congregation"; fourthly, "I will ascend above the heights of the clouds"; and finally, "I will be like the Most High." Thus, we can see the self-edification (represented by the five "I will" statements that caused the beautiful cherub of God, Lucifer, to become the diabolical creature known as Satan or the Devil. The apostle John provides more details of Satan's fall:

> *And there was war in heaven; Michael and his angels fought against the dragon, and the dragon fought and his angels, and prevailed not, neither was their place found any more in heaven. And the great dragon was cast out, that old serpent, called the Devil and Satan, who deceiveth the whole world; he was cast out into the earth, and his angels were cast out with him. And I heard a loud voice saying in heaven, Now is come salvation, and strength, and the kingdom of our God, and the power of his Christ; for the accuser of our brethren is cast down, who accused them before our God day and night...Woe to the inhabiters of the earth and of the sea! For the devil is come down unto you, having great wrath, because he knoweth that he hath but a short time (Revelation 12:7-10, 12; NSSB).*

So Lucifer, **The Day Star**, became the **Devil**. The reference to Lucifer as the **Devil** is the Greek word **diabolos**, meaning the **accuser** or the **slanderer**. He who was the epitome of light became the

epitome of darkness.[3] The Greek word for Satan is **satanas**, which simply means **adversary**.[4] Lucifer, in his rebellion, drew a multitude of angels with him in his rebellion and became Satan. He reigns over a kingdom of darkness that is organized in opposition to God (Matthew 12:26). The angels following Satan became the demons or evil spirits, Satan's minions.[5]

## A PROBING LOOK AT THE WORD "DEMON"

Demonology probably had its beginning when Lucifer (later to be referred to as Satan) fell from heaven. The fallen angels followed him from the realm of heaven. However, before this can be stated with probability, more probing is required to understand the word **demon** and the works of demons. The Greek word **daimon** means, "A demon, signified among pagan Greeks as an inferior deity, whether good or bad. In the N.T. it **denotes** an evil spirit. It is used in Matthew 8:31 mistranslated 'devils'."[6] The Zondervan Encyclopedia cites:

> The Eng. word 'demon' is derived from the Gr. daimon, which was used of rather anonymous influences whether of good or bad variety. When the concept of a supernatural spirit or intelligence subsequently developed in Gr. circles, the word gradually acquired a malign connotation, and was used as a general designation, of malevolent powers and characteristic functions.[7]

Dr. John L. Nevius, author of **Demon Possession**, says that Rev. James Gall, in his work entitled, **Primeval Man Unveiled**, declares that the **Authorized English Version of the New Testament** is not as clear as the revised version in its translation of the words **diabolos**, **daimonion**, and **daimon**. In the former, all three words are translated devil. In the revised version, only the word **diabolos** is translated **devil**, and the other two, **daimon** and **daimonion**, are translated demon, thus preserving the important distinction of the original Greek. The Greek words **daimon** and **daimonion** are used very frequently in the New Testament, both in their singular and plural state, but never interchangeably with **diabolos**, and always in a different sense than **diabolos**, which means the **accuser**. The synonym of **daimon** is **kakos**, (meaning *evil*), and of **daimonion** is **akathartos**, (meaning ***unclean spirit***). In the scripture, there is only one Devil, but there are many, many demons.[8]

## HISTORICAL EVIDENCES OF DEMONS

Who are these demons and where did they come from? We find references to them dating back to earliest times--the thought or belief in demons seems to be universal. Unger believes that earliest religious history demonstrates a universal belief in the Devil and his demons; that according to the Bible, degeneration from monotheism (belief in one God) to polytheism (belief in more than one God), resulted in Satan's blinding men, thus causing the most despicable forms of idolatry.[9] This degeneration is verified by what the apostle Paul says in Romans:

> *Because, when they knew God, they glorified him not as God, neither were thankful, but became vain in their imaginations, and their foolish heart was darkened. Professing themselves to be wise, they became fools, and changed the glory of the incorruptible God into an image made like corruptible man, and birds, and four-footed beasts and creeping things. Wherefore, God also gave them up to*

*uncleanness through the lusts of their own hearts, to dishonor their own bodies between themselves, who exchanged the truth of God for a lie, and worshiped and served the creature more than the Creator, who is blessed forever. Amen. For this cause God gave them up unto vile affections; for even their women did exchange the natural use for that which is against nature; and likewise also the men, leaving the natural use of the woman, burned in their lust one toward another, men with men working that which is unseemly, and receiving in themselves that recompense of their error which was fitting. And even as they did not like to retain God in their knowledge, God gave them over to a reprobate mind, to do those things which are not seemly, being filled with all unrighteousness, fornication, wickedness, covetousness, maliciousness; full of envy, murder, strife, deceit, malignity; whisperers, backbiters, haters of God, insolent, proud, boasters, inventors of evil things, disobedient to parents, without understanding, covenant breakers, without natural affection, implacable, unmerciful; who, knowing the judgment of God, that they who commit such things are worthy of death, not only do the same but have pleasure in them that do them (Romans 1:21-32; NSSB).*

By the time of Abraham (c. 2000 B.C.), men had digressed into a dark polytheism which encompassed belief in and worship of all kinds of evil spirits and demons. Archaeological discoveries in Sumeria and Babylon reveal abundant evidence of the use of exorcisms, spells, incantations, and magical texts, as well as evidence of other demonic activity. Studies of the ancient Greek, Egyptian, Chaldean, Assyrian, and Roman cultures provide much information on this activity. The gods worshipped by these people of old were invisible demons represented by manmade idols and images.[10] As George W. Gilmore, in his book **Demon, Demoniac**, declares, "The entire religious provenience out of which Hebrew religion sprang is full of demonism."[11]

Early religions, including Judaism, involved belief in the existence of demon spirits. Christianity, in its earliest stages, sought to rescue its converts from the bondage of Satan and his demon servants (Ephesians 2:2; Colossians 1:13). Unger says that, to an amazingly large degree, the history of religion is an account of demonically controlled religion, especially in its clash with the Hebrew faith and later with Christianity.[12]

The Greeks used the word **demon** to designate the disembodied spirits of deceased men.[13] Unger believes the precise identity of demons is impossible to determine because the Word of God is silent on the issue. Scripture does not state exactly who the demons are, or how they came to exist. Many theories, however, have been proposed to account for their origin.[14] All nations since the time of the Greeks have incorporated into their cultures the belief in the existence of demonizing spirits. The scriptures do not specifically indicate who these demons are, but the most generally accepted opinion is that they were beings originally with the Holy Angels, who fell from their original state by sinning against God.

Some scholars disagree and believe that these demons must be distinguished from the angels that sinned, the angels who "kept not their first estate." They contend that while the heavenly beings who joined Satan in his revolt against God are fallen angels, the demons are disembodied spirits of physical and mortal creatures who once lived upon the earth. Even these Bible scholars disagree with one another regarding an exact identification of the demons. Some identify the demons as the spirits of

27

pre-Adamite beings similar to man, while others identify them as the spirits of the giants who were destroyed in the great flood of Noah's time. (Genesis 6:4)

Nevius comments that Rev. Gall believes Satan and his demons are the disembodied spirits of a pre-Adamite race which once lived on this earth. Rev. Gall proposes that this race sinned and fell from its original state, just as the human race did. He believes that the consequences of their sin involved suffering physical death.[15]

Unger differs with him, saying, "Demons are not the disembodied spirits of a pre-Adamite race of humanity of the earth."[16] He believes that the whole idea of a pre-Adamite human race to be nothing but pure conjecture and unbiblical.

He also discounts another theory: that demons are the unnatural offspring of angels and ante-diluvian women. He declares that two premises (which he believes to be false) would be necessary to establish that theory. The first premise would be that **the sons of God** of Genesis 6:2 (whom Unger believes to be the fallen angels) had sexual intercourse with human women. (**The sons of God** were called **nephilim**, which in Hebrew means *fallen ones*.) The second premise would be that their union with the human women produced **giants**. However, this Hebrew term refers not so much to strength and human size as it does to *earth born* **(the Greek gengenes).**

Unger also does not believe, as some scholars do, that these sons of God are godly descendants of Seth. He does believe that these **sons of God** are indeed angels, and that this belief is supported by the uniform use of that term in the Old Testament (Job 1:6; 2:1; 38:7) where it refers only to angelic beings.[17]

It seems to be only pure speculation that such monstrous offspring of fallen angels and corrupt ante-diluvian women would become disembodied spirits or demons after their bodies were destroyed in the flood. The New Testament reveals that the fallen angels who thus sinned were consigned to Tartarus (II Peter 2:4-9; Jude 6, 7), but states nothing regarding the fate of any *mongrel offspring*.

Richard W. DeHaan declares in his book, **Satan, Satanism and Witchcraft** that many Bible students reject interpreting Genesis 6 to mean that half-human creatures formerly existed. The existence of such creatures would have required that angels, who are non-material beings, create physical bodies for themselves capable of impregnating a female member of the human race. This would have required a creative miracle, and the Bible declares that only God has that kind of power, which was only exemplified in the Virgin Mary's miraculous conception of the Savior, Jesus Christ. DeHaan believes it is not necessary for us to interpret the statements in Jude 6, 7 and II Peter 2:4 as a reference to sexual sin on the part of the fallen angels. He proceeds to attempt to convince his readers that Jude's use of the expression *going after strange flesh* may just be figurative language representing spiritual fornication. He believes the prophets often compared Israel's unfaithfulness to God to spiritual fornication. He also strives to show the reader that Peter's statement concerning the angels who had sinned being assigned to Tartarus may just have been a method for showing that all sinning angels have been designated to this place, and that they are even now under chains of moral and spiritual darkness.[18]

Unger, in **Demons in the World Today**, clarifies a great number of things about the biblical interpretation of who the demons are and what they are doing. He declares that in view of the Bible's silence pertaining to the origin of demons, that the best-supported deduction from the scriptural hints that are available is that demons are fallen angels. He makes every effort to show that when Lucifer rebelled and injected sin into a universe that had previously been sinless, he drew with him a great number of lower celestial beings. Matthew 25:41 and Revelation 12:4 seem to support his theory. These fallen demons are free to roam the heavens and the earth under leadership of Satan, who is also in scripture called **Beelzebub**, *Prince of the Demons* (Matthew 12:24), and **the Dragon** (Revelation 12:7). The demons are his subjects and helpers, an idea suggested in Matthew 12:26. These demons are so numerous that Satan's power is practically everywhere. The demons are well-organized, and Satan strategically uses them as effectively as a commander-in-chief would a great army, which is a concept evidenced in Ephesians 6:11-12.[19]

According to Luke, demons are spiritual beings or personalities. "A spirit hath not flesh and bones" (Luke 24:39). This means that demons do not possess a material body, yet they can act upon the human body and soul. Demons have the capabilities of entering and assuming control of a human body, and operating and acting through it as if it were their own property.[20] Charles Hodge, author of **Systematic Theology**, believes that demons are depraved and malevolent, showing that they are personalities, and that the human race is the prime target of their evil works.[21]

The Bible makes numerous references to the fact that demons <u>are</u> spirits. "When the evening was come, they brought unto him many that were possessed with <u>demons;</u> and he cast out the <u>spirits</u> with his word" (Matthew 8:16). When Christ sent out the seventy and they had returned, their response was joyfully declared, "Lord, even the <u>demons</u> are subject unto us" (Luke 10:17). The Lord Jesus replied, "Notwithstanding, in this rejoice not, that the <u>spirits</u> are subject unto you" (v. 20). The lunatic boy had the <u>demon</u> cast out of him in Matthew 17:18, an account of which may also be found in Mark 9:25. In this passage the demon is referred to as a <u>foul spirit</u>. In Ephesians 6:12, the apostle Paul declares that Satan and his <u>demons</u> are <u>spirits</u>. The apostle John wrote in Revelation 16:14 that <u>demons</u> are <u>spirits</u>.

Unger, in his book **Demons in the World Today**, makes it very clear that he believes demons are personalities:

> The fact that demons are spirits, and thus immaterial and incorporeal, does not in the least suggest that they lack individuality, with all the elements of personality such as will, feelings, and intellect. Like all God's creatures, they were constituted with self-determining choice. Created originally sinless, they joined Satan in a chosen course of rebellion. Their decision was deliberate and in the full knowledge of their Creator. This is why they are incorrigible and confirmed in their depravity with no hope of repentance or change. Like Satan's, their choice is irretrievable; their doom is sealed.[22]

Apparently, these demons are personalities without bodies, and they are highly organized. As damned and fallen spirits, they desire to dwell in a body in order to manifest themselves and accomplish their intent (Acts 19:11-20). It can be concluded from the study of scripture that they are angry with God

because of their fallen state. Their prime objective is to destroy what God loves or creates, especially man (Genesis 3; Luke 4:1-13).

We find in studying the Word of God that Satan's base of operation is not in Hell, but that he, along with his demons, is conducting his warfare on God's people from heavenly realms. This is not to say that he is in the third heaven, or heaven of heavens (II Corinthians 12:2). It is important for us to understand that out of hundreds of occurrences of the word **heaven** in the English Bible, there are translations of two words. The first is the Hebrew word **shamyim** and it literally means *the heights*. The second is the Greek word **ouranos** and it literally means *that which is raised up*. When the word **heaven** is used in the Bible, except when it is used figuratively, it is referring to one of three realms, (1) **the first heaven**, which consists of the realm where the clouds and atmospheric space are immediately above us, (2) **the second heaven**, called **celestial**, which consists of the realm where the stars and planets are located, and (3) to **the highest heaven**, the realm of *the abode of God*.[23] In the third heaven or heaven of heavens, Christ is seated "far above all principality, and power, and might, and dominion" (Ephesians 1:20,21).

Satan was expelled from the highest heaven, evidently not at the time of his primeval fall (Job 1:6), but after Christ had completed his redemptive work and glorious ascension.[24] Satan is "prince of the power of the air" (Ephesians 2:2), and he and his wicked demons are now confined to the first and second heavens. The Bible declares that during the great tribulation, Satan and his demons will be cast down to earth (Revelation 12:7-12), where they will make their last futile effort to seize control of man and the earth (Revelation 19:19; 20:2-3).

In summary, little information is found in the Bible regarding the actual origin of demons. However, it can be stated with absolute certainty that they are fallen spirit-beings who have committed themselves to Satan, who hate God, and who seek to harm His people and to do everything possible to render them inoperative. We can make no clear distinction between fallen angels and demons, for they are all evil spirits. Some questions must remain unanswered, because the Bible does not reveal many details pertaining to their origin.

**HISTORY OF DEMONOLOGY IN GREECE**

Greek culture reflects an open acceptance of demonology. The writings and cultural history of Greece include references to all kinds of superstitions, demons and disembodied entities. In the writings of Homer, the word **daimon** was commonly used to refer to divinity, deity, or divine power, whereas the word **theios** was used to denote *a god in person*. A **daimon**, to the Greeks, was a major deity who had the power to exert some influence upon human life. In **Hesiod** (a Greek writing) the **daimon** was regarded at different times as one of the souls of men from the *golden age* that formed some kind of connecting link between mortals and gods. We find consistent credence given to the idea of a guardian spirit being given to watch over a Greek individual from his birth--this guardian spirit being good or bad. Evil demons were presented as attaching themselves to an individual to insure his untimely death.[25]

Among the Greek philosophers, we find many writings pertaining to demons or evil spirits. Thales held that "All things are full of gods," and Herrclitus refined the concept of an indwelling and controlling deity by his statement, "Character is each man's demon." Empedocles was given credit for

describing the way by which wicked demons could be rehabilitated through various phases and stages of reincarnation. Socrates indicated that he was often dissuaded from following a particular course of action by receiving a divine sign or warning. Plato believed that demons, which he identified with souls of the dead, served as interpreters between man and the gods. Aristotle believed that all men had demons which accompanied them throughout life. Epicurus denied the very existence of demons and believed, that if by chance, they did exist, they could in no way communicate with humans. The Stoics of ancient Greece strongly advocated demonism.[26] We cannot pinpoint the beginning of demonology in Greece, but we can see how prevalent it seemed to be.

## HISTORY OF DEMONOLOGY IN MESOPOTAMIA

From the beginning Mesopotamia was full of superstition, which greatly influenced the natural environment, the living conditions, and the religious projections. Sumerian mythology held many allusions to the underworld gods or **anunnaki**, and the seven evil **asakki**, or demons, which inhabited the Nether regions. Popular belief held that demons were responsible for man's misfortunes, particularly in the areas of disease and illness. They believed demons gained entrance into man through the internal organs. This is why they wore amulets (jeweled ornamentations) and resorted to magical incantations. Magical incantations and spells were used to invoke **Ea**, the god of the waters. Ea became the patron deity of priestly orders that were trained in exorcism, knowledge of spells, formulating incantations, and interpreting dreams and omens. Sumerians particularly dreaded the spirits that came from people who had been buried without the appropriate burial rites, or who had died in violent or mysterious circumstances. These ghosts were known as **etimmu**, and it took a certain kind of exorcist-priest (called an **ashipu**), to recite the proper incantations that would dispel their attacks.[27]

The Mesopotamians gave names to demons they feared. Some were given the names of actual diseases, while others were given the names of hostile, natural powers. One of the demons was given the name **Rabisu**, which means *the croucher* because he was thought to lie in wait secretly for his enemies. It seems that the Sumerians and the Semites of Babylonia put great emphasis on the magical power of names.[28] Like the Greeks, the Mesopotamians seem to have believed in demons, their existence and their power from the very beginning of their culture. Again, it is impossible to find an absolute beginning of demonology.

## HISTORY OF DEMONOLOGY IN EGYPT

The Egyptians believed in the presence of great hordes of demons which marshaled the powers of magic. Though they believed in many demonic forces, they did not catalog their devils and evil spirits like other civilizations by giving them a vast number of different names. They did, however, name the demons according to their function: *the cutter, the archer, the ripper* and so forth. Furthermore, such celestial phenomena as floods and storms, which elsewhere were accepted as the work of demons, were attributed to the gods themselves by the Egyptians. They feared the disembodied demon from the dead more than any other demon. Demonology in Egypt was similar to the demonology of other nations in some ways: the belief in astrology and horoscopes, the belief in demons responding to chants, the belief in the ability to control a particular demon by the use of its correct name.[29]

## JEWISH AND RABBINIC VIEWS ON DEMONOLOGY

The difference between satanology or demonology of the Rabbis and of the New Testament are of marked differences. In general, we note that, with the exception of the word Sammael (another word for Satan), none of the names given to the great enemy in the New Testament occurs in Rabbinic writings. Most important still, Rabbini's writings contain no mention of a kingdom of Satan. The power of evil is not contrasted with that of good nor Satan with God. Moreover, Satan is presented rather as the enemy of man than of God and of good. The New Testament presents two opposing kingdoms or principles which tug at mankind. Since Rabbinism viewed *the great enemy* only as the envious and malicious opponent of man, the spiritual element is entirely eliminated.[30]

Alfred Edersheim, in his book, **The Life and Times of Jesus the Messiah**, says that based on Rabbinic view, the fall of Satan and his angels took place subsequently rather than antecedently to the creation of man. As related to **Pirgé de R. Eliezer, chapter 13**, this view presents the Rabbinic view of the fall of Satan and his angels as quite different from that of the Bible. This view presents the stand that this fall followed the creation of man because of the angels' opposition to such a creation. According to this view, while the angels disputed over the creation of man, God created man, and then addressed the angels: "Why dispute any longer? Man has already been created." The angels saw then that the man God had created was superior, shown by man's ability to name all the creatures. Therefore, the angels devised a plot against Adam, so that by his fall they might obtain supremacy of the earth. This Rabbinic tradition holds that Sammael was first of all angel-princes. He rebelled, taking the company of angels subject to him and coming down upon the earth and selecting the serpent, through which he would tempt the woman. The serpent at that time could speak. He had hands and feet and looked like a camel. Sammael entered into and took possession of the serpent, thus giving Sammael absolute control over him. Then Sammael, acting through the serpent, deceived the woman by showing her that he could touch the tree and not die. When the woman touched the tree of life, she saw the death angel coming against her. Afraid that she would die and that God would give another wife to Adam, she led her husband, Adam, to disobedience.[31]

In Jewish legend, the origin of evil spirits brings forth different opinions. Edersheim states:

> According to Ab. 12b, Ber. R. 7, they were created on the eve of the first Sabbath. But since that time their numbers have greatly increased. For, according to Erub. 18b. Ber. R. 20 (ed. Warsh. p. 40b), multitudes of them were the offspring of Eve and of male spirits, and of Adam with female spirits or with Lillith (the queen of the female spirits), during the 130 years that Adam had been under the ban, and before Seth was born (Gen. v. 3): comp. Erub 18.b, again their number can scarcely be limited, since they propagate themselves (Chag. 16a) resembling men in this as well as in their taking of nourishment and dying. On the other hand, like the Angels, they have wings, pass unhindered through space, and know the future. Still further, they are produced by a process of transformation from vipers, which, in the course of four times seven years, successively pass through the forms of vampires, thistles and thorns, into Shedim (Bab. K. 16 a)--perhaps a parabolic form of indicating the origination of Shedim through the fall of man. Another parabolic idea may be implied in the saying that Shedim sprung from the backbone of those who have not bent in worship (u.s.).[32]

In studying biblical accounts, as well as the Greek, Mesopotamian, Egyptian and Rabbinic traditions on the subject of the origin of demons, it becomes apparent that none of them give an absolute starting point. Of all the accounts, the Bible presents the most logical and systematic information about demons and their origin. I believe that this part of the study can best be summarized by a quote from Dickason's book, **Demon Possession and the Christian**:

Support for the fact that demons are fallen angels is sufficient. First, they have a similar relation to Satan as do Satan's angels. The parallel expressions "the devil and his angels" (Matt. 25:41), "the dragon and his angels" (Rev. 12:7), and "Beelzebub the ruler of the demons" (Matt. 12:24, 26) support this.

Second, when Satan is designated "ruler of the demons," the term that is used is **archonti**, which has the basic meaning of "first." "As 'first among demons' he is their ruler" [which he quoted from Charles R. Smith's "The New Testament Doctrine of Demons," Grace Journal 10 (Spring 1969):32.] This same relationship may be seen in that demon-locusts, released from the pit during the Tribulation, have over them an angel named Abaddon or Apollyon (destroyer, who may be Satan (Rev. 9:11).

Third, demons and angels have similar essence. Angels are termed "spirits" (Ps. 104:4; Heb. 1:14), and so are demons (Matt. 8:16; Luke 10:17, 20).

Fourth, they carry out similar activities. Demons seek to enter and control men (Matt. 17:14-18; Luke 11:14-15). So also may evil angels such as Satan (Luke 22:3; John 13:27). Evil angels, just as demons, join Satan in war against God and man (Rev. 12:7-17; Mark 9:17-26; Rev. 9:13-15).

Fifth, the ranks of angels and demons are similar, if not identical (Rom. 8:38-39; Eph. 6:10-12; Col. 1:16; 2:15).

The above reasons seem quite sufficient to identify demons as fallen angels subservient to Satan, carrying out his plans. If that is not the case, then we have no biblical evidence for determining the origin of demons.[33]

## NOTES

1. Lester Sumrall, <u>Demons The Answer Book</u>, p. 29.
2. Jack R. Taylor, <u>Victory Over the Devil</u>, p. 10.
3. <u>Ibid.</u>, p. 13.
4. Kenneth S. Wuest, <u>Word Studies in the Greek New Testament</u>, p. 320.
5. Merrill F. Unger, <u>Demons in the World Today</u>, p. 8.
6. W. E. Vine, <u>An Expository Dictionary of New Testament Words</u>, p. 291.
7. Merril C. Tenney, <u>The Zondervan Pictorial Encyclopedia of the Bible</u>, Vol. II, p. 92.
8. John L. Nevius, <u>Demon Possession</u>, p. 263.
9. Merrill F. Unger, <u>op</u>. <u>cit</u>., p. 10.
10. <u>Loc</u>. <u>cit</u>.
11. George W. Gilmore, "Demon, Demoniac," <u>New Schaff-Herzog Encyclopedia of Religious Knowledge</u>, Vol. III, p. 399.
12. <u>Loc</u>. <u>cit</u>.
13. G. Pember, <u>Earth, Earliest Stages</u>, pp. 70-73.
14. Merrill F. Unger, <u>op</u>. <u>cit</u>., p. 13.
15. John L. Nevius, <u>op</u>. <u>cit</u>., p. 270.
16. Merrill F. Unger, <u>op</u>. <u>cit</u>., p. 14.
17. <u>Loc</u>. <u>cit</u>.
18. Richard W. DeHaan, <u>Satan, Satanism and Witchcraft</u>, p. 25.
19. Merrill F. Unger, <u>op</u>. <u>cit</u>., p. 15.
20. <u>Ibid</u>., p. 22.
21. Charles Hodge, <u>Systematic Theology</u>, pp. 28-32, 37, 38.
22. Merrill F. Unger, <u>op</u>. <u>cit</u>., p. 22.
23. Merril C. Tenney, <u>The Zondervan Pictorial Encyclopedia of the Bible</u>, Vol. III, pp. 60,61.
24. Merrill F. Unger, <u>op</u>. <u>cit</u>., p. 15.
25. Merril C. Tenney, <u>op</u>. <u>cit</u>., Vol. II, p. 92.
26. <u>Ibid</u>., p. 93.
27. <u>Loc</u>. <u>cit</u>.
28. <u>Ibid</u>., p. 94.
29. <u>Ibid</u>., pp. 95,96.
30. Alfred Edersheim, <u>The Life and Times of Jesus the Messiah</u>, Vol. II, pp. 756,757.
31. <u>Loc</u>. <u>cit</u>.
32. <u>Ibid</u>., pp. 759,760.
33. C. Fred Dickason, <u>Demon Possession and the Christian</u>, pp.24, 25.

# CHAPTER TWO
# OLD TESTAMENT SCRIPTURAL ACCOUNTS OF DEMONS

## DEMONS AND OLD TESTAMENT PEOPLE

The Old Testament is filled with references to demons, as shown by Satan's temptation of man and the resulting fall of man in the Garden, after which God's people have continually been the object of Satanic attack (Genesis 4:1-8; 6:1-7). The pagan nations which surrounded Israel manifested the full gamut of demonic practices and beliefs. They constantly clashed with Israel, which held a monotheistic (belief in one God) faith. The enlightened Israelites regarded idols as demons worshiped by man (Baruch 4:7; Psalm 96:5, Septuagint; I Corinthians 10:20). The **sheddim** (Deuteronomy 32:17; Psalm 106:36-37) and **seirim** (Leviticus 17:7; II Chronicles 11:15, Isaiah 13:21; 34:14) were considered demonic conceptions.[1] William Alexander in his book, **Demon Possession in the New Testament** declares that the Old Testament refers to demons time and time again, but that its rigid application of the monotheistic principle relegates the demons to an unimportant position. Some of the demons mentioned seem to be mere shadow-figures (**Rahab**, Job 9:13; **Tannin**, Isaiah 27:1; **Leviathan**, Isaiah 27:1; the **Sea Serpent**, Amos 9:3); others are degraded gods (**Kazab**, a Hebrew word meaning *lies*, Amos 2:4; **No-god**, Jeremiah 16:20; **Pegar**, a Hebrew word meaning *carcasses*, Leviticus 26:30; **Tohuw**, a Hebrew word meaning *emptiness*, I Samuel 12:21; **Elil**, a Hebrew word meaning *nothing*, Psalm 96:5); another one is a possessing spirit (I Samuel 16:16; 18:10; 19:9).[2]

Why demons are called **demons** in the New Testament but called **evil spirits or familiar spirits** in the Old Testament? Keep in mind that the Old Testament was originally written in Hebrew, and the New Testament in Greek. **The Zondervan Pictorial Encyclopedia of the Bible** states that the earliest Hebrew sources had no specific word or term equivalent to the Greek word which is translated *demon*. In situations where supernatural phenomena occurred and needed to be described, the word elohim was commonly translated *god*. An inspired man was a **man of elohim**, meaning a *godly man*, an expression which found its counterpart in the Hittite phrase man of the gods, meaning seer. **Elohim** was quite often used to describe an awesome power as in Genesis 30:8, **great wrestlings** (the Hebrew word for **great** is **elohim**), and as in Jonah 3:3, **an exceeding great city** (the Hebrew word for exceeding is **elohim**). In the same neutral sense, the idea of a divine spirit (**ruah-elohim**) possessing a person was used to account for extraordinary phenomena such as the prophetic activities of Balaam (Numbers 24:2) and of Saul (I Samuel 10:11, 19:20). **Elohim** is used in connection with an evil spirit in II Samuel 16:23; it was wrongly ascribed to God in the English versions. Actually, the use of this generic term for god was merely intended by the author to describe the evil spirits as powerful without any inherent demonism being conveyed.[3]

The first reference to spirits, other than Satan, in the Old Testament is made in Genesis 6, where the sons of God came and cohabited with the daughters of men.[4] Another reference to a demon spirit is found in Judges 9:23,24. God sent an evil spirit to punish Abimelech for his part in murdering Gideon's seventy sons, and the men of Shechem for aiding him:

Then God sent an *evil spirit* between Abimelech and the men of Shechem; and the men of Shechem dealt treacherously with Abimelech, in order that the violence done to the seventy sons of Jerubbaal might come, and their blood might be laid on Abimelech their brother, who killed them, and on the men of Shechem, who strengthened his hands to kill his brothers.[5]

There are a number of indications that the Old Testament mentions many **demon** or **god names**. The Old Testament contains some references to the popular demonology of pagan nations, particularly in the context of cultic worship.[6] In post-biblical Hebrew, the word **sed** became the common name of a malignant spirit, but the reference to it in Deuteronomy may imply only the Assyrian word **shedu** or *guardian spirit*. Zondervan says, "While 'sed' could be given a demonic interpretation, the concrete use of the term suggests a heathen deity...."[7]

Another reference to pagan gods occurred in Leviticus 17:7 where the term **hairy ones** refer to **satyrs**. The literal meaning of the word is **goats**, but pagans deemed the *hairy ones* to be sylvan gods, or demons which inhabited waste places (Isaiah 13:21; 34:14). (Goat worship, accompanied by evil rituals, was very much in existence in Lower Egypt, and was very familiar to the Israelites of pre-exodus times.) The Zondervan Encyclopedia suggests that **hairy ones** merely mean *wild goats* and not **demons**. Isaiah refers to the familiar **akkad**, a female demon, **lilitu** (Isaiah 34:14). Zondervan states:

> Many demons referred to by name or titles in literature from the ancient Near East are also mentioned in certain OT passages. There is a problem of interpretation, since the fact that all such allusions occur in poetic sections. This raises the question as to whether they are actually anything more than mere figures of speech.[8]

Using poetic language, God's prophets long and vigorously ridiculed the claims of the heathen divinities. These so-called divinities were exposed as false gods and their worship in Israel was instantly discredited. Thus deprived of public recognition and support, they sank to a vague position, which according to Eastern conventions, was assigned to demonic creatures. For the true worshipers of Jehovah, however, they were considered practically non-existent--impotent shedim and mere nothings. In Deuteronomy 32:17 and Psalm 106:37, the heathen gods are reduced to the rank of demons.[9]

## GOD'S WARNING AGAINST INVOLVEMENT WITH EVIL OR FAMILIAR SPIRITS

Although many scriptures make fun of the heathen **gods** and demons, God repeatedly warned His people to stay away from them. Worshipping or seeking a **familiar spirit** brought death by stoning. The seriousness of this matter is evidenced in Deuteronomy 17:1-5, Exodus 20:1-5, and Leviticus 20:6, 27. God clearly shows that these gods and demons were much more than figures of speech. They were a very real danger to His people.

In the Old Testament, we find a clearly-drawn distinction between the angels of God (as seen in Psalm 91 and Daniel 9:21), and the fallen angels (as in Genesis 6)--both are understood to be immaterial beings. There is no connection at all between good and evil spirits. Unlike in the animistic and the spiritistic cults, and unlike Greek philosophy, the demons or evil spirits in the Bible cannot play a double role with good spirits. The so-called **spirits of the dead** play only a very small part in the Old Testament.[10] While searching the scriptures, we find that spirits of the dead are neutrally mentioned in I Samuel 28 and in Isaiah 8:19 but elsewhere, we find that talking with the departed is bracketed together with sorcery and forbidden by the threat of death.[11] Deuteronomy 18 is an excellent example of this:

> *When thou art come into the land which the Lord thy God giveth thee, thou shalt not learn to do after the abominations of those nations. There shall not be found among you any one that maketh his son or his daughter pass through the fire, or who useth divination, or an observer of times, or an enchanter, or a witch, or a charmer, or a consulter of mediums, or a wizard, or a necromancer. For all that do these things are an abomination unto the Lord; and because of these abominations the Lord thy God doth drive them out from before thee. Thou shalt be perfect with the Lord thy God. For these nations, whom thou shalt possess, hearkened unto observers of times, and unto diviners; but as for thee, the Lord thy God hath not permitted thee so to do (Deuteronomy 18:9-14; NSSB).*

Demonic operations in relation to God's servants can be traced throughout all of history. Once we clearly comprehend the existence of the unseen host of evil spirit-beings which are actively engaged in deceiving and misleading men, we can better discern the deceiving works of Satan during Old Testament times, works which were previously hidden from our knowledge. David was deceived by Satan into numbering Israel because he failed to see that the suggestion that came to his mind had come from a satanic source (I Chronicles 21:1). Job was deceived when he believed that the fire which had fallen from heaven was from God (Job 1:16) and that all the calamities which befell him-- the loss of children, wealth, and home--came directly from the hand of the Lord. The early part of the book of Job clearly shows that Satan was the primary cause of his trouble. In Daniel 10, Satan actively opposed the messenger of God who had been sent to Daniel to enable him to understand God's counsel for His people.

J. Stafford Wright, in his book, **Christianity and the Occult**, says that the first known occurrence of the term *familiar spirits* in English literature is found in the **Geneva Bible of 1560**. This translation was made by exiled Protestants during Queen Mary's reign. Wright explains that the word **familiar** comes from Latin, meaning **servant**. During the latter half of the sixteenth century, there were many references to familiars as demons in the form of animals. The *familiar spirits* were to have been given to a witch who had made a pact with the devil. The familiar spirit served her by performing magical spells and was rewarded for his service by sucking blood from some spot on the witch's body. This type of account of familiar spirits is almost entirely of English and Scottish origin. While it is not mentioned in Queen Elizabeth's Statute against Witchcraft in 1563, the James I Statute of 1604 refers to any person who shall "entertain, employ, feed, or reward any evil and wicked spirit to or for any intent or purpose."[12] Many of God's people, through contact with others who were under Satan's power, were deceived into communicating with *familiar spirits*. They were persuaded to use **divination** and other occult powers of darkness, even though God's laws warned against them.

## ANIMISM VERSUS SPIRITISM

The basis for ancestral worship found in Asiatic cultures is found in such animistic thought, together with spiritistic beliefs. **Animism** comes from the word **anima** meaning *soul or life*, and is the doctrine that objects in nature possess, or are possessed by souls or spirits. The word **demon** in the Greek language has strong connections with the idea of **animism**. **Animism** also embraces the idea of *pantheism*, meaning "God and the universe are one." Souls and spirits are considered to be those of the departed, and are regarded as having no physical substance and intermediary beings. **Spiritism** is based on the view that departed spirits can communicate with the living, usually through a medium. The animist and spiritist believe that these spirits can be either good or evil. The animist offers sacrifices of food to spirits, and the spiritist attempts to talk to the dead.[13]

It is not surprising to find the Word of God teaches that magic and sorcery are offensive to God, and are intimately related to demonic forces. They are not to be received as harmless games with which to experiment or as a stimulant for jaded metaphysical appetites. God's chosen people, because of the danger of witches to the moral life and the redemptive purposes of God, were told that it was not permitted for witches to live: "Thou shalt not suffer a witch to live" (Exodus 22:18). We find in Deuteronomy 18:10-12 that sorcerers and wizards are also offensive to God. It is obvious that black magic and witchcraft were widely practiced in Canaan; this practice is evidenced by the inscriptions on the Ras Shamra tablets.

The biblical attitude toward any attempt to communicate with departed spirits is unquestionably negative. God says:

> *And the soul that turneth after such as have familiar spirits, and after wizards, to play the harlot after them, I will even set my face against that soul, and will cut him off from among his people. A man also or a woman who hath a familiar spirit, or who is a wizard, shall surely be put to death: they shall stone them with stones; their blood shall be upon them (Leviticus 20:6, 27; NSSB).*

God condemns those who consult mediums (these have *a control spirit or familiar spirit*). He also condemns wizards and necromancers (Deuteronomy 18:9-14, quoted previously in this chapter). In I Samuel 28 Saul is found using forbidden means of inquiry. In I Chronicles 10:13 we see that Saul's death occurred because he disobeyed God's word against seeking a familiar spirit.[14] "So Saul died for his transgression which he committed against the Lord, even against the word of the Lord, which he kept not, and also for asking counsel of a medium, to inquire of her." God's prophet Isaiah also recorded the emphatic warning and bitter condemnation of such spiritistic practices:

> *And when they shall say unto you, Seek unto those who are mediums, and unto wizards that peep, and that mutter: should not a people seek unto their God? Should they seek on behalf of the living to the dead? To the law and to the testimony; if they speak not according to this word, it is because there is not light in them (Isaiah 8:19-20; NSSB).*

This should make the God-fearing, God-abiding person give serious consideration to what the Word of God says about communication with the spirit world.

It is unfortunate that the King James Version is not as clear as it should be in its use of the term **familiar spirits**. The manner in which the term is used tends to divert the reader's thoughts from mediumship to witchcraft.[15] While *mediumship* is communications between the living and *familiar spirits* representing the dead, **witchcraft** is the power or practices of witches, sorcery, black magic, and enchantments. The King James Version translators, thinking of the then-current witch trials, extended the Geneva Bible's references to *familiar spirits* (Leviticus 19:31) to be included with witchcraft. This resulted in the medieval and early post-reformation worlds completely misunderstanding the meaning of witchcraft as referred to in God's Word. Not until the return of spiritism and mediumship in the 19th Century did the world start to know what the Bible really meant by the term witchcraft.[16] Looking at the terms in our modern versions of the Bible, the previous errors become obvious.

There are two Hebrew words that should be noted. Firstly, the word **ob** (the "o" is long, and the "b" is softened with an "h" and pronounced almost an "av") is always translated *familiar spirit* in the King James Version. Secondly, **yiddeoni** (with the final "o" and "i" being long) is always translated as *wizard* in the King James Version. The precise meaning of "ob" is uncertain, but a similar word found in the Arabic language means *to return*. The second word is almost certainly connected with the Hebrew verb *to know*. An observance of their usage reveals that both words refer to a communicating spirit.[17]

In view of what has been said about the King James Version's use of the term **familiar spirits**, I will, for study purposes, substitute these two Hebrew words (which are used in the original manuscripts) into the appropriate places in passages from the King James Version. For those who do not know Hebrew endings, the plural will be made by adding the English "s":

> *Regard not them that have (**obs**), neither seek after (**yiddeonis**), to be defiled by them: I am the Lord your God (Leviticus 19:31).*

> *And the soul that turneth after such as have (**obs**), and after (**yiddeonis**), to play the harlot after them, I will even set my face against that soul, and will cut him off from among his people (Leviticus 20:6).*

> *A man also or woman who hath (**an ob**), or who is a (**yiddeoni**), shall surely be put to death: they shall stone them with stones; their blood shall be upon them (Leviticus 20:27).*

> *...or a charmer, or a consulter of (**obs**), or a (**yiddeoni**), or a necromancer (Deuteronomy 18:11).*

> *...and Saul had put away those who were (**obs**), and the (**yiddeonis**), out of the land (I Samuel 28:3).*

> *Then said Saul unto his servants, Seek me a woman who is (**an ob**), that I may go to her, and inquire of her...there is a woman who is (**an ob**) at Endor (I Samuel 28:7).*

*So Saul died for his transgression which he committed against the Lord...for asking counsel of (an **ob**), to inquire of her (I Chronicles 10:13).*

Among Manasseh's sins, we find that he uses an **ob** and a **yiddeoni** (II Kings 21:6). In this passage referring to Manasseh, we find both singular and plural forms of the words. In the corresponding passage in II Chronicles 33:6, we find their singular form.

*Moreover, the (**obs**), and the (**yiddeonis**)... (II Kings 23:24).*

*And when they shall say unto you, Seek unto those who are (**obs**), and unto (**yiddeonis**) that peep, and that mutter: should not a people seek unto their God (Isaiah 8:19)?*

*...and thy voice shall be, like (an **ob**)... (Isaiah 29:4).*

Wright believes that as we take a closer look at the passages listed, that **ob** and **yiddeoni** can usually be assumed to be titles of communicating spirits. Since **ob** is used occasionally by itself, and **yiddeoni** is always linked with an **ob**, it could be regarded that the **ob** is the main control spirit and that the **yiddeoni** is the other spirit that is called up by the control spirit. Most of today's mediums appear to have one or two main controls of this kind.[18] Regardless of the exact meaning of any single passage; the Old Testament definitely speaks of demons, and bans any attempt to contact the dead. When a person uses a medium, he is dealing with someone who has demons and is disobeying God's Word, which strictly forbids His people to call on demons for help in talking to the dead. Deuteronomy 18:11-12, Isaiah 8:19 and Leviticus 20:6 plainly shows God's opposition to spiritism.

While the story of the witch of Endor is the subject of much debate, one thing is for certain: Saul received his death sentence for visiting the spiritist (I Samuel 28). In like manner, King Ahaziah received his death sentence for sending messengers to Ekron to consult Baal-zebub as to whether or not he would recover from his disease (II Kings 1:2).

## DEFINITION OF DIVINATION

The word **divination** means *the art of soothsaying* in its widest sense. It is the unveiling of hidden things of the past, present, and future and is practiced by charmers, wizards, augurs, necromancers and dowsers. Divination was the most prevalent occult activity practiced in ancient pagan cultures. The Old Testament contains a number of references to divination: Genesis 44:5; Leviticus 19:31; 20:6,27; Deuteronomy 18:10-12; I Chronicles 10:13; Isaiah 44:25; Jeremiah 29:8; Ezekiel 21:21; Hosea 4:12; Micah 3:6; Zechariah 10:2. Throughout these texts we find various forms of divination such as soothsaying by cup, wand, arrows, lots, liver, dreams, the cry of birds, days of ill omen, and many other signs. We especially notice the worship of stars through astrology (Deuteronomy 17:2-5; II Kings 17:16; Isaiah 47:9-14). The Word of the Lord pronounces the death penalty on those who practice heathen divination (Exodus 22:18; Leviticus 20:27; Deuteronomy 17:5). God's directive regarding heathen magic in Israel is unequivocal: "Regard not them that have familiar spirits, neither seek after wizards, to be defiled by them: I am the Lord your God" (Leviticus 19:31).

Dr. Kurt Koch, a German evangelist, counselor, student of the occult for fifty years and author of **Christian Counseling and Occultism**, believes that all magic and divinatory practices mentioned in the Old Testament are viewed in the light of the first and second commandments. God was not dealing with Israel simply for her involvement with Asherah images and demons. God was dealing with Israel about her violation of the commandments to have no other gods or graven images before them. She was being called to accountability about her heathenistic practices, with an appeal for her to choose--whether Yahweh was Lord, or not. God wants man to occupy himself only with Him, and not to allow him to be lured away by spirits or demons. Koch states, "Magic in the Old Testament is therefore not a matter of demons, but a matter which has to do with God. This is clear, not only from the first commandment but in other connections."[19] Koch is not denying the existence of demons in the Old Testament; he is simply saying that God wanted His people's total worship. As we study God's Word carefully, it becomes apparent that failure to obey God in this area often brought demonic results and/or self-destruction.

At this point, I find it necessary to comment about Christians performing magic tricks. While on the surface the tricks may appear to be harmless, they are associated with deception and trickery. Magical art stirs most people's curiosity. Some viewers of the Christian magician may not be the slightest bit interested in learning any of the tricks. However, there are others who become captivated by the craft, and these can be carried further into its deceptive arts--out of the Christian arena. Give Satan an inch and he readily takes miles. Thus, I firmly believe that Christians participating in any magic tricks, are stumbling blocks to weaker brethren.

## ASTROLOGY IS DEMONIC

Astrology involves demonic deception--it is a type of pagan divination inviting the activity of demon spirits into a person's life. It includes worshipping the stars and seeking secret knowledge, practices in opposition to God's Word and to His divine will. When an Israelite became involved in star worship, the sentence of death by stoning was pronounced upon him, emphasizing his flagrant violation of the first commandment:

> *Thou shalt not sacrifice unto the Lord thy God any bullock, or sheep, wherein is blemish, or any evilfavoredness: for that is an abomination unto the Lord thy God. If there be found among you, within any of thy gates which the Lord thy God giveth thee, man or woman, that hath wrought wickedness in the sight of the Lord thy God, in transgressing his covenant, and hath gone and served other gods, and worshipped them, either the sun, or moon, or any of the host of heaven, which I have not commanded; and it be told thee, and thou hast heard of it, and inquired diligently, and behold, it be true, and the thing certain, that such abomination is wrought in Israel: then shalt thou bring forth that man or that woman, which have committed that wicked thing, unto thy gates, even that man or that woman, and shalt stone them with stones, till they die.[20] (Deut. 17:1-5)*

> *And God spoke all these words, saying I am the Lord thy God, which have brought thee out of the land of Egypt, out of the house of bondage. Thou shalt have no other gods before me. Thou shalt not make unto thee any graven image, or any likeness of any thing that is in heaven above, or that is in the earth beneath, or that is in the*

*water under the earth: Thou shalt not bow down thyself to them, nor serve them: for I the Lord thy God am a jealous God, visiting the iniquity of the fathers upon the children unto the third and fourth generation of them that hate me;... (Exodus 20:1-5 KJV)*

Satan and his demons want to draw men away from God into idolatry, and brazenly use the creation of God's stars to accomplish their goal. We see evidence of the interference of demonic powers in Ephesians: "In which in time past ye walked according to the course of this world, according to the prince of the power of the air, the spirit that now worketh in the sons of disobedience" (Ephesians 2:2). The prophet Jeremiah admonished the people not to be dismayed by the signs of the heavens "for the heathen are dismayed at them" (Jeremiah 10:2 KJV)!

## EXAMPLES OF OLD TESTAMENT SAINTS CONTROLLED BY DEMONS

Demon possession in the Old Testament is another controversial subject among Bible scholars. Alexander cites King Saul as an example of demon possession in the Old Testament. He allows that it has been repeatedly claimed, however, that *possession* is unknown in the Old Testament. "But the case of Saul is undoubtedly to be regarded as one of possession by an evil spirit."[21] Alexander allows that Keim and Dr. F. B. Meyer declared possession as a modern disease among the Jews.[22]

## CASE #1, KING SAUL

Unger, in his book What **Demons Can Do to Saints**, states that the case of Saul is certainly a good example of an Old Testament saint being possessed by an evil spirit. The evil spirit terrifies Saul (I Samuel 16:14); when it leaves him, he is well (I Samuel 16:23); when it returns, he is ill (I Samuel 18:10); it causes him to prophesy (rave) in his house (I Samuel 18:10-11); it incites him to murder (I Samuel 19:9-10). The language and details of the narrative confirm the opinion that Saul's illness was regarded as demonic in nature.[23] **The Zondervan Pictorial Encyclopedia of the Bible**, differs, however, and makes this statement about the demon possession of King Saul:

> Similarly the expression 'ahazani hassabas' (II Sam. 1:9) has been claimed by some scholars to denote seizure or possession by an evil power whereas in actual fact Saul was describing an attack of giddiness due to extreme emotional exhaustion.[24]

Unger believes that nowhere in the scripture is it declared a believer may not be invaded by demon power. He believes, however, that God's Word contains scriptural implication that the powers of darkness have the right to invade the believer but only under certain conditions.[25] He believes that Saul was a believer because of the reference to God's giving him "another heart" (I Samuel 10:9), and to his receiving the anointing of God's Spirit. However, because of sin and disobedience, he became invaded by a demon spirit (I Samuel 16:14). He states that the demon is called "an evil spirit from the Lord" (I Samuel 16:14: cf. v. 23) because God used it as a chastening tool upon His disobedient child.

Taylor believes that Saul is the most apparent case of demonization in the Old Testament. He points out Saul's partial, subtle disobedience in I Samuel 15, where he uses his own judgment instead of obeying God's commandment. When Saul tried to use the cause of God as an excuse for his disobedience, Samuel replied, "Behold, to obey is better than sacrifice, and to hearken than the fat of rams. For rebellion is as the sin of witchcraft, and stubbornness is as iniquity and idolatry" (I Samuel 15:22, 23).[26]

I agree with Unger: to argue that Saul was not a believer is to argue that the Spirit of God may anoint an unbeliever and that God would appoint an unbeliever over His inheritance (I Samuel 10:1,10). The exact reason why King Saul was invaded by a demon is not stated. Samuel declared, "Rebellion is as the sin of witchcraft" (I Samuel 15:23), and in the very next chapter (I Samuel 16:14,23), Saul was invaded by a demon.[27] I believe that the reason is apparent--in stubborn rebellion, Saul turned his focus away from God.

## CASE #2, THE KING'S PROPHETS

Of the four hundred prophets of the Lord in I Kings 22:20-22, one would think that the majority were believers. Despite the fact that they were the Lord's prophets, they had become controlled by deceptive spirits as a result of their compromising to please wicked Ahab. The scripture plainly declares that these prophets thought they were telling the truth by the Spirit of God. Zedekiah, under demonic control, struck Micaiah, who was controlled by God's Spirit, on the cheek. Unger says that Zedekiah "...was not joking when he said, 'How did the Spirit of the Lord pass from me to speak to you?'" (I Kings 22:24, NASB) [28] Zedekiah was actually deceived into believing he was speaking by the "Spirit of the Lord," and that he was a true prophet of the Lord.

As we look at the scripture in I Kings, this scene evidently depicts the whole realm of both good and bad in the supernatural world:

> *And Micaiah said, therefore, hear the word of the Lord. I saw the Lord sitting on His throne, and all the host of heaven standing by Him on His right and on His left. And the Lord said, Who will entice Ahab to go up and fall at Ramoth-gilead? And one said this while another said that. Then a spirit came forward and stood before the Lord and said, I will entice him. And the Lord said to him, How? And he said, I will go out and be a deceiving spirit in the mouth of all his prophets. Then He said, You are to entice him and also prevail. Go and do so. Now therefore behold, the Lord has put a deceiving spirit in the mouth of all these your prophets; and the Lord has proclaimed disaster against you (I Kings 22:19-23).[29]*

In reference to this scripture, Unger says, "...the incident is a vivid illustration from the Old Testament and of the New Testament revelation that demons inspire false prophets and give them deceptive teaching and predictions" (I John 4:1).[30]

As we have looked at these case studies, I believe the reader will agree with Unger and me that these Old Testament saints were invaded by demons. The reader must understand that I am not going into major detail on each of these cases because doing so would make this book an enormous catalog of details. However, if the reader wants a few more examples, I would suggest purchasing the book **What Demons Can Do to Saints,** by Unger.

## NOTES

1. Merrill F. Unger, <u>Demons in the World Today</u>, p. 9.
2. William M. Alexander, <u>Demonic Possession in the New Testament</u>, p. 13.
3. Merril C. Tenney, <u>The Zondervan Pictorial Encyclopedia of the Bible</u>, Vol. II, p. 95.
4. Jack R. Taylor, <u>Victory Over the Devil</u>, p. 43.
5. The Lockman Foundation, <u>New American Standard Bible</u>, Judges 9:23-24, p. 366. (All future references to this work will be referred to within the text with the scripture reference followed by NASB.)
6. Merril C. Tenney, <u>op</u>. <u>cit</u>., p. 95.
7. <u>Loc</u>. <u>cit</u>.
8. <u>Ibid</u>., p. 96.
9. William M. Alexander, <u>op</u>. <u>cit</u>., p. 18.
10. Kurt Koch, <u>Demonology Past and Present</u>, p. 27.
11. <u>Ibid</u>., p. 28.
12. J. Stafford Wright, <u>Christianity and the Occult</u>, p. 106.
13. Kurt Koch, <u>op</u>. <u>cit</u>., p. 24.
14. John P. Newport, <u>Demons, Demons, Demons</u>, p. 133.
15. J. Stafford Wright, <u>op</u>. <u>cit</u>., p. 106.
16. Basil Atkinson, "Commentary on Leviticus", <u>Pocket Commentary on the Bible</u>, p. 27.
17. J. Stafford Wright, <u>op</u>. <u>cit</u>., p. 108.
18. <u>Ibid</u>., p. 110.
19. Kurt Koch, <u>Christian Counseling and Occultism</u>, p. 269.
20. <u>The Holy Bible</u>, King James Version, Deuteronomy 17:1-5, p. 187. (All future references in this edition will be referred to with the scripture reference followed by KJV.
21. William M. Alexander, <u>op</u>. <u>cit</u>., p. 20.
22. <u>Loc</u>. <u>cit</u>.
23. Merrill F. Unger, <u>What Demons Can Do To Saints</u>, pp. 122, 123.
24. Merril C. Tenney, <u>op</u>. <u>cit</u>., p. 95.
25. Merrill F. Unger, <u>op</u>. <u>cit</u>., p. 9.
26. Jack R. Taylor, <u>op</u>. <u>cit</u>., p. 45.
27. <u>Ibid</u>., pp. 88, 89.
28. Merrill F. Unger, <u>op</u>. <u>cit</u>., p. 124.
29. The Lockman Foundation, <u>New American Standard Bible</u>, I Kings 22:19-23, p. 527.
30. Merrill F. Unger, <u>op</u>. <u>cit</u>., 125.

# CHAPTER THREE
# NEW TESTAMENT SCRIPTURAL ACCOUNTS OF DEMONS

## JESUS' PRESENCE BRINGING WARFARE AGAINST SATAN

The New Testament describes a war between the kingdom of the Devil and the Kingdom of God. This war involves direct attacks against God's people, for Ephesians 6:12 says, "For we wrestle not against flesh and blood, but against principalities, against powers, against the rulers of the darkness of this world, against spiritual wickedness in high places." I Peter 5:8 goes on to say, "...your adversary, the devil, like a roaring lion, walketh about, seeking whom he may devour."

The appearance of our Savior, Jesus Christ, brought the very dawning of the Kingdom of God on earth. This kingdom presents itself in the new realities of salvation: the blind see, the lame walk, the lepers are healed, the deaf hear, the dead are raised, and the poor receive the Gospel (Matthew 11:5). Prisoners are loosed; the oppressed are freed; the year of the Lord and all His good pleasure has come (Luke 4:18-19). Satan organized his forces for the demonic counter-attack against God's Kingdom.[1] Satan set everything submitted to his control in motion against Christ, including the Jewish authorities, theologians, priests and people (John 8:12-59). Knowing his kingdom was threatened; Satan summoned his demonic forces for a great counter-attack against the power of the Son of God.[2] Eventually, Christ's very own disciples and the Roman rulers turned against Him.

The very nature of Jesus' mission on earth supplies the answer to the question, "From whence comes all this deadly hostility?" and clarifies the enigma regarding the powers of darkness. Karl Heim writes in his book, **Jesus Der Weltvollender**:

> The removal of confusion which has arisen through Satan's rebellion is therefore the ultimate meaning of the mission of Jesus on the earth. If this Satanic revolution against God had not taken place, the mission of Christ on earth would not have resulted.[3]

Heim sees this truth of the mission and ministry of Christ in the writings of Paul in I Corinthians 15. There it is stated that Christ must continue to exercise kingly rule until He has put all enemies under His feet as a foot-stool. Then Christ will have finished His mission and given back to God the Father what has been committed to Him as the Son. Jesus Christ exercised great authority over his enemies during His ministry which throws light on the power of His adversary, the Devil. Understanding the powers of darkness in the New Testament revolves around understanding the Christ; in short, the question of demons is a question of Christ.[4]

There are many references to demons in the earliest Christian literature, particularly in the Gospels, but few in the Epistles. For the most part, they were generally referred to by the term **daimonion**, a diminutive form of **daimon**, and the two words being used interchangeably. In contrast to the Greeks, who frequently thought of **daimon** in a good sense, the New Testament writers always thought of devils or demons as spiritual beings hostile to both God and men. The controller or prince

of these evil beings was named Beelzebub, or more accurately, Beelzebul. The demons were generally regarded as his agents in human society (Mark 3:22; Acts 17:18; I Corinthians 10:20-21; Revelation 9:20).

## SOME PHILOLOGICAL FACTS ABOUT DEMONS

It is necessary to mention a few philological facts about demons in the New Testament. The noun **demon** occurs only once in the New Testament (Matthew 8:31). On the other hand, the adjective demonic occurs more than fifty times in the Gospels. **Unclean or evil spirits** are mentioned in the New Testament twenty-eight times, but **spirits of the dead** are not mentioned once. The **angels of God** are mentioned in Matthew 25:31, Luke 12:8, 12:10, and in John 1:51; and the **angels of Satan** are mentioned in Matthew 25:41, II Corinthians 12:7, and in Revelation 12:7. The types of angels are still sharply contrasted as they are in the Old Testament, and contact with the strong powers of Satan through participation in heathen rites and sorcery is also condemned as it was previously (Galatians 5:19-20; Revelation 9:21, 18:23, 22:15).[5]

The word **demon** can be traced back to a custom practiced in some cultures for many years--that of eating the dead. This word **demon** contains the Greek root **dia** or **daiomai**, meaning *to divide, to tear, or to portion out*. People who ate their dead were therefore called demons or dividers. This derivation of the word is found in the dictionary of, Kittel's **Dictionary of Greek**. Another area of heathenism throws even more light on the origin of the word. The cannibals of New Guinea actually go as far as to call the souls of the dead **demons**. The use of the word **demon** is connected with cannibalism practiced by primitive tribes in South America and in East Africa. Koch says, "...this custom is most pronounced among the Pacaas Novos, a tribe of Indians living on the border between Brazil and Bolivia." Unfortunately, this grisly custom of eating human flesh exists even today.[6]

During New Testament times, there was apparently no significant difference between the usage of the words for demons, **evil spirits (ponera),** and **unclean spirits (akatharta),** since in the case of the Gadarene demoniac, the terms *unclean spirits* and *devil* were used interchangeably (Luke 8:27-29). In Luke 11:24-26, the *unclean spirit* which went out of a man returned with seven other spirits of a more wicked, though still kindred nature. In the New Testament, demons and evil spirits were regarded as one cause of disease (Mark 1:23; 7:25). It is very interesting to note that such possession did not defile the sufferers morally or spiritually, since they were not excluded from the synagogue or the temple precincts. The possessing spirits were uniformly regarded as evil, and had to be expelled on all possible occasions, for they were considered allies of Satan, and thus hostile to man and God alike.[7]

As the Bible student explores the New Testament, he will find that the Gospel records are full of references to the workings of evil spirits. Wherever the Lord Jesus moved, the messengers of Satan sprang into active manifestation in the bodies and minds of those in whom they lived. The ministry of Jesus Christ and His Apostles was directed actively against them. Again and again, the record states that He went throughout synagogues preaching and casting out **demons** (Mark 1:39). Mark 1:34 says He "cast out many **demons**; and permitted not the demons to speak, because they knew Him." Mark goes on to say, "*Unclean spirits*, when they saw Him, fell down before Him, and cried, saying, Thou art the Son of God" (Mark 3:11). When Jesus sent out the twelve and then the seventy, He gave them power over the **demons** (Mark 6:7; Luke 10:17).[8]

Dr. Augustus H. Strong, author of **Systematic Theology**, believes that Satan takes away the seed sown and sows tares, and that he controls many subordinate *evil spirits*; there is only one Devil, but there are many *angels or demons*, and through their agency, Satan may accomplish his purposes.[9]

In conclusion we can see there is one Satan--one Devil--one Prince of the demons--directing all the multitudes in opposition to Christ and His people. The horde of *wicked spirits*, whether they are called *demons, lying spirits, foul spirits, unclean spirits, or deceiving spirits*, are at work against mankind. The Christian, however, can praise God for the victory found in I Corinthians 15:57: "But thanks be to God, who giveth us the victory through our Lord Jesus Christ." Therefore, as we learn more about the demonic, we can rest in total peace that the Christian has victory over Satan and his demons!

## JESUS' RECOGNITION OF THE WORK OF SATAN

The Word of God reveals that Jesus recognized the Devil as the energizer behind the opposition of the Pharisees (John 8:44); the "hour and the power of darkness" (Luke 22:53); and behind His persecutors at Calvary (Luke 22:1-6). Jesus said that His mission was "to preach deliverance to the captives" (Luke 4: 18). He revealed who the captor was on the eve of His crucifixion when He said, "Now is the judgment of this world; now shall the prince of this world be cast out" (John 12:31). Later, He said that the prince would find nothing in Him as ground for his power (John 14:7, 30).[10]

The scriptures show that Jesus encountered people with demons that affected them physically. In Matthew 17:14-21 an epileptic boy was delivered of a demon and cured completely. In Matthew 9:32-34, a dumb man was healed by Jesus when the demon was cast out. In Luke 13:10-17, the case of a woman with a serious case of spinal curvature is recorded. Jesus healed her, informing the people that the Devil had kept her bound for many years.

In Mark 1:34, it says: "And He healed many that were sick of diverse diseases, and cast out many demons." "And He preached in their synagogues throughout all Galilee, and cast out demons" (Mark 1:39). In the scriptures, we can see that the instances of Jesus' dealing with demons is often the rule rather than the exception. Mark 3:10-11 says: "For He had healed many; insomuch that they pressed upon Him to touch Him, as many as had plagues. And unclean spirits, when they saw Him, fell down before Him, and cried, saying Thou art the Son of God." The Lord Jesus delivered thousands of people by His power and authority. Taylor believes that there must have been many cases of mass deliverances and says, "This would lead us to believe that demonization was indeed common in Jesus' day."[11]

## TEN CASE STUDIES OF DEMONIZATION OR DEMON POSSESSION

The New Testament records ten specific cases of demonization, eight incidents in the Gospels and two in the book of Acts. Before we look at these ten cases, I want the reader to know that I believe that all the cases are exactly what the Word of God says they are--cases of people who were demonized. Let's carefully look at each of them.

## CASE #1, THE CAPERNAUM DEMONIAC

> *And they went into Capernaum; and straightway on the sabbath day he entered into the synagogue, and taught. And they were astonished at his doctrine; for he taught them as one that had authority, and not as the scribes. And there was in their synagogue a man with an unclean spirit; and he cried out, saying Let us alone! What have we to do with thee, thou Jesus of Nazareth? Art thou come to destroy us? I know thee, who thou art, the Holy One of God. And Jesus rebuked him, saying, Hold thy peace, and come out of him. And when the unclean spirit had torn him, and cried with a loud voice, he came out of him. And they were all amazed, insomuch that they questioned among themselves, saying, What thing is this? What new doctrine is this? For with authority commandeth he even the unclean spirits, and they do obey him. And immediately his fame spread abroad throughout all the region round about Galilee (Mark 1:21-28; NSSB).*

This is the first recorded case of a demonized man in the New Testament. Taylor describes the demoniac as one who had evidently been worshipping along with the rest of the Jews.[12] Alexander, however, believes the demoniac was an outside intruder in the synagogue, and that he took the worshipers completely by surprise. How he got there remains unexplained; there is no mention of the details in the scripture.[13] Alexander says that Keim boldly asserts that "the incident bears all the marks of invention," while Holtzmann believes that the incident shows "the glorification of miracles."[14] Alexander attempts to prove in his book that the cure of the demoniac was the beginning of miracles of this type in Christ's ministry and says, "The case is one of epileptic insanity" but it also meets his guideline of being supernaturally caused.

Alexander goes on to say, "The confession of Jesus as the Messiah or the Son of God is therefore the classical criterion of genuine demonic possession."[15] Therefore, he believes that it was a genuine case of a demonized person only if an unclean spirit spoke out and acknowledged that Jesus was the Son of God. In studying all the cases, however, we clearly see there were times when Jesus allowed the demons to speak, such as in this case of the demonized Capernaum, and other times in which He prevented them from speaking and declaring their knowledge of Him. Evidence of Jesus silencing them is found in Mark 1:34 where we read, "...he healed many that were sick of diverse diseases, and cast out many demons; and permitted not the demons to speak, because they knew him" (NSSB).

Merril C. Tenney in the, **Zondervan Pictorial Encyclopedia of the Bible** states that the madman of Capernaum spoke as though he were a victim of multiple personalities. He believes that the demonized man's convulsive interlude during the healing might have resulted from the discharging of long-repressed emotion in the subconscious mind.[16]

I believe the demonized man in the synagogue who had the voice crying out of him, was a Jew and a child of God by the standards of Old Testament law. He was tormented by the presence of Christ. The Lord Jesus Christ treated him as one of His own. He took authority over the demon and told him to stop his babblings and leave the man. From this time forth in God's Word, we find Jesus taking authority and dealing with the demonized.

## CASE #2, THE GERASENE DEMONIAC

*And when he was come to the other side into the country of the Gerasenes, there met him two possessed with demons, coming out of the tombs, exceedingly fierce, so that no man might pass by that way. And, behold, they cried out, saying, what have we to do with thee, Jesus, thou Son of God? Art thou come here to torment us before the time? And there was a good way off from them an herd of many swine feeding. So the demons besought him, saying, If thou cast us out, permit us to go away into the herd of swine. And he said unto them, Go. And when they were come out, they went into the herd of swine; and, behold, the whole herd of swine ran violently down a steep place into the sea, and perished in the waters. And they that kept them fled, and went their ways into the city, and told everything, and what was befallen to those possessed with the demons. And, behold, the whole city came out to meet Jesus; and when they saw him, they besought him that he would depart from their borders (Matthew 8:28-34; NSSB).*

Tenney expresses a number of opinions about this demoniac. He believes that the Gerasene demoniac behaved as though a personality separate from his own were speaking through his mouth and using destructive physical strength. He asserts that the demoniac's psychosis was deeply entrenched, and that his self-imposed name of Legion perhaps furnishes a hint as to the origin of the shock which precipitated his illness--namely, some atrocity committed in the area by the Roman legion, possibly the massacre of children. Whether or not this is actually the case, the sufferer spoke as though possessed in the most literal sense, and the phenomena which accompanied the demoniac's cure did nothing to dispel this notion in the minds of those who witnessed Jesus' healing the man.[17]

Alexander thinks that the demoniac suffered from acute mania, but that the demoniac's confession of Jesus as the Messiah or the Son of God is therefore the classical criterion of genuine demonic possession.[18]

According to Edersheim, a demonic person is characterized by an incapability to separate his own consciousness and ideas from the influence of the demon. The conduct and language of the demonized must always be regarded as a mixture of the human being and the demon. In this demonized state, a man's identity was not superseded, but controlled.[19]

Regarding this most famous of all demonization cases in the New Testament, Taylor says, "He [the demoniac of Gadara] is the exception instead of the rule. In fact, he is the only one of his kind mentioned (in one case, two are mentioned as being present on that occasion). He was a man truly possessed."[20]

There are three major things that I believe stand out in the case of the demoniac of Gadara. First, Jesus dealt with the man by dealing with the demons. That means He accepted the reality of the demons being present. Secondly, the man's mania was healed when the demons were cast out. Jesus did not treat the demoniac as if he were insane, but dealt with him in the spiritual realm, and saw him freed and restored to his right mind. Thirdly, Jesus sent the man back among his people as a missionary with a message: Jesus heals and sets the captives free. Once again we see the Lord's power and authority come against the demonic world and win the conflict.

## CASE #3, THE EPILEPTIC IDIOT

> *And when he came to his disciples, he saw a great multitude about them, and the scribes questioning with them. And straightway all the people, when they beheld him, were greatly amazed and, running to him, greeted him. And he asked the scribes, What question ye with them? And one of the multitude answered and said, Master, I have brought unto thee my son, who hath a dumb spirit; and wherever he taketh him, he teareth him; and he foameth, and gnasheth with his teeth, and pineth away. And I spoke to thy disciples, that they should cast him out, and they could not. He answereth him, and saith, O faithless generation, how long shall I be with you? How long shall I endure you? Bring him unto me. And they brought him unto him; and when he saw him, straightway the spirit convulsed him; and he fell on the ground, and wallowed foaming. And he asked his father, How long ago is it since this came unto him? And he said, From a child. And often it hath cast him into the fire, and into the waters, to destroy him; but if thou canst do anything, have compassion on us, and help us. Jesus said unto him, If thou canst believe, all things are possible to him that believeth. And straightway the father of the child cried out, and said with tears, Lord, I believe; help thou mine unbelief. When Jesus saw that the people came running together, he rebuked the foul spirit, saying unto him, Thou dumb and deaf spirit, I charge thee, come out of him, and enter no more into him. And the spirit cried, and convulsed him greatly, and came out of him; and he was like one dead, insomuch that many said, He is dead. But Jesus took him by the hand, and lifted him up; and he arose. And when he was come into the house, his disciples asked him privately, Why could not we cast him out? And he said unto them, This kind can come forth by nothing, but by prayer and fasting (Mark 9:14-29; NSSB).*

Alexander believes that the son's sickness was possibly congenital, or that his convulsions had begun very early in life and had been frequent. He does not believe that the son was demon-possessed, but rather that he was an epileptic idiot. He goes on to say that for a case to be classed as demon possession, it must meet the criterion of genuine demonic possession. Since the confession from the demons did not take place, this particular case does not meet Alexander's criterion.[21] I totally disagree with Alexander's diagnosis that this case is dealing strictly with a medical condition.

**The Criswell Study Bible**, indicates that this type of demonic possession affected the son both spiritually and physically, with side effects in the form of seizures.[22] Taylor also believes that the boy was an epileptic, but that he was delivered of a demon and was completely cured by the Lord Jesus.[23] I believe in this case, however, that there is much more involved with the epileptic son than just a demon, and I will speak to this in a later chapter as I address the subject of ancestral demons and how to deal with them through biblical counseling and church ministry.

At this point I will make only a few comments on the remaining seven cases since much of the material is repetitious. However, I will deal more thoroughly with these cases toward the end of this chapter.

## CASE #4, THE SYROPHENICIAN GIRL

*And from there he arose, and went into the borders of Tyre and Sidon, and entered into an house, and would have no man know it; but he could not be hidden. For a certain woman, whose young daughter had an unclean spirit, heard of him, and came and fell at his feet...the woman was a Greek, a Syrophenician by nation...and she besought him that he would cast forth the demon out of her daughter...and he said unto her, For this saying go thy way; the demon is gone out of thy daughter. And when she was come to her house, she found the demon gone out, and her daughter lying upon the bed (Mark 7:24-26; 29-30; NSSB).*

Alexander says, "...the diagnosis here is thus epileptic idiocy," and because of the criterion he sets, there is no demon possession.[24]

## CASE #5, THE DUMB DEMONIAC

*As they went out, behold, they brought to him a dumb man possessed with a demon. And when the demon was cast out, the dumb spoke; and the multitudes marveled, saying, It was never so seen in Israel. But the Pharisees said, he casteth out demons through the prince of demons (Matthew 9:32-34; NSSB).*

## CASE #6, THE BLIND AND DUMB DEMONIAC

*Then was brought unto him one possessed with a demon, blind, and dumb; and he healed him, insomuch that the blind and dumb both spoke and saw. And all the people were amazed, and said, "Is not this the son of David? But when the Pharisees heard it, they said, this fellow doth not cast out demons, but by Beelzebub, the prince of demons (Matt. 12:22-24; NSSB).*

Alexander, in dealing with the dumb demoniac and the blind and dumb demoniac, says that these two cases are not to be treated as duplicates of the same case; they are, however, both diagnosed by him as idiocy or mental deficiency.[25] The narratives concerning the demoniacs who were blind and dumb are too vague to admit pronouncements concerning the nature of the affliction.[26]

## CASE #7, MARY MAGDALENE

*And it came to pass, afterward, that he went throughout every city and village, preaching and showing the glad tidings of the kingdom of God; and the twelve were with him, and certain women, who had been healed of evil spirits and infirmities: Mary, called Magdalene, out of whom went seven demons; (Luke 8:1-2; NSSB)*

Alexander believes that the number seven attested to the severity of Mary's disorder, showing proof that it surpassed the skill of ordinary practitioners; nevertheless, his diagnosis of her is acute mania.[27]

## CASE #8, THE INFIRM WOMAN

> *And he was teaching in one of the synagogues on the sabbath. And, behold, there was a woman who had a spirit of infirmity eighteen years, and was bowed together, and could in no way lift herself up. And when Jesus saw her, he called her to him, and said unto her, Woman, thou art loosed from thine infirmity. And he laid his hands on her; and immediately she was made straight, and glorified God. And the ruler of the synagogue answered with indignation, because Jesus had healed on the sabbath day, and said unto the people, There are six days in which men ought to work; in them, therefore, come and be healed, and not on the sabbath day. The Lord then answered him, and said, Thou hypocrite, doth not each one of you on the sabbath loose his ox or his ass from the stall, and lead him away to watering? And ought not this woman, being a daughter of Abraham, whom Satan hath bound, lo, these eighteen years, be loosed from this bond on the sabbath day? (Luke 13:10-16; NSSB)*

Alexander regards this case as an extreme instance of spinal disease, in the form of "Pott's curvature."[28] Alexander also allows that Trench indicates there was a deeper spiritual root to the woman's calamity, based on her description as one "...whom Satan has bound." He says, "Her sickness, having its first seat in her spirit, had brought her into a moody melancholy state...her outward condition was but the sign and the consequence."[29] Alexander believes that neither the symptoms of this case, nor the testimony of Christ, can be construed to be proof of demonic possession.[30]

## CASE #9, THE PHILIPPIAN PYTHONESS

> *And it came to pass, as we went to prayer, a certain maid possessed with a spirit of divination met us, who brought her masters much gain by soothsaying. The same followed Paul and us, and cried, saying, These men are the servants of the Most High God, who show unto us the way of salvation. And this did she many days. But Paul, being grieved, turned and said to the spirit, I command thee, in the name of Jesus Christ, to come out of her. And he came out the same hour (Acts 16:16-18; NSSB).*

The young woman with divinatory gifts, who was little more than a fortune-teller or a sooth-sayer, certainly falls into a different category than those with mental afflictions. Alexander makes several points in his evaluation of the case. He believes that this woman should not be considered anything other than a common ventriloquist or fortune-teller, in which case there would be no genuine demonic activity. He forms his opinion from this information: the woman belonged to the order of the Puthones. The Puthones were formerly called Eurukleis, after Eurukles [who was mentioned by Aristophanes]. Eurukles was a famous ventriloquist, who was supposed to deliver true oracles. Alexander goes on to assert that the apostle Paul may not have been fully emancipated from the traditions of the fathers, and that he may have used an ethnic formula without endorsing ethnic doctrine.[31] He believes Paul was wrong in treating her as a demonic, and asserts that he responded to the Jewish traditions of that day in blaming this woman's actions on a demon.

**The New Testament and the Wycliffe Bible Commentary** makes a very good point in its reference to a spirit of divination's literally meaning python spirit. A person having a python spirit was thought to be inspired by Apollo. The commentary goes on to state, "This girl was demon-possessed, and her uncontrolled utterances were regarded as the utterances of a god."[32]

## CASE #10, THE EPHESIAN DEMONIAC

*And God wrought special miracles by the hands of Paul, so that from his body were brought unto the sick handkerchiefs or aprons, and the diseases departed from them, and the evil spirits went out of them. Then certain of the vagabond Jews, exorcists, took upon them to call over them who had evil spirits the name of the Lord Jesus, saying, we adjure you by Jesus, whom Paul preacheth. And there were seven sons of one Sceva, a Jew, and chief of the priests, who did so. And the evil spirit answered and said, Jesus I know, and Paul I know; but who are ye? And the man in whom the evil spirit was, leaped on them and overcame them, and prevailed against them, so that they fled out of that house naked and wounded (Acts 19:11-16; NSSB).*

William Alexander considers this man to be another "sufferer from epileptic insanity." He believes that the mention of the names of Jesus and of Paul has nothing to do with supernatural knowledge.[33]

The Zondervan Encyclopedia makes a couple of points about this case: (1) In antiquity, the widespread conception of exorcism was that of "power of the name," and was based on the assumption that the name was not only a personal designation, but also represented an integral part of the bearer's personality. (2) In the time of Christ, the Jewish custom was to commence a magical incantation against a demon with the words, "I conjure you by the name of 'whatever name represented power or authority to them.'" This custom was reflected in Acts 19:13, where certain Jewish exorcists took it upon themselves to pronounce the name of the Lord Jesus Christ over those who were possessed with evil spirits. They used the formula, "We adjure you by the Jesus whom Paul preaches" which produced entirely unexpected results.[34]

## THE THEOLOGICAL DEBATE, DEMON POSSESSION

Reviewing these past ten cases of demon possession in the New Testament, Unger proposes the answer to the question, "What is demon possession?" He believes that it is a condition in which one or more evil spirits inhabit the body of a victim and can take complete control of his will. They do this by blotting out the victim's consciousness. The demon can speak and act through the victim, using him as his complete slave. Also, the inhabiting demon (or demons) can come and go at will. The condition of the afflicted person in the possessed state varies greatly. Sometimes it is marked by depression and deep melancholy; sometimes by vacancy and stupidity that resembles idiocy. At other times, the victim may be ecstatic or extremely spiteful and wildly ferocious. During the transition from the normal to the abnormal state, the victim is frequently thrown into a violent reaction, often falling to the ground unconscious, foaming at the mouth with symptoms similar to epilepsy or hysteria.[35]

We must remember that demon influence (or temptation), as Unger has said, may vary from mild harassment to extreme subjection, when body and mind become dominated and held in slavery by the spirit agent. In demon influence, evil spirits exert power over a person short of actual possession.[36] Demon possession is the step beyond influence, to actual possession; that is, a person yielding frequently to Satan.

Regarding demonic possession, **Strong's Systematic Theology** says that Meyer believes in the existence of Satan but not of demons. Though the Old Testament refers to them as familiar spirits, he argues against their existence. He also believes that they do not exist in the present age. He declares that there is no evidence of demonic possession in the Gospel of John, even though Satan's being allowed to overcome is clearly mentioned (as he entered into Judas' mind and took control--thus playing a part in the Messiah's work [John 13:27]). As would be expected, he believed the so-called demoniacs are not of a diabolic temper and filled with extreme ill will toward Christ.[37]

Alexander says that Farrar believes, since so many good and capable orthodox writers with the same data before them have arrived at different conclusions on this question, any certainty regarding it seems to be impossible. This uncertainty leads him to state: "I have shown that the Jews, like all unscientific nations in all ages, attributed many nervous disorders and physical obstructions to demoniac possession which should be attributed to natural causes."[38] He also says, however, that he is not prepared to deny that in the first advent of Christ, there may have been forms of madness attributed to evil powers. He personally finds no difficulty in accepting such a belief. He says that he has only been arguing against the "uncharitable and pernicious attempt to treat it as a necessary article of faith for all. The subject is too obscure (even to science) to admit of dogmatism on either side."[39]

It is the opinion of Professor Wendt that Jesus followed traditional ideas in regard to supernatural beings, even though He took quite a different view from that of His Jewish contemporaries regarding the significance of those beings affecting man's health. Professor Wendt believes that as far as the existence, nature, and ordinary mode of activity of these spiritual agents is concerned, Christ simply accepted the current ideas of His countrymen. The view that demoniac influences aim, not at immorality, but at the misery of man, was not original on the part of the Lord Jesus.[40]

Alexander concludes that Gould doubts the reality of demoniacal possession. He thinks the most serious argument against it is that the phenomena are mostly natural, not supernatural. It was the unscientific habit of the ancient mind to account for abnormal and uncanny things--such as lunacy and epilepsy--supernaturally, and that in such cases outside the Bible; these diseases are ascribed to natural causes. He discusses another serious difficulty: that lunacy and epilepsy are as common in the East as elsewhere, and yet, Jesus is not found healing these disorders as such, but is found healing cases of demoniacal possession in which these were symptoms. He states: "The dilemma is very curious. Outside the New Testament, no demoniacal possession, but only lunacy and epilepsy; in the New Testament, no cases of lunacy and epilepsy proper, but only demoniacal possession."[41]

Nevius believes that the scriptures do not confuse demon-possession with diseases, but uniformly make a clear distinction between them. The Bible says, "He cast out the spirits with his word, and healed all that were sick" (Matthew 8:16). In Matthew 4:24 it says, "They brought unto him all sick people that were taken with divers diseases and torments, and those who were possessed with demons, and those who were epileptics, and those who had the palsy; and he healed them." In the above passage, demon-possession is differentiated from all sickness or disease; also from divers diseases and torments, and specifically from epilepsy and paralysis.[42]

**Strong** states that the time of Christ, popular belief undoubtedly exaggerated the influence of evil spirits, perhaps causing many to see *a demon behind every bush*. Because of the fall of man, however, Satan and his demons do affect man's welfare with a limited amount of God-given power. Satan sometimes exercises a God-measured control over physical (natural) phenomena, such as using the weather for his purposes (Job 1:12, 16, 19; 2:7; Luke 13:11, 16; Acts 10:38; II Cor. 12:7; I Thess. 2:18; Heb. 2:14).

More commonly, however, we find that demons subject man's soul to temptation (Gen. 3:1; Matt. 4:3; John 13:27; Acts 5:3; Eph. 2:2; I Thess. 3:5; I Peter 5:8). The possession of man's being, either physically or spiritually, by demons is recognized in the scriptures. Savage says in, **Life After Death**:

> While God was at a distance, the demons were very, very near. The air about the earth was full of these evil tempting spirits. They caused shipwreck at sea, and sudden death on land; they blighted the crops; they smote and blasted in the tempests; they took possession of the bodies and the souls of men. They entered into compacts, and took mortgages on men's souls.[43]

Scriptural accounts of personal encounters between Christ and the demons cannot be interpreted as symbolic. Farrar says, "...in the temptation of Christ and in the possession of the swine, imagination could have no place."[44] Strong says that Trench believes possession is distinguished from mere temptation by the complete or incomplete loss of the sufferer's reason or power of will. His actions, words, and thoughts are mastered by the evil spirit, until the sufferer's personality seems to be destroyed, or at least so overtaken as to produce the consciousness of a two-fold will within him like that in a dream. He believes that the ordinary assaults and temptations of Satan overcome the individual and cause him to yield consciously. By yielding gradually, the individual assumes--without losing his apparent freedom of action--the characteristics of the Satanic nature. Farrar says, "It is solicited, urged, and persuaded against the strivings of grace, but it is not overborne."[45]

In an opposing view, Strong quotes T. H. Wright, saying, "The finger of God argues that Jesus, in his mention of demoniacs, accommodated himself to the beliefs of his time."[46] Strong also quotes Maclaren, however, in **Sunday School Times**, 1904, who had this to say:

> We are told by some that this demoniac was an epileptic. Possible; but if the epilepsy was not the result of possession, why should it take the shape of violent hatred of Jesus? And what is there in epilepsy to give discernment of his character and the purpose of his mission?[47]

Taylor believes that we can see by the New Testament record that even the most fervent liberals of Christ's day believed in the existence of demons.[48] The scribes are recorded in Mark 3:22 (KJV) as saying, "He hath Beelzebub, and by the prince of devils casteth he out devils." Taylor says, "This word devils should be properly translated 'demons.'"[49]

Strong believes possession is distinguished from bodily or mental disease, though such disease often accompanies possession or results from it. He also believes that the demons speak in their own persons with a supernatural knowledge, and that they are directly addressed by Jesus.

Christ recognizes Satanic agency in these cases of possession and rejoices in the casting out of demons, as a sign of Satan's downfall. These facts render it impossible to interpret the narratives of demoniac possession as a popular description of abnormal physical or mental conditions. Demon possession may be manifested either in physical maladies, as in the recorded case of the demoniac of Gadara (Mark 5:1-20), or in spiritual disorders as in the case of the maid with a spirit of divination (Acts 16:16) where the body does not seem to have been affected.[50]

Strong makes it very clear to the Bible student that the evil spirits are neither omnipotent, omniscient, nor omnipresent.[51] pertaining to the works of evil spirits, he points out two general conclusions:

> First, the power of evil spirits over men is not independent of the human will. This power cannot be exercised without at least the original consent of the human will and may be resisted and shaken off through prayer and faith in God. Secondly, their power is limited, both in time and in extent, by the permissive will of God.[52]

## DEMONIZATION AS THE RESULT OF CONTROL BY ONE OR MORE DEMONS

I must mention at this point that the term **demon possessed** is probably a very unfortunate misnomer. It is an incorrect translation of a Greek word meaning to **demonize**, a word signifying various degrees of demonic influence or control. [The term *demon possessed* invites misconceptions of who may be subjected to demon influence.[53]] Unger, who does a thorough job of discussing demon possession, believes that both demon invasion and demon possession are more accurately defined biblically as demonization (**daimonizomai**, in the Greek, meaning *being demonized, under the control of one or more demons.* [Matthew 4:24, Mark 1:32, and Luke 8:30]). Also, the Greek expression **echei daimonion** means *to have a demon* (Luke 7:33; John 7:20). The scriptures speak of people being demonized or having a demon or demons, while the popular terminology speaks of demon possession. The more scripturally accurate definition is **demonization as the result of control by one or more demons.**[54]

The Holy Scripture shows that Jesus shared His gift of exorcism with His followers at the time of the mission of the Twelve (Luke 9), and that he gave the Seventy authorities and power over all demons (Luke 10). The Apostles dealt with the demons of the invisible world. We can see the evidence of this from the records of the Acts of the Apostles and from other references in the Epistles. Peter quickly recognized Satan's work in Ananias (Acts 5:3); he saw how *unclean spirits* came out in his presence as they had come out in his Lord's presence (Acts 5:15,16). Philip, too, encountered the evil spirits as he proclaimed the Gospel of Christ to the people (Acts 8:5-8). The apostle Paul knew the power of the name of the Risen Lord in dealing with the evil power (Acts 19:11,12). If the Word of God is divinely inspired as it is claimed to be, then it is the only authoritative guide we need to answer the questions which have been raised about demon possession.

There are basically five theories held by professing Christians about demon possession or demonization in the New Testament. Before we look at these five theories, I want to establish that I believe that the first four theories are in error. The first theory holds that the Lord Jesus and His disciples were victims of a primitive and unscientific generation; at least, pertaining to the subject of demon possession. This theory holds that they, like their contemporaries, erroneously accepted and believed in the doctrine of demons--doing so through ignorance and superstition. This theory is totally in opposition to the teachings of Jesus Christ and the words of scripture--conflicting with the view held by the Church concerning the authenticity and divine origin of the scripture.

The second theory is one which has been embraced by a number of those who are regarded as some of the most intelligent and orthodox Christian scholars of today, and which seems to be a compromise between scientific and theological orthodoxy. This theory maintains that the Lord Jesus was not suffering from the ignorance and superstition of His generation, but was in accordance with the accepted ideas of His time and the ordinary use of the language; He chose to speak in the same manner as His contemporaries in reference to demon possession. The holders of this theory allude to the belief that Jesus recognized that the men and women who were brought to him as ones supposedly being possessed by demons only had different forms of bodily disease.

Since, however, the people spoke of it as demon possession rather than sickness, Jesus did also. He *allowed* the people to believe that the casting out of demons healed their sicknesses. When he gave power to His disciples to heal, He also accommodated His language to support this popular belief--calling it the power to cast out demons.

The third theory, held by a number of prominent Christians in the local church today, acknowledges the reality of demon possession, but they believe it was limited to the apostolic age. Those who believe this theory hold little or no interest in the possibility or probability of demons existing in today's age. They do believe that divine knowledge or inspiration is needed to determine what is real or unreal in cases of demon possession.

Regarding this third theory, Nevius makes four observations: (1) This theory represents Jesus as deceiving His disciples, as well as encouraging superstition. (2) This theory represents the Lord Jesus lying to His disciples. The Bible shows that the Lord Jesus regarded demons as being the agents and representatives of Satan, and the casting out of demons as being open war upon Satan's dominion. When Jesus talked to the Seventy upon their return, He said, "I beheld Satan as lightning fall from heaven" (Luke 10:17-18). Are we for the moment to regard the Lord Jesus as sanctioning and encouraging the belief that demon possession was to be referred to as a Satanic agency, when in fact, all along, He knew that there was no such thing as demon possession? (3) This theory presents the Lord Jesus in a light entirely inconsistent with His character as a divine teacher. It represents Him not only as speaking of diseases as being a result of possession by demons, but as personifying diseases, and actually addressing them as demons, having formal conversations with them and receiving answers from them. How can we accept the fact that Jesus would voluntarily adopt a course which could only tend to confuse and mislead His disciples? (4) This theory represents the Lord Jesus as making use of unfounded superstition to substantiate His claim of divine authority. When He sent forth the Twelve and the Seventy, He is said to have given them authority over all demons, which, according to this theory, would have been a lie.[55] Nevius also believes this view is inconsistent with facts stated in the Scripture, and says:

Nearly every case which the Bible presents to us is brought to our Savior as a case of 'possession', the fact of its being such having been decided not by our Savior or his disciples, but by the people. We read of no instance of our Savior's informing the people that they were mistaken in their diagnosis of the case; no intimation that they were incompetent to decide upon these cases; or that there was any serious difficulty in so doing. There may have been many cases in Judea in which the symptoms were not sufficiently marked to indicate their character unmistakably, but those brought to Christ seem to have been clearly developed and pronounced.[56]

The fourth theory is that the records of the Gospel writers were colored and distorted so that they were not accurate. Those holding this theory would say that Jesus simply cured diseases, never speaking of them as possessions, nor regarding them as such; but that His disciples wrote the narratives of these events in a form which was in accordance with their own beliefs.

This theory is presented in, **Chamber's Encyclopedia of Religious Knowledge**. The article, in essence, is saying that the disciples reported the healing Jesus did on the people who were brought or came to Him, in language intelligible to their age and in harmony with its general notions. This same theory is presented by Dr. A. D. White, formerly of Cornell University.[57]

The above theory will at once be rejected by those who hold even the least belief in the inspiration and authenticity of the Bible because the Word of God in II Timothy 3:16 says, "All scripture is given by inspiration of God, and is profitable for doctrine, for reproof, for correction, for instruction in righteousness."

Aside from being contrary to scripture (Luke 9:1, 10:17; 11:20; 13:31-33), this theory that the gospel writers colored the truth is shown to be false by five considerations (according to Nevius): (1) It thrives on the assumption that the Jews regarded mental diseases as possession by demons. This assumption has been shown to be inconsistent with facts. (2) This theory is totally inconsistent with the minute circumstantial details of the Gospel narrative. How could the disciples, without an overwhelming sense of guilt because of falseness and dishonesty, give details of imaginary conversations with demons, recording the very words used by both parties? (3) This theory is also inconsistent with the Gospels. If the Gospel's authors recorded facts as they saw and heard them, then this theory proclaims that they lied. (4) If Jesus Christ never spoke of demon possession, but only of disease, how could the disciples have failed to notice this special teaching on the part of Jesus? (5) If this theory is true, how do we account for the fact that such misrepresentation of the records and perversion of the truth went unchallenged or unrebuked by the contemporary eye-witnesses of the events, whether they were Christians or Jews?[58]

The fifth theory is put forth from Christians like me who believe that after viewing all the facts, the language of the Bible in reference to demon possession or demonization is to be interpreted in its ordinary literal sense. There were unseen spirits in Judea which sought opportunities to invade the bodies of men, and indeed did so. Those bodies invaded by demons gave unmistakable evidence of it. The demons communicated by the human tongue of those they controlled, and not only gave evidence of having their own personalities, desires, and fears, but acknowledged God's authority over them. Our Lord Jesus Christ cast out the demons by His word, and gave that same authority to His disciples and His Church.

The Lord Jesus was fully knowledgeable of the whole subject of demonology, and calmly dealt with the demons as matter of fact. I believe that the Church today must follow His example in order to be scripturally sound. God's people need to stop allowing Satan to deter by tempting them to debate endlessly, and need to, by faith, believe God's Word and proceed with the ministry to which they have been called. My prayer is that the information I have shared will help bring this to reality.

## NOTES

1. Kurt Koch, <u>Christian Counseling and Occultism</u>, p. 270.
2. <u>Ibid</u>., p. 271.
3. Karl Heim, "Jesus Der Weltvollender", p. 84.
4. Kurt Koch, <u>op</u>. <u>cit</u>., p. 271.
5. Kurt Koch, <u>Demonology Past and Present</u>, p. 28.
6. <u>Ibid</u>., p. 23,24.
7. Merril C. Tenney, <u>op</u>. <u>cit</u>., p. 98,99.
8. Jessie Penn-Lewis, <u>War on the Saints</u>, p. 35.
9. Augustus H. Strong, <u>Systematic Theology</u>, p. 455.
10. Jessie Penn-Lewis, <u>op</u>. <u>cit</u>., p. 35.
11. Jack R. Taylor, <u>Victory Over the Devil</u>, p. 49.
12. <u>Loc</u>. <u>cit</u>.
13. William M. Alexander, <u>Demonic Possession in the New Testament</u>, p. 66.
14. <u>Ibid</u>., p. 65.
15. <u>Ibid</u>., p. 150.
16. Merril C. Tenney, <u>The Zondervan Pictorial Encyclopedia of the Bible</u>, Vol. II, p. 99.
17. <u>Ibid</u>., p. 101.
18. William M. Alexander, <u>op</u>. <u>cit</u>., pp. 80, 150.
19. Alfred Edersheim, <u>The Life and Times of Jesus the Messiah</u>, Book III, pp. 607-609.
20. Jack R. Taylor, <u>op</u>. <u>cit</u>., p. 49.
21. William M. Alexander, <u>op</u>. <u>cit</u>., p. 150.
22. W. A. Criswell, <u>The Criswell Study Bible</u>, Mark 9:18, p. 1171.
23. Jack R. Taylor, <u>op</u>. <u>cit</u>., p. 50.
24. William M. Alexander, <u>op</u>. <u>cit</u>., p. 88.
25. <u>Ibid</u>., p. 90.
26. Merril C. Tenney, <u>op</u>. <u>cit</u>., p. 101.
27. William M. Alexander, <u>op</u>. <u>cit</u>., p. 92.
28. <u>Ibid</u>., p. 94.
29. <u>Ibid</u>., p. 95.
30. <u>Ibid</u>., p. 96.
31. <u>Ibid</u>., p. 160.
32. <u>The Wycliffe Bible Commentary</u>, ed. Charles F. Pfeiffer, Everett F. Harrison, p. 443.
33. William M. Alexander, <u>op</u>. <u>cit</u>., pp. 101, 162.
34. Merril C. Tenney, <u>op</u>. <u>cit</u>., p. 99.
35. Merrill F. Unger, <u>Demons in the World Today</u>, p. 102.
36. <u>Ibid</u>., p. 113.
37. Augustus H. Strong, <u>Systematic Theology</u>
38. William M. Alexander, <u>Demonic Possession in the New Testament</u>, p. 4.
39. <u>Loc</u>. <u>cit</u>.
40. <u>Ibid</u>., p. 6.
41. <u>Ibid</u>., p. 8.
42. John L. Nevius, <u>Demon Possession</u>, p. 181.
43. Augustus H. Strong, <u>op</u>. <u>cit</u>., p. 455.

44. <u>Ibid.</u>, p. 456.
45. <u>Loc</u>. <u>cit</u>.
46. <u>Loc</u>. <u>cit</u>.
47. <u>Loc</u>. <u>cit</u>.
48. Jack R. Taylor, <u>op</u>. <u>cit</u>., p. 45.
49. <u>Loc</u>. <u>cit</u>.
50. Augustus H. Strong, <u>op</u>. <u>cit</u>., p. 456.
51. <u>Ibid.</u>, p. 458.
52. <u>Ibid.</u>, p. 457,458.
53. Jack R. Taylor, <u>op</u>. <u>cit</u>., p. 48.
54. Merrill F. Unger, <u>What Demons Can Do To Saints</u>, pp. 86, 87.
55. John L. Nevius, <u>op</u>. <u>cit</u>., pp. 247-248.
56. <u>Ibid.</u>, p. 249.
57. <u>Ibid.</u>, p. 251.
58. <u>Ibid.</u>, p. 254.

# PART II

## GOD'S GIFT
## OF
## RECONCILIATION

# CHAPTER FOUR
## THE FALL AND RESTORATION OF MAN

**THE CREATION OF MAN**

Looking at the Word of God we see that on the sixth day of creation God created man in His own image and gave him dominion over all the earth. God placed Adam in Eden, a garden that was like a paradise. He set man over His garden to have stewardship of it and to live by its sustenance (Gen. 1:26, 27; 2:7-17). God provided food for Adam to eat and to be full. He placed every kind of fruit tree there--everything necessary for his needs.

**MAN GIVEN A CHOICE**

God also planted two very special trees in His garden. One was in the very middle of the garden and was called the **tree of life**. Next to it was the **tree of knowledge of good and evil**. God told Adam that he could eat of all the trees in the garden except one, which was the **tree of knowledge of good and evil**. Why did He do this? This was God's way of allowing man to have a choice to obey or not to obey Him. In giving Adam and Eve a choice, we see that God created man with a free will--an ability to make choices. Otherwise, God would have created robots who automatically obeyed His will.

**INNOCENCE IN THE GARDEN**

Adam and Eve were innocent before God. There was nothing within Adam's and Eve's nature that would lead them in even the **direction** of sin. So we see that sin could only be brought into the world if they chose to submit to temptation, which could only come from a source other than God. This is where Satan entered the scene.

Lucifer, **the day star**, had become Satan, the dreadful **adversary** or **accuser** opposing the Lord and all His purposes. In the garden Satan became that **old serpent** by entering into the body of this **most clever** of all the beasts of the field in order to speak to Eve. He tempted Eve concerning God's not allowing her to eat of that one forbidden thing in the garden, the fruit of the **tree of knowledge of good and evil**. The serpent first tempted her to question God's authority and goodness, then worked to distort and dilute God's Word. It is understandable that he is called the **father of lies**. He even went beyond altering and diluting God's Word, and began calling God a liar. God had warned Adam and Eve that if they ate of the fruit they would die, and Satan disputed God's Word saying, "Ye shall surely not die." Satan also suggested to Eve that God was afraid they would learn too much.

Satan then told Eve that if she and her husband believed and obeyed him, "Ye shall be as gods." Pride was the very same thing that Isaiah 14:13, 14 tells us resulted in Satan being thrown out of heaven. Satan tempted Eve in the three areas described in I John 2:16: "For all that is in the world, the lust of the flesh, and the lust of the eyes and the pride of life, is not of the Father, but is of the world." Satan tempted her to look upon the only forbidden thing in the entire garden. When Eve looked, she saw that the tree was **good for food**--temptation to her physical appetite; secondly, that it was **pleasant to**

the eyes--temptation to her emotions; and thirdly, that it was **desirous to make one wise**--temptation to her mind.

## THE FALL OF MANKIND

So Eve gave in, and regarding her own feelings as more important than her obedience to God, she chose of her own free will to submit to Satan. She ate of the forbidden fruit and then went to find Adam. Like so many humans in the world today, Eve felt compelled to propagate her sin, leading her husband to buy into the same sin. Eve readily brought Adam some of the fruit, enticing him to participate in her sin, and he ate of the forbidden fruit. It can only be surmised that she probably also fed Adam the same lines that Satan had fed her. However, based on the Word of God, we know that Adam "was not deceived" (I Tim. 2:14). We might not know what all this means this side of Heaven, but we do know that despite Adam's not being deceived, he chose of his own free will to disobey God.

## THE CURSE BROUGHT UPON MANKIND

When Adam and Eve chose to believe Satan's lie over God's truth, they fell under the curse of sin, which affected all of mankind and all of creation. God's covering of righteousness fell from them, and Adam and Eve saw themselves as naked and hid from God, knowing He would see the exposure of their sinful condition.

## THE FIRST BLOOD SACRIFICE

As God walked in the cool of the day and sought His usual fellowship with Adam and Eve, He found them behind a tree, hiding in shame (Gen. 3:8-13). After God confronted them about their sin, in His mercy He killed animals to make coverings for them. Those bloody skins held a symbolic meaning-- the merciful covering and cleansing of man and woman from their wickedness and nakedness of sin (Gen. 3:21). Here is the first recorded death and blood sacrifice--there in God's garden--which God was to require from that time forth for the covering for sin. God's Word in Hebrews 9:22 records this requirement: "And almost all things are by the law purged with blood, and without shedding of blood is no remission." We see this requirement being fulfilled by God's sending His Son as our sacrifice in Ephesians 1:6-7:

> *To the praise of the glory of His grace, through which He hath made us accepted in the Beloved. In whom we have redemption through His blood the forgiveness of sins, according to the riches of His grace.*

## THE CURSE UPON THE SERPENT AND SATAN

After God had confronted Adam and Eve, He then confronted "that old Serpent called the Devil" (Rev. 12:19). We find the confrontation recorded in Genesis 3:14:

> *And the Lord God said unto the serpent, Because thou hast done this, thou art cursed above all the cattle, and above every beast of the field; upon thy belly shalt thou go, and dust shalt thou eat all the days of thy life.*

This marked the beginning of the spiritual warfare which will continue until the end of this age. This earth had been originally placed under the dominion of Adam, but because Adam had chosen to believe Satan and disobey God's Word, his dominion was now forfeited to Satan. We can see proof of the transfer of this dominion in II Corinthians 4:4 when the Word tells us that Satan is the "god of this world."

Satan, no doubt, had high hopes for his future. Dr. Henry M. Morris, in his book **The Genesis Record**, says that Satan probably thought he could get mankind to align itself with him and his fallen angels (or demons) to oppose God and perhaps to even dethrone and vanquish Him. Morris also believes at this point that Satan was anxious to use the woman because she had already demonstrated her control over the man. Satan also saw that the child-bearing woman could be his potential means to control the human reproduction under his control. This would give Satan time to create an innumerable host of servants that would perhaps obey him at his bidding.[1]

However, God was not going to allow Satan this awesome right--the woman was not going to be his willing ally--for God said in Genesis 3:15, "And I will put enmity between thee and the woman and between thy seed and her seed; he shall bruise thy head, and thou shalt bruise his heel." This first gospel message was God's great promise that He would send a Savior who would come from woman to destroy Satan and his power. This prophecy pointed generations ahead to the cross and to the empty tomb and to the last judgment, when Satan will be thrown into the lake of fire and completely crushed under the foot of the woman's triumphant Seed (Jesus).

Even though Adam and Eve forfeited living in the garden paradise where they had walked daily with God and had to work by the sweat of their brow and deal with the thorns and thistles of life, Satan would not win out. Although the first conflict of man with Satan gave him an apparent victory, it was not to be permanent. God had said that the woman's Seed would eventually bruise Satan's head.

**SPIRITUAL TRUTHS ABOUT THE WORD "SEED"**

Now look at Genesis 3:15. What does God mean by the word **Seed** in speaking of the **woman's Seed** and the **serpent's seed**? Even though the word seed has a biological connotation, in this context that meaning does not apply. Here, the word **Seed** means **spiritual offspring**. Satan is a spirit, and because of the woman's physical makeup, she and the Devil could not produce physical seed in its actual sense. The serpent's seed are those who willfully choose to be enemies of the Seed (Christ) of the woman. They take on the very characteristics of the adversary (John 8:44; Eph. 2:2-3), and seek to oppose God's purposes in creation and redemption.

On the other hand, the seed of the woman would refer, first, to the human family which is brought into right relationship and fellowship with God. We also learn that prophecy foretold a generational conflict between the children of God and the children of the wicked one. This began with Cain and Abel (Matt. 13:37-40; I John 3:8-12) and will continue to the end of the age (Rev. 12:17). But there are additional meanings of the word **seed**. The **seed** of the serpent will soon be coming in the future as the "son of perdition" (II Thess. 2:3)--the antiChrist--to whom the Dragon gives his powers, throne, and authority (Rev. 13:2). Morris says "The primary seed of the woman is, of course, the Lord Jesus Christ; and it is not the seed of the serpent, but Satan himself who battles and is destroyed by this Seed, according to Genesis 3:15".[3]  It is clear that verse fifteen refers to the Seed being fulfilled in Jesus Christ.  On the cross, Jesus Christ the Son of God was the second Adam; He became the curse that was placed upon Adam (Galatians 3:13).  In responding to the curse of man, Morris says:

> *The curse of man was fourfold (1) sorrow, resulting from continual disappointment and futility; (2) pain and suffering, signified by the 'thorns' which intermittently hinders man in his efforts to provide a living for his family; (3) sweat, or tears, the strong crying of intense struggle against a hostile environment.  And finally, (4) physical death, which would eventually triumph over all man's efforts with the structure of his body returning to the simple elements of the earth[4] (NSSB).*

There is coming a day when we will dwell with God.  Revelation 21:4 says:

> *And God shall wipe away all tears from their eyes; and there shall be no more death, neither sorrow, nor crying, neither shall there be any more pain; for the former things are passed away (NSSB).*

In Revelation 22:3, we also read, "And there shall be no more curse, but the throne of God and of the Lamb shall be in it, and His servants shall serve Him."

The complete and final removal of the sin and its curse cannot happen until Christ returns and brings about the needed change on earth (II Pet. 3:10; Rev. 20:11; 21:1).  Until that time occurs, we find ourselves removed from God's paradise, for God could not permit it to be used as a garden of sin.  In God's wonderful love and mercy, He didn't allow mankind to stay there and eat of the tree of life, for he would have lived forever in a fallen, evil state.  We see this truth in Genesis 3:22-24:

> *And the Lord God said, Behold, the man is become as one of us, to know good and evil; and now, lest he put forth his hand and take also of the tree of life, and eat and live forever.  Therefore the Lord God sent him forth from the Garden of Eden, to till the ground from where he was taken.  So he drove out the man; and he placed at the east of the Garden of Eden, Cherubim, and a flaming sword which turned every way to guard the way of the tree of life. (NSSB)*

So God closes the garden of paradise to mankind, but out of loving mercy, He puts man into a different environment where he will have opportunities to search out and know God and His ways if he so chooses.

## THE SECOND ADAM RESTORES FALLEN MAN TO A LOVING GOD

The Word of God speaks of two Adams.  In the first part of this chapter, I gave a thumbnail sketch of the first Adam whom God created and placed in the garden.  Sadly, the first Adam fell and forfeited earth's dominion to His enemy, Satan.  The first Adam, created from dust and made flesh, became spiritually dead by the curse of sin, resulting in his expulsion from the Garden of Eden.  Since the first Adam was the head of creation and the human family, he ancestrally passed down the Adamic or sin nature to all of mankind. We see in Romans 5:12: "Wherefore, as by one man sin entered into the world, and death by sin, and so death passed upon all men, for all have sinned."

This brings us to the second Adam, Jesus Christ, the head of all creation. He is the head of the heavenly family, which is the Church of the living God. He, like the first Adam, was tempted in all areas, but sinned in none. John 1:14 says "And the word was made flesh and dwelt among us...." Hebrews 4:15 states "For we have not an high priest who cannot be touched with the feelings of our infirmities, but was in all points tempted like as we are, yet without sin." When tempted, the first Adam fell, but the second Adam remained sinless. God's Law required a blood sacrifice without blemish, as we see stated in I Peter 1:18-19:

> *Forasmuch as ye know that ye were not redeemed with corruptible things, like silver and gold, from your vain (manner of life) received by tradition from your fathers...but with the precious blood of Christ, as of a lamb without blemish and without spot (NSSB).*

We see that the first Adam died because of his sin; the second Adam, who was perfect, became mankind's sin, "For he hath made him who knew no sin, to be sin for us that we might be made the righteousness of God in him" (II Cor. 5:21). Through the second Adam, all can be made alive. Romans 5:17, 18 states:

> *For if by one man's offense death reigned by one; much more they who receive abundance of grace and of the gift of righteousness shall reign in life by one, Jesus Christ. Therefore as by the offense of one judgment came upon all men to condemnation; even so by the righteousness of one the free gift upon all men unto the justification of life (NSSB).*

The truth is, the second Adam is the Son of God, the Son of man. He is a life-giving Spirit. He did not receive life from another as did the first Adam, for He is life. We learn this from John 1:4, "In Him was life; and the life was the light of men."

Because Adam was born of the flesh, all he could produce was flesh (John 3:6). But, Jesus Christ, God's Eternal Word (John 1:1), born of a virgin, took on a body of flesh (John 1:14) and in that earthly body, He conquered the world, the flesh, the Devil, death, the grave, and Hell. In doing so, He made it possible for man to become a new creation, which is Spirit. We understand this by what II Corinthians 5:17-18 says:

> *Therefore, if any man be in Christ, he is a new (creation); old things passed away, behold, all things are become new, and all things are of God, who hath reconciled us to Himself by Jesus Christ, and hath given to us the ministry of reconciliation (NSSB).*

We see in John 3:6b, "...that which is born of the Spirit is spirit." Paul wrote to the believers at the church of Ephesus:

*And you hath he made alive who were dead in trespasses and sins. In which in times past ye walked according to the course of this world, according to the prince of the power of the air, the spirit that now worketh in the (sons) of disobedience; among whom also we all had our (manner of life) in time past in the lusts of our flesh and of the mind and were by nature the children of wrath, even as others. But God who is rich in mercy for His great love with which he loved us, even when we were dead in sins, hath (made us alive) together with Christ (by grace ye are saved), and hath raised us up together and made us sit together in heavenly places in Christ Jesus (Ephesians 2:1-6; NSSB).*

Paul wanted the believers to know that only through the second Adam could man move from death to life. The spirit of the unregenerate man is dead toward God. He cannot see or understand spiritual truth, no matter how intelligent or educated he might be. As John 3 tells us, "Man must be born again" through the miracle of new birth, if he is ever to truly understand the Word or things that pertain to God.

We can understand why Jesus Christ would have to be virgin born; otherwise, this promised Seed would inherit the Adamic nature and the iniquity of the fathers. This is not to say that Mary was a sinless person but God found favor with her and chose her to bring forth His Son and Savior of the world. Jesus Christ was one-hundred percent man, but void of the Adamic sin nature and one-hundred percent God, with all of His nature. Jesus was born to an earthly life under the dominion of Satan, but was lacking the weakness of the first Adam. He was able to battle the serpent and emerge victoriously--bruising or crushing the serpent's head. Having done this, He sets the captive free and liberates the bruised. Although the battle has been won by Jesus Christ our Savior, man must of his own volition accept the sacrifice the Savior has made if he is to be redeemed from the curse. Romans 3:23-26 says:

*For all have sinned, and come short of the glory of God, being justified freely by His grace through the redemption that is in Christ Jesus, whom God hath set forth to be a propitiation through faith in his blood to declare his righteousness for the remission of sins that are past through the forbearance of God, to declare, I say, at this time his righteousness, that he might be just and the justifier of him who believeth in Jesus (NSSB).*

Jesus Christ is the propitiation (or satisfaction) for sin. Only by our repenting of our cursed nature and inviting the Lord Jesus into our hearts can we be saved and free. Romans 10:9, 13 tells the lost person:

*That if thou shalt confess with thy mouth the Lord Jesus, and shalt believe in thine heart that God hath raised Him from the dead, thou shalt be saved...for whosoever shall call upon the name of the Lord shall be saved (NSSB).*

Even though God put man out of the garden, He invited him back into His presence through man's acceptance and belief in His blood sacrifice, Jesus Christ, God's only Son, who was raised from the dead and sits at the right hand of the throne of God.

## SECURITY OF THE CHRISTIAN

God the Father did not allow His only Son to die the cruel death of the cross so that man could be saved, only to have man fall from that salvation because of further sin. The word of God in I Corinthians 1:30 says that when we were saved, God granted us salvation through Jesus Christ. If I'm saved, then I'm sanctified, or, in other words, I am a **saint** (I Corinthians 1:2,30; 6:11). Unger allows that the word **saint** comes from the same Greek root word as **holy** or **sanctified**, and that it is used sixty-two times in the New Testament to designate the believer. He says that it always **denotes** what the Christian is in Christ, never denoting what the Christian is in himself.[5] Being a **saint** doesn't mean that my goodness comes from me, but that it stands totally on what God has done for me. So, man's security is based on what God did for us and not on what we do for Him.

Throughout my years of counseling I have, from time to time, met counselees who believed Satan's lie--that Christians can lose their salvation--by their own doing or even by someone else's. In cases where those holding that false belief were demonized, the demons repeatedly refused to leave, claiming they held ground by the person's believing that lie. Until the counselee confesses that false belief as sin, repents and claims back the ground, the demons don't have to leave. The truth is that when the Lord Jesus Christ died on that cruel tree with all its curse, He vicariously became all the believer's sins--not just some of them, but all of them--past, present, and future (I John 2:1, 2). Jesus Christ is our substitute. John 3:18 and Romans 8:1 say Christ's atoning work removes all condemnation forever. Once we have accepted Him as our Savior, we are His children forever, even if we choose to be rebellious children and try to escape His presence. Prayerfully read this beautiful passage found in John 10:14-18, 27-31:

> *I am the good shepherd, and know my sheep, and am known of mine. As the Father knoweth me, even so know I the Father; and I lay down my life for the sheep. And other sheep I have, that are not of this fold; them also I must bring, and they shall hear my voice; and there shall be one fold, and one shepherd. Therefore doth my Father love me, because I lay down my life, that I might take it again. No man taketh it from me, but I lay it down of myself. I have power to lay it down, and I have power to take it again. This commandment have I received of my Father...My sheep hear my voice, and I know them, and they follow me. And I give unto them eternal life; and they shall never perish; neither shall any man pluck them out of my hand. I and my Father are one. My Father, who gave them to me, is greater than all, and no man is able to pluck them out of my Father's hand. I and my Father are one. Then the Jews took up stones again to stone Him (NSSB).*

Please understand that this truth of **once saved, always saved** (the believer's security) is not to be held with arrogance, but rather with humble gratitude and confidence. Examining the previous scripture closely, we see it clearly denies that we can lose our salvation, including those who say that while God may not quit them, they can quit God. You are either a man or a woman, aren't you? That doesn't leave anyone out. Therefore, when the Lord says that **no man** can pluck them out of His hand, He is speaking about each one of His children being secure. Romans 8:35-39, echoes that truth, saying that nothing can separate us from the love of God.

While I have neither the time nor space to share all of the scripture that has been misused and abused in attempts to prove man can fall again to the point of being lost, I will address the one used the most. Galatians 5:4 is pulled out of context, ignoring the rest of the scripture pertaining to it. Let's take a look at God's full truth surrounding verse four in Galatians 5:1-12:

> *Stand fast, therefore, in the liberty with which Christ hath made us free, and be not entangled again in the yoke of bondage. Behold, I, Paul, say unto you, that if ye be circumcised, Christ shall profit you nothing. For I testify again to every man that is circumcised, that he is a debtor to do the whole law.* <u>*Christ is become of no effect unto you, whosoever of you are justified by the law; ye are fallen from grace.*</u> *For we through the Spirit wait for the hope of righteousness by faith. For in Jesus Christ neither circumcision availeth anything, nor uncircumcision, but faith which worketh by love. Ye did run well; who did hinder you that ye should not obey the truth? This persuasion cometh not of him that calleth you. A little leaven leaveneth the whole lump. I have confidence in you through the Lord, that ye will be none otherwise minded; but he that troubleth you shall bear his judgment, whosoever he be. And I, brethren, if I yet preach circumcision, why do I yet suffer persecution? Then is the offense of the cross ceased. I would they were even cut off who trouble you (NSSB).*

Not only in these twelve verses but also in the entire book of Galatians, Paul clearly is dealing with **law versus grace**. In the preceding scripture, he is addressing those people who are insisting that the Christian must keep the law of circumcision to assure their salvation. Paul is correcting their error in thinking that they must keep God's law in order to maintain their salvation, for having to do such would render Christ's death on the Cross meaningless. His law is a guide to godly living. While Jesus Himself urged Christians to obey the law, which He came not to destroy but to fulfill, our keeping it or not keeping it had nothing to do with our souls being saved. We see that clearly in Ephesians 2:8-9 which says, "For by grace are ye saved through faith; and that not of yourselves, it is the gift of God, not of works, lest any man should boast." Dr. Spiros Zodhiates, author of **The Complete Word Study New Testament**, comments:

> The key to understanding the phrase 'are you fallen from grace' is seen in the verb **exepesate** which is better translated 'have fallen'. It does not mean that the grace of God was evident at one time and then was lost. Rather, this person deviates from the true path of grace by choosing justification by law instead of by grace. Grace has a law associated with it, but the law has no grace, only restrictions.[6]

Paul wants the people to see that the more they depend on themselves to keep the Law of Moses, the further they are from their salvation's hinging on God's grace. The whole key to salvation is appropriating God's grace by faith. We see this in Romans 5:1 and 2, where Paul speaks:

> *Therefore, being justified by faith, we have peace with God through our Lord Jesus Christ, by whom also we have access by faith into the grace in which we stand and rejoice in hope of the glory of God (NSSB).*

Paul was furious at those who preached the false doctrine of **law plus grace**. As you read earlier, he said in Galatians 5:12, "I would that they were even **cut off** who trouble you." The word **cut off** is the Greek word **apokopto** and it means to **amputate** or **mutilate (the private parts)**.[7] Watch carefully. Paul is a perfect example of one walking in God's Spirit and will concerning, "Be angry, and sin not" (Eph. 4:26a). He had a righteous indignation toward this destructive, false teaching. He not only desired those preaching false doctrine to be severed from the realm of preaching, but he was so angry that he thought it would benefit God's Kingdom if those preaching unsound doctrine would sever their own reproductive organs from themselves. This way, they could not multiply this false doctrine through their children and generations to follow. Look what **The New Testament and Wycliffe Bible Commentary** says about this:

> Paul found offense not in the cross but in those who unsettled his converts--**which trouble you**. His indignation led him to make a strong statement: **I would they were even cut off**, or better, would mutilate themselves (RSV). As an emasculated man has lost the power of propagation, so should these agitators be reduced to impotence in spreading their false doctrine? Such is the fervent wish to which the Apostle Paul gives expression.[8]

While Paul did not resort to seeing that such physical action was taken, as he preached he drew attention to the truth that the keeping of the law was not a requirement for keeping our salvation. Salvation is the gift of grace.

In II Thessalonians 2:3 and 12 we see the apostasy, or the falling away (rebellion or departure) of those who reject Christ and seek to achieve salvation through the works of their hands, a means contrary to believing in Jesus Christ, God's gift of grace. Those choosing to rebel and take pleasure in unrighteousness condemn themselves before God. For Christian readers who believe they can lose their salvation, I pray they repent, renounce this belief as false, and claim back the ground, the latter being explained in the next chapter.

In conjunction with the fact that the Christian cannot lose his salvation, I think it is imperative that we look even more closely at the blessed security of the believer. We read in Ephesians 4:30, "And grieve not the Holy Spirit of God, by whom ye are sealed unto the day of redemption."

## SEALED BY THE HOLY SPIRIT

We must first understand what the word sealed actually means. Research shows that the Hebrew word **chotham** is equivalent to our word seal or signet; **chotham** means signet ring; and **chatham** means to seal. The Greek words, **sphragizo** and **katasphragizomai**, **mean to seal**. As far back as the 4th millennium B.C., ones in positions of authority used seals as their personal signatures on important documents. The seals signified the finalization of an important transaction. The seal was a signet such as a ring with an engraved gem displaying a symbolic design, similar to a family crest. For instance, after purchasing a parcel of land, soft clay or wax would be placed upon the document and the owner would press his seal into it, leaving his mark of ownership.

In the story of Queen Esther, letters had been spread abroad calling for the destruction of her people-- God's people. She made an appeal to King Ahasuerus to set her people free from the condemnation. The king answered her plea and drew up a decree (writing) reversing the orders: "...the writing which is written in the king's name, and sealed with the king's ring, may no man reverse" (Est. 8:8). This parallels so beautifully our **sealing** at the time of our salvation. Look at Ephesians 1:13-14:

> *In (Christ) whom ye also trusted, after ye heard the word of truth, the gospel of your salvation; in whom also after ye believed, ye were sealed with that Holy Spirit of promise, who is the earnest of our inheritance until the day of redemption of the purchased possession, unto the praise of his glory (NSSB).*

How comforting it is for the Christian to have the same assurance that Job did, who gratefully expressed, "My transgression is sealed up in a bag, and thou sewest up mine iniquity" (Job 14:17). How awesome it is to know that we are sealed with the Holy Spirit until the day of redemption. Scripture also reveals that our eternal security is written down and sealed in the most valuable of documents. John recorded in the book of Revelation that there are sealed scrolls and books in heaven which only Jesus, the Lion of Judah, is authorized to open in His due time. In Revelation 20:12,15, we read that there is a "...**book of life**...and whosoever is not found written in the book of life will be cast into the lake of fire."

While Christians can rejoice over the fact that we will not be cast into the lake of fire and that we have the power to overcome the Devil and his demons who tempt and seek to devour us, look carefully at what Luke 10:17-21, 23 says to us:

> *And the seventy returned again with joy, saying, Lord, even the demons are subject unto us through thy name. And he said unto them, I beheld Satan as lightning fall from heaven. Behold, I give unto you the power to tread on serpents and scorpions and over all the power of the enemy; and nothing shall by any means hurt you. Notwithstanding, in this rejoice not, that the spirits are subject unto you; but rather rejoice, **because your names are written in heaven**. In that hour, Jesus rejoiced in [the Spirit], and said, I thank thee, O Father, Lord of heaven and earth, that thou hast hidden these things from the wise and prudent, and has revealed them unto babes...and he turned unto his disciples, and said privately, Blessed are the eyes which see the things that ye see.*

## NOTES

1. Henry M. Morris, <u>The Genesis Record</u>, pp. 119-120.
2. Alma E. Guinness, Editor, <u>ABC's of the Human Body</u>, pp. 268, 290-293.
3. Henry M. Morris, <u>op</u>. <u>cit</u>., p. 121.
4. <u>Ibid</u>., p. 127.
5. Merrill Unger, <u>What Demons Can Do To Saints</u>, p. 29.
6. Spiros Zodhiates, Th.D., <u>The Complete Word Study New Testament</u>, p. 625.
7. <u>Ibid</u>., <u>Greek Dictionary of the New Testament</u>, p. 14.
8. Charles F. Pfeiffer and Everett F. Harrison, <u>The Wycliffe Bible Comment Bible Commentary</u>, p. 714.

# CHAPTER FIVE
## RESTORING TRUE WORSHIP

**INTRODUCTION**

The previous chapter briefly covered the fall of man: what it cost him, and what it cost God to restore man to Himself. The cost to man was becoming separated from God and spiritually dead. The cost to God was the giving of His only Son to be put to death to pay for mankind's sins. Jesus arose from the grave and this living Lord and His life's blood enable us to have fellowship with God and the ability to worship Him. Not only must we ask God to forgive us, but we must also use the authority we have in Jesus and in His life-giving, shed blood to claim back ground lost to Satan. Do people today actually worship God the way He intends? To answer that question I would first of all stress the importance of studying the Bible in its entirety. Secondly, I would suggest a careful study of Josiah in the Old Testament.

**UNDERSTANDING THE WHOLE BIBLE**

While the Bible is one book, it is also a library of books; while it has one Author, it also has many authors. The Bible has a great central theme: salvation through Jesus Christ. It is the only record of God's redeeming love. There is a scarlet thread (representing Jesus' blood) that runs throughout the Bible from Genesis through Revelation. This scarlet thread begins in Genesis 3:15, where God promises salvation to man through His Son Jesus Christ and God also declares war against Satan. A great Bible teacher said of the Old and New Testaments, "...the new is concealed in the old and the old is revealed in the new."[1] Hester, in his book, **The Heart of the New Testament**, quotes Dr. W. O. Carver, the author of, **Why They Wrote the New Testament**:

> Without the Old Testament, the New Testament could never have been. Given the Old Testament, if its apparent source, significance and claim were true and genuine, the New Testament had to be. They supplement and explain each other. The old anticipates the New; and the New presupposes and uses the Old. Each in part explains and interprets the other.[2]

Working with both Old and New Testament scriptural principles, Jehovah is seen as the same God, "yesterday, today, and forever" (Hebrews 13:8). When we understand the relationship between the Old and New Testaments, we see the importance of studying both records. Without knowledge of God's dealings with His people in centuries prior to the coming of Jesus Christ, we cannot fully appreciate and interpret the work and teachings of Jesus. Without doubt, a good Bible student needs to begin the study of the New Testament with an accurate knowledge of Old Testament and Hebrew history. Sad but true, I believe such teachings are greatly neglected in all too many New Testament churches today.

In 1976, God convicted me to read the Bible from Genesis through Revelation in thirty days. For the first time in my life, I saw God's works through the ages in total context. Seeing this blessed my life.

75

After I had completed reading the whole Bible, He instructed me to make a daily practice of reading nine chapters in the New Testament and seven chapters in the Old Testament from that time forward. This practice takes me through the New Testament once a month and the Old Testament, twice a year. Reading the entire Bible as you would a newspaper helps guard against being blown to and fro with every wind of unsound doctrine, such as is commonly blowing about these days.

Sincere people hungering to grow in the Lord are often deceived and fall into big trouble by readily believing everything any Christian tells them. Many such people get into serious trouble by watching some of today's Christian television programs, because those leading them may teach doctrine contrary to God's Word. Many viewers assume that because these television teachers are in leadership positions they are trustworthy. This makes the viewers easy prey for wrong teachings. This can easily happen if they are not reading the Bible in its proper context and in its entirety to see if the teachings properly align with God's Word.

## KING JOSIAH AND HIS ANCESTORS

For the New Testament Christian, the background study of King Josiah in II Chronicles 33-35 and II Kings 21-23 displays a perfect example of restoring true worship. King Josiah was only eight years old when he began to reign. At the age of sixteen, he turned toward God (II Chronicles 34:3). He had a heart for God and totally turned his life over to Him. At age twenty he began to purge the high places (II Chronicles 34:3). Then at age twenty-six he proclaimed the need to repair the Temple of God (II Chronicles 34:8). This is when Hilkiah, the high priest, found the Book of the Law. Hearing its words, Josiah humbled himself before God and repented for his sinful acts and for those of God's people (II Chronicles 34:18, 19). He reigned for thirty-one years in Jerusalem, and consistently did what was right in the eyes of God, "...he did not turn right or left..." (II Chronicles 34:2).

Like King Josiah, we must have consistently godly lives if we are ever going to be used effectively by God. If we love Him, we will trust and obey Him. We cannot be used by God in an awesome way if we waver in our obedience to Him. Consistency in our fellowship with Him through prayer and Bible reading is essential. Josiah was a good example of one who was consistent in His determination to hear from and obey God. God later said there was not another one like him, despite the fact that Josiah did disobey and fail later in the narrative.

I want you to see that no matter how much God does in and through your life, you will never reach a point where you don't need to stay **snuggled up** to Him. One of the biggest problems I see today in counseling people, whether they are staff members, pew sitters, or brand-new Christians, is that they often feel they have **arrived** and **don't need His continual guidance**. They have forgotten "from whence [they have] fallen" (Rev. 2:5), and what God saved them from and have an arrogant attitude of being **holier than thou** and **super-spiritual**. God's Word shows us this attitude even in Josiah. God warned Josiah not to go out and meddle in a situation, but he disobeyed, and Pharaoh-Necho killed him at the age of thirty-nine (II Kings 23:29).

I recognize that if I don't stay **snuggled up** to God moment by moment I could become the murderer, rapist, or adulterer you hear of on television or read about in the newspaper. Anyone who says they aren't capable of doing such things is a prime target for trouble. The moment you awake in the morning, Satan and his demons would like to destroy your life that day. When I awake in the mornings determining to consistently obey God, surely the demons scream "Oh, no, he's awake!" and set out to sidetrack me. Since Satan is not a respecter of persons, will he not pick on you also?

As people struggle with major difficulties in their lives and seek God's help, He will make His Word come alive for them and help them apply it to their lives. I have observed that the closer we come to the end of the age, the more books are written on the Rapture and the Second Coming of the Lord. Likewise, the more Satan reveals himself in this age, the more books are written about the Devil, Satan worship, witchcraft, and even demons and how to deal with them. Since we must surely be living in the last days, God has likewise unveiled the scripture, helping to free His people to be what He wants them to be during these last crucial days.

Let us consider the application of what we have just learned to restore true worship. So many people ask, "Joe, where do you get the term **claiming back the ground**?" I will explain this through the Old Testament King Josiah's life, and will share seven major steps to restoring true worship.

King Josiah's great-grandfather, Hezekiah, was told by God to get his house in order because he was going to die. Hezekiah, like many of today's self-centered, spoiled Christians, turned his face to the wall and pouted, cried, and moaned to God, reminding God of all he had done for Him. Hezekiah did not fully love and trust God, and therefore fought against His will. Even so, God gave him his heart's desire by granting him fifteen more years to live. Within that fifteen-year span, he bore Manasseh, who after Hezekiah died, began to reign in his place at the age of twelve.

Just as Hezekiah entreated God and received his wish, some Christians today believe and teach that you can command God to do things and that He will do them. I have heard, "If it's in the Word, name it and claim it. Push Him against the wall and get it because God can't lie." Many have taken various scriptures sorely out of context, attempting to get their own way. They readily quote, "If ye shall ask anything in my name, I will do it" (John 14:14), deleting the previous verse 13, "...whatever ye shall ask in my name, that will I do, that the Father may be glorified in the Son." Jesus will only do it if it brings glory to the Father. They ask what they will, ignoring I John 5:14, "...this is the confidence that we have in him, that, if we ask any thing according to his will, he heareth us." In Psalm 106:15 God says of persons begging contrary to His will, "...he gave them their request but sent leanness into their souls." How much more wise and blessed to trust God enough to say, "Lord, I really want what you want for my life, no matter what." Neither you nor I have enough sense to know what we need; only God knows what is really best for us in the long run.

Let's assume that I learn I have terminal cancer. I have several ways to deal with this news. I should begin by going to God and praying, "Lord, if this is being caused by demons and Satan is putting this on me to hinder me, by the power of the Lord Jesus Christ, I want it taken from my life. In your name, I rebuke those demons." In such a case, the cancer would disappear. However, another essential step would be to pray, "Lord, if cancer has come upon me so you can get my undivided attention and deal with sin in my life, please convict my heart of what that sin is. I repent and ask your forgiveness." It's important to know that while God sometimes uses "negatives" to get His people in right fellowship with Him, He does not always remove the chastening instrument. This is where our trust in Him, His love and wisdom, should ultimately rest.

Another important step to consider is that God also allows afflictions and sickness in our lives as a testimony for the glory of God. Just because we get saved doesn't mean we won't suffer afflictions or sicknesses. Other people aren't really going to know how to live and die in peace if they don't see Christians demonstrating the knowledge and confidence they have in Christ, their Savior. This earth is not our final home, for we're just sojourners, pilgrims. "...It is appointed unto men once to die..." (Hebrews 9:27b).

Concerning calling the elders to lay hands on you when you're sick, it is appropriate to call upon godly elders, those sound in doctrine. As they meet with you, they have opportunity to see whether the illness is caused by sin and offer appropriate counseling. They can request healing but must trust the Lord to know what's best for you. Many people have inward struggles and confusion in their lives today from running here and there allowing any Christian to lay hands on them. Carelessly allowing any Christian to lay hands on you brings potential danger of picking up demons and familiar spirits. I believe this is why James 5:13-16 instructs the one with problems to call the elders. I would surely want to know each person's true walk with the Lord before letting him lay hands on me!

Concerning Hezekiah's rebellious prayer, it's essential to recognize that God in His foreknowledge already knew how Hezekiah would respond when He told him to put his house in order. Hezekiah did not change the mind of God. When he chose not to agree with God, God demonstrated His permissive will and allowed him freedom of choice. God also knew Manasseh would be born and the evil he would do upon taking his father's throne. Do not attempt to sell God short. He knew it all before the foundations of the world. He knows everything about us: sees from our beginning right on into eternity, and works everything together for our good even though we may not understand it. God says in I Corinthians 3:18-21a:

> *Let no man deceive himself. If any man among you seemeth to be wise in this age, let him become a fool, that he may be wise. For the wisdom of this world is foolishness with God. For it is written, He taketh the wise in their own craftiness. And again, The Lord knoweth the thoughts of the wise, that they are vain. Therefore, let no man glory in men (NSSB).*

In II Chronicles 33:1-9, we see that Hezekiah's son Manasseh, who began to reign at age twelve, brought heartbreak:

> *...he reigned fifty-five years in Jerusalem; but he did that which was evil in the sight of the Lord, like unto the abominations of the nations, whom the Lord had cast out before the children of Israel (vv. 1, 2; NSSB).*

In other words, Manasseh chose to go right into Satan worship, "...for he built again the high places which Hezekiah, his father, had broken down, and he reared up altars for Baalim, and made idols, and worshipped all the hosts of heaven, and served them (v. 3)." If you begin to worship something, it will soon rule you. Manasseh sought guidance from the stars, which is our modern day astrology and astroguide. He worshipped the hosts of heaven and served them. Anytime you look to anyone or anything for wisdom, power, or authority besides the Trinity of God, you are worshipping Satan. Manasseh not only worshipped and served other gods but also went a step further:

> *Also he built altars in the house of the Lord, of which the Lord had said, In Jerusalem shall my name be forever. And he built altars for all the hosts of heaven, in the two courts of the house of the Lord. And he caused his children to pass through the fire in the valley of the son of Hinnom (vv. 4-6a; NSSB).*

Yes, Manasseh actually offered some of his children as burnt sacrifices to Satan. Then, as we read on, we see:

> *Also, he observed times, and used enchantments, and practiced sorcery, and dealt with a medium (or familiar spirit), and with wizards; he wrought much evil in the sight of the Lord, to provoke Him to anger. And he set a carved image, the idol which he had made, in the house of God, of which God had said to David and to Solomon, his son, In this house, and in Jerusalem, which I have chosen before all the tribes of Israel, will I put my name forever; neither will I any more remove the foot of Israel from out of the land which I have appointed for your fathers, if only they will take heed to do all that I have commanded them, according to the whole law and the statutes and the ordinances by the hand of Moses. So Manasseh made Judah and the inhabitants of Jerusalem to err, and to do worse than the nations, whom the Lord had destroyed before the children of Israel (vv. 6b-9; NSSB).*

Did you notice in the Old Testament that God's people moved to a place in their life when they did worse than the godless, heathen nations God had thrown out so that they could have the land? We see those Israelites' actions as being so horrible, but as we continue to study, we find the actions of today's local churches being just as bad.

For example, it saddens me that many Christians flippantly participate in Halloween activities and many churches have Halloween parties. Halloween is one of the most unholy nights for Satan and his demons, yet some churches invite it in and play with it as if it were just another innocent child's game. Some churches lovingly offer alternative parties in order to help protect precious souls that have not been taught the truths concerning Halloween. They substitute costumes of Bible characters and Noah's ark animals for the usual Halloween costumes. But other churches join right in with Satan and his band by having haunted houses with scary pranks and blood-like gory, gruesome games. They do it all in the name of church programs and ministry, even inviting the public as a love gesture. Condoning the worship of other gods is not loving people; quite the contrary, it is sending them a dangerous message that Satan and his evil band are just harmless and imaginary.

I recognize there are many Christians who have never been taught the deception underlying Halloween, an ancient festival originated by pagans honoring the Celtic **god of death**, Samhain. During this holiday, saturated with divination and soothsaying, the pagans worshipped the dead, whom they believed rose annually and wandered from house to house demanding contributions of food. Today's **trick or treaters** wearing **death masks** and carrying **lanterns** mimic the demanding, wandering gods of death. The pagans believed harm would come to them if they did not feed them, so they offered burned sacrifices of foods, animals and even humans. They used the ashes from these sacrifices in fortune-telling. Many commercial Halloween items seen today are representative of their worship and witchcraft. In reality, these pagans are Satanists, who not only continue these annual festivals, but daily worship Satan, praying for the downfall of God's Church.

Manasseh, too, chose to worship Satan, but even after he had rejected God, God continued to deal with him. II Chronicles 33:10-11 states:

> *...the Lord spoke to Manasseh, and to his people, but they would not hearken. Wherefore, the Lord brought upon them the captains of the host of the king of Assyria, who took Manasseh in chains, and bound him with fetters, and carried him to Babylon (NSSB).*

If you have studied any Bible history of the Old Testament concerning the Gentile world, you will have learned about the extreme cruelty of the Assyrians. They staked out people alive by running a spear down their throats and hanging them upside down around their fortresses for everyone to see. They also skinned people alive, leaving them in the sun to die. It is important to acknowledge that the culprits behind such cruelties are Satan and his demons (Ephesians 6:12).

Out of rebellion Manasseh and his people chose not to walk with God. So God, in His wisdom and mercy, released them to Satan to suffer the consequences of their sins that they might see the reality of their spiritual condition. Likewise, when we don't have a heart for God and stubbornly rebel against Him, we set Satan free to have his way with us. But God uniquely uses those predicaments set up by Satan to get our attention that we might repent. After Manasseh rebelled against God and Satan bound him in fetters and carried him to Babylon, Manasseh chose to repent:

> *...when he was in affliction, he besought the Lord, his God, and humbled himself greatly before the God of his fathers, and prayed unto him; and he was entreated by Him, and heard his supplication, and brought him again to Jerusalem into his kingdom. Then Manasseh knew that the Lord, he was God (II Chron. 33:12-13) (NSSB).*

I have heard people say all too often that the God of the Old Testament was mean, tough, and hard, and that only Jesus loves them. This is simply not true. The God of the Old Testament is one with Jesus. We can clearly see Jehovah God's mercy was upon Manasseh. Manasseh had done everything evil against God, His house, and His people; yet when he cried out and asked God to forgive him, God was there, ready to forgive and restore. Not only did God forgive him but--praise God for His mercy--God also "...brought him again to Jerusalem into His kingdom," and restored him. It is sad that God sometimes has to let us almost drown in our own juice before He can get our attention!

Therefore, we see that mercy and grace abound in the Old Testament, just as they do in the New. Indeed, we can learn much from what God shows us through His Old Testament people. Many denominations rob themselves of God's words of wisdom by never opening the Old Testament. One cannot fully understand the New Testament without the Old nor understand the Old in all its completeness without the Cross. Jesus verified that by saying: "Think not that I am come to destroy the law, or the prophets; I am not come to destroy, but to fulfill" (Matthew 5:17).

When God allows hard times to come, we would be wise not to look at them as negative times, but rather to look at each as an "I love you" from God--an instrument that He uses either for a testimony of our faith to others, or to change us for the good. Hard times teach us to **snuggle up** more closely to God. It's wonderful to be **snuggled up** continually with the Lord, for in doing so; we only get to know Him better. That's exactly what Manasseh learned after he repented, for then "Manasseh knew that the Lord, he was God." He **snuggled up** to Him and got to know Him better. Then what did Manasseh do?

> ...*he took away the foreign gods, and the idol out of the house of the Lord, and all the altars that he had built in the mount of the house of the Lord, and in Jerusalem, and cast them out of the city. And he repaired the altar of the Lord, and sacrificed on it peace offerings and thank offerings, and commanded Judah to serve the Lord God of Israel (II Chronicles 33:15, 16; NSSB).*

However, even though Manasseh repented, **snuggled up** to the Lord, and testified to others to do likewise, he neglected a critical issue. Although he removed all the foreign gods and idols from the Lord's house, "Nevertheless, the people did sacrifice still in the high places, yet unto the Lord, their God, only" (II Chronicles 33:17). Yes, they were worshipping God, but where? The high places spoken of were the groves, not the Lord's house.

The old King James version of the Bible uses the word **groves**, but newer translations use the word **Asherah**. The high places or groves were previously dedicated and used for worshipping other gods, Baal and Astarti, the sex goddess, and others. Male and female prostitutes had sex orgies there and worshippers offered their babies as burnt offerings. Manasseh failed to pull down, indicating that worship there was all right: they just couldn't worship Satan there anymore--they would only worship God. That was compromise and hypocrisy. They were worshipping God on unholy ground.

This may come as a shock to some of you, but many in the average church today are worshipping no differently than those Old Testament people were--they are worshipping God on unholy ground. They are worshipping God on the same ground upon which they had previously been worshipping Satan. For example: When a Christian gathers with other Christians to worship the Lord, yet at the same time is having an affair and living in adultery--that is compromise and hypocrisy. Satan delights when this self-destructive route is followed. To enjoy God's abundant life, it is essential to cleanse the place of worship, God's temple (I Corinthians 3:16; 6:19; Romans 8:1,2). God forgave Manasseh didn't he? But Manasseh failed to pull down the high places--to go all the way with God! Oh, that God's people would go all the way with Him and find the abundant life. Let's examine the following seven major steps to restoring true worship which assure abundant living:

## SEVEN MAJOR STEPS TO RESTORING TRUE WORSHIP:

## I. THE WORD OF GOD (II Timothy 4:1-2; Hebrews 4:12)

Hearing God's Word, as Josiah and the nation of Israel did, is vital to each individual. God teaches Christians in Hebrew 10:25 not to forsake the assembling of ourselves together. Anyone who says worshipping God out in the woods is sufficient, and that there is no need to assemble together in a church home with other Christians, is acting in direct violation to God's Word and purpose for gathering His people together. Many Christians violate God's Word in this matter simply out of too little love for God and out of ungrateful hearts. Numerous Christians have allowed themselves to be turned away by the hypocrites and trouble-makers Satan has planted in the churches, rather than keeping their eyes on Jesus and helping good win out. Some Christians are simply selfish, self-centered, and non-caring of other souls. Others don't gather at church because they have a lot of unfinished business with God, or even have a demonic stronghold in their life and/or a shattered personality. (Strongholds and shattered personalities will be discussed later in this book.) There are also both attenders and non-attenders (members) who are actually lost, only professing to be Christians.

Why is the preached word so essential to restoring true worship in the house of God (II Kings 23:2; Romans 10:17; 15:4; II Timothy 3:16; 4:1-4; Hebrews 4:12)? The God-breathed Word is given to us to be preached: for reproof, for rebuke, for correction, for teaching--to guide us into becoming what God created us to be and to show us how God wants us to live. Through the Word of God, one finds peace and joy. Please look at II Timothy 4:1,2:

> *I charge thee, therefore, before God, and the Lord Jesus Christ, who shall judge the living and the dead at his appearing and his kingdom: Preach the word; be diligent in season, out of season; reprove, rebuke, exhort with all long-suffering and doctrine (NSSB).*

As surely as we are to reprove and rebuke, we are also to exhort people--encourage them. For example, in rearing children, it is essential to properly balance the negatives and positives; to discipline and to love; to withhold and to give rewards. Doesn't God both chastise and reward us? Once a person has gotten his life right with God, he must take care not to have a critical, condemning spirit to those who have not yet gotten their acts together. Often times, a kind word of encouragement or exhortation helps bring that person to repentance, and he begins to improve by leaps and bounds.

How powerful is God's Word? Look at Hebrews 4:12:

> *For the word of God is living, and powerful, and sharper than any two-edged sword, piercing even to the dividing asunder of soul and spirit, and of the joints and marrow, and is a discerner of the thoughts and intents of the heart. (NSSB)*

The preached word from both the Old and New Testaments can do major surgery to mend lives--can bring about healing and restoration. Paul says this in Romans 15:4: "For whatever things were written in earlier times were written for our learning, that we, through patience and comfort of the scriptures, might have hope" (NSSB). Yes, even the account of Josiah's life was included in the scriptures that we might have hope! We are given everything we need to offer hope and to help restore people.

Let us now look closely at what God wants to teach us through the life of Josiah.

## II.    REPENTANCE--AN EXAMINATION OF KING JOSIAH'S LIFE

> *Josiah was eight years old when he began to reign in Jerusalem one and thirty years. And he did that which was right in the sight of the Lord, and walked in the ways of David, his father, and declined neither to the right hand nor to the left. For in the*

*eighth year of his reign, while he was yet young, he began to seek after the God of David, his father... (II Chron. 34:1-3a; NSSB).*

Josiah, at only sixteen years of age, was seeking after God. Too often, we cut young people short. The best time in a person's life to begin serving God is in their youth. As I shared before, I was saved at age ten and called to preach at age eighteen, but ran from God's call until age thirty-three, due to believing Satan's lies, which convinced me that I was inferior. The last five years of my fifteen-year run, while I was a drunk, I was very successful in the eyes of the world. I was driving expensive cars and well on my way to becoming very wealthy, yet I hid from God in as much as three fifths of Vodka on some days during those five years. At the end of those five years, I had to deal with a great deal of junk in my life.

God led me to sit down with a legal-size pad and make a list of all that I was guilty of during my run from His will. As He revealed all the unconfessed sins in my life, it took almost the entire pad to write them all down. When the list was complete, I dealt with each sin before the Lord. The only thing I didn't do at that time was to go back and get the ground back from Satan. In time, I learned that if we are to be totally free, it is essential for us not only to confess our sins, but also to take back the ground we've given to Satan. This process is not to be taken lightly. One is not to flippantly say, "I'm sorry, God, for all I've done."

Although God can use me very effectively now, I surely wasn't supposed to drink and commit sinful acts in order to be used by Him to help people in like sins. He would rather have used me from the point of His first calling me--at age eighteen. He and I would both have been spared a lot of heartache. I wish I could tell you that I was not saved when I was deep in sin, but I was saved, just being disobedient and rebellious to my Father. I listened to and obeyed Satan rather than God. In doing so, demons infiltrated my life, destroying my testimony for a time.

What was Josiah doing at the young age of twenty?

> *...in the twelfth year he began to purge Judah and Jerusalem from the high places, and the idols, and the carved images, and the melted and cast images. And they broke down the altars of Baalim in his presence; and the images, that were on high above them, he cut down; and the idols, and the carved images, and the cast images, he broke in pieces, and made dust of them, and scattered it upon the graves of them who had sacrificed unto them. And he burned the bones of the priests upon their altars, and cleansed Judah and Jerusalem. And so did he in the cities of Manasseh and Ephraim, and Simeon, even unto Naphtali, in their ruins round about. And when he had broken down the altars and the idols, and had beaten the carved images into powder, and cut down all the idols throughout all the land of Israel, he returned to Jerusalem. Now in the eighteenth year of his reign, when he had purged the land, and the house, he sent Shaphan, the son of Azaliah, and Maaseiah, the governor of the city, and Joah, the son of Joahaz, the recorder, to repair the house of the Lord, his God (II Chron. 34:3b-8) (NSSB).*

Keep in mind that Hezekiah is Josiah's great-grandfather, Manasseh is his grandfather, and Amon is his father. Amon reigned two years before his constituents assassinated him; then Josiah began to reign.  Now, bear with me a moment as at first there will be a little repetition, but it's necessary for us to read the following from the book of II Kings:

*Josiah was eight years old when he began to reign, and he reigned thirty and one years in Jerusalem.  And his mother's name was Jedidah, the daughter of Adaiah of Bozkath.  And he did that which was right in the sight of the Lord, and walked in all the way of David, his father and turned not aside to the right hand or to the left.  And it came to pass in the eighteenth year of King Josiah, that the king sent Shaphan, the son Azaliah, the son of Meshullam, the scribe, to the house of the Lord, saying, Go up to Hilkiah, the high priest, that he may reckon the amount of the silver which is brought into the house of the Lord, which the keepers of the door have gathered of the people; and let them deliver it into the hand of the doers of the work, who have the oversight of the house of the Lord; and let them give it to the doers of the work who are in the house of the Lord, to repair the breaches of the house (II Kings 22:1-5b; NSSB).*

In order for us to gain more essential data, let us also read:

*And Hilkiah, the high priest, said unto Shaphan, the scribe, I have found the book of the law in the house of the Lord.  And Hilkiah gave the book to Shaphan, and he read it.  And Shaphan, the scribe, came to the king, and brought the king word again, and said, Thy servants have gathered the money that was found in the house, and have delivered it into the hand of those who do the work, who have the oversight of the house of the Lord.  And Shaphan, the scribe, showed the king, saying, Hilkiah, the priest, hath delivered to me a book.  And Shaphan read it before the king..  And it came to pass, when the king had heard the book of the law, that he tore his clothes. And the king commanded Hilkiah, the priest, and Ahikam, the son of Shaphan, and Achbor, the son of Micaiah, and Shaphan, the scribe, and Asaiah, the king's servant, saying, Go ye, inquire of the Lord for me, and for the people, and for all Judah, concerning the words of this book that is found; for great is the wrath of the Lord that is kindled against us, because our fathers have not hearkened unto the words of this book, to do according unto all that which is written concerning us.  So Hilkiah, the priest, and Ahikam, and Achbor, and Shaphan, and Asaiah, went unto Huldah, the prophetess, the wife of Shallum, the son of Tikvah, the son of Harhas, keeper of the wardrobe (now she dwelt in Jerusalem in the second quarter), and they talked with her.  And she said unto them, Thus saith the Lord God of Israel, Tell the man who sent you to me;  Thus saith the Lord, Behold, I will bring evil upon this place, and upon its inhabitants, even in all the words of the book which the king of Judah hath read, because they have forsaken me, and have burned incense unto other gods, that they might provoke me to anger with all the works of their hands; therefore, my wrath shall be kindled against this place, and shall not be quenched.  But to the king of Judah who sent you to inquire of the Lord, thus shall ye say to him:  Thus saith the Lord God of Israel, As touching the words which thou hast heard; because thine heart was tender, and thou hast humbled thyself before the Lord, when thou heardest what I spoke against this place, and against its inhabitants, that they should become a desolation and a curse, and hast torn thy clothes, and wept before me, I also have heard thee, saith the Lord. Behold, therefore, I will gather thee unto thy fathers, and thou shalt be gathered into thy grave in peace; and thine eyes shall not see all the evil which I will bring upon this place. And they brought the king word again (vv. 8-20; NSSB).*

All the people heard the reading of God's Word. While Josiah had a repentant heart, apparently the people as a whole did not; thus God told Josiah that He was not going to make him suffer through seeing all the things He would have to do to unrepentant Israel.

Upon hearing the Word preached, Josiah cried out and repented. Josiah then allowed God's house to become the house of prayer that God intended it to be (Isaiah 56:7; Jere. 7:11; Matt. 21:13; Mk. 11:17; Lk. 19:46; John 2:13-17). Josiah tore his clothes, an outward display of his repentant heart. Then the prophetess sent word that Josiah's prayers had been heard, that he had been forgiven and that he was in right standing with God. When the people assembled themselves and heard the Word, they repented and began to communicate with God through prayer. You cannot pray effectively without repentance and a total surrender of your will. A total **letting go to God** brings a total life change. A total life change in Josiah's life required repentance and claiming back ground by removing the high places (claiming back the ground given to Satan).

## III. TOTAL COMMITMENT TO GOD (Matthew 6:33)

Matthew 6:33 tells us to seek God with everything that we have: "...seek ye first the kingdom of God, and His righteousness, and all these things shall be added unto you." Following salvation, our number-one priority should be to seek God and His will--and, by faith, to trust and obey Him. Did not Jesus instruct His disciples to pray for God to bring down to earth His will in heaven (Matthew 6:10; 16:19)? God has a wonderful plan for each of us that is completed as far as God is concerned; we have the choice whether or not to appropriate that plan. He never takes away our freedom of choice to obey or disobey Him, but stands ready to enable us to fulfill our callings. Satan wants us to think we will be unhappy in God's plan, when actually that is where we will be happiest. As we willingly obey God with a total commitment, He faithfully supplies all we need, plus any additional luxuries that He deems good for us.

Josiah got serious about doing business with God. He experienced revival and committed his heart to God to the point that he turned not from God, neither right nor left. Look at II Kings 23:3:

> *And the king stood by a pillar, and made a covenant before the Lord, to walk after the Lord, and to keep his commandments and his testimonies and his statutes with all his heart and all his soul, to perform the words of this covenant that were written in this book. And all the people joined in the covenant (NSSB).*

Even though the people joined in the covenant, they went back to their old, ungodly ways after Josiah's death. Why? The people had their eyes only on Josiah, not God. They **went along for the ride** in what they said, but not in what they believed in their hearts. It grieves me that many people today get their eyes on their preacher rather than on God. This is why God said:

*...Thou shalt love the Lord thy God with all thy heart, and with all thy soul, and with all thy mind, and with all thy strength: this is the first commandment, and the second is this: Thou shalt love thy neighbor as thyself. There is no other commandment greater than these (Mk. 12:30-31; NSSB).*

When I get in tune with the fact that God really cares for me--loves me unconditionally--I become secure in Him. Then I can love you unconditionally and be a channel of God's love flowing toward you.

When you **love God with all your heart**, obeying God is actually not so difficult. For after you get saved and are baptized--which is the first act of obedience following your salvation--God only requires two things of you for the rest of your life: One is availability and the other is obedience. While those two things really cover everything, you don't have to have a computer to figure out what you can and can't do. God simply wants you to consistently, willingly stay **snuggled up** to Him. Being sensitive to His voice, you can obey His will, both written and unwritten.

When Moses was not sensitive and obedient to God's voice, as in Exodus 2:5-4:17, he quickly demoted himself to a **wilderness**. He was assured of becoming Pharaoh of Egypt. However, believing he was the deliverer of God's Hebrew people from captivity, he rushed ahead of God--took matters into his own hands and killed an Egyptian and buried him in the sand. Hebrew witnesses rebuked him; and, the next thing we know, he was running, out of fear for his life, and spending forty years tending sheep in a wilderness.

Then one day Moses was heading toward home with all his sheep and Moses saw a bush burning, yet it was not consumed by the fire. When Moses **turned aside** to see it, God had his full attention--he was available to God. As a result, he heard God command him to do something: "Take your sandals off, Moses, for you are standing on holy ground." God can work through us when we make ourselves available and follow with obedience. Moses chose to obey for we see that he kicked his sandals off. However, when God told Moses that He had heard the cry of His rebellious people in Egypt and wanted him to go down and get them, Moses started backtracking. Immediately he gave God a bunch of excuses! "Oh, but God, I'm slow-tongued; you don't know me; I was born on the wrong side of the tracks."

Reader, not only was I insecure in the past, but I thought I was dumb, ugly, and a sure loser. I thought I had to **be somebody** with great abilities--such as a great intellect, a wide vocabulary, a great education and a great personality--but all I had to do was submit myself to God to be available for Him to use and trust that God could use me. As I've said before, none of us has enough sense to do anything without God, and He wants to do the things He desires through us. Running from Him for fifteen years, I gave Him the excuse that He couldn't use a ninth-grade dropout. The moment I stopped running and turned things over to Him, God amazed me as He enabled me to earn four degrees, including a doctor's degree in the ministry of counseling. I'm so grateful He kept loving me and pursuing me until I quit running. Here I am 60 years of age (in 1997 at the time of this writing) and He's using me more now than He ever has. I once asked, "God, why did you wait so long to use me so much?" He said, "You were just slow about moving forward!" If I don't fully trust, submit, and commit my life to the Lord, I cannot live a life that will be an effective testimony. Oh, that we would more readily make ourselves available and obedient!

## IV. LIFESTYLE-CHANGING REFORMS (II Kings 23:4-25; Roms. 12:1-2)

Now I have not **arrived**, for I, like Paul, am the chief of sinners and the least of the saints; but because I love Him and want to be in the center of His will, each morning I pray:

> *Lord, I submit to you my will; my rights; my life; my family; my ministry; my finances; my needs; my desires; my direction; and my flesh. 'Lord, search me, try me, see if there be any wicked way in me.' Remove those things that need to be removed from my life and bring into my life those things that need to be brought in. For, I confess to you that you are all I have and all I want and all I need.*

How much do you love Him? If you choose not to let your will become His will, then you are telling Him that you want <u>your</u> will done instead of His. In such cases, as God warns, Satan's plan begins to unfold and leanness comes to one's soul, perhaps even leading to a reprobate mind (Romans 1:28). God truly has a good plan for each of us. If we trust Him and let His desires become our desires, we will enjoy an abundant life; for God, our Potter, does know what's best for us. II Kings 23:4-25 covers this subject, as does Romans 12:1-2:

> *I beseech you therefore, brethren, by the mercies of God, that ye present your bodies a living sacrifice, holy, acceptable unto God, which is your reasonable service. And be not conformed to this world, but be ye transformed by the renewing of your mind, that ye may prove what is that good, and acceptable, and perfect, will of God (NSSB).*

God has shown us this in the New Testament--now watch what He did with Josiah in the Old Testament. When Josiah began doing God's will, look what he did in II Kings 23:5-7:

> *...he put down the idolatrous priests, whom the kings of Judah had ordained to burn incense in the high places in the cities of Judah, and in the places round about Jerusalem, and them also who burned incense unto Baal, to the sun, and to the moon, and to the planets, and to all the host of heaven (Zodiac). And he brought out the idol from the house of the Lord, outside of Jerusalem, unto the brook, Kidron, and stamped it small to powder, and cast the powder of it upon the graves of the children of the people. And he broke down the houses of the sodomites that were by the house of the Lord, where the women wove hangings for the idol (NSSB).*

When God started dealing with Josiah concerning the things in the house of God, look closely at what Josiah did in verse four:

> *And the king commanded Hilkiah, the high priest, and the priests of the second order, and the keepers of the door, to bring forth out of the temple of the Lord all the vessels that were made for Baal, and for the idol, and for all the host of heaven; and he burned them outside of Jerusalem in the fields of Kidron, and carried their ashes unto Bethel (NSSB).*

Josiah is restoring true worship, which brings about lifestyle changes. Through Josiah, God shows us what the New Testament declares in I Corinthians 3:16-17; 6:19-20; Acts 19:11-20. The first thing that had to happen was the cleansing of the Temple, God's house. In the New Testament, each person repenting of his sins and accepting the Lord Jesus as his Savior becomes the temple of God, because the Holy Spirit of God actually comes to dwell within his heart at the time of his salvation (I Corinthians 3:16-17; 6:19-20). Josiah's lifestyle changes illustrate the changes we need to make with regard to God's temples, our bodies.

## A. IDENTIFYING IDOLATRY

Josiah dealt with idolatry--worship of Baal, Venus, the Sun and other gods--and then all the paraphernalia that had been used in worship. Look what the **Zondervan Pictorial Dictionary and Encyclopedia** says of idolatry:

> *Ancient man believed that the image was the dwelling place of the superhuman force or being, or was the deity itself. Idols were made of wood, stone, or clay and sometimes of gold or silver. For the Hebrews, idolatry included the worship of anything other than Jehovah...Idolatry was the embodiment of human desire and thought. Idols, though made in many shapes and sizes, really represented the image of man, for they expressed his thoughts, desires, and purposes. Man's pride caused him to trust himself rather than God, hence, his idols were really expressions of self-worship (Isa. 2:8-22).*[3]

This passage means that worshipping anything that is not God (Jehovah or Yahweh--the Father, Son, and Holy Spirit) is worshipping Satan. In counseling, one of the biggest strongholds I see is self-idolatry. Often people say, "Oh, but, Joe, you don't understand. I can't help myself. I don't have a choice. I can't overcome my habit. I'm not Jesus!" If you think you can't resist all temptations, you believe Satan's lie. However, it is also possible that you are using that as an excuse to hang onto your sins--your gods.

Many people struggle while trying to break the cigarette habit because nicotine is a drug. Addicts freed from cocaine and heroine have an even more difficult time kicking the nicotine habit. Be it nicotine, drugs, alcohol, sex, anger, etc, you can't blame its stronghold on the fact you're **only human**. The Bible repeatedly depicts man as debasing himself when he worships what he has made with his own hands. We must put off all sins and habits in order to live godly lives. If you walk in the flesh long enough, Satan will build a stronghold, perhaps even bringing in some demonic company to make their abode within you.

The Israelites found that the Canaanites worshiped El, Baal, and Astarti. "The chief Canaanite deities were El, the creator of the earth; Baal, the controller of storms (both were symbolized by **the bull** and its procreative powers); and the fertility goddess Astarti, biblical Ashtaroth." The Canaanite religion as a whole involved worship of the sex-goddess, Astarti.[4] In the worship of Astarti, as well as in most cults and in the occult, you always find perverted sex. Why are sexually-transmitted diseases at near-epidemic heights today? It's simple: Satan has long been perverting sex to destroy God's creation. So many people have flippantly obeyed Satan's perverted lies about sex, and, while one may not be involved in a Satanic cult or in the occult, the sinful acts are just as evil, and still hold the same destructive consequences. God created sex for good, and for our protection from disease, He gave clear guidelines in His word concerning the proper use of it within the marriage bed.

## B.    CLEANSING THE TEMPLE OF GOD

People worshipped Baal, Venus, and the Sun not only in the high places but also in God's Temple. As part of their "worship," sex orgies with male and female prostitutes took place in shrines and ritual booths. Josiah took action as we have already read in II Kings 23:6-7:

> *And he brought out the idol from the house of the Lord, outside of Jerusalem, unto the brook, Kidron, and burned it at the brook, Kidron, and stamped it small to powder, and cast the powder of it upon the graves of the children of the people. And he broke down the houses of the sodomites that were by the house of the Lord, where the women wove hangings for the idol (NSSB).*

While Josiah reigned, sex orgies and sinful acts ceased but the booths still stood. Knowing that was wrong, "...he broke down the houses of the sodomites that were by the house of the Lord, where the women wove hangings for the idol." He destroyed the consecrated things and places of familiar spirits.

Since every Christian's body is God's temple, one would have to ignore reality to say sex sins aren't going on in the temple (house) of God today. It is grievous that numerous Christians today are captivated by perverted sex--masturbation, oral sex, adultery, prostitution, homosexuality, bestiality, etc. Until one is willing to let God clean up His temple and oust the idols, self-destruction is imminent. God warns us firmly in Colossians 3:5 to "Mortify, therefore, your members which are upon the earth: fornication, uncleanness, inordinate affection, evil desire, and covetousness (which is idolatry)...." It was vital that Josiah cleanse the Temple of the Old Testament; it is equally vital that Christians cleanse their New Testament temples.

## C.    CLAIMING BACK GROUND LOST BY SEXUAL SIN

You may be bombarded with impure thoughts, perhaps even while praying, reading your Bible or hearing a sermon. Guilt may overwhelm you, and you wonder how such thoughts could occur. God says in I Corinthians 6:13, "Foods for the body and the body for foods; but God shall destroy both it and them. Now the body is not for fornication, but for the Lord; and the Lord for the body." The word **fornication** from the Greek is **porneia**. What English word is similar to porneia? Yes, pornography! That's where it came from. God warns us to "Flee fornication, every sin that a man doeth is outside the body; but he that committeth fornication sinneth against his own body."

Satan has convinced so many people to sin against their very own bodies. Loose sexual lives are so prevalent today; many believe its okay for males to **sow their wild oats**, and for two consenting persons to have sex as long as outsiders don't get hurt. God says it's not okay--someone always gets hurt because fornication is a sin against one's self. This is the only place in the New Testament where God categorizes a sin, not only for what it does to others, but also for what it does to the individual. If sexual sin is a stronghold in your life and you want peace and joy, go to the cross and pray:

> Lord Jesus, you took my place on Calvary and became my sexual promiscuity, my junk. You became my sin of sleeping with my wife/husband before I married them. Lord, I'm sorry for it and ask you to forgive me. I release my feelings of insecurity, inferiority, and rejection, as well as my suspicions and jealousies, which led to this sin. I release to the cross the pain, shame, and condemnation resulting from it. Forgive me for violating my commitment to my marriage through these sins. I release all of this to the cross. And, Satan, I command you by the authority of the Lord Jesus Christ and the power of His shed blood, that you give me back the ground that the sexual promiscuity gave you in my life. Lord Jesus, permeate that ground with your precious blood; heal it, cleanse it, and totally restore it. Heal my mind, body, soul and spirit. Lord Jesus, heal my memories involving my sexual impurities. I want no negative effect on my life nor my family's life, present or future. Any demon spirits that have been able to stand on this ground to harass me, I claim back that ground. Lord Jesus, by your blood and your name, send them and their network to the pit. Lord, seal the doorway to that part of my mind so they can never come back to harass me and lead me through the gutter again. Lord Jesus, I praise you and thank you that you have done all this for me and healed my memory. Thank you for restoring that torn part of my soul. I love you. I thank you and praise you for working all things together for my good.

It is then handled forever. We are to exercise our authority and rights as children of God, recognizing the blood of Christ is living and applicable to every area of our lives today. It's peaceful to live in a clean temple!

If you slept with your mate before marrying them, take your mate by the hand and kneel together, saying, "I'm sorry for sinning against you and making you sin and stumble. Will you forgive me, please?" I assure you, the result can be a fresh new beginning, a new honeymoon for you. Cleansing your temple places a security in your marriage that will help you work through any other difficulties that may be in your marriage. Try it...try Him, His way! It works if you do it from your heart.

It is crucial for people to understand that prostitutes and homosexuals are demonized. Most female and male prostitutes and homosexuals have been abused by both sexes, and sell or give their bodies to be in control and to return abuse. If you lead such a person to the Lord but don't deal with the demonic stronghold in his or her life, they will return to their sinful lifestyle most of the time.

You say, but Joe, why is that so? It is so for the same reason Josiah reclaimed the ground and cleansed the Temple even though the actual acts were not going on at the time. After God cleanses His temples, we are to continually do as I Peter 1:13a says, "...gird up the loins of your mind"--remain on guard against future temptation from Satan.

90

### D.    PUTTING AWAY IDOLATRY

Oh, that our churches today would recognize the urgency for judgment to begin at the house of God! In verse eight we read:

> *And he brought all the priests out of the cities of Judah, and defiled the high places where the priests had burned incense, from Geba to Beersheba, and broke down the high places of the gates that were in the entrance of the gate of Joshua, the governor of the city, which were on a man's left hand at the gate of the city (NSSB).*

I Peter 4:17 states, "For the time is come that judgment must begin at the house of God; and if it first begin at us, what shall the end be of them that obey not the gospel of God?" We cannot expect to be effective witnesses and counselors in the world for Christ if our hearts and lives are not clean before God in every area. If you gossip, curse, tell dirty jokes, those sins are just as evil before God as other sins, and are hindrances to witnessing.

During Josiah's reign, judgment began at the house of God in Jerusalem; but then, it moved out to Judah, and then to Samaria (II Kings 23:4, 8, 19). Jesus taught His disciples to begin spreading the gospel in Jerusalem; then in Judah, in Samaria, and into the uttermost parts of the earth (Acts 1:8). As we allow God to do a major work in our lives that work overflows as a testimony to others. However, if we allow Satan to do a major work in our lives, that work also overflows, touching others. Some people are even glad to know Christians sin, for it eases their consciences, giving them excuses to lounge in their sin. Sinning Christians also turn others away from Christ, causing Christianity to appear as a sham, and Christians to appear no different from dishonest, corrupted non-Christians.

Josiah didn't miss a thing. II Chronicles speaks of stables of horses and two chariots used by the kings to ride out, morning and evening, to worship the Sun-god. The horses were esteemed like gods and kept next to the house of God. Josiah relegated the horses to common labor and burned the chariots, destroying them. It's essential to deal with all ground.

In Josiah's day, there were two types of priests: those appointed by the kings to conduct sexual orgies, and the supposedly-godly Levite priests. Some of the Levite priests got involved in sex orgies. Josiah allowed them to sit with the other brethren but they could not serve in the Temple. Likewise, when Christian brethren fall, Church fellowship must be withdrawn until that person chooses to repent and be restored. They can come and hear the preaching and teaching of the Word, but should neither serve nor enjoy casual fellowship. Also, there are times when preachers and deacons can sin in areas that disqualify them from being used according to God's original calling. One such an example is divorce and remarriage which violates God's guidelines stipulated for pastors and deacons (I Timothy 3; Titus 1). Any pastor or deacon having a poor reputation according to God's Word--a bad name--falls into the category of disqualification. However, if they are truly repentant, God can use them in other areas of ministry.

Solomon had lusted after hundreds of women, received all their false gods, and built groves and high places. The word **iconoclasm** means **the act of breaking images; attacking cherished beliefs as shams**. The word **iconoclast** means **the breaker of images**. Josiah was an **iconoclast**, defaming and desecrating all the altars, sacred places, and paraphernalia of Satan. He ground them to powder and scattered the ashes away from the city, making sure everything was clean. He even burned the bones of the dead satanic priests appointed by the king (II Kings 23:5). These were not the Levite priests. Josiah claimed back the ground! Now let's look at II Kings 23:9-20:

> *Nevertheless, the priests of the high places came not up to the altar of the Lord in Jerusalem, but they did eat of the unleavened bread among their brethren. And he defiled Topheth, which is in the valley of the children of Hinnom, that no man might make his son or his daughter to pass through the fire to Molech. And he took away the horses that the kings of Judah had given to the sun, at the entrance of the house of the Lord, by the chamber of Nathanmelech, the chamberlain, which was in the precincts, and burned the chariots of the sun with fire. And the altars that were on the top of the upper chamber of Ahaz, which the kings of Judah had made, and the altars which Manasseh had made in the two courts of the house of the Lord, did the king beat down, and broke them down from there, and cast the dust of them into the brook, Kidron. And the high places that were before Jerusalem, which were on the right hand of the mount of corruption, which Solomon, the king of Israel, had builded for Ashtoreth, the abomination of the Sidonians, and for Chemosh, the abomination of the Moabites, and for Milcom, the abomination of the children of Ammon, did the king defile. And he broke in pieces the images, and cut down the idols, and filled their places with the bones of men. Moreover, the altar that was at Bethel, and the high place which Jeroboam, the son of Nebat, who made Israel to sin, had made, both that altar and the high place he broke down, and burned the high place, and stamped it small to powder, and burned the idol. And as Josiah turned himself, he spied the sepulchers that were there in the mount, and sent, and took the bones out of the sepulchers, and burned them upon the altar, and polluted it, according to the word of the Lord which the man of God proclaimed, who proclaimed these words. Then he said, What marker is that that I see? And the men of the city told him, It is the sepulcher of the man of God, who came from Judah, and proclaimed these things that thou hast done against the altar of Bethel. And he said, Let him alone; let no man move his bones. So they let his bones alone, with the bones of the prophet who came out of Samaria. And all the houses also of the high places that were in the cities of Samaria, which the kings of Israel had made to provoke the Lord to anger, Josiah took away, and did to them according to all the acts that he had done in Bethel. And he slew all the priests of the high places who were there upon the altars, and burned men's bones upon them, and returned to Jerusalem (NSSB).*

These things had been proclaimed in I Kings 13:1, 30-31, and in I Kings 13:11, 31. Look more closely at the references to the high places in I Kings 14:24. A good description of these booths is seen in **The Pulpit Commentary of I & II Kings**:

> Verse 7--And he brake down the houses of the sodomites; literally, of the consecrated ones...and note that the male prostitutes or Galli, who consecrated themselves to the Dea Syra, formed an essential element in the Astarte-worship, and accompanied it wherever it was introduced.) Dollinger says ('Jew and Gentile,' vol. i. pp. 430, 431)

of these wretched persons, "To the exciting din of drums, flutes, and inspired songs, the Galli cut themselves on the arms; and the effect of this act, and of the music accompanying it, was so strong upon mere spectators, that all their bodily and mental powers were thrown into a tumult of excitement, and they too, seized by the desire to lacerate themselves, deprived themselves of their manhood by means of potsherds lying ready for the purpose. Thereupon they ran with the mutilated part through the city, and received from the houses which they threw them into, a woman's gear. Not chastity, but barrenness, was intended by the mutilation. In this the Galli only desired to be like their goddess. The relation of foul lust, which they thenceforeward occupied towards women, was regarded as a holy thing, and was tolerated by husbands in their wives.[5]

It is clear that Satan tempts in order to distort and destroy God's original purpose for His human creations. These men wanted to be like their goddess.

If I were to point out paraphernalia in your house which you need to dispose of, for instance a sundial-god or objects with your astrological sign on them, you probably wouldn't be upset. You'd readily **purge** your house to claim back ground. Yet, if I were to instruct you to allow God to reveal such things in your mind and heart, you might hesitate. For your sake, ask God to show you any booths and high places in your lifestyle, allowing Him to cleanse His temple.

If the average person will apply what I'm sharing, he will probably have no need for counseling. While many have come to me who have not had fragmented personalities and have not been full of demons, many others have had fragmented personalities with demonic strongholds. The latter almost always require help from a pastor or Christian counselor. This book is to be used not only as preventative maintenance and self-help for those who can benefit, but also as encouragement for those who do need deeper counseling to seek it. If you are deep into problems, there is help and hope for you.

## E.    DEFILING THE HIGH PLACES

Is there anything in your heart that is put above God? Any place where God is not worshipped, idols will be set up in His place and become a mount (high place) of corruption. Our hearts and our beings will become mounts of corruption if we allow God to be dethroned. Are you loving Him and serving Him with all your heart, mind, soul, and strength? If not, self is being worshipped above God.

If anyone holds unforgiveness toward someone, self is on the throne of their life. Many sexually-abused people say that they cannot forgive their abuser, insisting they must suffer through the hurt for a period of time. They feel no one understands the cruelty that was done to them. I ask, "When Jesus Christ died on Calvary two thousand years ago, and His blood fell, how many sins did He die for?" All. Think of the results from those sins: the hurt, shame, pain, rejection and condemnation. Jesus took those upon Himself on the cross. Reject your freedom in Christ and you are choosing to convert those hurts done to you into self-inflicted hurts. Jesus Christ died for the abuser as well as for the abused. He became the sin of that sexual abuse and the emotional trauma resulting from it. He appeals to the abused and the abuser alike to allow His truths to set them free to be what He created them to be.

Forgiveness of the abuser is essential, or the root of bitterness will soon devour the holder. Jesus' death on the cross brought healing to those who accept the truth, "...by His stripes we are healed." They are healed of all the results of sin. Our perfect Lord Himself forgave all; who are we not to do likewise? As I shared before, my dad died before I was one, my mother gave me away the day before I turned two, and the man who took me to rear died when I was eight years old. His wife had to take a job, and left me alone for weeks at a time from ages nine to twelve. I understand rejection, hurt, fear, and anger. For thirty-seven years that hurt grew into hatred for my mother.

I once wanted to be another Percy Foreman, a successful attorney (now deceased), so that I could represent and defend the abused. God had a different but similar plan. When God called me to preach, I felt insecure and scared, and I ran from His plan for fifteen years. However, the day came when I ceased running and reclaimed the ground I had given Satan through hanging onto my hurts, anger and hatred, and my insecurities and fears. I'm living proof of how Jesus can heal all the hurt and memories. I went to the cross and claimed back my ground. I was already saved, but became more usable because I let God's truths set me free. Now by God's grace I stand to offer liberty and represent and defend those abused by Satan.

## F.    GUARDING AGAINST IDOLATRY IN OUR LIVES

The Age of Idolatry is not past (Colossians 3:5). Some worship the church building and its programs instead of God. Some even worship the preacher above God. Today we see the worship of self, the worship of nature, the worship of money, the worship of power (even in the ministry), the worship of knowledge, the worship of science, and many other forms of idolatry. We should be relentless in our thoroughness to let high thoughts be mightily brought down, and proud imaginations abased (II Corinthians 10:4-5). In I Samuel 15:23, God tells us that rebellion is as the sin of witchcraft and stubbornness is as iniquity and idolatry--a chosen lifestyle and example to others. Like many who succumb to the lure to worship the creation rather than the Creator, at one time I changed my focus from the Lord to my preaching position. I **walked in the flesh** in the pastorate, ministering to people only from the pulpit and referring those needing counseling to others. Impatiently I wondered why people couldn't just get their act together with God and go on with their lives. I failed to love God's people with God's heart. So God in His mercy got my undivided attention by removing me from the pastorate, and putting my family and me in a scummy motel for an entire year. We shared the motel with a vast, ever-increasing population of large, brown roaches, and the carpet reeked with the odor of urine from a previous cat resident. Every time it rained, the parking lot filled with water and seeped into the room, moistening the carpet and strongly enhancing the odor the cat had left behind. My family walked with me through that time, and I thank God that none of them ever complained of the mess we were in. They daily walked beside me--unquestioningly--with trusting hearts.

During that year, God taught me that He loved me anyway-- unconditionally--with no strings attached. He didn't love me a dime less when I was a drunk wallowing in my own vomit, nor a dime more when I surrendered to Him and preached His Word. He just loved me and wanted me to love others in turn. He pointed my preaching-god out to me and asked, "Joe, what if I just put you on a shelf, never take you down and never let you preach again? What if I just want to set you there and admire you? Would you still love Me as much as you say you love Me?" Three months later, still sitting in that scummy motel, I answered, "Yes, Lord!" I'm so grateful that God drew my undivided attention, and that I chose to let Him clean the junk out of my life.

## V.    APPLYING THE SHED BLOOD

After Josiah tore down the booths and high places and reclaimed the ground, what actions did he then take?

> *And the king commanded all the people, saying, Keep the Passover unto the Lord your God, as it is written in the book of this covenant. Surely there was not held such a Passover from the days of the judges who judged Israel, nor in all the days of the kings of Israel, nor of the kings of Judah (II Kings 23:21-22; NSSB).*

After he claimed back the ground from Satan, the first thing Josiah did was to re-institute the Passover--apply the blood as atonement for sin. He did this according to God's Old Testament Law, observing Passover in a way not seen since the days of the Judges. (That includes the time of David and Solomon!) Josiah dotted every "i" and crossed every "t," for he knew that it was necessary to cleanse the people from all sins and reclaim the ground. What cleanses our sins today? The shedding of blood!

For Josiah and Israel, the shedding of the blood of the spotless lamb at Passover atoned for sin. For New Testament Christians, believing in and applying the shed blood of the Lamb of God, the Lord Jesus Christ, atones for our sins (Ephesians 1:3-9; Hebrews 9:11-22; I Peter 1:18,19). We see in Revelation 12:11 that "...they overcame him (Satan) by the blood of the Lamb, and by the word of their testimony; and they loved not their lives unto the death." The most powerful weapon we have is Jesus Christ--the blood of the Lamb. It is grievous that so many moderates and liberals try to remove the blood out of theology and out of Bibles and hymnals, for Jesus' blood is our only power over Satan! Satan delights in such heresy, for he hates the blood. When I'm counseling and start reading scripture about, praying about or singing about the wonderful power we have in the blood of our Lord, demonic persons often put their fingers in their ears and shout, "No, no, no! Not the blood!" The power of the blood of Christ is awesome! Without it, we are lost and hopeless, indeed.

## VI.    A PERSONAL ENCOUNTER WITH GOD FROM THE HEART (II Kings 22:16-20; 23:25-27)

As we've learned, Josiah did not turn right nor left in his allegiance to God. He determined in his heart to claim back the ground that Satan had claimed. In that day, the people had to follow and obey King Josiah, but they followed him only physically and verbally, not with their hearts. Many people today go to church, but don't really worship and serve the Lord with their hearts. A pastor asked me one day, "Joe, why do you think your counseling ministry appears to bring more victories in people's lives than your preaching ministry?" I answered, "There are probably individuals out in the congregation like this, but people coming for counseling are hurting and desperate for help. They don't care what it takes, no matter how hard the truths are that I have to tell them."

A precious man once told me that he didn't think Christians could have demons. And then I counseled his son who had been a homosexual and drug addict since the age of seventeen. The son was about thirty-two years old when he came to see me and had been in every type of rehabilitation

95

center imaginable. I led him to the Lord, but he kept wandering back into the homosexual lifestyle. Finally, I appealed to his parents explaining, "Your son is still a single person and is still submitting himself to your authority in many ways. So, I beseech you to reconsider the possibility of this young man's having demons, and pray with me and permit me to deal with them."

The father answered, "Joe, I don't understand any of this. I know my son got saved but he's still not free to be what God intended him to be. And, since telling you years ago that I didn't believe Christians could have demons, I have come to the point that I trust you. So as his parental authority, I give you permission to do whatever God tells you and that's good enough for me." **He got desperate with God.**

I have witnessed so many people religiously carrying their notebooks, "ever learning but never growing." In the past, Christians such as Bill Gothard, the head of **Basic Youth Conflict**, have disagreed with me over whether or not Christians can have demons, but then later have grasped the truth that Christians can. At one of Gothard's all-day ministers' conferences he said that God had shown him that, indeed, Christians can have demons, and that it is essential to reclaim the ground, or that Satan will beat you to death with the past. I was grateful to have the opportunity to stand in his conference, confirming from counseling experience that if people don't get in touch with past emotions and sins and deal with them, plus regain ground lost to Satan, they would remain miserable, saved, but forfeiting peace and joy and the abundant life.

## VII.  PULLING DOWN STRONGHOLDS AND CLAIMING BACK GROUND

When people ask me where I get my scriptural authority concerning Christians having demons, one of the scriptures I show them is 1 Corinthians 5:5 where Paul teaches about delivering stubbornly sinful members of the church to Satan for the destruction of the flesh. The one released to Satan doesn't lose his salvation, but, due to his stubbornly unrepentant heart, he loses his peace and joy and is subjected to the demonic. While God does not force His will upon anyone, He does allow things to happen that will cause a rebellious person to see that his wrong choices are carrying him to self-destruction. It is very essential to always remember that God's purpose is restoration.

More evidence of Christians being subjected to the demonic is found in Matthew 18:34-35. Here Jesus told Peter that unless he forgave every brother their trespasses, God would deliver him to the **tormentors**. The word **torment (basanos)** means **torture** and is associated with disease (Matt. 8:6). Those who torment (vex), through diseases are devils (Matt. 17:14-18). Once again, we see that God will deliver a stubbornly rebellious Christian to **tormentors**.

I always show further scriptural authority on the subject of warfare which is found in II Corinthians 10:4-5 where all Christians are addressed:

> *For the weapons of our warfare are not carnal, but mighty through God to the pulling down of strongholds, casting down imaginations, and every high thing that exalteth itself against the knowledge of God, and bringing into captivity every thought to the obedience of Christ (NSSB).*

God warns all of us that we are involved in warfare, like it or not. Didn't He tell us to put on the whole armor of God so that we can stand against the wiles of the Devil (Ephesians 6:10-18)? Where do those strongholds that we are to pull down take root? In our minds. That's why God instructs us to cast down any imaginations--thoughts that come in the form of Satan's ideas and temptations. The word **imagination** means **the act or power of forming mental images of what is not actually present; the act or power of creating mental images of what has never been actually experienced, or of creating new images or ideas by combining previous experience.**[6] Deep rooted and consistent remembrances of past hurts combined with imaginations, readily give birth to fragmented personalities. Do we have a way to pull down these strongholds and cast down the imaginations? You'd better believe we do! Our weapon, Jesus, is mighty through God. God says He will supply all our needs (Philippians 4:19). Isn't this a need? God has supplied it. How many things can we do in Him? All things (Phil. 4:13). We're more than conquerors!

Look carefully at Galatians 5:1: "Stand fast, therefore, in the liberty with which Christ hath made us free, and be not entangled again with the yoke of bondage." This clearly says Christians can be put in bondage. If a Christian lounges in sin, Satan establishes ground. God says, "Be angry, and sin not; let not the sun go down upon your wrath; neither give place to the devil" (Ephesians 4:26-27). God means we can be angry at the sin and at Satan, but not at the sinner. We must forgive and not give Satan a loophole or foothold by which to ensnare us!

It grieves my heart that many **professional** psychiatrists and psychologists, even Christian ones, tell poor souls it will take **years** for them to **work through** and overcome their abusive past. I believe this is a lie that causes them doubt and robs their hope. Few professionals speak of the necessity for their client to forgive, and the truth that they can move on with their lives. Instead, they often use physical elements for a tolerant rather than God for solutions. Please understand that I am not saying that there is not a temporary time necessary for medication. I believe that there are times that it is needed to bring a person's body and emotions under control so that they can begin dealing with the underlying spiritual and other issues. However, I must stress that medication should only be used temporarily. Typically, the foremost **helper** of professionals is **medication**, only suppressing emotions and memories that need to be healed. Medication is commonly their answer for depressed, suicidal, and uncontrollable patients, and it, in itself, cannot bring the true hope, freedom, peace and joy of an abundant life.

Recently, a patient killed a Houston doctor and his assistant by throwing them down an elevator shaft. I believe the man was demonic. The demonic have great strength, as we see in the Bible. God is the sole solution to all problems--demonic and otherwise--for through Him all strongholds and imaginations can be torn down. God wants to help us rise above our past:

> *In which in times past ye walked according to the course of this world, according to the prince of the power of the air, the spirit that now worketh in the sons of disobedience; among whom also we all had our manner of life in times past in the lusts of our flesh, fulfilling the desires of the flesh and of the mind, and were by nature the children of wrath, even as others. But God, who is rich in mercy, for his great love with which he loved us, even when we were dead in sins, hath made us alive together with Christ (by grace ye are saved), and hath raised us up together, and made us sit together in heavenly places in Christ Jesus (Eph. 2:2-5; NSSB).*

Clearly, God does not want former sins affecting us. Even if the whole world has abused and rejected us, the most important One, our Potter, loves and accepts us: "To the praise of the glory of his grace, through which he hath made us accepted in the Beloved" (Ephesians 1:6) and "In whom we have boldness and access with confidence by the faith of him" (Ephesians 3:12)!

Healing for the personality that has fragmented begins with acceptance and hope. Freedom then comes from dealing with that wounded person's past, which will be covered in coming chapters.

Many unloved and abused persons move into a Peter Pan syndrome--not wanting to grow up. Many who were abandoned or wounded verbally, physically, and/or sexually as children have personality fragments holding deep emotional hurts and angers. The Church should be equipped to help heal these trauma victims. While many psychiatrists and psychologists allow these fragmented victims to remain divided, the Church can counsel them as to how to become one--whole again. Now let us look at seven essential steps to help victims reclaim ground:

### A.    CONFIRM AND AFFIRM YOUR SONSHIP IN CHRIST

John 1:12 says, "But as many as received him, to them gave he power to become the children of God, even to them that believe on his name." The only way to freedom is through the power of the blood of Christ and in order to experience that power, you must belong to Him. You begin by confirming your sonship in Christ by praying: "I am a child of God and have the right and authority through Jesus' blood to do what You have given me permission to do."

### B.    BREAK ALL ANCESTRAL AND GENETIC TIES

All ancestral and genetic ties should be renounced as far back generationally--on both the dad's and mom's sides--which God deems necessary. In Exodus 34:6-7, the Lord said:

> *The Lord, the Lord God, merciful and gracious, long-suffering, and abundant in goodness and truth, keeping mercy for thousands, forgiving iniquity and transgression and sin, and who will by no means clear the guilty, visiting the iniquity of the fathers upon the children and upon the children's children, unto the third and to the fourth generation (Also Ex. 20:5; Num. 14-18; Deut. 5:9).*

### C.    RENOUNCE ALL WORKINGS OF SATAN (See example, Acts 19:18, 19; II Corinthians 4:2)

In dealing with people who have been involved in witchcraft, cults and other religions with ritualistic acts (such as Mormonism and Free Masonry), it is not unusual to have to go back further than the third and fourth generations. Why are some people so easily lured to such organizations, some even selling their souls to Satan? They desire the position and power it offers. It's a matter of pride, again, the very reason Satan fell.

As Satan, through his human followers, seeks to hinder God's work, we must take seriously their evil plots, for some even cast curses on God's people. Jesus says, "Love your enemies, bless them that curse you, do good to them that hate you, and pray for them who despitefully use you, and persecute you" (Matt. 5:44). How are we to handle attacks from our enemies? Even if they are cursing you, your end goal is to witness to them that they might be saved. If you experience afflictions and illnesses, check to see whether or not they are there due to sin in your life. Then see if God will remove them, or if He will leave them as a testimony that Jesus' grace is sufficient. After making sure all sins are confessed from the heart, you may pray a prayer similar to one I pray:

> Lord, in your name and the power of the blood you shed for me, I cancel out, renounce and sever, every word of curse or sorcery that has been worked or spoken against me, my family, my ministry, my pastor, his family, everyone connected with me that Satan would like to hurt. ....I ask you to send the curses back on them to demonstrate your almighty power that they might come under conviction, repent and accept you.

While one is ministering to ex-witches and ex-Satan worshippers, their previous cohorts sometimes work overtime sending demons to attack. They would delight in God's servants being maimed or killed, but would rather drag them through the gutter, destroying their testimony for Christ, just as they did Jimmy Swaggart's. The grievous thing about Jimmy Swaggart is that he preaches that we can lose our salvation if we sin. His Pentecostal, Armenian faith also claims that we can sin to such a degree that we must get **re-saved**. Yet, when he repented of his sin of visiting the prostitute, he only asked for forgiveness from God, his family, the Church, and the public, never once saying anything about being lost and getting **re-saved**. He simply said that the demons of hell had drawn him to pornography and then to the prostitutes, and that he had been afraid to tell anyone in the Church. You see, many Pentecostals, like so many Baptists and those of other faiths, refuse to believe that Christians can have demons.

A high percentage of my counselees have had demons as a result of their involvement in pornography, which leads to perverted sexual involvement. Frequently, I deal with precious Christians, including pastors and deacons, who have been enslaved for fifteen or twenty years by pornography. They are too terrified to let their Church family know for fear of rejection. How tragic! When they come to see me they are desperate, weary of the junk in their lives, and ready for God's truths.

I have counseled people who speak in tongues, another area in which many people can give ground to Satan. I believe that all the gifts of the Spirit are active, but God cautions us to test the spirits. So I test the tongue with my counselees for their protection. Some, in spite of being enveloped in serious problems, won't let you test their tongue because they falsely believe that would be blaspheming the Holy Spirit of God. They do not understand that a Christian cannot blaspheme the Holy Spirit. Blasphemy of the Holy Spirit can only be done by an unbeliever--blasphemy is not believing God, refusing to believe on the Lord Jesus Christ as Savior. Many who speak in tongues feel so edified by their "gift" that they won't allow it to be tested to see if it's a demon tongue, an emotional tongue, or the real one--one that shares the Gospel of Jesus Christ with the lost. So, they keep the tongue, and run the risk of its being a false one.

Let's take a moment and define the **unpardonable sin, blasphemy**. It has an acceptable definition that means **defiant irreverence**. Let's look to God's Word for some clarification concerning the terms **unpardonable sin** or the **blasphemy of the Holy Spirit**. When we look at Matthew 12:22-

32, we see the occasion on which the Lord Jesus spoke to the issue of the unpardonable sin of blasphemy against the Holy Spirit. Jesus had healed one who was possessed with a demon, and the Pharisees had said that Jesus had cast out the demon by the power of Beelzebub. They accused the Lord of performing this work through the power of the Devil, or the prince of demons. Therefore, Jesus responded:

> *Wherefore, I say unto you all manner of sin and blasphemy shall be forgiven men but the blasphemy against the Holy (Spirit) shall not be forgiven men. And whosoever speaketh a word against the Son of Man, it shall be forgiven him, but whosoever speaketh against the Holy (Spirit) it shall not be forgiven him, neither in this (age), neither in the age to come (NSSB).*

We must keep in mind that the Pharisees were talking to Jesus in person, and that this was the only time in history when Jesus would walk on earth as a man. The Pharisees--with their own eyes and ears--directly witnessed the miracles and heard Jesus proclaim that He was the Son of God. The Pharisees had the opportunity to witness the undeniable evidence that God's Son was performing miracles in the power of the Holy Spirit. Even though Christians work today in the Spirit of Christ Jesus, He is not bodily in the world as He was with the Pharisees. Dr. Stanley says, "I agree with a host of biblical scholars that this unique circumstance cannot be duplicated today."[7]

One must also keep in mind that Jesus had already spoken about the Pharisees as being of their father the Devil (John 8:33-59). Jesus had already told the Pharisees, that they, as a whole, were lost and belonged to the Devil. This means that He was not talking to God's children about the possibility of their losing their salvation. He was talking to the lost about their not believing in Him.

Therefore, there is no unpardonable sin besides unbelief in the Lord Jesus Christ as Savior. Dr. Stanley speaks to this issue when he says, "Although there is no unpardonable sin, there is an unpardonable state--the state of unbelief. There is no pardon for a person who dies in unbelief."[8] So we see that since the Christian is saved and sealed by the Holy Spirit of God, he cannot blaspheme Him.

People have come to me who do automatic writing; something takes control of their hand and they can't stop their hand from writing. A woman came to me who was frequently awakened during the night to write **love letters to Jesus**, for hours and hours, telling Him of His greatness. In counseling, demons spoke from her, bragging that they were **demons of religiosity** with a purpose to tire her out, waste her time, and make her feel pious. Thus, it is essential to test the spirits, even if they have **religious connotations**.

Another crucial issue by which ground can be given Satan is that of drinking alcoholic beverages. Many Christians, including Baptists, drink alcoholic beverages against God's teachings and examples (Genesis 9:20-29; Leviticus 10:9-10; Numbers 6:3,4; Proverbs 20:1; 23:29-35; 31:4,5; Isaiah 5:11-13; Daniel 1:8-20; Habakkuk 2:15,16; Luke 1:15; Romans 14:19-21; Ephesians 5:18). In spite of alcoholic beverages being contrary to God's Word and a drug which surely negatively affects a person's mind and reflexes, many Christians try to justify drinking simply because they want to drink. Many people drink to relax instead of turning to God for calmness. Many Christians even take scriptures out of context in an attempt to ease their consciences and in hopes of gaining God's approval to drink. The truth is that Jesus neither drank nor served alcoholic wine. He served fresh fruit juice from the vine--unfermented grape juice.

There are two reasons that it is wrong for a Christian to drink alcoholic beverages. One reason is that it can alter the mind and reflexes, and the other is that it is a stumbling block to others. For example, someone sees a Christian drink a beer or glass of wine and thinks that since he's an alright guy who lives a pretty clean life, it is surely okay for them to drink. They begin drinking and they and/or their children end up alcoholics. Some then reason that it's okay to drink behind closed doors--in the privacy of their homes. Wrong. It is still a stumbling block, for when they are asked their belief concerning drinking, their testimony should be true on both sides of the door. We are our brother's keeper. God says that out of our unselfish love for a potentially weaker brother or sister, we should be willing to refrain from being a stumbling block (I Corinthians 8:9-13).

I encourage you to pray to renounce any ground you may have given Satan, and also to make a commitment to follow and obey Christ. On the following page is a sample prayer to help you. (I will explain the ancestral demon mentioned in the prayer in future chapters.) You may have someone witness your signing of this to help encourage you to keep your commitment:

## THE RENUNCIATION AND AFFIRMATION COMMITMENT

As God is my eternal witness, Savior, and judge, I do hereby affirm that I am a child of God who has been purchased with the precious blood of the Lord Jesus Christ (Rms. 6:3-11). I confess Him as my Lord and Savior and by my own volition, I specifically renounce Satan as my lord and god. As one completely acknowledging and accepting the finished work of Christ on the cross for my redemption and my only hope of eternal life, I now renounce all ancestral and genetic ties, back as many generations on my dad's and mom's sides that God needs to go. Because I have, through the Lord Jesus Christ's own shed blood, been redeemed and delivered from the power of darkness and translated into the kingdom of God's dear Son (Col. 1:13), I now cancel out and nullify all demonic power or effect that has been passed down to me from my ancestors, including the ancestral demon that carries my formal name and his network. Also, I cancel out any other ancestral demons and their networks.

Because the Lord Jesus Christ became a curse for me by dying the death on the tree (Gal. 3:13), I use my authority that is found in Him to cancel every spell or curse that may have been placed on me with or without my knowledge. As God's child, covered by the precious blood of the Lord Jesus Christ, and trusting totally in the atoning power of that blood (Eph. 1:7), I cancel, renounce, sever, and nullify every agreement or pact I have made with Satan or anyone else, including blood pacts. I renounce and sever any and every way that the Devil has gotten ground in my life and all ground that I have ever given to Satan that gave him power or claim over me. I cancel, renounce, sever, and nullify any powers, gifts, or workings in me which are not of my Heavenly Father or pleasing to Him.

I confess that I belong totally to the Lord Jesus Christ. As one who has been crucified (Gal. 2:20) and raised with Christ and now sits with Him in the heavenly places (Eph. 2:5-6), I sign myself eternally and completely over to the Lord Jesus Christ. It is my desire to pray daily that my Lord Jesus will have total control of my life. All of these things I do in the precious name of my Lord and Savior, Jesus Christ and by His absolute authority over all things, rulers, authorities, principalities, and powers (Eph. 1:18-23), and with a childlike faith, I thank you that it's done. Amen.

DATE: _____

FULL NAME: _____
(If you are a married woman, include your maiden name.)

WITNESS: _____

WITNESS: _____

**D.    TAKE TO THE CROSS ALL REVEALED SINS AND CONFESS HOW YOU HAVE WRONGED OTHERS AS WELL AS HOW OTHERS HAVE WRONGED YOU.  BE SPECIFIC (I John 2:1, 2).**

Our salvation experience is going to the Cross with a repentant heart and receiving Christ as our Savior.  From that time forth, *going to the Cross* means appropriating, by faith, forgiveness for all future daily sins, including any unresolved issues.  It is sad that some people choose to hold onto sins that Christ took to the cross with Him, something that He died for.  Some people say with their mouths that they forgive people, but if they don't forgive with their hearts by going to the cross with the offenses, they will not be free.  For example, I experienced a lot of hurt in the past from pastors, my fellow brethren.  I held onto the hurt and anger, and was not free until I prayed this with my heart:

> Lord, you became their sin on the cross, so I ask you not to lay that sin to that pastor's charge.  Forgive him; he really didn't know what he was doing to me.  And, Lord Jesus, by the power of your blood, I forgive him and release to the cross all the shame, pain, hurt, rejection, and condemnation that was brought on my life and my family.  I release it to the cross where it belongs.

Can you pray (with your heart) about each person who has hurt you?  If so, then you can address Satan to reclaim your lost ground (as I did about each of the pastors):

> Satan, I command you by the authority of Jesus to give me back the ground that my root of bitterness toward that pastor gave you in my life.  I claim back that unforgiveness and resentment--that will to hold onto the hurt.  You give me back that ground by the authority of Jesus.

Then you can appropriate the blood of Jesus to cleanse that ground:

> Lord Jesus, permeate, saturate that ground with your precious blood.  I want you to heal, cleanse, and totally restore me.  Heal my mind, body, soul, and spirit.  Lord Jesus, heal my memories (of what others did to me and/or what I did to them).  I want no negative effects upon my family and me, present or future.  Any demon spirits that have been able to stand on that ground and harass me, to manipulate me, or control me, they no longer have the ground.  By the authority of Jesus Christ and His shed blood, I want them in the pit.  Now, Lord Jesus, seal the doorway to my mind where that memory is, so that harassing memories and feelings can never return or allow any demons within.  And, Lord Jesus by the power of your blood, I confess that you have healed my memories and restored my torn soul.

This cleanses the ground in your mind, heart, and emotions from those roots of bitterness, unforgiveness, resentment, and hurt.  What comfort, victory and joy are found in Psalm 23:

> *The Lord is my shepherd; I shall not want.  He maketh me to lie down in green pastures; he leadeth me beside the still waters.  He restoreth my soul; he leadeth me in the paths of righteousness for his name's sake.  Yea, though I walk through the valley of the shadow of death, I will fear no evil; for thou art with me; thy rod and*

*thy staff they comfort me. Thou preparest a table before me in the presence of mine enemies; thou anointest my head with oil; my cup runneth over. Surely goodness and mercy shall follow me all the days of my life; and I will dwell in the house of the Lord forever (NSSB).*

What a peace and joy we forfeit for holding onto hurts from the past. Satan tells you that you've been maimed and handicapped by your abusers and that you have a right to hold on to those feelings. I often find this belief prevalent with those who have had abusive parents. Who gave them their parents? God. If they're angry with their parents, they're also angry with God! What a big stronghold! Once I was angry with God, shook my fist at Him and said, "God I don't need you and I don't need your people", and I felt that way for five years. I was miserable until I dealt with it and got back Satan's stronghold.

### E. MAKE SURE YOU TAKE TO THE CROSS ALL UNFORGIVENESS, BITTERNESS AND REJECTION (I John 2:1, 2; I Thess. 5:18; Romans 8:28-29).

Make certain you deposit on the cross all unforgiveness, bitterness and rejection, dealing with it as I have shared previously.

### F. ADDRESS SATAN AND BY THE NAME AND BLOOD OF JESUS CLAIM BACK ALL THE GROUND YOU HAVE GIVEN HIM (Rev. 12:1).

Stand against him by the word of the testimony that you've been to the cross; stand against him with the blood; overcome him with the Lamb's blood and take back your ground.

### G. REDEDICATE TO GOD THE GROUND CLAIMED BACK

After rededicating the ground, ask Him to permeate it with the blood of Jesus Christ and ask God to heal your body, soul, spirit, and mind. Also ask Him to restore your torn soul.

If you will take the truths that you've read in this chapter, check them out with the Spirit of God and His Word, and apply them to your life, you will sense yokes of bondage drop from your heart and life.

Some examples of prayers follow that may help a person in claiming back his or her ground.

# PRAYER FOR CLAIMING BACK THE GROUND OF OTHERS' SINS AGAINST ME

**IF GOD SHOWS YOU SOMETHING THAT SOMEONE HAS DONE TO YOU, TAKE HIS / HER SIN TO THE CROSS AND PRAY:**

Lord Jesus, by the power of Your blood, on the cross You became (<u>name the person and their specific sin against you</u>). I ask You not to lay that sin to (<u>person's</u>) charge. I ask you to forgive (<u>person</u>), for he/she really doesn't fully know what he/she did to me." And, Lord Jesus, by the power of your blood, and only through Your power, can I, and do I choose to forgive (<u>person</u>) for what he/she did to me.

**THEN, PRAY UNLOADING ALL THE EMOTIONS SURROUNDING THIS INCIDENT:**

Lord, I want to dump on the cross the (<u>any and all emotions you are in touch with--or remember--relating to their sin against you</u>).

**THEN, COMMAND SATAN AND CLAIM BACK YOUR GROUND:**

Satan, by the power of the blood of the Lord Jesus Christ, I command that you give me back the ground that (<u>the person and their sin</u>) gave you in my life.

**THEN, ASK THE LORD FOR HEALING, CLEANSING, AND RESTORATION:**

Dear Lord Jesus, please saturate the ground with Your precious blood. Heal it, cleanse it, and totally restore it. Heal my mind, body, soul, and spirit. And, dear Lord Jesus, please heal my memories. I let go of all the negative feelings and negative fallout from this memory. I want no negative effects affecting my life or my family's life, present or future. Any demon spirits that have been able to stand on this ground to emotionally and mentally harass or manipulate me, I want them in the pit (the abyss, not hell) by the authority of the Lord Jesus (Luke 8:31; Revelation 9:1-12). Now, Lord Jesus, please seal the doorway to that part of my mind; heal those damaged emotions; restore that torn part of my soul.

**FINALLY, RELEASE IT ALL TO CHRIST, AND PRAISE HIM FOR WHAT HE'S DONE IN YOUR LIFE:**

Lord, I want to praise You and thank You that You have, and that You will, work all of this together for my good. I release it to You. Lord Jesus, by faith I let go of it. I no longer have to carry around its negative effects. I praise and thank You for the victory and the deliverance. Amen.

**CONTINUE TO LET GOD SHOW YOU EACH PERSON AND HIS / HER SIN AGAINST YOU, TAKING EACH TO THE CROSS UNTIL ALL GROUND IS RECLAIMED.**

# PRAYER FOR CLAIMING BACK THE GROUND OF MY SINS

**IF GOD SHOWS YOU SOMETHING THAT YOU HAVE DONE, GO TO THE CROSS WITH IT AND PRAY:**

Lord Jesus, by the power of Your blood, You became my sin of (name it--be specific) on the cross, and I call it sin. I ask You to forgive me and cleanse me, and I gratefully receive Your forgiveness and cleansing.

**THEN, UNLOAD ALL THE EMOTIONS SURROUNDING THIS INCIDENT:**

Lord, I want to dump on the cross the (shame, guilt, pain, etc--any and all emotions you get in touch with relating to this sin).

**THEN, COMMAND SATAN TO GIVE YOU BACK THE GROUND:**

Satan, by the power of the blood of the Lord Jesus Christ, I command that you give me back the ground that (that specific sin) gave you in my life.

**THEN, ASK THE LORD FOR HEALING, CLEANSING, AND RESTORATION:**

Dear Lord Jesus, please saturate that ground with your precious blood. Heal it, cleanse it, and totally restore it. Heal my mind, body, soul, and spirit. And dear Lord Jesus, please heal my memories. I let go of all the negative feelings and negative fallout from this memory. I want no negative effects affecting my life or my family's life, present or future. Any demon spirits that have been able to stand on this ground to emotionally and mentally harass or manipulate me, I want them in the pit by the authority of the Lord Jesus. Now, Lord Jesus, please seal the doorway to that part of my mind, heal those damaged emotions, and restore that torn part of my soul.

**FINALLY, RELEASE IT ALL TO CHRIST, AND PRAISE HIM FOR WHAT HE HAS DONE FOR YOU:**

Lord, I want to praise and thank You that You have, and that You will, work all of this together for my good. I release it all to You. Lord Jesus, by faith I let go of it. I no longer have to carry around its negative effects. I praise and thank You for the victory and the deliverance. Amen.

**CONTINUE TO LET GOD SHOW YOU EACH SIN, TAKING EACH TO THE CROSS UNTIL ALL YOUR GROUND IS RECLAIMED.**

## NOTES

1. Dr. E. E. Elliott, Trinity Theological Seminary, <u>New Testament Survey</u>, Cassette #1.
2. H. J. Hester, <u>The Heart of the New Testament</u>, p. 17.
3. Merrill C. Tenney, <u>The Zondervan Pictorial Encyclopedia of the Bible</u>, Volume Three, pg. 242.
4. Merrill C. Tenney, <u>The Zondervan Pictorial Encyclopedia of the Bible</u>, Volume One, p. 392.
5. Very Rev. H. D. Spence, MA., D.D., <u>Pulpit Commentary</u>, Volume 5, p. 453.
6. Webster's New Twentieth Century Dictionary, Second Edition p. 907.
7. Charles Stanley, <u>Forgiveness</u>, Appendix A, pp. 192-194.
8. <u>Loc</u>. <u>cit</u>.

# CHAPTER SIX
# THE MYSTERY OF OUR BODY'S SOUL UNVEILED

When Christians finally face the reality that Christians can have demons, they still shudder--understandably so--at the thought of the evil Devil slithering up alongside the Holy Spirit. They rationalize that the two surely must be in separate compartments. But are these thoughts founded on scriptural truths, human reasoning, or traditional beliefs? To find out, let's prayerfully step back a moment and examine some scriptural truths. I'm certain you agree that God is omnipresent (everywhere at the same time). No one can escape His presence. He is inescapable as Psalm 139:7-10 tells us. He even promises never to leave or forsake us (Heb. 13:5b). He said, "Lo, I am with you always, even unto the end of the age" (Matt. 28:20).

At the same time, Satan is with us, in our midst, coming and going at will. He is called "the prince and power of the air" (Eph. 2:2), but of course no glory should be given him for his position. Keep in mind, while he is called a prince, he is only "Beelzebub, the prince of the demons" (Matt. 9:34; 12:24; Mk. 3:22), a fallen prince. He is not The Prince, The Prince of Peace, The Prince of Life, Jesus Christ who will return as King of all kings. This fallen prince has been in direct, face-to-face communication with God since long before the Garden of Eden (Isa. 14:12): from the time of his creation and residence in heaven, and continuing throughout his days of being an outcast power in the air (Job 1:6-12; Rev. 12:7-12). It's essential that we understand that our God--the Father, Son, and Holy Spirit--is temporarily tolerating the presence of the traitor prince in the air space between heaven and earth, just as He tolerated the presence of Pharaoh in Egypt before freeing His people. Satan does not have air space that excludes God. And right up to the time of Satan's doom's day, Satan will be communicating with God, running back and forth to God's throne, day and night accusing the brethren (Rev. 12:10). Why?

To better understand why, it is very important that we remember God created him and immediately allowed him to enjoy living in the **third heaven, paradise** (II Cor. 12:2-4). There, however, Satan and his angel followers chose to rebel against God; thus, were made to leave the **third heaven** where corruption was not permitted. We are in the reverse position. God created us to live on earth first, to be free to make our choice as to whether or not we want to live with God in His heavenly home. Satan, hating God for kicking him out, is trying to get back at God in the only possible way--through us, God's children. He lies to us, hoping we will believe and obey him instead of God. So he's actually using us to get back at God. What is he saying about us to God as he runs back and forth? In spite of his knowing that God already knows what we're doing, he is continually taunting and mocking, throwing in God's face the unbelief and disobedience of His children. Satan can only taunt and mock because of the sins we choose to commit.

## TWO VOICES IN OUR EARS

Although Satan is temporarily **mouthing off** to God, he has no power over God, and God is surely not afraid of him. As we've previously established, Satan has no power over us unless we give it to him by our choices of unbelief or disobedience to God (I Corinthians 10:13; Galatians 5:16;

Colossians 2:6, 9-10). Satan only has power to tempt us, to voice evil suggestions and false accusations; however, he can gain further power to manipulate us if we choose to yield our listening mind, will, and emotions to him. That's why it is so essential that we constantly tune our ears to God and listen and heed what He says. God also warned us and gave us written instructions about how to stand our ground against this airborne tempter. Ephesians 6:12-18 states:

> *For we wrestle not against flesh and blood, but against principalities, against powers, against the rulers of the darkness of this world, against spiritual wickedness in high places. Wherefore, take unto you the whole armor of God that ye may be able to withstand in the evil day, and having done all, to stand. Stand, therefore, having your loins girded about with truth, and having on the breastplate of righteousness, and your feet shod with the preparation of the gospel of peace; above all, taking the shield of faith, with which ye shall be able to quench all the fiery darts of the wicked. And take the helmet of salvation, and the sword of the Spirit, which is the word of God; praying always with all prayer and supplication in the Spirit, and watching thereunto with all perseverance and supplication for all saints (NSSB).*

Prayerfully studying this, we see that a Christian's unwavering belief--his total trust--in the Lord is the key to being able to resist any **fiery darts** of temptation. The Christian has the Holy Spirit of God within him, who stands ready to aid him in this war against the prince of the air. When a Christian has permitted a demon to invade his life, only his human reasoning could imagine that the Holy Spirit would be enveloped or defiled by a demon--that demons **can get Him dirty**. To the contrary, Jesus--and therefore His Spirit--have no sin. We read in Hebrews 4:15, "For we have not an high priest who cannot be touched with the feeling of our infirmities, but was in all points tempted like as we are, yet without sin." The demons cannot affect the Holy Spirit in any way; however, it's a sobering truth that the unbelief and disobedience of His children does affect Him. It grieves Him. That should make us shudder! Ephesians 4:30 urges us, "...grieve not the Holy Spirit of God, by whom ye are sealed unto the day of redemption." Even if we grieve Him, however, we remain sealed, saved, and unforsaken. The Holy Spirit doesn't reject and abandon His child. Rather, He remains with him, ready and able to evict the demons upon the person's giving Him permission to do so! Philippians 4:13 says the war can be won: "I can do all things through Christ, who strengtheneth me." Romans 8:37-39 says:

> *...in all these things we are more than conquerors through him that loved us. For I am persuaded that neither death, nor life, nor angels, nor principalities, nor powers, nor things present, nor things to come, nor height, nor depth, nor any other creation, shall be able to separate us from the love of God, which is in Christ Jesus, our Lord (NSSB).*

How awesome it is to know that we cannot be separated from the love of God, which is in Christ Jesus, our Lord. We have established that our God, the Father, Son, and Holy Spirit, is in this warfare with us all the way. Someone once said how amazing it is that our God is large enough to create this universe, yet small enough to dwell within each of our hearts. In our hearts? The Lord did say, "...I am in my Father, and ye in me, and I in you" (John 14:20). And God said, "...I will dwell in them, and walk in them..." (II Cor. 6:16; NSSB). That draws us to question <u>where</u> God's Holy Spirit actually dwells within us, and <u>where</u> the demons of a demonized Christian or non-Christian dwell.

## SOUL, SPIRIT, AND SPIRITUAL HEART, ONE OR SEPARATE PARTS?

As you know, surgeons have never reported finding a soul or spirit within a body, and the physical heart they see is merely a pump. While no one argues that our body is only temporary, for ages there have been varied opinions on the subject of whether or not the soul and spirit of a person are **separate parts or one and the same**. Many people have a hard time accepting the fact that we **humans don't have a really good part of us** worthy of going to heaven. Some rationalize, considering that perhaps the soul is bad and the spirit is good. Much to our own egos' disappointment, the reality is: there is no good part in us that deserves heaven. Often even sincere scriptural attempts to prove the soul and spirit are separate parts only complicate and cloud the issue. While this is not a critical doctrinal issue, I believe it should be looked at closely to help eliminate confusion.

It is my opinion that the soul, spirit, and spiritual heart are one, for after much biblical study, I find that they all reflect the same functions. Our soul, spirit, and spiritual heart are like unto the temporary body in which we are housed. Our body is one unit, complex from exterior to interior, but, nevertheless, one. When we say our body is exhausted, we mean the whole thing. Body, mind, will, and emotions agree and readily rest as one.

Look how the words heart, soul and spirit compare with one another in W. E. Vine's book An Expository Dictionary of New Testament Words:

### HEART, HEARTILY

**Kardia**, the heart (Eng., cardiac, etc.), the chief organ of physical life ('for the life of the flesh is in the blood,' Lev. 17:11), occupies the most important place in the human system. By an easy transition the word came to stand for man's entire mental and moral activity, both the rational and the emotional elements. In other words, the heart is used figuratively for the hidden springs of the personal life. 'The Bible describes human depravity as in the 'heart,' because sin is a principle which has its seat in the centre of man's inward life, and then 'defiles' the whole circuit of his action, Matt. 15:19, 20. On the other hand, scripture regards the heart as the sphere of Divine influence, Rom. 2:15; Acts 15:9...The heart, as lying deep within, contains 'the hidden man,' I Pet. 3:4, the real man. It represents the true character but conceals it' (J. Laidlaw, in **Hastings' Bible Dictionary**).

As to its usage in the N.T. it **denotes** (a) the seat of physical life, Acts 14:17; Jas. 5:5; (b) the seat of moral nature and spiritual life, the seat of grief, John 14:1; Rom. 9:2; 2 Cor. 2:4; joy, John 16:22; Eph. 5:19; the desires, Matt. 5:28; 2 Pet. 2:14; the affections, Luke 24:32; Acts 21:13; the perceptions, John 12:40; Eph. 4:18; the thoughts, Matt. 9:4; Heb. 4:12; the understanding, Matt. 13:15; Rom. 1:21; the reasoning powers, Mark 2:6; Luke 24:38; the imagination, Luke 1:51; conscience, Acts 2:37; I John 3:20; the intentions, Heb. 4:12, cp. I Pet. 4:1; purpose, Acts 11:23; 2 Cor. 9:7; the will, Rom. 6:17; Col. 3:15; faith, Mark 11:23; Rom. 10:10; Heb. 3:12.

The heart, in its moral significance in the O.T., includes the emotions, the reason and will.

2. **Psuche**, the soul, or life, is rendered "heart" in Eph. 6:6 (marg., "soul"), "doing the will of God from the heart." In Col. 3:23, a form of the word psuche preceded by ek, from, lit., 'from (the) soul,' is rendered "heartily."[1]

## SOUL

**Psuche denotes** the breath, the breath of life, then the soul in its various meanings: The N.T. uses may be analyzed approximately as follows: (a) the natural life of the body, Matt. 2:20; Luke 12:22; Acts 20:10; Rev. 8:9; 12:11; cp. Lev. 17:11; 2 Sam. 14:7; Esth. 8:11; (b) the immaterial, invisible part of man, Matt. 10:28; Acts 2:27; cp. I Kings 17:21; (c) the disembodied (or 'unclothed' or 'naked,' 2 Cor. 5:3, 4) man, Rev. 6:9; (d) the seat of personality, Luke 9:24, explained as == 'own self,' ver. 25; Heb. 6:19; 10:39; cp. Isa. 53:10 with I Tim. 2:6; (e) the seat of the sentient element in man, that by which he perceives, reflects, feels, desires, Matt. 11:29; Luke 1:46; 2:35; Acts 14:2, 22; cp. Ps. 84:2; 139:14; Isa. 26:9; (f) the seat of will and purpose, Matt. 22:37; Acts 4:32; Eph. 6:6; Phil. 1:27; Heb. 12:3; cp. Num. 21:4; Deut. 11:13; (g) the seat of appetite, Rev. 18:14; cp. Ps. 107:9; Prov. 6:30; Isa. 5:14 ('desire'); 29:8; (h) persons, individuals, Acts 2:41, 43; Rom. 2:9; Jas. 5:20; I Pet. 3:20; 2 Pet. 2:14; cp. Gen. 12:5; 14:21 ('persons'); Lev. 4:2 ('any one'); Ezek. 27:13; of dead bodies, Num. 23:10; Jud. 16:30; Ps. 120:2 ('me'); 2nd person, 2 Cor. 12:15; Heb. 13:17; Jas. 1:21; I Pet. 1:9; 2:25; cp. Lev. 17:11; 26:15; I Sam. 1:26; 3rd person, I Pet. 4:19; 2 Pet. 2:8; cp. Ex. 30:12; Job 32:2, Heb. 'soul,' Sept. 'self'; (j) an animate creature, human or other, I Cor. 15:45; Rev. 16:3; cp. Gen. 1:24; 2:7, 19; (k) 'the inward man,' the seat of the new life, Luke 21:19 (cp. Matt. 10:39); I Pet. 2:11; 3 John 2.[2]

## SPIRIT

**Pneuma** primarily **denotes** the wind (akin to pneo, to breathe, blow); also breath; then, especially the spirit, which, like the wind, is invisible, immaterial and powerful. The N.T. uses of the word may be analyzed approximately as follows: (a) the wind, John 3:8) where martg. is, perhaps, to be preferred); Heb. 1:7; cp. Amos 4:13, Sept.; (b) the breath, 2 Thess. 2:8; Rev. 11:11; 13:15; cp. Job 12:10, Sept.; (c) the immaterial, invisible part of man, Luke 8:55; Acts 7:59; I Cor. 5:5; Jas. 2:26; cp. Ecc. 12:7, Sept.; (d) the disembodied (or 'unclothed,' or 'naked,' 2 Cor. 5:3, 4,) man, Luke 24:37, 39; Heb. 12:23; I Pet. 4:6; (e) the resurrection body, I Cor. 15:45; I Tim. 3:16; I Pet. 3:18; (f) the sentient element in man, that by which he perceives, reflects, feels, desires, Matt. 5:3; 26:41; Mark 2:8; Luke 1:47, 80; Acts 17:16; 20:22; I Cor. 2:11; 5:3, 4; 14:4, 15; 2 Cor. 7:1; cp. Gen. 26:35; Isa. 26:9; Ezek. 13:3; Dan. 7:15; (g) purpose, aim, 2 Cor. 12:18; Phil. 1:27; Eph. 4:23; Rev. 19:10; Cp. Ezra 1:5; Ps. 78:8; Dan. 5:12; (h) the equivalent of the personal pronoun, used for emphasis and effect: 1st person, I Cor. 16:18; cp. Gen. 6:3; 2nd person, 2 Tim. 4:22; Philm. 25; cp. Ps 139:7; 3rd person, 2 Cor. 7:13; cp. Isa. 40:13; (i) character, Luke 1:17; Rom. 1:4; cp. Num. 14:24; (j) moral qualities and activities: bad, as of bondage, as of a slave, Rom. 8:15; cp. Isa. 61:3; stupor, Rom. 11:8; cp. Isa. 29:10; timidity, 2 Tim. 1:7; cp. Josh. 5:1; good, as of an adoption, i.e., liberty as of a son, Rom. 8:15; cp. Ps. 51:12.[3]

Sometimes the use of the terms--**heart, soul, or spirit**--simply depends on how they are being used in a sentence or on circumstances surrounding their use. We say a lost person is spiritually dead, not soulishly dead; yet when they die, we grieve that their soul went to Hell. Scripture, in expressing hope of our being comforted, alternates between addressing our hearts, souls, or spirits.

God encourages us to yield our spirit, soul, and heart--our entire being--to His control. In Psalm 51:17, we read, "The sacrifices of God are **a broken spirit; a broken and a contrite heart**, O God, thou wilt not despise." Proverbs 16:32 says, "He who is slow to anger is better than the mighty; and he who ruleth his spirit, than he that taketh a city." I Peter 4:19 says, "Wherefore, let them that suffer according to the will of God **commit the keeping of their souls** to him in well-doing, as unto a faithful Creator." And Proverbs 4:23 says, "**Keep thine heart with all diligence**; for out of it are the issues of life."

I agree with and appreciate what Dickason says about heart, soul, and spirit being one and the same. Dickason comments that while some people hold to the tripartite view (that man has three parts: body, soul, and spirit) most standard theologians agree this has little biblical support. He also states that only one place in the Bible mentions the three together (I Thessalonians 5:23), and he adds:

> Those who hold this view say...that the soul contains the rational facilities for contact with ourselves and persons around us and that the spirit provides contact with God. No where does the Bible say such a thing. How shall we understand the reference by Christ to the command, 'and you shall love the Lord your God with all your heart, and with all your soul, and with all your mind, and with all your strength' (Mark 12:30)? Why did He omit the supposed most important part of man in relation to God, the spirit? What are these other terms--heart, mind, strength? Are these to be taken as parts of man?
>
> We may better understand that man is two parts--body and spirit, and that his whole being is termed soul. This fits Genesis 2:7: 'Then the Lord God formed man of dust from the ground [body], and breathed into his nostrils the breath of life [spirit]; and man became a living being [soul; Heb., nephesh].' This latter term is used also of the whole of man (Gen. 12:5; 46:15, etc) and of animal life (Gen. 9:4). Genesis clearly presents man as material body, related to the earth, and as spirit, related to God.
>
> ...it is very difficult to differentiate between spirit and soul. They are both spiritual in nature according to the tripartite theory. How may there be two spiritual entities, both human, within man? But some point to Hebrews 4:12. This is supposed to see a division of spirit and soul by the Word of God. However, the Greek term (diikneomai) means to penetrate or pierce, as of missiles. It does not mean to separate two different parts. The idea is that the Word of God penetrates the deepest recesses of man's being. Note the judging of the 'thoughts of the heart,' another reference to man's innermost being, an expansion of the same concept of penetration without any hiding of an inner secret from God.
>
> ...when Jesus said, 'That which is born of the Spirit is spirit,' He was not defining the part of man that was missing or impaired but describing the nature of the birth: it was

not to be confused with the physical, or merely human. New birth is from God, not man...our whole spiritual natures are born again, not just part of our person. Scripture never speaks of just the spirit renewed and not the soul.

...we cannot support from the Bible that man's spirit is nonexistent or totally inoperative before the new birth. The total man is dead with respect to God and spiritual truth in that he is separated from God and does not operate in God's moral sphere (Eph. 2:1-3). Are men less than total humans until regeneration? Neither does the Bible suggest that anything in the human being is perfect now. Our legal standing and acceptance is perfect through the provision of the righteousness of Christ, but we must be developed into the totality of our person now awaiting rapture or resurrection for the perfecting of both body and spirit (I John 3:1-2, 5; Phil. 3:20).[4]

It's essential to realize that when God created our minds, wills, and emotions, enveloping them with our very own unique personalities, He created permanent souls. When people see our body in action, they see our personality--what we are inside. Our body's actions and language reflect what we think, desire, and feel. We show forth what is sometimes called our "countenance." Often, you can read a person's **inner mood** by their expression, their facial countenance.

When a lost person dies, his permanent soul--his total inner being--leaves his temporary clay vessel behind and he enters Hades, the place of torment where he remains until he is to appear before God's great white throne of judgment (Rev. 20:11-15). When a Christian dies, he goes into the presence of Christ until the end of the age (I Cor. 15:50-58; II Cor. 5:1-10). The Christian's permanent soul (personality/soul/spirit/spiritual heart) goes to heaven, leaving the clay body and sinful fallen nature behind. He is given a new eternal body that houses his personality, mind, will, and emotions that God originally created in him. And, what will our new bodies be like? The Bible says, ***"Beloved, now are we the children of God, and it doth not yet appear what we shall be, but we know that, when he shall appear, we shall be like him..."*** (I Jn. 3:2). We shall have new, eternal bodies with our original minds, wills, and emotions like Jesus' mind, will, and emotions--not corrupted! While on earth, however, our minds can be corrupted if we permit them to be.

**WHERE THE EVIL INVADERS CAN SQUAT**

Mankind is born totally depraved, having the Adamic nature (Rom. 5:12). That means he has a fallen mind, a fallen will, and fallen emotions, all of which make up the soul of man. Within our mortal bodies, our soul's mind, will, and emotions function together as a whole; thus, that is the only area susceptible to invasion and possession by evil spirits. God says of us, "...as he thinketh in his heart, so is he" (Prov. 23:7), and "...Jesus, knowing their thoughts, said, Why think ye evil in your hearts?" (Matt. 9:4). On what and on whom we choose to fix our mind and heart determines whether or not the demonic can invade our mind and heart.

A lost person chooses for or against God from their soul's mind, will, and emotions, as God lovingly convicts and Satan deceitfully lies. If he chooses to receive Christ as his Savior he will then have the new nature of Jesus Christ living within his heart, soul, and spirit. "And you, being dead in your sins and the uncircumcision of your flesh, hath he made alive together with him, having forgiven you all trespasses" (Col. 2:13). He will be blessed with the indwelling of the Holy Spirit, with God's teaching and guiding him into all truths. However, he is not a programmed robot, for he still has his old mind, will, and emotions. He can choose from which mind, will, and emotions he wants to operate. Hopefully he will choose to put on the new man and put off the old man (Eph. 4:17-5:1).

Perhaps the following four illustrations will help to simplify and plant the truth concerning this often confusing issue. In a future chapter, I will explain how to counsel persons with ancestral demons and/or lifestyle demons, flip-side and/or fragmented personalities, demon-produced personalities and/or demons masquerading as personalities which you will see mentioned on these illustrations. All of these can take up residence in the soul area. This explains why we see some people who get saved still walking, most of the time, in their old lifestyle. Until these deeply imbedded strongholds are dealt with in their soul area, the person can be manipulated and controlled by them. Examine the following illustrations carefully:

# THE MAKE-UP OF OUR BODY AND SOUL

♥ = SOUL     ♡ = HOLY SPIRIT     ♠ = FLIP-SIDE PERSONALITY

● = DEMONIC INFLUENCE     ◈ = FRAGMENTED PERSONALITY

◆ = DEMON/DEMON NETWORKS     ▲ = LIFESTYLE DEMON

◆ = ANCESTRAL DEMON     ✳ = DEMON-PRODUCED PERSONALITY

**AN ETERNAL LIVING SOUL, SPIRITUALLY DEAD ("LOST"):**

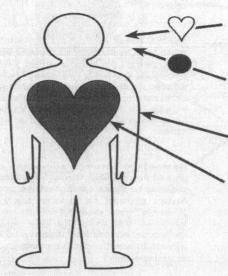

**God's Holy Spirit** lovingly convicting the soul of his lost state and sins in order for him to be saved.

**Demonic influence (temptation)** seeking to deter the soul from knowing and trusting God.

**A clay body,** temporarily housing the soul.

**Eternal living soul with a personality, mind, will, and emotions thought up by God:** spiritually dead without Christ; possessing the fleshly ("old man"; "carnal") Adamic nature inherited from ancestors fallen nature; living lifestyle in accordance with his lost, unbelieving nature; retaining his freedom of choice to accept or reject Christ.

**AN ETERNAL LIVING SOUL, SPIRITUALLY DEAD ("LOST") AND DEMONIC:**

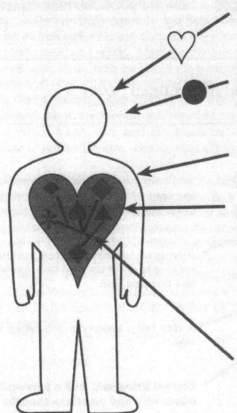

God's Holy Spirit lovingly convicting the soul of his lost state and sins in order for him to be saved.

Demonic influence (temptation) seeking to deter the soul from knowing and trusting God.

A clay body, temporarily housing the soul.

Eternal living soul with a personality, mind, will, and emotions thought up by God: spiritually dead without Christ; possessing the fleshly ("old man"; "carnal") Adamic nature inherited from ancestors fallen nature; living lifestyle in accordance with his lost, unbelieving nature; retaining his freedom of choice to accept or reject Christ.

Demonized through ancestral sins passed down and/or through repeatedly yielding to Satan's temptations, giving Satan ground to govern his life. (Possible forms: ancestral demons and/or lifestyle demons; flip-side and/or fragmented personalities; demon produced personalities and/or demons masquerading as personalities.)

117

**AN ETERNAL LIVING SOUL, SEALED AND SPIRITUALLY ALIVE ("SAVED"):**

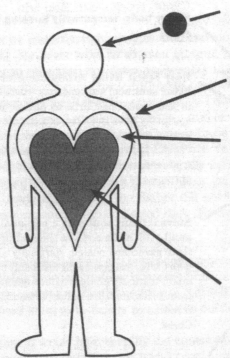

Demonic influence (temptation) seeking to deter the soul from trusting and obeying God.

A clay body, temporarily housing the soul.

Holy Spirit living within the eternal living soul: soul was repentant – believing in and accepting Christ as Savior; now spiritually alive in Christ; sealed forever; having the mind, will, and emotions of Christ within to teach and guide him in all truth and to enable him to walk in God's purpose and will for his life if he chooses.

Eternal living soul with a personality, mind, will, and emotions thought up by God: saved and sealed; spiritually alive with Christ; still possessing the fleshly ("old man"; "carnal") Adamic nature inherited from ancestors fallen nature; retaining his freedom of choice to obey or disobey Christ.

**AN ETERNAL LIVING SOUL, SEALED AND SPIRITUALLY ALIVE ("SAVED")
BUT DEMONIC:**

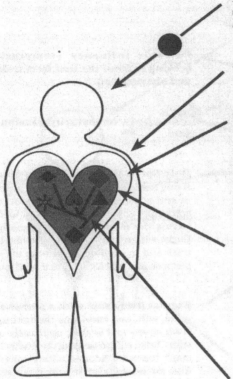

**Demonic influence (temptation)
seeking to deter the soul from trusting
and obeying God.**

**A clay body, temporarily housing the
soul.**

**Holy Spirit living within the eternal
living soul:** soul was repentant – believing
in and accepting Christ as Savior; now
spiritually alive in Christ; sealed forever;
having the mind, will, and emotions of
Christ within to teach and guide him in all
truth and to enable him to walk in God's
purpose and will for his life if he chooses.

**Eternal living soul with a personality,
mind, will, and emotions thought up by
God:** saved and sealed; spiritually alive
with Christ; still possessing the fleshly ("old
man"; "carnal") Adamic nature inherited
from ancestors fallen nature; retaining his
freedom of choice to obey or disobey
Christ.

**Demonized through ancestral sins
passed down and/or through repeatedly
yielding to Satan's temptations, giving
Satan ground to govern his life.**
(Possible forms: ancestral demons; flip-
side personalities; lifestyle demons;
fragmented personalities; demon produced
personalities; demons masquerading as
personalities.) Freedom and victory is
available through Christ if he chooses to
believe and apply it.

## WALKING IN THE SPIRIT

God encourages His children to make the right choices. Galatians 5:19-25 states:

> *Now the works of the flesh are manifest, which are these: adultery, fornication, uncleanness, lasciviousness, idolatry, sorcery, hatred, strife, jealousy, wrath, factions, seditions, heresies, envyings, murders, drunkenness, revelings, and the like...but the fruit of the Spirit is love, joy, peace, long-suffering, gentleness, goodness, faith, meekness, self-control; against such there is no law. And they that are Christ's have crucified the flesh with the affections and lusts. If we live in the Spirit, let us also walk in the Spirit (NSSB).*

When we make the right choices, God can more effectively help us to **walk in the Spirit**. He never asks us to even <u>attempt</u> to do good works of ourselves, but rather to relinquish our entire personality to be used by him, with His mind, will, and emotions being enacted through our beings. When Jesus was called **Good Master**, you recall that He answered, "...I do nothing of myself; but as my Father hath taught me, I speak these things. And he that sent me is with me. The Father hath not left me alone; for I do always those things that please him" (John 8:28b, 29). Now, if Jesus said that He could do nothing of Himself, how can any Christian say they can behave in a godly fashion and do good works--walking in the Spirit--except through Christ? They can't say this without lying. Jesus said that it was evident that the Father did not leave Him alone, for He was able to behave in a manner that pleased Him. He desired to obey His Father, thus fulfilling the Father's will for His life.

Remembering this, we can better comprehend the meaning of John 15, concerning His being the Vine, and our being the branches. Since only God is good, and Jesus clearly stated that He did nothing of Himself but by way of His Father, it is surely impossible for us to do any good works outside our Lord, Jesus Christ.

Perhaps it would help simplify the concept of **walking in the Spirit** by picturing a person's clay housing (his body) containing the inner personality of a Christian enveloped in a beautifully-tailored, indestructible White Glove, which represents the Holy Spirit. While growing up, you probably viewed a variety of puppet shows which used glove-like creations called **hand puppets**. Picture our earthly life as a hand puppet stage, where the Christian is free to perform whatever program in life he chooses to follow. There are two scripts: the one influenced and written by the heavenly Father, the other by Satan. **While the Father faithfully shares His Best-For-Us script all along, He never takes away our choice to rebel and choose another script.**

A Christian is only capable of fulfilling God's wonderful plan for his life if he chooses to **walk in the Spirit**--walk <u>within</u> the White Glove, the Holy Spirit. The Christian is free to slip out of the White Glove at will and walk in his flesh, but let me quickly say again that the Holy Spirit does not leave him, but remains securely within his housing, ready and able to help. Of course when a Christian chooses to walk in the flesh, he makes himself vulnerable to be penetrated and used by Satan and his demons, who intend to spoil the program, sometimes through the use of other people. God warns, "Beware lest any man spoil you through philosophy and vain deceit, after the tradition of men, after the rudiments of the world, and not after Christ" (Col. 2:8). Jesus encourages each of us to follow

His example, allowing His Holy Spirit to enable us to follow the plan God so wisely designed for our unique personality.

## WALKING IN THE SPIRIT WITHOUT FEAR

When we choose to allow the Holy Spirit to live through us and to fulfill our purpose in life, it is important for us to realize that we have no cause to be afraid. While Jesus alerted us to the fact men would attack us as they had Him, and that He was sending us forth as sheep amidst wolves (Matt. 10:16), He also told us not to fear anyone but God. Matthew 10:26-28 says:

> *Fear them not, therefore; for there is nothing covered that shall not be revealed; and hidden, that shall not be known. What I tell you in darkness, that speak in light; and what ye hear in the ear, that proclaim upon the housetops. And fear not them who kill the body, but are not able to kill the soul; but rather fear him who is able to destroy both soul and body in hell.*

The Lord was telling his disciples to obey and preach the Gospel without fear of what man could do to them physically. At the same time, He was emphasizing the importance of their reverential fear of God, who has the power to destroy both the soul and body. He was not saying that God was going to destroy a disobedient Christian's body and soul in hell; He was declaring that God has the power to destroy an unbeliever's body and soul. This truth served not only to dispel the disciples' fear of man but also to proclaim the news from the housetops in hope of instilling an awesome, reverential fear of God in the lost listeners' ears and drawing them to trust in Christ.

## FOR THE ABUNDANT LIFE, WE MUST LABOR

The moment a Christian chooses not to **walk in the Spirit**, Satan and his demons readily await opportunity to **attain ground**. God appeals to us in Hebrews 3 and 4 not to allow our hearts to become hardened due to the deceitfulness of sin. He urges us not to fall into the sin of unbelief as God's Old Testament people did, who then had to wander in the wilderness. While the Israelites went to heaven when they died, they missed out on the abundant life while on earth--Canaan's rest--because of their lack of faith, their unbelief. God gives us that example of His discipline in order that we might not fall into that same sin which brought the discipline. Hebrews 4:11 reads, "Let us labor, therefore to enter into that rest, lest any man fall after the same example of unbelief." As Christians, we are cautioned to reverentially fear the Lord, obey Him, and not fall short of our rest--the abundant life. May we purpose in our hearts to labor to attain that rest, so that our testimony for Christ will be fruitful. I encourage you, my brothers and sisters in Christ, to **"...be strong in the Lord, and in the power of His might"**! (Eph. 6:10)

## NOTES

1.    W. E. Vine, <u>An Expository Dictionary of New Testament Words</u>, pp. 206- 207.
2.    <u>Ibid</u>., p. 54.
3.    <u>Ibid</u>., p. 62.
4.    C. Fred Dickason, <u>Demon Possession and the Christian</u>, pp. 136-137.

# PART III

## GOD'S TRUTHS
## FOR
## COUNSELING TODAY'S BRUISED

# CHAPTER SEVEN
## CAN DEMONS INVADE CHRISTIANS OF TODAY?

Today, many people believe that Satan and his demons are merely figments of one's imagination; like travelers on **a yellow brick road**, they are placed amidst fairy tales. Sadly enough, The Encyclopedia Britannica (published in 1910) reports them as such in its article on the Devil:

> It may be confidently affirmed that belief in Satan (and obviously his demonic cohorts) is not now generally recognized as an essential article of the Christian faith, nor is it found to be an indispensable element of Christian experience.[1]

According to this article, Satan and his demons are gone. Therefore, when Jesus attributed the cause of disease and insanity to evil spirits, He was merely accommodating the way of thinking of the people of that day. Many skeptics look upon the demonic accounts only as reflections of the ignorance and the superstition which were prevalent during the time of our Lord's ministry on earth.

The New Testament, however, was written for today as well as for yesteryear, and it disagrees with this premise and describes various persons afflicted with what can be termed as **demon possession** or **demonization**. It is evident from the Gospels and the book of Acts that Christ and His apostles readily accepted the reality of evil spirits. They taught Christians to flee from them and their temptations (I Tim. 6:11, 12). Many people today suffer from the **ostrich syndrome**--putting their heads in the sand to escape reality. Out of fear, they refuse even to consider being educated about the existence of the wiles, the cunning schemes, and temptations of Satan and his demons. Yet these forces are as destructive and real as cancer, a dread disease with which they would quickly deal.

In previous chapters, a person who is demonized is described as one who has been invaded by evil spirits. In the invasion, the demons can cause physical afflictions, as well as control the person's mind and body, exhibit extremely immoral behavior and speech, and supernatural strength. It is imperative to let scriptures explain exactly what demon possession or demonization is, how human responsibility is involved, and what the believer is supposed to do when encountering a demonized person. The Bible cites a number of demon-produced illnesses that have all the characteristics of known diseases. The Gospel writers carefully discerned between natural and demon-caused afflictions, as evidenced in Mark 1:32,34. When the Lord restored health to the individual and the healing had nothing to do with the demonic, Jesus did not mention demons. If the person's illness was demon-produced, Jesus healed those individuals by commanding the demons to leave their bodies.

For many early, as well as late, twentieth-century theologians, the demonic was but an ancient superstition, and faded almost entirely out of existence under the strong light of human reasoning, man's common sense. However, with evil behavior on the rise over the last few decades, many theologians are again examining the possibility of the existence of the demonic. In the theological arena, many liberal and moderate theologians continue to deny the existence not only of Satan, but also of angels and demons as well. They believe that the demonic is merely the reflection of either the sub- or super-conscious within man. To them, the biblical stories pertaining to demonization simply infer Jesus was a reflection of His own time and was holding to primitive beliefs concerning the supernatural. Modern liberal and moderate scholars believe that demons take possession only in the form of mental illness. Koch in his book **Demonology Past and Present** says, "Reports of possession are uncomfortable for our modern, liberal scholars. They do not quite fit into their rationalistic scheme of the world."[2]

## DEMONIC INFLUENCES: IN TODAY'S LIFESTYLES

Demonic influences can be seen in the realm of parapsychology, and the resulting use of psychics even among top-named people, including the wife of one of our recent presidents. Recently, there has been a vast increase in sexual promiscuity and racism; in the number of people addicted to drugs, and suffering from eating disorders; as well as in occultism and Spiritism. The Church is being tainted by theological heresy, and many other practices such as the use of demonic meditation in some of the martial arts fields.

Pastors and biblical counselors see much chaos and despair from the increase in demonic activity. Why does one see so much increase in this activity? The clearest, most precise answer to the chaotic condition of our times is found in God's Word. The world is apparently in the midst of what scripture calls **the last days**. One can see this through passages in I and II Timothy:

> *Now the Spirit speaketh expressly that in latter times some shall depart from the faith, giving heed to seducing spirits, and doctrines of (demons), speaking lies in hypocrisy, having their conscience seared with a hot iron (I Timothy 4:1,2; NSSB).*

> *This know, also, that in the last days perilous times shall come. For men shall be lovers of their own selves, covetous, boasters, proud, blasphemers, disobedient to parents, unthankful, unholy, without natural affection, trucebreakers, false accusers, incontinent, fierce, despisers of those that are good, traitors, heady, high-minded, lovers of pleasures more than lovers of God (II Timothy 3:1-4; NSSB).*

No one can deny we are surrounded by people living ungodly lifestyles, which are the results of their yielding to Satan. The present century can only be coped with and understood in the light of the Word of God. As the believer observes the world through God's eyes, he can see that Satan is mobilizing all his forces for a final, all-out attack on the world and especially on God's Church.

Koch says, "We are living in the days of a demonic nature!"[3] He gives a vivid example of this as he tells about counseling a theological student. As he was praying for him, the student fell into a trance and Koch heard voices speaking out of him in foreign languages. When Koch asked who they were, they replied in English, "We are fifty demons." As he commanded the demons to come out, the demonic voices cried out, "The Lord is coming soon with the holy angels. Give us more time. We will be finished when He comes."[4] Satan and his demons know that God will someday cast them into "the lake of fire" (Revelation 12:12; 20:10).

## DEMONIC INFLUENCES: SEEN IN CHRISTIAN COUNSELING

Demonic influences can also be seen in the area of Christian counseling. Koch, up to the time of his death, had been counseling for more than fifty years in the area of occultism. In dealing with thousands of cases, he found that demonically-oppressed people exhibit the same symptoms today as did the possessed Gadarene almost two thousand years ago. Therefore, he believes demon possession has remained the same in its effects since the time of Christ, despite what the modernists say to the contrary.

In finding a possessed person in Haiti behaving in the same way as a possessed person in New Guinea, he saw two constants: the first constant being that neither time, age, nor epoch affect the demonic phenomenon; the second constant being that neither geographical, national, racial, nor cultural factors affect its outworking.[5] During my years of counseling, I have observed that demons are demons, no matter where one encounters them. However, I have also observed that they do such an underground, deceptive work that sometimes one does not see the same outpouring of symptoms as were seen in the Gadarene demoniac.

What are the conclusions that we can draw from Koch's two observations? The psychologist might be tempted to write the matter off by referring to the principle of archetypes. The Webster's Dictionary that carries the title of **The New Lexicon of the English Language** defines archetypes in this manner:

> The model from which later examples are developed, or to which they conform, a prototype (the assumed example or perfect model which inferior examples may resemble but never equal). One of the inherited unconscious patterns which Jung held to constitute the fundamental structure of the mind.[6]

Yet, this term that Professor Jung has formulated fails to do justice to the phenomenon.

Demonization, in all its different facets, fails to fit into the normal, psychological and psychiatric pattern. It should be noted that although the theories of psychiatry and psychology change from time to time, the fact of demonization does not change. In fact, many who practice in these two fields of science are, to some degree, indifferent to Christian beliefs. The demonized person, however, is not indifferent to Christian beliefs, but often reacts strongly when faced with true biblical counsel. This reaction is called the **phenomenon of resistance**. Koch cites a case of a demonized woman who could not even look at a Bible or a crucifix during the occasions of her demonic attacks.[7] Many times, as I have read the Bible, sung Christian songs, or talked about the blood of Jesus, the demonized person has put his fingers in his ears or screamed to shut out the message.

The **phenomenon of resistance** is not known among the **standard** mentally ill. However, the **phenomenon of resistance** can be clearly viewed in truly demonic people like the Gadarene demoniac. When the Gadarene demoniac saw Jesus, the demons began to cry out saying, "What have we to do with thee, Jesus, thou Son of God? Art thou come here to torment us before the time" (Matthew 8:29)? This seems to be the typical emotional response to the things of God by demonized people all over the world.

This resistance is seen in a case described by Koch: that of a Swiss woman he had counseled. Every time this woman entered a Christian's home, she always began to feel sick. Also, if she were traveling through an unfamiliar town, she would always begin to feel sick when passing a church--even if she were unaware of the church's being there--even if it were at night. In spite of all these strange symptoms, the woman's intellectual powers remained intact. Koch comments, "Her state of

126

possession had in fact been brought about only by her persistent practice of spiritism over a good number of years."[8]

I have found such a case of resistance in my own counseling. I invited a counselee who was an SRA (satanically, ritualistically abused) victim to visit at our church one Sunday morning. As Christians greeted her, shook her hand or hugged her, she pulled away. I later asked her why she pulled away from them. She answered that when the Christians touched her, the demons burned her painfully.

## DEMONIC INFLUENCES: HUMAN RESPONSIBILITY

With regard to human responsibility for demonization, Bible students have a difficult time agreeing. As one reads Mark 9:14-29, however, we can see an example of an individual who was in no way responsible, nor could he have been held accountable for the invasion of his personality. The son had suffered from **seizures since early childhood**. If the Bible student checks out the Greek, he will find that the Greek word **paidiothen**, meaning **infancy**, gives a different meaning to the word **childhood**. We have to accept the fact that this physical affliction came upon the child at such an early age, that he could not have been held responsible for the demonic invasion of his body.

With regard to this case, DeHaan, in his book **Satan, Satanism, and Witchcraft**, points out that even though the Bible account does not seem to point to any responsibility on the part of the father's son, there are those who would disagree. He allows that there are many who believe God would not permit evil spirits to take over a human's body unless the person had done something to allow the demon in.[9] If we accept this answer, then all those who are violent, unclean, blasphemous, or consistent failures in their Christian walk because of demonization, must be held totally responsible for their present state. We would have to conclude that they all make themselves susceptible to demonic invasion of their personalities by persisting in sinful and immoral practices.

I want to go on record as saying that I believe that people are not always responsible for any demonization that may have occurred. However, I believe that there are many more times when Christians are responsible for the demonization of their personalities. Of course this was not true in the boy's case (Mark 9), as it is not true in numerous other demonic cases. I will explain this more in detail in a future chapter concerning dealing with ancestral demons. I firmly believe that the boy in Mark 9 was suffering from attacks of an ancestral demon, and that the demonization of his personality was not of his making.

One must recognize there are legitimate illnesses which have no connection whatsoever to the demonic world. One must be careful not to link all seizures to the demonic. Nonetheless, more people in the world today are suffering from the effects of the demonic world than psychiatrists and other counselors of mental health, as well as modern theologians, would care to admit. Koch says, "I have heard several Christian psychiatrists in areas where occultism is rife, affirm that sometimes more than half the inmates of their psychiatric clinics are demonically oppressed rather than mentally ill."[10]

## DEMONIC INFLUENCES: THE OCCULT REVIVAL

Satan and his demons did not exist only in Bible times. In fact, the powers of darkness are enjoying a heyday in the occult movements and Satan worship which has been springing up like mushrooms in a rainy season in these last days.[11] It seems that skepticism, along with an ignorance of the Word of God, is fueling an increase in demonic activity. Those denying the existence and activity of Satan and demons show how much they reject biblical teachings. Leaving the safe ground of God's Word, many liberal and conservative churchmen, as well as untrained Christians, become ensnared in the fast-moving currents of the occult, fortune-telling, spiritism, magic, and false cults.

An example of such entanglement with the occult is seen in the alleged communication of the late Bishop James A. Pike with his deceased son in September, 1967 (the son had committed suicide). A televised séance was directed by a well-known medium, Arthur Ford (now deceased), who, at that time, was a Disciple of Christ Minister. This sensationalized séance shocked people around the world. Hopefully, this alerted Christians to the reality of twentieth-century occultism.[12] Through His Word God reveals His general plan for both the saved and unsaved, but it is not His purpose, nor is it in our best interest, for His people to know all the details of their tomorrows.

> *Come now, ye that say, Today or tomorrow we will go into such a city, and continue there a year, and buy and sell, and get gain; whereas ye know not what shall be on the next day. For what is your life? It is even a vapor that appeareth for a little time, and then vanisheth away. For ye ought to say, If the Lord will, we shall live, and do this, or that (James 4:13-14; NSSB).*

God's condemnation of the occult leaves Christians, as well as the lost, without excuse; yet many are falling into Satan's occult snare by disobeying His Word and consulting witches, mediums, clairvoyants, and astrologers. One finds the teachings of ones like Jean Dixon and Edgar Cayce more well-known than the teachings of God's Word. Isaiah's warning to God's people about the occult is just as fresh and relevant today as it was in his day.

> *And when they shall say unto you, Seek unto those who (are mediums), and unto wizards that peep, and that mutter: should not a people seek unto their God? Should they seek (on behalf of) the living to the dead? To the law and to the testimony; if they speak not according to this word, it is because there is no light in them (Isaiah 8:19-20; NSSB).*

Taylor believes that along with the revival of the occult in America, there has been a sharp rise in known cases of demonization. He also points out that another reason for this increase is a growing awareness of the presence of demonic spirits and an ever increasing knowledge of the power of the Christian to deal with them authoritatively.[13] Unger points out that the scope and power of modern occultism staggers the imagination. Millions are unwittingly oppressed and enslaved by the occult which causes mental and emotional problems to increase at an alarming rate.[14] A medical doctor recently shared that forty percent of the patients he saw had physical symptoms that were directly demonic, not even taking into consideration those who had psychosomatic symptoms.[15]

There are so many different areas of the occult that can ensnare a person, especially a child of God. Even though only a few areas can be covered at this time, one can be assured that all facets of the occult are demonically inspired and controlled. The apostle Paul warned believers that the Devil is so clever that he can make himself or his demons appear as **angels of light** (II Corinthians 11:13-15).

## DEMONIC INFLUENCES: IN SPIRITISM

World-wide spiritism is conservatively estimated to have at least seventy million adherents. Koch enumerates sixteen different varieties of spiritistic practices. All of these must be carefully weighed and understood if one is to accurately understand and evaluate spiritism.[16] While time will not allow for full details about occult spiritism, I will strive to give you an idea of what occultic snares to avoid. Here is a short statement from Unger:

> Spiritistic phenomena may be conveniently divided into the following categories: (1) physical phenomena, (levitations, apports, and telekinesis); (2) psychic phenomena (spiritistic visions, automatic writing, speaking in a trance, materializations, table lifting, tumbler moving, excursions of the psyche); (3) metaphysical phenomena (apparitions, ghosts); (4) magic phenomena (magic persecution, magic defense); (5) cultic phenomena (spiritistic cults, spiritism among Christians).[17]

It can be seen from what Unger had to say about spiritism that talking to the dead is but one of many spiritistic practices. Some people believe that people survive death as spirits, and that they can communicate with the living through a medium. A medium is a person who supposedly has a special psychic gift. An individual seeking to communicate with the dead is called a **necromancer**. Such an attempt to communicate with the dead is a practice synonymous with sorcery. DeHaan says, "The fact has been established that nearly one hundred million people in the world today have participated with some regularity in efforts to receive messages from the dead."[18]

DeHaan tells that Raphael Gasson, a former medium who is now a believer in the Lord Jesus Christ, published a work entitled, "The Challenging Counterfeit." In this work he sets forth the idea that demons, by impersonating the dead, are able to deceive those who attend séances in hope of contacting the spirits of their dead loved ones.[19] DeHaan also shares about Victor Ernest, in his work, telling the story of his early life as a member of a spiritualistic family. Now as a minister of the Gospel, he declares unequivocally that the religion of his childhood contained supernatural elements and that it was dangerous and wicked.[20]

The Word of God clearly denounces any efforts to communicate with the dead and leaves no ground for anyone to claim that it is all right to do so. In Leviticus 19:31 God says, "Regard not them that have familiar spirits, neither seek after wizards, to be defiled by them: I am the Lord your God." The Lord has shown in His Word that experimenting with the occult will bring about the same moral and spiritual corruption that had come to the Canaanites:

> *When thou art come into the land which the Lord thy God giveth thee, thou shalt not learn to do after the abominations of those nations. There shall not be found among you anyone who maketh his son or daughter pass through the fire, or who useth divination, or an observer of times, or an enchanter, or a witch, or a charmer, or a*

*consulter of (mediums) or a wizard, or a necromancer (Deuteronomy 18:9-11; NSSB).*

Also, in Leviticus 20:27, God told His people what to do with a witch: the penalty for practicing witchcraft was death by stoning. These Old Testament verses should be sufficient to convince anyone that any effort to communicate with the dead is forbidden by God Almighty.

## DEMONIC INFLUENCES: FORTUNE-TELLING

When examining the occult, one must deal with **fortune-telling or soothsaying**. Koch, in his book **Occult ABC**, does a great job of explaining the six forms of fortune-telling. The oldest form of fortune-telling is by means of the **rod and pendulum**, a practice which can be traced back six thousand years. Diviners normally use a forked willow twig, although some use a rod of fish bone or steel. There are a number of diviners who use no instrument at all, but simply spread out their fingers to detect the **earth rays**. Some use a pendulum, that is, a metal weight attached to a thread. Since the rod and pendulum are used in similar ways, the societies of water diviners and pendulum users have been merged to form the Society of Radiaesthesia.

The second oldest form of fortune-telling is **astrology**, which is the interpretation of human destiny (i.e., a man's future) by reference to the position of the stars at the moment of his birth. Astrology has existed for five thousand years. Job stated, "...yea, the stars are not pure in His sight" (Job 25:5). In the fourth chapter of Deuteronomy, God clearly gave the command not to worship the stars. Yet, the Sumerians, Accadians, the Chaldeans, Babylonians, Greeks, and Romans all had their astrologers.

The third form of fortune-telling is **palmistry**, which can be traced back about four thousand years. Palmistry was practiced by the priests of ancient Babylon. This is perhaps the most common form of fortune-telling practiced by the occult. It is simply the practice of reading palms.

The fourth form of fortune-telling is that involving the **use of cards**. The Romans had little wax tablets with symbols carved on them, which they used for telling the future.

The fifth form of fortune-telling is **psychometry**. The fortune-teller holds in his hand an object belonging to a certain person, and then gives information concerning that person.

A sixth form is fortune-telling with the aid of a **crystal ball**. This type of fortune-telling is practiced by the nationally known Jeane Dixon.[21]

The last form of fortune-telling discussed by Koch is that using the **Ouija Board**. In 1890, Robert Fuld marketed a device called an Ouija Board. The name **Ouija** comes from a combination of the French and German words for "yes." Newport, in his book **Demons, Demons, Demons**, allows that Neff states that many have gotten into serious psychological trouble through the use of the Ouija Board. He warns those who would treat it as if it were an innocent toy, that it is not. Many other counselors believe that evil spirits influence the results, and that the spirits purposely lead people into occult demonism.[22]

Every pagan nation practices some form of fortune-telling. The Bible shows that God hates it, for it leads to destruction. All forms of fortune-telling promote superstition and idolatry; therefore, divination of any sort is condemned and rigidly banned for God's people by the Word of God. Spiritistic fortune-tellers, clairvoyants, witches, charmers, consulters with familiar spirits (mediums), and necromancers were subject to the death penalty in Israel (Leviticus 19:31, 20:6, 27). The same stringent prohibition runs throughout the scriptures (cf. I Chronicles 10:13; Isaiah 8:19, 44:25; Jeremiah 29:8; Ezekiel 21:21-23; Micah 3:6, 7; Zechariah 10:2). The New Testament takes the same firm stand (Acts 16:16-18; Galatians 5:20).

## DEMONIC INFLUENCES: OTHER OCCULT PRACTICES

There are a few more well-known occult practices such as witchcraft, which is experiencing one of the greatest revivals in history. The Middle Ages seem to have come alive in our very midst. There are many forms of witchcraft including: communicating with the dead, calling up the Devil (to benefit from his powers and/or to worship him), reciting incantations, using certain herbs for magical purposes, and casting spells.

Another occult practice is the reading of occult literature. Witchcraft has its own bible, **The Book of Shadows**, and is characterized by a misuse of biblical terms and concepts. Its supreme characteristics include the concept of the union between Christ and Satan.[23] Christians should rid home and office of such materials, including objects and trinkets imported from lands where demonization is rampant if the objects are demonic in character.

Besides astroguides, occult and witchcraft books, objects bearing symbols contrary to Christ such as zodiac signs, Buddha, and sun-dials, should be discarded. Any style of inverted and/or broken crosses that represent opposition and mockery to Christ should not be in one's possession. While some are easily recognizable, like the German **swastika**, others are deceptive. For instance, the "**Ankh**", an upright **cross has a loop on top** representing Isis the sex goddess. Another demonic symbol is the pentagram, a circle with a five-point star with its point upward, used for black or white magic. Other objects and jewelry bear stars similar to this with drawings or writings on them that pertain to supernatural powers. These are called **talismans** or **amulets**. The **baphomet** is the **pentagram upside down**, with the point downward, and stands for a goat head representing Satan. Another satanic symbol, the **hexagram**, a six-point star, is deemed the most powerful symbol in the occult. The symbol of a quarter moon positioned with points upward and a star above represents the moon goddess **Dianna** and **Lucifer, the Morning Star**, and is used in witchcraft and Satanism. Various other symbols representing supernatural powers are found on objects pertaining to secret organizations such as Free Masonry.

An additional occult practice is the wearing of amulets for good luck, a practice which simply amounts to a compensation for a lack of faith in God. It may surprise you to learn that even the age-old custom of a team's having a **mascot** began in ancient times, when these **mascots** were believed to bring aid from the supernatural world.[24]

The Bible consistently associates occultism and sorcery with mediumistic abilities. One finds examples in Deuteronomy 18:10-12 and Leviticus 20:6, 20:27. Paul in Acts 16 considers as demonic the mediumistic power of the girl who was a fortune-teller. In light of what Paul says by the leadership of the Holy Spirit, it is not right to regard these abilities as some kind of new field for scientific research, much less as a gift from God. The evil nature of mediumistic powers is further evidenced by the way they come into being. They originate in one of three ways: by heredity, occult participation, or occult transference. Occult powers and mediumistic tendencies can be passed down from generation to generation.

Unger believes that the cruelty and bondage resulting from occult practices can cause lasting problems. He shows that violence, suicide, and insanity almost always run through a whole family line where the magical arts have been cultivated and practiced. Such tragic events often involve as many as four generations (Exodus 20:1-7; cf. I Corinthians 10:10).[25] Many occult-oppressed people, however, find it almost impossible to believe in Christ. Unbelief is one of the results of the sins of sorcery, and the sins need to be renounced by the victim. Koch says, "I often pray what one can call a prayer of renunciation with the person concerned."[26] II Corinthians 4:2 reads, "...we...have renounced the hidden things of dishonesty." Renunciation should be done before witnesses. There is to be a breaking away from the ties to objects of sorcery:

> *And many that believed came, and confessed and showed their deeds. Many of those also who used magical arts brought their books together, and burned them before all men; and they counted the price of them, and found it fifty thousand pieces of silver. So mightily grew the word of God, and prevailed (Acts 19:18-20; NSSB).*

**DEMONIC INFLUENCES: DISTINGUISHED FROM DEMONIZATION**

As we study the demonic, we can see that there is a difference between demon influence (temptation) and demon possession. In demon influence, evil spirits can exert great power over a person just short of actual possession. This demon influence may vary from mild harassment to extreme subjection where the body and mind become dominated and held in slavery by spirit agents. Christians, as well as non-Christians, can be so influenced, oppressed, vexed, depressed, hindered, and bound by demons that the demon influence resembles demon possession. Influence and possession are not, however, the same.

The Word of God reveals some of the results of demon influence. The demon influence may manifest itself in spiritual blindness and hardness of heart toward the Word of God and the Gospel of Christ (II Corinthians 4:4). It can produce antagonism toward God and cause a departure from the faith, resulting in open apostasy (I Timothy 4:1) or in doctrinal corruption and perversion of the truth, evident in the Babel (conversations of lies) of cults which brings Christian disunity (I John 4:1-2). Demon influence in doctrine leads to corrupt conduct and practice (I Corinthians 10:16-22), loving pleasure more than God (II Timothy 3:4) and indulging in defiling lust (II Peter 2:10-12). If an orthodox creed is embraced, demon influence may show itself in empty adherence to the letter of the law without the spirit of the law, or in ritualistic formalism (II Timothy 4:2-4).

Demonization, on the other hand, is a condition in which one or more evil spirits or demons inhabit the body of a human being and can take complete control of their victim at will. By temporarily blotting out his consciousness, they can speak and act through him, using him as their complete slave and tool. A question often raised is the following: how can one tell if a person has demons? From the study of demoniacs (particularly the demoniac of Gadara), a number of symptoms of demonic possession are listed below:

(1)      The Incapacity for Normal Living. The demoniac of Gadara found that he was unable to live a normal life. He wore no clothes and lived among the tombs.

(2)      The Suffering of Chronic Fears. Fear is one of the most common characteristics of demonization. Many saved as well as unsaved people are rendered totally inoperative by fear.

(3)      The Suffering of Chronic Loneliness. The demoniac of Gadara lived alone among the dead. People who are demon possessed seem to suffer from extreme loneliness.

(4)      Exhibition of Superhuman Strength and Violence. A demonized person can exhibit unusual strength. It is written of the demoniac of Gadara, "neither could any man tame him." With no real difficulty he broke the fetters and chains that bound him. Koch tells of a frail young man in the Philippines who was severely demonized. "When the super-natural rage struck him, he sometimes needed some grown men to hold him down."[27] Earnest Rockstad (deceased), a conference speaker and counselor in the area of the demonic, said, "We have known a slender girl of thirteen who could be restrained by four adults only with difficulty."[28]

(5)      Personality and Behavior Problems. Those who exhibit these problems show a visible conflict in their personality. There is a dual personality in the life of a demonic person, causing conflict within himself. The demon spirit wars against the human spirit, which causes mental suffering.

(6)      Opposition to the Things of God. "What have you to do with me?" the demoniac of Gadara cried out. Koch tells of a student at Manila crying out each time he addressed him in the name of Jesus, "Don't mention that name, I can't stand it."[29]

(7)      The Gift of Clairvoyance and/or Foreign Languages. The demoniac of Gadara immediately knew who Jesus was when he saw Him, even though he had never met Him. He also spoke with voices that were not his own. One cannot categorize this case as **schizophrenia** (meaning **to divide the mind; a mental disorder characterized by indifference, withdrawal, hallucinations, and delusions of persecution**), for in many instances the voices actually use foreign languages which the victim does not know. No mentally ill or hysterical person can suddenly start speaking in a foreign language which he or she has never learned. Newport believes that demonized people also display prophetic, clairvoyant, and telepathic abilities, including speaking in foreign languages which they have never had an opportunity to hear.[30]

Unger tells about a Baptist minister's wife who wrote him a letter pertaining to what has been discussed in the above text. Here are a few excerpts from her letter:

In 1967, a friend gave me a book about speaking in tongues. My spiritual life was at low ebb, and I was intensely seeking after God. I knew I was saved but there seemed to be an emptiness in my soul.

After reading the book, I began to believe that the experience of tongues was necessary to fill the spiritual void. For six years I asked for the experience. I contacted a charismatic Baptist minister and received the laying on of hands, which brought a most ecstatic experience...undoubtedly super-natural. I had never experienced such a wonderful feeling--too different to be merely psychological. I felt certain no one had ever been so happy, contented, and filled with joy...

Tongues did not come to me with the laying on of hands, but I kept asking for them. Two months later they came, accompanied with unusual happenings. Each day was a new and wonderful experience. Prayers were answered, miraculously, and always in the name of Jesus. One of the greatest deceits is the other Jesus spirits, who do not confess Jesus Christ as Savior and Lord (John 4:2, II Corinthians 11:4).

The tongues were new and exciting, and I used them frequently at first. I knew the physical happenings were demonic, but I thought Satan was trying to defeat the wonderful experience of the Holy Spirit. When the glory of the 'high' was over after each tongues experience, the presence of evil was more prominent...

Fourteen months after receiving the tongues, I was ready to take my life. Although I had lent myself through ignorance to the influence of the evil powers of Satan, the Lord in love continued to draw me out of the snare of the enemy. It has been a long journey back from the realm of darkness into which I had gone so deeply, but the grace of the Lord Jesus Christ has been sufficient to meet every need.[31]

I have found over the years that many people pick up demons while **seeking the gift of tongues or by being slain in the spirit**. If while I am gathering data from a counselee, I hear them say that they have the gift of tongues, I ask their permission to test their gift. God's Word tell us to test the spirit to see if it is really from Him (I John 4:1). Most of the time, they allow me to test the tongue and, most of the time, we find a demon tongue.

How can you test the spirit--test the one who speaks in tongues? I pray and ask God to protect us from being deceived by an emotional or demonic tongue. I also ask the Lord to make the demonic tongue speak in English when I need to ask him questions. Then, I ask the person submitting to the test to begin speaking in tongues. When this occurs, I command in the name of Jesus and by the power of His blood that he tell me whether or not Jesus Christ is his Lord. Of course, if the tongue is an emotional tongue, he cannot tell me anything. He only babbles. I Timothy 1:6 reveals that some Christians stepped away from sound doctrine and **"...turned aside unto vain jangling."** The word **jangling** is defined as babbling with empty and fruitless conversation and vain, foolish talking. The warning for Timothy to be cautious against such **jangling** applies to us as well.

If there is a demonic tongue, the demon almost always tries to fool me. He typically speaks in a soft voice with a phony, spiritual-like tone. When I ask the usual question, "Is Jesus your Lord?," he avoids the question. Sometimes he speaks in tones of mockery, lying by telling me that he loves Jesus and that Jesus provides for him and answers his prayers. I respond to such comments by saying, "I didn't ask you that! By the authority of Jesus Christ, is Jesus your Lord?" I have frequently heard the demon speak in a language that cannot be understood and suddenly switch to English and shout vulgarities and declare, "I don't have to tell you anything!"

If the person speaks in the true tongue, he/she will answer in a loving, sweet and soft tone, "Yes, Jesus is my Lord. I bring praise and honor and glory to the name of the only Son of God, Jesus Christ." Even upon hearing that, to be on the safe side, I test further by asking a number of times "Will this stand as truth before the eternal throne of God?" In all my years of testing the tongue, I have only found two that I deemed legitimate. However, I regret to say that looking back after many years of experience, I am not confident that they really were true tongues.

(8)     The Sudden Deliverance. Another sign that a person is demonized is sudden deliverance. Psychiatrists know so well how long and tedious the treatment for mental illness can be. Demonized people, on the other hand, can be delivered almost instantaneously upon coming in contact with the Lord Jesus Christ.[32]

(9)     The Phenomenon of Transference. Demons in a demonized person may be transferred to other persons, to animals, or, in some cases, to the abyss, the prison of the demons (Luke 8:31; NASB).[33] I believe demon transference can occur while having sex contrary to God's will, such as in dating relationships, prostitution, and even rape cases. I also believe demon transference can happen through allowing people **to lay hands on you to get the gift of tongues or to receive healing, or by being slain in the spirit**. This is why it is essential to know that the person laying hands on you has a **godly walk and is doctrinally sound**. In my opinion demon transference can also occur through reading, or looking at pornographic material, as well as through listening to certain rock music, using the Ouija board, and viewing occult video games.

(10)    An Abnormal Sex Life. Homosexuality and other sex perversions are symptomatic of demonic possession. The demons also work to produce uncontrollable heterosexual drives. Taylor says, "I have little doubt that behind cases of **unnatural sex** there are demon powers."[34]

As one can see from this study, demons can not only impart physical energy to their victim, but also can cause physical and mental oppression of their victim. They can produce physical disabilities and sicknesses unrelated to organic disorders, which medicine or natural therapy cannot alleviate.[35]

**DEMONIZED CHRISTIANS: WITNESSED HERE AND ABROAD**

In pagan lands where demonic activity has raged unchecked for thousands of years, many Christian missionaries declare that demons can and do invade and control believers who open the door by compromising their beliefs, by tampering with the occult, and by participating in idolatry and sin.

They also believe that a demon-harassed person often finds that being regenerated--saved through Christ--does not always result in deliverance from their demonization. Newport shows in his book that reports of demonic influence and possession of Christians flow in from dozens of sources. Foreign mission boards in the United States continue to receive reports of such demonic activity.[36]

An exhaustive study of demon possession in China by Nevius is based on numerous questionnaires sent to missionaries and Chinese Christians before the Communist take-over.[37] Nevius concludes that demon possession is just what the name suggests: it cannot be equated with ordinary physical or psychological derangements. Similar reports have poured in from Korea, Indonesia, Africa, and South America.[38]

Lester Sumrall, in his book **Demons the Answer Book**, replies to the question, "Can a Christian have a demon?": "I am of the opinion that evil spirits can invade and enter the life of a believer."[39] However, Newport believes that only God knows the heart of man. Some, who profess to be Christians may have never been really converted, and perhaps the true Christian is only oppressed, not possessed. He also believes that in order to cure a believer of pride or arrogance, God may allow him to undergo a temporary period of possession. In I Corinthians 5:1-5, Paul tells of a believer's being delivered up to Satan with the purpose of purging and saving him for service. Turning one over to the Devil does not always mean death. Paul wanted a sinful Christian turned over to Satan strictly for the purpose of drawing the person to repentance. Death was only the last resort and totally in God's hands.

Newport believes that if a Christian is possessed, the possession is surely only a severe form of affliction and trial through which he has to temporarily pass.[40]

In the case studies listed in his books**, Demonology Past and Present** and **Christian Counseling and Occultism**, Koch repeatedly states that Christians can have demons. In his book **Demonology Past and Present**, he makes an awesome statement about demonic problems that can be brought into the Christian life:

> There is another problem facing us today which is especially prevalent in the United States. It is that many Christians teach that when one becomes a Christian all one's problems are solved. In answer to this idea I can only turn to the literally thousands of Christians who have come to me in counseling sessions, who have carried their occult subjection over with them into their Christian lives. It is true that with a deep conversion a person can be delivered from all such oppressions of the devil, but this does not often take place. This can be illustrated by a simple analogy. If a young man, for example, contracts venereal disease before he becomes a Christian, although as a result of turning to Christ his sins may be forgiven, the effect of his sins will nevertheless almost certainly remain. So it is with occultism. A person can quite easily carry the effects of either his own or his ancestors' sins of sorcery over into his Christian life. And it is a person like this who needs the counsel of an experienced Christian worker. It is shocking to find in our Bible Schools and training colleges that hardly any time is devoted to preparing intending Christian workers for the problems they will surely meet in this field.[41]

Jessie Penn-Lewis, in her book **War on the Saints**, makes this statement about Christians and demon possession:

> The fact of the demon possession of Christians destroys the theory that only people in 'heathen countries,' or persons deep in sin, can be 'possessed' by evil spirits. This unexamined, unproved theory in the minds of believers, serves the devil well as a cover for his workings to gain possession of the minds and bodies, of Christians in the present time. But the veil is being stripped off the eyes of the children of God by the hard path of experience; and the knowledge is dawning upon the awakened section of the Church that a believer baptized in the Holy Ghost, and indwelt by God in the inner shrine of the spirit can be deceived into admitting evil spirits into his being; and be possessed, in varying degrees, by demons, even whilst in the centre he is a sanctuary of the Spirit of God; God working in, and through his spirit, and the evil spirits in, or through, mind, or body, or both.[42]

Dr. Irwin Rocky Freeman, in his book **Victory Flight Over Powers of Darkness**, responds to the question:

> Let me state that in all of our work, for over thirty-two years, we have only dealt in this area with two people who proved to be unsaved or non-Christians. One was a pastor's wife and the other a registered nurse. Both did confess Christ and the final demon spirits were forced to leave their lives. All others that we have counseled or helped have confessed Christ as Saviour and Lord. After the demonic spirits were gone, they still confessed Him. There was never any wavering with them concerning their relationship to the Lord Jesus Christ. Many of these were or are Christian workers with long years of faithful service.[43]

Dickason, in his book **Demon Possession and the Christian**, has this to say about Christians having demons:

> These case studies taken from my personal written and taped records demonstrate that genuine believers can and indeed were inhabited by demons. Those demons manifested themselves and were recognized as persons distinct from the believer. They were not so-called multiple personalities. Instead, they identified themselves as spirit beings under Satan and as enemies of Christ defeated by His blood. Most of the demons had invaded before the person had received Christ. Many of them came in as the result of ancestral sins. They could not prevent the person from receiving Christ, but they stayed on hoping to distract, defeat, and destroy the believer. Under pressure of the authority of Christ, they confessed Christ as their victor and the believer as their victor in Christ. Upon confrontation with Scripture and in the Savior's authority, there was significant relief and, in most cases, removal of the wicked spirits from the Christian. For this we can thank God.
>
> Again, clinical evidence found by qualified counselors has helped us answer in the affirmative the question; can genuine believers in Christ be inhabited by demons?[44]

Dr. Mark I. Bubeck, in his book **The Adversary**, has this to say about Christians and the term **demon possession:**

>It is my conviction that no believer can be possessed by an evil spirit in the same sense that an unbeliever can. In fact, I reject this term altogether when talking about a believer's problem with the powers of darkness. A believer may be afflicted or even controlled in certain areas of his being, but he can never be owned or totally controlled as an unbeliever can...
>
>The moment a person becomes a believer, the Holy Spirit brings birth to his spirit...The spirit of the Christian is reborn, regenerated, possessed, and sealed by the Holy Spirit in a way not enjoyed by the rest of man's being as yet. The spirit of man thus reborn becomes the Holy Spirit's unique center of control and operation within man. [45]

This is what noted author and Bible teacher, Charles R. Swindoll, says in his booklet on **Demonism** about the question of a Christian being demonized:

### Can a Christian Be Demonized?

>For a number of years I questioned this, but I am now convinced it can occur. If a 'ground of entrance' has been granted the power of darkness (such as trafficking in the occult, a continual unforgiving spirit, a habitual state of carnality, etc.), the demon(s) sees this as a green light--okay to proceed (II Corinthians 2:10-11; I Corinthians 5:1-5; Luke 22:31-32). Wicked forces are not discriminating with regard to which body they may inhabit. I have worked personally with troubled, anguished Christians for many years. On a few occasions I have assisted in the painful process of relieving them of demons.
>
>Perhaps a clarifying word of assurance is needed here. The believer has the Holy Spirit resident within. Therefore, the alien, wicked spirit certainly cannot claim 'ownership' of the Christian. He is still a child of God. But while present within the body (perhaps in the region of the soul) that evil force can work havoc within the life, bringing the most extreme thoughts imaginable into his or her conscious awareness. Couldn't this explain how some believers can fall into such horrible sins? And how some could commit suicide? [46]

Dr. Neil T. Anderson, in his book **The Bondage Breaker**, makes this statement about demonic control of the saints:

>It is critical that Christians understand their vulnerability to demonic influence. Those who say a demon cannot control an area of a believer's life have left us with only two possible culprits for the problems we face: ourselves or God. If we blame ourselves we feel hopeless because we can't do anything to stop what we're doing. If we blame God our confidence in Him as our benevolent Father is shattered. Either way, we have no chance to gain the victory which the Bible promises us. In reality we are in a

winnable war against principalities and powers from the defeated kingdom of darkness. But their lies can gain a measure of control if we let them.

Here are several indications in Scripture that believers can lose control or come under bondage. Luke 13:10-18; 22:31-34; Eph. 6:10-17; James 3:14-16; I Tim. 4:1-3; I Cor. 5:1-13; Eph. 4:26-27; I Pet. 5:6-9; Acts 5:1-11.[47]

Unger, in his book **What Demons Can Do to Saints**, points out that nowhere does the scripture expressly declare that a believer may not be invaded by demonic power. Also, he shows that God's Word contains intimations that the powers of darkness may invade the believer under certain conditions.[48] on the subject of demonic invasion he comments:

> But who dares assert that a demon spirit will not invade the life of a believer in which the Holy Spirit has been grieved by serious and persistent sin and quenched by flagrant disobedience? The demon enters, it is true, as a squatter and not as an owner or a questor, as one who has a right there, but he comes in as an intruder and as an invader and enemy. But come he does if the door is opened by serious and protracted sin.[49]

This is like unto a Christian who owns his vehicle but by his own choice, hands the keys over to someone else to drive it. While the other person is in possession of the vehicle, he is not the owner. Possession does not institute ownership.

Unger, however, stresses that demons cannot indwell a Christian in the same sense that the Holy Spirit indwells. He explains that while God's Spirit enters a believer at salvation never to leave again, a demon, by contrast, enters as a squatter and an intruder and is subject to eviction.[50]

I have dealt with hundreds of precious Christians who have had demons. In future chapters, I will share some of these cases in detail. I believe, based on all the facts presented by this goodly number of qualified men of God, the answer to the question as to whether or not demons can control, invade, and demonize Christians in the twentieth century is a unanimous, yes. I feel it necessary to emphasize that one who is truly a child of God cannot be possessed by demons in the sense that the demon powers of darkness could take ownership of him. When one comes to believe that demons are real, that they are present today, and that Christians can have them as well as the lost, one needs to learn how to confront and help demonic people.

## NOTES

1.    Edward Langton, <u>Satan, A Portrait</u>, p. 118.
2.    Kurt Koch, <u>Demonology Past and Present</u>, p. 32.
3.    <u>Ibid.</u>, p. 37.
4.    <u>Ibid.</u> p. 38.
5.    <u>Loc. cit.</u>
6.    Webster's Dictionary, <u>The New Lexicon of the English Language</u>, p. 48.
7.    Kurt Koch, <u>op. cit.</u>, p. 39
8.    <u>Ibid.</u>, p. 40.
9.    Richard W. DeHaan, <u>Satan, Satanism and Witchcraft</u>, pp. 31, 32.
10.   Kurt Koch, <u>op. cit.</u>, p. 42.
11.   Merrill F. Unger, <u>What Demons Can Do To Saints</u>, p. 102.
12.   Merrill F. Unger, <u>Demons in the World Today</u>, p. 17.
13.   Jack R. Taylor, <u>Victory Over the Devil</u>, p. 50.
14.   Merrill F. Unger, <u>op. cit.</u>, p. 18.
15.   Jack R. Taylor, <u>op. cit.</u>, p. 50.
16.   Kurt Koch, <u>Between Christ and Satan</u>, pp. 123, 124.
17.   Merrill F. Unger, <u>op. cit.</u>, p. 38.
18.   Richard W. DeHaan, <u>op. cit.</u>, p. 52.
19.   <u>Ibid.</u>, p. 53.
20.   <u>Loc. cit.</u>
21.   Kurt Koch, <u>Occult A B C</u>, pp. 70, 185.
22.   John P. Newport, <u>Demons, Demons, Demons</u>, p. 117.
23.   Jack R. Taylor, <u>op. cit.</u>, p. 60.
24.   <u>Ibid.</u>, p. 59.
25.   Merrill F. Unger, <u>op. cit.</u>, p. 51.
26.   Kurt Koch, <u>Demonology Past and Present</u>, p. 153.
27.   <u>Ibid.</u>, p. 138.
28.   Ernest B. Rockstad, <u>Symptoms of Demonic Invasion</u>, p. 1.
29.   Kurt Koch, <u>Demonology Past and Present</u>, p. 138.
30.   John P. Newport, <u>op. cit.</u>, p. 73.
31.   Merrill F. Unger, <u>What Demons Can Do To Saints</u>, pp. 83, 84.
32.   <u>Ibid.</u>, p. 135.
33.   <u>Ibid.</u>, p. 136.
34.   Jack R. Taylor, <u>op. cit.</u>, p. 61.
35.   Merrill F. Unger, <u>Demons in the World Today</u>, p. 27.
36.   John P. Newport, <u>op. cit.</u>, p. 66.
37.   <u>Loc. cit.</u>
38.   <u>Loc. cit.</u>
39.   Lester Sumrall, <u>Demons The Answer Book</u>, p. 103.
40.   John P. Newport, <u>op. cit.</u>, p. 66.
41.   Kurt Koch, <u>op. cit.</u>, 49, 50.
42.   Jessie Penn-Lewis, <u>War on the Saints</u>, p. 97.
43.   Irwin Rocky Freeman, <u>Victory Flight Over Powers of Darkness</u>, p. 67.
44.   C. Fred Dickason, <u>Demon Possession and the Christian</u>, p. 213.

45.   Mark I. Bubeck, <u>The Adversary</u>, p. 87.
46.   Charles R. Swindoll, <u>Demonism</u>, pp. 18, 19.
47.   Neil T. Anderson, <u>The Bondage Breaker</u>, pp. 174-177.
48.   Merrill F. Unger, <u>What Demons Can Do To Saints</u>, p. 88.
49.   <u>Ibid</u>., p. 51.
50.   <u>Loc</u>. <u>cit</u>.

# CHAPTER EIGHT
## UNWANTED INHERITANCE

In this chapter I want us to take a fresh look at what the term **iniquity of the fathers** actually means, how it passes down, and how to overcome it. In order to do that, we must fully understand the meaning of the word **iniquity**.

## WHAT IS INIQUITY?

Let's begin by looking at the original meaning of the word. Look at three Hebrew words for iniquity and their Greek equivalents:

(1)    **Awon**; a depraved action (Gen. 13; 44:16), perversity, perverseness, sin, guilt, a crime, a fault, iniquity, mischief (Ps. 31:10). This noun is derived from awah...often the results of past misdeeds against God and man.[1]

**Awon** is the Hebrew word used in Exodus 20:3-6; 34:6,7; Leviticus 26:39; Numbers 14:18, 30-34; Psalm 51:5; Jeremiah 3:24,25; 9:12-15; 32:18; and Lamentatations 5:7.

(2)    **Awah**; to be bent, make crooked; to writhe; to act perversely, sin, do wrong, commit iniquity, be perverse, subvert (to distort, twist), to turn upside down; to make impassable. Its essential meaning is to deviate from the proper path.[2]

(3)    **Awen**; this is an important Hebrew word for sin. It means vanity, breath, vainness, nothingness, falseness, falsehood, idol, idolatry, sin, wickedness, sorrow, distress, hardship, toil.[3]

**Awen** is the word used in Isaiah 32:6; Job 21:19; and Psalm 7:14, and seems to mean internalized wickedness.

The Greek word for iniquity is a noun, **anomia**, having a meaning of **transgression of the law**. The Greek adjective, **anomos**, has a meaning **of not having or knowing or acknowledging the law**. When these Greek words and definitions are considered, the word **iniquity** takes on a meaning of **opposition to or contempt for the will of God**.[4] We find this Greek word **anomia** in the following scriptures: Matthew 7:23; 13:41; 23:28; 24:12; Romans 4:7; 6:19; II Cor. 6:14; II Thessalonians 2:7; Titus 2:14; Hebrews 1:9; 8:12; 10:17; and I John 3:4.

Most people mistakenly view the words **sin** and **iniquity** as one and the same. Even in dictionaries, we find that some treat the word **iniquity** as a synonym for **sin**. I have found that the meaning of the word **iniquity** goes far beyond the meaning of the word **sin**. God gives us the correct meaning in the scriptures. **Iniquity** involves choosing one's own will over God's will. Iniquity is consistently doing anything--whether good or bad--outside the will of God. Choosing to totally ignore God's will and

His commands, one's continued disobedience can lead to a sinful, self-pleasing lifestyle--**a lifestyle of iniquity.**

Gothard says, "Iniquity is doing my own will even though it is something good"[5] He cites King Saul's disobedience in I Samuel 13-15 as an example. In studying those passages and considering King Saul's life, we see that acts of self-will always seem to cause further sinning. We seem all too ready to follow our own human reasoning.

**HOW DOES GOD VIEW INIQUITY?**

How does our <u>human</u> reasoning compare to <u>God's</u> <u>wisdom</u> concerning iniquity? We learn the answer when we see God's condemnation of iniquity in Exodus 20:3-6:

> *Thou shalt have no other gods before me. Thou shalt not make unto thee any carved image, or any likeness of anything that is in heaven above, or that is in the earth beneath, or that is in the water under the earth; Thou shalt not bow down thyself to them, nor serve them; for I, the Lord thy God am a jealous God, visiting the iniquity of the fathers upon the children unto the third and fourth generation of them that hate me; and showing mercy unto thousands of them that love me, and keep my commandments (NSSB).*

We see in Exodus that everyone has the freedom to choose whether to hate and disobey God, or to love and obey Him. Just as God promised our ancestors, He visits the iniquity of the fathers upon us, their children, unto the third and fourth generations of those who hate and disobey Him. God told His people that their love and obedience to Him was very important, so important that if they would only love and obey Him, He would show mercy to them. This information, no doubt, was so vital for the protection of His people, He repeated it many times. I find it essential for us to look very carefully at the following quotes. I will make only a few comments between each to avoid breaking our focus on God's important messages, then comment afterward. Here, we see God meeting with Moses:

> *And the Lord passed by before him, and proclaimed, The Lord, The Lord God, merciful and gracious, long-suffering, and abundant in goodness and truth, keeping mercy for thousands, forgiving iniquity and transgression and sin, and who will by no means clear the guilty, visiting the iniquity of the fathers upon the children, and upon the children's children, unto the third and to the fourth generation (Exodus 34:6, 7; NSSB).*

The Lord told the Israelites that their chastening would be dispersion into the land of the enemy:

> *And they who are left of you shall pine away in their iniquity in your enemies' lands; and also in the iniquities of their fathers shall they pine away with them (Lev. 26:39; NSSB).*

The Lord told Moses and the Israelites that they must spend forty years in the wilderness:

*The Lord is long-suffering, and of great mercy, forgiving iniquity and transgression, and by no means clearing the guilty, visiting the iniquity of the fathers upon the children unto the third and fourth generation...Doubtless ye shall not come into the land, concerning which I swore to make you dwell therein, except Caleb, the son of Jephunneh, and Joshua, the son of Nun. But your little ones, whom ye said should be a prey, them will I bring in, and they shall know the land which ye have despised. But as for you, your carcasses, they shall fall in this wilderness. And your children shall wander in the wilderness forty years, and bear your harlotries, until your carcasses be wasted in the wilderness (Num. 14:18, 30-34; NSSB).*

God spoke of Ahaziah the son of Ahab the king of Israel:

*And he did evil in the sight of the Lord, and walked in the way of his father, and in the way of his mother, and in the way of Jeroboam, the son of Nebat, who made Israel to sin; for he served Baal, and worshiped him, and provoked to anger the Lord God of Israel, according to all that his father had done (I Kings 22:52, 53; NSSB).*

God told of Ahaziah the son of Jehoram the king of Judah:

*He also walked in the ways of the house of Ahab; for his mother was his counselor to do wickedly. Wherefore, he did evil in the sight of the Lord like the house of Ahab; for they were his counselors after the death of his father, to his destruction (II Chron. 22:3, 4; NSSB).*

Job spoke of iniquity being laid up for the children:

*God layeth up his iniquity for his children; he rewardeth him, and he shall know it (Job. 21:19; NSSB).*

The Psalmist speaks on iniquity and wickedness:

*Behold, I was shaped in iniquity, and in sin did my mother conceive me (Ps. 51:5; NSSB).*

*The wicked are estranged from the womb; they go astray as soon as they are born, speaking lies (Ps. 58:3; NSSB).*

God warned of the destruction of Babylon:

*Thou shalt not be joined with them in burial, because thou hast destroyed thy land, and slain thy people; the seed of evildoers shall never be renowned. Prepare slaughter for his children for the iniquity of their fathers, that they do not rise, nor possess the land, nor fill the face of the world with cities (Isa. 14:20, 21; NSSB).*

God showed how the children are taught and suffer because of the iniquity of the fathers:

*For shame hath devoured the labor of our fathers from our youth; their flocks and their herds, their sons and their daughters. We lie down in our shame, and our*

145

*confusion covereth us; for we have sinned against the Lord, our God, we and our fathers, from our youth even unto this day, and have not obeyed the voice of the Lord our God (Jere. 3:24, 25; NSSB).*

*Who is the wise man, that may understand this? And who is he to whom the mouth of the Lord hath spoken, that he may declare it? Why is the land perished and burned up like a wilderness, that none passeth through? And the Lord saith, Because they have forsaken my law which I set before them, and have not obeyed my voice, neither walked in it, but have walked after the imagination of their own heart, and after Baalim, which their fathers taught them. Therefore, thus saith the Lord of hosts, the God of Israel, behold, I will feed them, even this people, with wormwood, and give them water of gall to drink (Jere. 9:12-15; NSSB).*

*Thou showest loving-kindness unto thousands, and recompensest the iniquity of the fathers into the bosom of their children after them; the Great, the Mighty God, the Lord of hosts, is his name (Jere. 32:18; NSSB).*

Jeremiah spoke about the iniquities:

*Our fathers have sinned, and are not, and we have borne their iniquities (Lament. 5:7; NSSB).*

We easily saw that God is serious about His promises, which came true regarding the Israelites. As a Christian today, we must realize that God's promises hold true for us as well. Let's look a moment and learn from some of our Old Testament ancestors:

## WHAT CAN ONE LEARN ABOUT INIQUITY FROM THE LIFE OF KING DAVID?

In dealing with the phrase **iniquity of the fathers**, I want us to spend some time with King David in Psalm 51. I want to point out several truths in King David's cry of wisdom and sorrow. It is known that this is a Psalm of David that grew from the prophet Nathan's confronting him over his sin with Bathsheba. In verse two, David said, **"Wash me thoroughly from mine iniquity and cleanse me from my sin."**

It seems that David understood that there is a difference between **iniquity** and **sin**. Unlike the words **heart, soul, and spirit** that carry the same meaning, David uses both iniquity and sin in the same verse. In this case, he was not being redundant. Carefully consider what he is saying in verse five, "Behold, I was **shapen in iniquity**; and **in sin did my mother conceive me**." David was letting us know that he was aware of the **iniquity of the fathers** passing down to him as well as **his own sin nature.**

David then says of God in verse six: "Behold, thou desirest truth in the **inward parts**, and **in the hidden part**, thou shalt make me know wisdom." What is God telling us in that verse? God teaches us through David that He had convicted David's heart--which He wanted truth to prevail in his **inward parts**. The Hebrew word for **inward parts** is a combination of words that make up **tuwcah** which means to **smear or overlay**.[6] It also means as **being covered, the inmost thought**, and **to**

146

**cast down, forth or out**. David had learned that there was a **hidden part** of his life--the Hebrew word **for hidden part** is again a combination of words that make up **satham**, meaning **to repair, to keep secret, to be closed or shut out (up) or to stop**.[7] David concluded that God wanted truth to prevail to the point of **casting down or out, the secrets** that were **closed up** in his life. It is clear that God had used Nathan to help convict David regarding the condition of his heart. When David told God, "Thou shalt make me know wisdom" concerning the iniquity and sin in his life, he recognized his lifestyle had deteriorated severely, to the point of a demonic stronghold in his life. He had totally ignored the Word of God and His protective commandments.

## WHAT CAN ONE LEARN ABOUT INIQUITY FROM THE LINE OF JUDAH?

Better understanding King David and Psalm 51, let's move on to the first chapter of Matthew. Here, we find the genealogy of Judah, which includes Jesus Christ, the son of David, the son of Abraham. The second and third verses of Matthew state: "Abraham begot Isaac; and Isaac begot Jacob; and Jacob begot Judah and his brethren; and Judah begot Perez and Zerah of Tamar." Take a good look at this first-born of Jacob, known as Judah, and see if you see the iniquity being passed down.

Chapter thirty-eight of Genesis shows Judah making some critical wrong choices. Judah took a Canaanite woman--a heathen--named Shua, to be his wife, and had three sons by her, Er, Onon, and Shelah (vv. 2-5). However, when Judah's first-born was old enough, Judah did choose a wife for him who was not a heathen--Tamar (v. 6). Verses seven through eleven say:

> *...Er, Judah's first-born, was wicked in the sight of the Lord; and the Lord slew him. And Judah said unto Onan, Go in unto thy brother's wife, and marry her, and raise up seed to thy brother. And Onan knew that the seed should not be his; and it came to pass, when he went in unto his brother's wife, that he spilled it on the ground, lest that he should give seed to his brother. And the thing which he did displeased the Lord: wherefore he slew him also. Then said Judah to Tamar, his daughter-in-law, Remain a widow at thy father's house, till Shelah my son be grown: for he said, Lest perhaps he die also, as his brethren did. And Tamar went and dwelt in her father's house (NSSB).*

These verses let us see the iniquity (or the self-will and rebellion) of Judah's taking a heathen wife. Later, we see the iniquity of Judah's first-born son Er acting wickedly before the Lord, and being killed by the Lord for doing so. Following Jewish tradition, Judah gave Er's wife Tamar to his second son Onan. However, Onan also rebelled, refusing to raise up seed for his dead brother. Instead, Onan spilled his seed on the ground, an act which displeased God, who then killed him. Then, we see Judah's telling Tamar to leave and go to her father's house and wait there until his third son was old enough to be her husband. However, we later discover that Judah deceived her, keeping Shelah from Tamar out of fear that his third son might die also. Judah added the iniquities of fear and deceit to his iniquity of rebellion, and passed them down to the next generation. After Judah kept his third son from marrying Tamar, let's see what came from all this iniquity in verses 12-23:

> *And in the process of time the daughter of Shua, Judah's wife, died; and Judah was comforted, and went up unto his sheepsheareres to Timnah, he and his friend Hirah, the Adullamite. And it was told Tamar, saying, Behold thy father-in-law goeth up to*

*Timnah to shear his sheep. And she put her widow's garments off from her, and covered her with a veil, and wrapped herself, and sat in an open place, which is by the way to Timnah; for she saw that Shelah was grown, and she was not given unto him as his wife. When Judah saw her, he thought her to be an harlot; because she had covered her face. And he turned unto her by the way, and said, Come, I pray thee, let me come in unto thee (for he knew not that she was his daughter-in-law). And she said, What wilt thou give me, that thou mayest come in unto me? And he said, I will send thee a kid from the flock. And she said, Wilt thou give me a pledge, till thou send it? And he said, What pledge shall I give thee? And she said, Thy signet, and thy bracelets, and thy staff that is in thine hand. And he gave them to her, and came in unto her, and she conceived by him. And she arose, and went away, and laid by her veil from her, and put on the garments of her widowhood. And Judah sent the kid by the hand of his friend, the Adullamite, to receive his pledge from the woman's hand; but he found her not. Then he asked the men of that place, saying, Where is the harlot that was openly by the wayside? And they said, There was no harlot in this place. And he returned to Judah, and said, I cannot find her; and also the men of the place said that there was no harlot in this place. And Judah said, Let her take them to her, lest we be shamed: behold, I sent this kid, and thou hast not found her (NSSB).*

Judah's initial iniquity invited more iniquity--fornication and incest were involved. Judah's wife had died and he went to Timnah to shear his sheep, there seeing his daughter-in-law Tamar, disguised as a harlot. Not knowing her to be Tamar, he readily consented to have sex with her, and submitted his initialed ring, bracelets, and his staff as his pledge--his collateral. Later, we see Judah send a friend to pay Tamar for her services with a kid from his flock and to retrieve his belongings, but he cannot find her. At that point, the sexual act had cost Judah his pledge. We read the rest of the story in verses 24-30:

*And it came to pass about three months after, that it was told Judah, saying, Tamar, thy daughter-in-law, hath played the harlot; and also, behold, she is with child by harlotry. And Judah said, Bring her forth, and let her be burned. When she was brought forth, she sent to her father-in-law, saying, By the man, whose these are, am I with child; and she said, Discern, I pray thee, whose are these, the signet, and bracelets, and staff. And Judah acknowledged them, and said, She hath been more righteous than I; because that I gave her not to Shelah, my son. And he knew her again no more. And it came to pass in the time of her travail, that, behold, twins were in her womb. And it came to pass, when she travailed, that the one put out his hand: and the midwife took and bound upon his hand a scarlet thread, saying, This came out first. And it came to pass, as he drew back his hand, that, behold, his brother came out: and she said, How hast thou broken forth? This breach be upon thee: therefore his name was called Perez. And afterward came out his brother, that had the scarlet thread upon his hand: and his name was called Zerah (NSSB).*

Learning that his daughter-in-law had played the harlot and was with child, Judah was more than ready to pass judgment upon her and have her brought forth and burned. He became sorely aware of God's judgment upon him when she presented him with his signet, bracelets, and staff, proving he was the child's father. We see him confessing that she was more righteous than he, for he had broken his promise, deceived her and kept his son from her. It is interesting to find the descendants of the twins to which she gave birth in Old Testament times in a genealogy mentioned in the New Testament. In Matthew 1:3-7, knowing the lifestyles of Judah's descendants, we can see the iniquity of the fathers pass down:

> *And Judah begot Perez and Zerah of Tamar; and Perez begot Hezron; and Hezron begot Ram; and Ram begot Amminadab; and Amminadab begot Nahshon; and Nahshon begot Salmon; and Salmon begot Boaz of Rahab; and Boaz begot Obed of Ruth; and Obed begot Jesse; and Jesse begot David, the king; and David, the king, begot Solomon of her that had been the wife of Uriah; and Solomon begot Rehoboam; and Rehoboam begot Abijah; and Abijah begot Asa (NSSB).*

Again we can see iniquity in some of Judah's descendants marrying heathens. Only through God's permissive will and man's free choice, was Salmon able to choose to marry Rahab the harlot of Jericho. That marriage produced Boaz who also married a heathen woman--Ruth. From that marriage came Obed, who begat Jesse, who begat David, the king. In studying this trend, we can better understand what David meant in Psalm 51:2-5: "Wash me (thoroughly) from mine iniquity...behold I was shapen in iniquity and in sin did my mother conceive me."

The iniquity of the fathers had passed down to David, and his own iniquity of rebellion and self-will (revealed in his sin with Bathsheba), clearly passed down to his son Solomon. I Kings 11 shows evidence that Solomon had enormous self-will and an excessive, unsatisfiable sexual appetite:

> *But King Solomon loved many foreign women; in addition to the daughter of Pharaoh, women of the Moabites, Ammonites, Edomites, Sidonians, and Hittites, of the nations concerning which the Lord said unto the children of Israel, Ye shall not go in to them, neither shall they come in unto you; for surely they will turn away your heart after their gods. Solomon clung unto these in love. And he had seven hundred wives, princesses, and three hundred concubines; and his wives turned away his heart. For it came to pass, when Solomon was old, that his wives turned away his heart after other gods, and his heart was not perfect with the Lord his God, as was the heart of David, his father. For Solomon went after Ashtoreth, the goddess of the Sidonians, and after Milcom, the abomination of the Ammonites. And Solomon did evil in the sight of the Lord, and went not fully after the Lord, as did David, his father. Then did Solomon build an high place for Chemosh, the abomination of Moab, in the hill that is before Jerusalem, and for Molech, the abomination of the children of Ammon. And likewise did he for all his foreign wives, who burned incense and sacrificed unto their gods (NSSB).*

The iniquity of Solomon's self-will and rebellion passed down to his son Rehoboam, who caused the people of Israel to rebel against the house of David (I Kings 12:1-20).

I want to point out a couple of things about some of David's other wives' children. In II Samuel 3:2-5 *we read:*

149

*And unto David were sons born in Hebron: and his first-born was Amnon, of Ahinoam, the Jezreelitess; and his second, Chileab, of Abigail, the wife of Nabal, the Carmelite; and the third, Absalom, the son of Maacah, the daughter of Talmai, king of Geshur; and the fourth, Adonijah, the son of Haggith; and the fifth, Shephatiah, the son of Abital; and the sixth, Itream, by Eglah, David's wife. These were born to David in Hebron (NSSB).*

Looking at the account of the births of children, other than Solomon, I want the reader to notice the names of Amnon and Absalom. When we see these names appear in II Samuel 13, we also find a blood sister, Tamar, coming from the same marriage that produced Absalom. Amnon is a half-brother to Absalom and Tamar. We can see David's iniquity--rebellion, sexual sin, murder--passing down to other generations. Amnon, in his sinful attitude of self-will and rebellion, raped his half-sister Tamar. Absalom, in his fury, murdered Amnon for raping his sister.

I have taken some precious time to illustrate the iniquity of the fathers passing down to the children in Judah's line, in order to make it even clearer to God's people why Jesus Christ had to be virgin-born. A human <u>father</u> would have passed down all the ancestral sins and iniquities of the fathers, making it impossible for Jesus to have been the perfect sacrifice in our place.

## WHY DO WE NEED TO STUDY ABOUT INIQUITY?

The main purpose for the study of **iniquity** is for us to understand what it is so that we can stop it from passing down further in our future generations. It is vital to understand that Ezekiel 18:19-23 does <u>not</u> say that God has stopped the iniquity of the fathers from passing down. Ancestral sin is not done away with in the new covenant. The scripture puts the emphasis on taking responsibility--not on blaming ancestors and claiming helplessness. The new covenant makes each one responsible to deal with ancestral sin by repentance and claiming back ground that was given up through sin (II Cor. 4:1,2; Acts 19:13-20). We can see that even though children are not responsible or guilty for the iniquities of their fathers, they are affected by them.[8]

Iniquity is a stubbornly chosen lifestyle of sin lived outside the will of God. Self-will is being enacted instead of God's will. A few examples of such lifestyles may be consistently involving unbelief, worry, fear, rebellion, lust, occult worship, eating disorders, and self-idolatry. God has promised to visit such iniquity unto the third and fourth generations. The word visit shows that iniquity can be temporary. Once again we can see God's love and mercy for mankind.

## HOW IS INIQUITY PASSED DOWN?

I have learned that the iniquities of the fathers pass down in three major ways. (1) <u>Through learned behavior</u>. While we certainly did not evolve from anything, our fallen nature is prone to "monkey see, monkey do." Often if a parent screams while correcting his children, the children become screaming parents. If the parent abuses his children, whether sexually, emotionally, or physically, the children most likely will do the same thing to their children. (2) <u>Through genetic ties</u>. These ties range from inherited tendencies to worry and depression, to eating disorders, sexual perversion, and drugs and alcohol addiction. (3) <u>Through ancestral demons</u>. These are programmed to live out the iniquity in that generation.

God's promise to visit the iniquities of the fathers on the children is connected with the first and second commandments:

> *Thou shalt have no other gods before me. Thou shalt not make unto thee any carved images, or any likeness of anything that is in heaven above, or that is in the earth beneath, or that is in the water under the earth; thou shalt not bow down thyself to them, nor serve them; for I, the Lord thy God, am a jealous God, visiting the iniquity of the fathers upon the children unto the third and fourth generations of them that hate me; and showing mercy unto thousands of them that love me, and keep my commandments (Exodus 20:1-5).*

The New Testament states that if one is guilty of the least of the commandments, he is guilty of all (Matt. 5:19; Jms. 2:8), including the first two dealing with the passing down of the iniquity of the fathers. John said in II John 6, "...this is love that we walk after his commandments." Again in Matthew 22:37-40, the Bible says:

> *Jesus said unto him, Thou shalt love the Lord, thy God, with all thy heart, and with all thy soul, and with all thy mind. This is the first and great commandment. And the second is like it, Thou shalt love thy neighbor as thyself. On these two commandments hang all the law and the prophets (NSSB).*

## CAN WE DEAL WITH THE INIQUITIES AND STOP THEM FROM PASSING DOWN?

The picture is not hopeless. Not only is it possible for us to deal with the iniquities, but also it is possible for us to stop them from passing down. For our own sake, as well as for the well-being of future generations, we must face and deal with the iniquities in our own lives and stop them from passing down and hurting other generations. Bill Gothard, in his fourth journal on **Fulfilling Your Life's Purpose**, does a beautiful job in presenting a plan for dealing with our iniquities. (By the way, Gothard's material can be purchased by writing I.B.L.P. Publications Office, Box One, Oak Brook, Illinois 60522-3001, or by calling 708/323-9800.) He mentions four steps of action that Christians should take in order to deal with the iniquities of the forefathers. (1) Identify the precise iniquity that has been passed down. (2) Acknowledge your sin and your forefathers' iniquities. (3) **Reclaim ground and yield yourself to God**. (4) Cast down the strongholds or high places of Satan in your mind.[9] Gothard's information is great and has worked for many people. I listed the same types of helps in my chapter on Restoring True Worship. I must add, however, that if a person follows these instructions, but still continues to suffer with problems, these problems could be caused by ancestral demons or fragmented personalities and he should seek godly counsel.

## WHAT ROLE DO INIQUITY AND ANCESTRAL TIES PLAY IN COUNSELING?

Other counselors have found, as I have, the iniquity of the fathers playing a major part in counselees' lives, their needing to deal with it being essential to freedom. Look at the following quotes from counselors and writers concerning learned behavior, the iniquity of the fathers, and ancestral demons: The great preacher, Charles H. Spurgeon, in his study of Psalm 51:5, quotes Samuel Chandler in saying:

I doubt that parents, who are sinners themselves and much under the influence of bad affections and passions, will be very likely to produce children without transmitting to them some of those disorders and corruptions of nature with which they themselves are infected....[10]

Bubeck discusses transference in his book **The Adversary**:

What some have called transference is another way unwilling demonic possession of unbelievers may come. Demonic powers want to stay in families and ancestral blood lines. An ancestor who gives place to Satan is not only hurting himself, but he is opening the door of grave harm to his children, grandchildren, and on down the line. This ground of transference would seem to account for little children having to endure this invasion of the powers of darkness.[11]

Koch, in his book **Demonology Past and Present**, comments on ancestral background:

Through investigating the background of numerous families in which mediumistic abilities are in evidence, I have discovered that when someone has the ability to use a pendulum or to practice mesmerism, one can predict with almost absolute certainty that he has had either a grandparent or a great-grandparent who has practiced magic charming. Magical charmers have descendants in the third and fourth generation who are mediumistically endowed. It is a fulfillment of the second commandment: 'I will visit the iniquity of the fathers on the children to the third and fourth generation of those that hate me.'

It is true that such mediumistic abilities are not a sin in themselves to the one who inherits them, but they are a burden. The Swiss Christian, Markus Hauser, who carried such abilities himself, freely admitted this.

Many times I have been told by Christians that when a person is converted he loses any mediumistic abilities that he may previously have had. This, however, is simply not true.[12]

Francis Frangipane discusses ancestral demons in his book **The Divine Antidote**:

It is also true that we ourselves may not have sinned, but we might be living under the curse of ancestral sins. These are the sins which have been passed down to us from our parents. To break ancestral curses, we must identify the unchristlike behavior we have inherited from our forefathers and then renounce it. Submitting our hearts to Christ for cleansing and ongoing transformation, we determine to build our lives upon the nature of Christ.[13]

M. Scott Peck, in his book, **The Road Less Traveled**, describes children's learning their parents' sins:

If a child sees his parents day in and day out behaving with self-discipline, restraint, dignity and a capacity to order their own lives, then the child will come to feel in the deepest fibers of his being that this is the way to live. If a child sees his parents day in and day out living without self-restraint or self-discipline, then he will come in the deepest fibers of being to believe that that is the way to live.[14]

Freeman, in his book **Victory Flight Over Powers of Darkness**, discusses dealing with the sins of ancestors:

Parents should repudiate and renounce sins of their ancestors as a definite act of renunciation to any invasion to demonic workings. On the basis of the finished work of the Lord Jesus Christ, parents can declare that all demonic workings that have been passed to them through the ancestral corridor is destroyed and all 'doors' to their lives are closed. This will begin the battle for victory as the faith principle comes against the powers of darkness. The victory may not be immediate, but it will come![15]

James Friesen, in his book **Uncovering the Mystery of M.P.D.**, mentions family spirits encountered as he works with M.P.D. counselees:

**Family Spirits**. Another kind of experience with a profound effect on a child's identity is the entrance of a 'family spirit.' I have been told by adult survivors from cult families that when they were young they were called to the deathbeds of their grandparents or other relatives and were given spirits from the dying relative. Those are known as 'family' or 'familiar' spirits and are passed down as part of the child's heritage. That child, or at least one altar of that child, receives the demon and gives it a place to attach. The child believes that the continuing presence of the demon proves he or she will always belong to the demon, or to Satan. 'You are in the line of Satan's followers. It is in your blood.'

This kind of attachment can be called a 'demonic stronghold.' The person's own strong belief that he or she is in union with the demon combines with the demonic strength and presents a powerful entanglement. The demonic voice rings out like a bell in the victim's head: 'You belong to Satan. You will always belong to Satan. You will do as you are told.' The inner fear and confusion that result keep the person constantly off balance, and the demonic possession deepens. The person gets weaker and the evil spirit gets stronger.[16]

Dickason, author of Demon Possession and the Christian, talks about ancestral involvement:

**Ancestral involvement**: Bondage, mediumistic abilities, and demonization are not transferred by genetic reproduction. Certain inherited and/or conditioned weaknesses may contribute toward one's seeking self-satisfaction through the occult, but the bondage is not inborn. However, if the parents back to the third and fourth generation were involved in the occult or had demonic abilities, then the children may be affected or even invaded as a legal judgment from God. Such is the effect of the warning in the second commandment. It is an unclean and wretched thing to worship dirty demons instead of the true and living God and His Son, Jesus Christ. God considers this a major evil (Jer. 2).

Worship of idols, ancestors, spirits, or gods of any sort other than God the Creator and Redeemer revealed in the Bible is essentially the worship of demons (Ps. 106:36-38; I Cor. 10:20).

The same principle of God's visiting the sins of the ancestors upon their descendants is found in Jeremiah 32:18, which says that God 'repayest the iniquity of fathers into the bosom of their children after them.' We read of this law applied to the descendants of Jeroboam. Because of the evil he had done, more than all who were before him, and because of his blatant idolatry, God promised to cut off all of his males in Israel so as to make a clean sweep of filth (I Kings 14:9-10). The same judgment came upon the house of Baasha, king of Israel, who led them to sin as did Jeroboam. God said, 'I will consume Baasha and his house' (I Kings 16:1-3). The principle is repeated for the house of Israel. Their judgment in removal from the land of promise was due to the sins of their forefathers and their own sins (Jer. 16:10-13).

Nehemiah recognized the propriety of such judgment, for the people deserved it (Neh. 9:33-37).

Some mistakenly think that God has revoked this judgment connected with the second commandment. They quote Ezekiel 18:1-4 where God condemns the misuse of the proverb 'The fathers eat the sour grapes, but the children's teeth are set on edge.' God retorts, 'As I live...you are surely not going to use this proverb in Israel anymore. Behold, all souls are Mine; the soul of the father as well as the soul of the son is Mine. The soul who sins will die.' Note that God does not refer directly to the second commandment but to the proverb that the rebels in Israel used to cast the guilt for their judgment back on their ancestors. God is saying that they cannot ignore their own guilt and blame their fathers. They have enough of their own guilt to cause His judgment. Furthermore, we note that Ezekiel lived in the same period as Jeremiah, who spoke of God's removal of Israel on the basis of the second commandment.

Further evidence that this principle is in effect today comes from the Lord Jesus in Matthew 23:32-36. He warns the leaders of Israel who are rejecting Him: 'Fill up then the measure of the guilt of your fathers.' He says he is sending them messengers whom they will also reject,

> *'that upon you may fall the guilt of all the righteous blood shed on earth, from the blood of righteous Abel to the blood of Zechariah, the son of Berechiah, whom you murdered between the temple and the altar. Truly I say to you, all these things shall come upon this generation.'*

Romans 1:21-32 describes the rebellion of the race and its descent into idolatry. In God's judgment for this, He gave them over to further sin and the penalty that results. This involved continuing the effects of God's judgment to the children of the idolatrous rebels. The visiting the sin of the fathers upon third and fourth generations is presented by Paul as a continuing principle of God's judgment.

I have found this avenue of ancestral involvement to be the chief cause of demonization. Well over 95 percent of more than 400 persons I have contacted in my counseling ministry have been demonized because of their ancestors' involvement in occult and demonic activities. This may involve the above sins and immoral sins connected with idolatry.[17]

Grayson H. Ensign and Edward Howe, in their book **Counseling and Demonization**, describe children's being affected by their ancestors:

**Cases involving children**. One of the most startling discoveries in our deliverance work has been the fact that evil spirits have in some way been able to invade some children from early childhood or even at birth. By invasion we mean to be present in the body so as to exercise some physical, emotional, or mental control. Some have gone into wild rages and have attacked parents or have torn at their own faces, bodies, etc. In some cases they have struck walls with their hands or heads, and when the children were demonized they manifested another personality as clearly defined as that seen in some adults. The parents often say, 'That simply is not my child that is acting and speaking in that way.' In some cases the very mention of phoning an elder for help has brought on violent reaction, threatening, and shouted defiance: 'Don't you dare call him!' 'I will tear the phone off the wall!' In a few cases the child has been brought to the elders with great effort because of violent resistance due to demonization. Yet these same children are good friends who normally go to the elders and show affection.

Since children have not sinned as morally responsible persons at these early years, we have concluded that the evil spirits must have been handed down to the children as a consequence of the 'Law of Generations' in Exodus 20:5: 'I the Lord your God, am a jealous God, visiting the iniquity of the fathers on the children on the third and fourth generations of those who hate me.' This was the testimony of evil spirits (whatever value you may place in their word though it was carefully checked by the test of truth). They declared they had a right to occupy the individuals because of the sins of the ancestors which often involved witchcraft, other occult behavior, or violent rebellion against God.

To us it seems highly probable that this includes in some cases the power of the evil spirits to pass from the ancestors who committed these abominable sins before the Lord into the children of the third and fourth generations. In one case, unknown to the person we were working with, her grandmother lay dying in the same state institution in which she was a patient. Upon the death of the grandmother, a demon left her body and entered into the body of the granddaughter. Dr. Koch reported that he had many such cases in his ministry. This does not mean that it inevitably happens, because there is the grace of God mediated through prayer and through the godly members of the same family or of the body of Christ which may prevent invasion.

It is standard procedure with us now to ask the Lord in deliverance sessions to break and nullify the working of the Law of Generations in the individuals with whom we are working.  We regularly ask the Lord to force into manifestation any ancestrally-derived demons that He knows need to be dealt with.[18]

Often as confirmation of what the Lord has just taught me, I hear testimonies from other people of God who have learned the same lessons.  As you can see from the previous quotes concerning the iniquities of the fathers, this truth holds firm today.  I know the quotes were long, but I believe that we must see that the Holy Spirit of God has taught a number of godly men this truth, and that it plays a major part in **Liberating the Bruised**.

## NOTES

1. Dr. Warren Baker, <u>The Complete Word Study, Old Testament</u>, p. 2348.
2. <u>Ibid</u>., p. 2347.
3. <u>Ibid</u>., p. 2299.
4. Spiros Zodhiates, Th.D.; <u>The Complete Word Study New Testament Lexical Aids to the New Testament</u>, p. 883
5. Bill Gothard, <u>The Life Purpose Journal</u>, #4, p. 7.
6. Dr. Warren Baker, <u>op</u>. <u>cit</u>., <u>Hebrew and Chaldee Dictionary</u>, p. 45.
7. <u>Ibid</u>., p. 84.
8. Bill Gothard, <u>op</u>. <u>cit</u>., p. 10.
9. <u>Ibid</u>., p. 11-13.
10. C. H. Spurgeon, <u>Treasury of David, Vol. II.</u>, p. 464.
11. Mark I. Bubeck, <u>The Adversary</u>, p. 87.
12. Kurt Koch, <u>Demonology Past and Present</u>, pp. 61, 62.
13. Francis Fragipane, <u>The Divine Antidote</u>, pp. 68, 69.
14. M. Scott Peck, M.D., <u>The Road Less Traveled</u>, pp. 21, 22.
15. Dr. Irwin Rocky Freeman, <u>Victory Flight Over Powers of Darkness</u>, p. 62.
16. James G. Friesen, Ph.D., <u>Uncovering the Mystery of M.P.D.</u>, p. 257.
17. C. Fred Dickason, <u>Demon Possession and the Christian</u>, pp. 219-221.
18. Grayson H. Ensign and Edward Howe, <u>Counseling and Demonization the Missing Link</u>, pp. 201-203.

# CHAPTER NINE
## THE EVILS THAT LURK WITHIN

As you may have guessed, I consider evils that lurk within to be any demonic ground that Satan has been allowed to establish in a person. Since there is so much material to cover in this chapter, I have chosen to divide it into three parts. Part one will cover Information About Ancestral Demons, part two will cover Information About Fragmented Personalities (Multiple Personality Disorders), and part three will cover Information About Counseling Techniques (for both ancestral demons and fragmented personalities).

## PART I

### INFORMATION ABOUT ANCESTRAL DEMONS

One of those evils that can lurk within a precious child of God is the ancestral demon. It's important for us to examine the biblical basis for dealing with ancestral demons.

### BIBLICAL BASIS FOR ANCESTRAL DEMONS

Let's begin by looking at Mark 9:1-32:

> *And he said unto them, Verily I say unto you, There be some of them that stand here, who shall not taste of death, till they have seen the kingdom of God come with power. And after six days, Jesus taketh with him Peter, James, and John, and leadeth them up into an high mountain, apart by themselves; and he was transfigured before them. And his raiment became shining, exceedingly white like snow, as no fuller on earth can whiten them. And there appeared unto them Elijah with Moses; and they were talking with Jesus. And Peter answered and said to Jesus, Master, it is good for us to be here; let us make three booths: one for thee, and one for Moses, and one for Elijah. For he knew not what to say; for they were very much afraid. And there was a cloud that overshadowed them; and a voice came out of the cloud, saying, This is my beloved Son; hear him. And suddenly, when they had looked round about, they saw no man any more, except Jesus only with themselves. And as they came down from the mountain, he charged them that they should tell no man what things they had seen, till the Son of man were risen from the dead. And they kept that saying to themselves, questioning one with another what the rising from the dead should mean. And they asked him, saying, Why say the scribes that Elijah must first come? And he answered and told them, Elijah verily cometh first, and restoreth all things; and how it is written of the Son of man, that he must suffer many things, and be treated with contempt. But I say unto you, Elijah is indeed come, and they have done unto him whatsoever they desired, as it is written of him. And when he came to his disciples, he saw a great multitude about them, and the scribes questioning with them. And straightway all the people, when they beheld him, were greatly amazed*

*and, running to him, greeted him. And he asked the scribes, What question ye with them? And one of the multitude answered and said, Master, I have brought unto thee my son, who hath a dumb spirit; and wherever he taketh him, he teareth him; and he foameth, and gnasheth with his teeth, and pineth away. And I spoke to thy disciples, that they should cast him out, and they could not. He answereth him, and saith, O faithless generation, how long shall I be with you? How long shall I endure you? Bring him unto me. And they brought him unto him; and when he saw him, straightway the spirit convulsed him; and he fell on the ground, and wallowed foaming. And he asked his father, How long ago is it since this came unto him? And he said, From a child. And often it hath cast him into the fire, and into the waters, to destroy him; but if thou canst do anything, have compassion on us, and help us. Jesus said unto him, if thou canst believe, all things are possible to him that believeth. And straightway the father of the child cried out, and said with tears, Lord, I believe; help thou mine unbelief. When Jesus saw that the people came running together, he rebuked the foul spirit, saying unto him, Thou dumb and deaf spirit, I charge thee, come out of him, and enter no more into him. And the spirit cried, and convulsed him greatly, and came out of him; and he was like one dead, insomuch that many said, He is dead. But Jesus took him by the hand, and lifted him up; and he arose. And when he was come into the house, his disciples asked him privately, Why could not we cast him out? And he said unto them, This kind can come forth by nothing, but by prayer and fasting. And they departed from there, and passed through Galilee; and he would not that any man should know it. For he taught his disciples, and said unto them, The Son of man is delivered into the hands of men, and they shall kill him; and after he is killed, he shall rise the third day. But they understood not that saying, and were afraid to ask him (NSSB).*

Looking closely at the above scripture, we can see the **reality of progressive revelation**. I was taught in seminary that **progressive revelation** is the gradual revealing of scripture. The Bible is the Living Word of God, and as we mature in the Lord, scriptures will come alive in different ways. They have more meat to their meaning, and will be more clearly understood because of our having experienced their truths. Such revelation is a continual unveiling of God's wisdom--wisdom needed to help us apply the scriptures to our lives.

In this passage, we see that Jesus told Peter, James, and John not to tell the other disciples what they had seen and heard until after He had risen from the dead, for until after the resurrection, none of them would understand what Jesus was talking about. We see evidence of that lack of understanding by the fact that Peter, James and John pondered Jesus' words: "And they kept the saying to themselves, questioning one with another what the rising from the dead should mean" (v. 10). Until the disciples experienced the death, burial, and resurrection of Christ and the coming of His Holy Spirit, they would not understand the words of Christ. While experience is not doctrine, the Holy Spirit does teach us and gives us wisdom concerning even the deep things in the Bible as we are ready to understand them. If the reader looks closely at the last sentence in the above scripture, he sees that the disciples were not ready to understand, "...they understood not that saying, and were afraid to ask him" (v. 32).

After Jesus and His disciples had come down from the mountain, the Lord saw the disciples being surrounded by a group of people and being questioned by the scribes. Jesus was told a father had brought his demonic son to them and that the disciples had not been able to heal him. The son's father appealed to Jesus about his son's condition, and Jesus stated that the people were **a faithless generation**, an **unbelieving generation**. I believe that Jesus was talking of the iniquity of the fathers, the **unbelief** that plagued their generation.

We see Jesus asking the father how long his son had been in that condition. Jesus never asked a question because He didn't know the answer; rather He asked a question to provide insight to those listening and to future generations (Jn. 6:5, 6; Jn. 11:42). He wanted all of us to understand--by the father's answer--that his son had been afflicted since childhood (in the Greek language, **childhood meaning infancy**). This shows that demons don't just affect the lives of people who have chosen to walk in sin. So, how <u>was</u> this demon able to enter an infant's life?

Remember my mentioning **progressive revelation**? I experienced it with reference to this passage. Although I had read that scripture many times, it wasn't until I actually started dealing with ancestral demons that the Holy Spirit confirmed (through His Word) that this child had been suffering from an ancestral demon since infancy. Upon studying the scripture, we can surmise that the ancestral demon came by way of the father's iniquity of unbelief, and that it had been there since the boy's infancy. We can see the father's struggling with this unbelief: Jesus said to the father, "...If thou canst believe, all things are possible to him that believeth. And straightway the father of the child cried out, and said with tears, Lord, I believe; help thou mine unbelief" (vv. 23,24).

We can also see why the demon did nothing when the disciples had tried to cast him out. The demon could not hear and could not speak to tell them that he wasn't hearing. So we see Jesus first address the father (the boy's authority) concerning his iniquity of unbelief, and then, address the demon: "...Thou dumb and deaf spirit, I charge thee, come out of him and enter no more into him. And the spirit cried, and convulsed him greatly, and came out of him" (v. 25). When the boy was healed and Jesus was back in the house with His disciples, they asked Him why they couldn't heal the boy. Jesus told them that "...this kind can come forth by nothing but by prayer and fasting" (v.29). It is important to keep in mind that Jesus had not yet ascended into heaven and returned in the form of the Holy Spirit to indwell every Christian to teach and give them wisdom and to give them the power to overcome their unbelief and temptations.

Years ago I counseled a man who had had a number of demons from whom he had gotten free. About a year later, however, he returned for counseling and expressed that he was very angry with God and with me. He said he had followed my instructions, but that the demons were back. I had told him to pray and read his Bible daily, get involved in a strong Bible-preaching, believing church, and not to go back into the lifestyle where he had picked up the demons. Angrily, he told me that he had done everything I had told him to do, but that the demons were back and he wanted to know why. I didn't have the answer, but I wanted to <u>know</u> the answer, and to help him. I began to fast and pray. It was during my usual daily reading of seven chapters of the Old Testament and nine chapters of the New that God began to teach me. While reading Mark, chapter nine, God began showing me answers involving ancestral demons.

God continued teaching me about the ancestral demon through counseling sessions as He enabled me, through Christ, to demand that the demon tell me his works. The ancestral demon confirmed that when the fathers passed down their iniquities to the next generation, Satan once again had sought out a means to try to use the reproductive cycle to control mankind--just as he sought to do so after the fall in the garden. The ancestral demon does such a deceptive work in making the person believe that all his feelings, actions, and attitudes are just his own, that the demon causes the person to **beat up** on himself for being a failure or a weakling.

## DAMAGE IN THE SOUL AREA

As I share further about the ancestral demon and other evils that can lurk within a person, it is important for you to keep chapter six in mind, where I shared about the soul and spirit being one and the same, rather than two. The four drawings showed that the Adamic nature was passed down to us (Genesis 3) through the fall of our ancestor Adam and that both non-Christians and Christians can have demons which invade and live in the soul area.

Whenever a person is emotionally, physically, or sexually abused, he suffers in the soul area. When a demon invades a person, it operates from the soul area. The actions of a person depend on what a person allows to go on in the area of his soul. Hopefully, the lost person will choose to be saved, at which time the Holy Spirit will indwell and seal his soul. And, hopefully, he will choose to consistently walk in the Spirit. Galatians 5:16 says we should determine to "...walk in the Spirit, and ye shall not fulfill the lust of the flesh."

The reader must remember that the Christian will have the godly mind, will, and emotions of Christ ever-present within him. Anytime he chooses to submit to Christ's spiritual mind, will and emotions that are permanently sealed within him by the Holy Spirit, he will be able to properly deal with things. The body operates according to the Christian's choices--whether he chooses to allow **the old man** (walking in accordance with the old **Adamic nature**) or the **new man** (walking in the power of the Holy Spirit) to control his life. The Christian's choices must be made moment by moment. Remember, the **flesh** is not referring to our bodies but rather to **our mind, will, and emotions that operate from the soul area** (Galatians 5:16).

Since ancestral demons and their networks can take up residence in the soul area, one can understand why a person can get saved but still have strongholds in the soul area that can manipulate and control his life. As the Bible student searches the Word of God, there is considerable evidence that our soul can be shattered or fragmented. We must face the issue that we are clay vessels with breakable souls. Our souls or personalities can be broken or crushed. There is proof in the scriptures:

> *The Lord is nigh unto them that are of a broken heart and saveth such as be of a contrite spirit (Ps. 34:18; NSSB).*

> *Reproach hath broken my heart and I am full of heaviness: and I looked for some to take pity, but there was none; and for comforts, but I found none (Ps. 69:20; NSSB).*

> *Because that he remembered not to show mercy, but persecuted the poor and needy man, that he might even slay the broken hearted (Ps. 109:16; NSSB).*

*A merry heart maketh a cheerful countenance: but by sorrow of the heart the spirit is broken (Prov. 15:13; NSSB).*

*A merry heart doeth good like a medicine: but a broken spirit drieth the bones (Prov. 17:22; NSSB).*

*The Spirit of the Lord is upon me, because he hath anointed me to preach the gospel to the poor; he hath sent me to heal the brokenhearted, to preach deliverance to the captives and recovering of sight to the blind to set at liberty them that are bruised (Lk. 4:18; NSSB).*

The Greek word for **broken** used in Luke 4:18 is **suntribo** and it means **to crush completely, to shatter, break (in pieces), broken to shivers (hearted), bruise.**[1]

The Hebrew word for broken used in Psalm 34:18 and 69:20 is **shabar** and it means to **burst, break (down, off, in pieces, up), broken (hearted), bring to the birth, crush, destroy, hurt, quench...**[2] The Hebrew word for **broken** used in Proverbs 15:13 and 17:22 is **naka** and it means **to be smitten, afflicted: broken, stricken, wounded.**[3] The Hebrew word for **broken** that is used in Psalm 109:16 is **kaah** and it means **to despond; to deject: to be broken, be grieved, made sad.**[4]

## RESTORATION OF THE SOUL

Through these verses and definitions, we can see our soul can be crushed, broken, wounded, bruised and shattered. However, God identifies the culprit in His Word, and shows us how to deal with him. God, in His love, offers restoration and freedom. In Psalm 23 David speaks of the Lord restoring man's soul. Look at the Hebrew word for **restoreth**. **Shuwb** means **to turn back, fetch home again, get (oneself) back again.**[5] **Restoreth** carries the idea of returning to the point of departure, and fetching home or getting oneself back--the one that God thought up. To **restore one's soul**, the **prayer of renunciation** (concerning claiming back ground and given in a previous chapter) can be prayed. If someone prays this prayer but the problem still persists, then the person must undergo deeper counseling.

## THE ANCESTRAL DEMON TAKES THE VICTIM'S FORMAL NAME

God tells me in Jeremiah 33:3 and in James 1:5, that if I seek Him, He will teach me the deep things of God that I need to know. In time, God taught me another essential truth concerning the ancestral demon. I learned that it takes the victim's formal name, and creates a flip-side--a second personality that splits off from the core personality that was thought up by God. I must share at this point that I have attempted to contact all the people whose cases involved ancestral demons that I counseled before I knew about the demon assuming the formal name, to explain what God has shown me. After explaining what God has shown me about the ancestral demon's taking the person's formal name, I guide them to pray, asking God to remove from their life the ancestral demon carrying their formal name and his network, and send them to the pit. If the person senses a relief, then that work is completed. Most have been able to deal with it this simply and quickly. For those who still have

struggles, I must have them come in for further counseling, but few have had to come back. I believe that the fact that few have returned is the Lord's confirmation that what He has shown me is truth.

## EXISTENCE OF A "FLIP-SIDE" PERSONALITY (James 1:8, 4:8)

Where have I acquired scriptural authority concerning a **flip-side personality**? There is a Greek word **dipsuchos** which literally means **two-souled or split-souled**. The word is found only in two places in the entire Bible and both are in the book of James. The first is in James 1:8, the second, in James 4:8 and both are translated **double-minded**. It is very important for us to keep in mind that the book of James was written to Christians on the very critical subject of spiritual warfare. Thus, this helps us better understand what James is saying in these verses. If one makes a paradigm shift from just viewing this the way it has always been viewed (that a double-minded person is one who simply can't make up his mind or keeps changing his mind) to viewing this as a two-souled or split-souled person that James is referring to, it can take on the deeper concept of a flip-sided person.

If the iniquity of the fathers has passed down to an individual in the form of a curse or an ancestral demon, the ancestral demon is already there within the Adamic nature hoping to manipulate the core personality--the one God thought up--and split it off into a second personality, which I have chosen to call the **flip-side**. (In the clinical realm, they refer to the flip-side as the split or host personality.) When I find an **ancestral demon**, I find a **flip-side**; when I find a **flip-side**, I find an **ancestral demon**.

The ancestral demon holding the iniquities of the fathers passed down or visited on him, works to **program the flip-side** with his personality. I find it essential to look for the ancestral demon and the flip-side first in my counselees. If they are indeed present, their discovery alone helps alleviate a great amount of confusion and extra work.

Along with understanding the illustrations of body, soul and spirit shown in chapter six, we need to understand the illustration of the flip-side's being like a coin. Look at the face of a quarter. The person with **a flip-side is like a quarter, having two sides but being one whole**. If you look at an actual quarter, you will see that the flip-side of the coin is not only the back of the coin, but that it is upside down. One might say it's the negative side. (As stated previously, the Hebrew word **awah** means **iniquity and to turn upside down**.) If the flip-side is upright, the face is upside down, head first, just as Satan would have our lives. But let us remember, however, that when the coin is tossed in the air--whether it lands on its face or on its back--the value remains the same. The Bible tells us in Psalm 139:16 that each one of us is a thought of God--valuable, not a sexual happenstance.

We must realize that even before we were in the womb God already knew our formal names and whether or not we--our core personality--would accept or reject God's offer of salvation through Jesus Christ. When God thought us up, He had a very good plan for our lives--a godly lifestyle--if we chose to follow Him. His plan was complete (Acts 15:18; Hebrews 4:4). However, when each child is conceived in the womb, his core personality has the fallen Adamic nature, along with a free will to choose his own path. Of course Satan prefers that the child follow <u>his</u> alternate pathway.

Ancestral demons mimic God, trying to act out the role of God's ability to create. When an ancestral demon succeeds in creating a flip-side, this personality is activated and controlled by the ancestral demon. God revealed to me that the ancestral demon views the flip-side as his creation, even though it is really an intricate part of the core personality. From the womb the ancestral demon assumes and usurps the formal name of the core personality and leaves the flip-side without a formal name-- nameless or a degrading name. The flip-side becomes his formal ground, and he runs his operation from there. He can also cause fragmented personalities (which I will explain shortly) that you find in **M.P.D. (Multiple Personality Disorder)** counselees.

The **flip-side** has been there as long as the core personality has, and, usually, but not always has control over the core personality. The **flip-side personality** may range from a weak, insecure one, to an aggressive, demanding one. While it very seldom carries the core personality's name, it typically takes on names reflecting confusion, insecurity, and/or rebellion, such as "I don't have a name"; "I don't know my name"; "I don't know"; "I have no name"; "No name"; "No body"; "Just me"; "Anger"; "Bitterness"; etc. It may even create another personality and appoint it as a type of caretaker. An ancestral demon nearly always magnifies stress and panic, causing the personality to fragment further.

The ancestral demon stays hidden doing his work from the inside while the core personality is growing and developing his own lifestyle. If the **flip-side** yields to the demon's suggestions, the ancestral demon can program into the **flip-side** such things as manic-depressive; paranoia; schizophrenia; lust; anger; fear; bitterness; eating disorders; etc. The **demon programs the flip-side** to work against the core personality to cause confusion and to hinder the person's belief and trust in God.

When the core personality gets saved, the **flip-side** really starts causing confusion and opposition toward the core personality, who is now desiring to grow in Christ. All hell seems to break loose in the person's life; for, in most cases, the **flip-side** refuses to accept Jesus Christ and continues its work for the ancestral demon.

I don't want to confuse the reader, but until the **flip-side** is found, accepts the Lord Jesus just as the core personality did, and is fused and integrated, that person will never have a consistent, strong Christian walk and abundant life. This is why it is essential to deal with the ancestral demon and the **flip-side** first. **It is necessary for the flip-side to reclaim the ground and break all ancestral ties**, and for the ancestral demon to be thrown out. **The core personality usually isn't even aware of the flip-side or the ancestral demon**. Thinking he is just not capable of being a good Christian, he blames and beats up on himself. He tells himself that he should read and study the Bible more, go to church and give more, etc, yet none of these efforts make him feel better for long. I believe that this is why so many Christians become discouraged and easily backslide, with some ceasing to attend church altogether. Before we further discuss the flip-side and the ancestral demon, perhaps you will find the following chart helpful.

# "INIQUITY OF THE FATHERS"
# ADAMIC NATURE

## CORE PERSONALITY

Thought up and created by God from the beginning

Formal name

"For He has spoken in a certain place of the seventh in this way: And God rested on the seventh day from **all** his works."
(Hebrews 4:4)

"Your eyes saw my substance being yet unformed. And in your book they all were written, the days fashioned for me, when as yet there were none of them."
(Psalms 139:16)

Choice to accept God and salvation or to remain lost.

## FLIP-SIDE PERSONALITY

Activated and manipulated by the ancestral demon who uses the core personality's form name

Typical names flip-sides choose:

| | |
|---|---|
| I Don't Have A Name | Nobody |
| I Don't Know My Name | Just Me |
| I Don't Know | Anger |
| Bitterness | No Name |

Terms sometimes used in describing a flip-side:

| | |
|---|---|
| Manic Depressive | Paranoia |
| Schizophrenia | Eating disorders |

". . . For I, the Lord your God, am a jealous God, visiting the iniquity of the fathers upon the children to the third and fourth generations of those who hate me, but showing mercy to thousands, to those who love me and keep my commandments."
(Exodus 20:5-6; 34:7; Number 14:18; Deuteronomy 5:9)

## THE ANCESTRAL DEMON BUILDS A NETWORK

The **ancestral demon** carrying the formal name of the core personality is **usually not alone**. Typically, he has a **network of demons** with him to help carry out the program **in the flip-side's personality**. This network is directly under the authority of the ancestral demon carrying the core personality's formal name. The ancestral demon is a **power demon** working with the same kind of authority held by territorial demons, which are those assigned specifically to a particular area, such as a community, city, county, state, etc. The power demon is in charge of what goes on in the person's life through **using the flip-side** to control the individual. There can be other ancestral demons and lifestyle demons but they will all answer to the ancestral demon carrying the formal name.

I have found in working with counselees that there seem to be several kinds of demons in the average demonic person's life. There is an **ancestral demon** that carries the **formal name** and the demons he calls in to help him do his work. Then, there can also be **other ancestral demons and demon-produced personalities** of persons generations back from which the ancestral demons came. There can be **lifestyle demons** that are picked up as a result of the person's choosing a sinful lifestyle--such as demons acquired by involvement with the occult, those acquired from drug use and drinking, and those acquired during sexual promiscuity. The latter are often picked up during both voluntary and involuntary sexual acts, particularly those committed during incest. Often, lifestyle demons bring with them demon-produced personalities of the person from whom they transferred. There **can also be demons that masquerade as personalities**, trying to make the counselor believe that they are just fragmented personalities.

# PART II

## INFORMATION ABOUT FRAGMENTED PERSONALITIES (MULTIPLE PERSONALITY DISORDER)

### MULTIPLE PERSONALITY DISORDER, M.P.D.

At this point, let's talk about M.P.D. and how to deal with persons having it. I am grateful for the instructive teachings of Jerry Mugadeze, Ph.D., James G. Friesen, Ph.D., M. Scott Peck, M.D., C. Fred Dickason, Th.D., Kurt Koch, Th.D., and Grayson H. Ensign and his partner Edward Howe, from which I have gleaned much valuable information. Each of them has written material that is available for anyone desiring to study in-depth clinical terms and techniques. These men counsel people with Multiple Personality Disorders--the clinical name for a coping mechanism of dissociating into different personality states. They believe, as I do, that the main feature of this disorder is the existence of one or more distinct personalities living and operating from within a person. These personalities were brought into existence by some type of major trauma, by a destructive lifestyle, or perhaps by the work of an ancestral demon in the victim's life.

While there is a wide variety of technical names for different types of dissociation, I have felt impressed by the Lord to simplify the matter as much as possible, in order that even the most novice of counselors can understand and apply these methods to help set hurting souls free. I have found that the majority of my counselees work more readily with me in the realm of simplicity. I call all

dissociations from the core personality **fragmented personalities**, except for the **flip-side**, which I discussed previously.

Out of my years of ministry, I have learned that with the Lord Jesus Christ leading the counseling sessions, the most complicated cases can be made simple. In John 10:10 the Lord said "The thief cometh not but to steal, and to kill, and to destroy; I am come that they might have life, and that they might have it abundantly." As a Christian and a counselor, I believe and have experienced repeatedly what Jesus said about His being there for us. We see this in Matthew 18:20: "For where two or three are gathered together in my name, there am I in the midst of them." He has also consistently proved to me that I can do all things through Him (Phil. 4:13) and that He will provide for all my needs (Phil. 4:19). He also said if I am lacking wisdom, I am just to ask Him for it (Jms. 1:5), and He assures me that He has provided me with all spiritual blessings (Eph. 1:3) in order that His work might be done.

Paul even warned Christians against complicating things when he said, "But I fear lest by any means as the serpent beguiled Eve through his (craftiness) so your minds should be corrupted from the simplicity that is in Christ" (II Cor. 11:3). As we continue our journey through a subject that can be very complicated, the knowledge of everything I say and teach has come from the classroom of God's counseling course.

## UNDERSTANDING FRAGMENTED PERSONALITIES

Fragmented personalities are additional personalities created from the mind--the vulnerable imaginative part of the core personality--as a result of demonic influence during and/or after traumatic experiences. Fragmented personalities come about as some people's means of coping, or escaping into a fantasy world. They are much like actors and actresses role-playing, putting aside who they really are. If the core personality is to get well, the person must choose to assume responsibility for his life and to not hide from the reality of M.P.D.. Whether or not a person becomes demonic depends on a person's choices. While I have found fragmented personalities without demons and ancestral demons, that generally is not the case. Most of the time I also find ancestral demons and/or lifestyle demons.

God has shown me that the ancestral demon works from the inside of a person. For example, in **S.R.A. (Satanic Ritualistic Abuse)** victims, the satanic abuse from the outside causes trauma inside. Those performing the abuse hope to have the person create fragments (clinically known as alters), which can be programmed by demons to carry out the torment work. The ancestral demon, like satanic abuse and torment, can cause the fragmentation, but he often does it unnoticed from the inside, without the victim's or others' knowledge. If there is an ancestral demon in a person with M.P.D., he views that flip-side as his formal ground and the first fragmented personality as his first fruit and all the others as his offspring. Until the counselor discovers all the personalities, the ancestral demon has ground to stay.

## CASTING DOWN IMAGINATIONS FROM SATAN

Once again we see why God warned us of the necessity of casting down imaginations with which Satan bombards us. After a person has gone through a traumatic experience of any kind, God appeals to him to listen to and heed His solutions, while Satan offers his destructive advice. When some people consistently remain focused on the trauma and listen to Satan's imaginations, fragmented personalities can be created and demons can invade. Fragmented personalities have been created by Satan with the intent to destroy or at least prevent the core personality from fulfilling God's plan for his precious life.

If the core personality allows Satan to achieve these fragmentations, each new fragmented personality claims their age to be whatever age the core personality was at the time the trauma took place. They usually select names for themselves and perform a work related to the state of their emotions at the time of the trauma.

While some of these created personalities may not perform what we would consider evil actions, their behavior is not of God, and works as a hindrance to the core personality's becoming what God created him to be. For example, let's say a person experienced a trauma, feeling fearful and hopeless, instead of turning to the Lord, they chose to cling to the memories, withdraw from people and cry most of the time. On the other hand, the core personality who is falling apart on the inside may fragment, allowing a new personality to act tough and strong to get necessary jobs done. God doesn't want His child robbed of His fellowship and the peace and joy of walking in His will. The core personality is the one that God thought up, and is the only one that should be in existence if the counselee is to be totally healed--the core is the only one that can legitimately get saved.

Since fragments are formed from trauma, let's look at some situations we would consider traumatic. Trauma can be caused from a number of things, from mild stress to uncontrollable panic. For instance, trauma can range from a child's being **"the new kid on the block"** to being cruelly and sexually abused. Trauma can come from stress within or without the home, or both. Some trauma may come from being ridiculed and rejected by people for being too fat or two skinny. Intellectual weaknesses can cause poor grades and can result in a teacher embarrassing the child in front of classmates, causing more trauma--with the child now **feeling rejected and different--feeling he doesn't fit in.**

## DUTIES OF FRAGMENTED PERSONALITIES

As the counselor begins to identify **personalities**, they may start surfacing **in different types of categories**. While some fragments are enormous **hindrances**, some perform as **helpers**. While the onlooker may think the core personality is performing, the **fragmented personalities** are actually **up** and **executing the work**. The core is only functioning in cooperation with the fragments, much like a robot or one hypnotized. There are some fragmented persecutors who attempt to condemn and stifle the core personality's emotions altogether. The fragmented helper personalities might do the housework, cooking, sewing and other household duties. Some personalities perform sex, some keep finances in order, and some hold down a career. There are even those who hide memories from the core personality to protect the person from further hurt.

If there are a number of personalities, the counselor should first find the **delegator personality--such as a mother, baby-sitter, or caretaker who was created to control.** The delegator personality organizes, bosses, and takes care of all the other personalities. **The delegator usually creates a personality that controls and stays up a large portion of the time to run the person's life.** He usually views the core personality as incompetent. Most of the time he has a negative view of any kind of counseling, because of the threat of not being in charge or control. I have found that much of the time, the flip-side will do this work. I usually try to help heal this personality first in order to achieve a more positive, non-competitive mode.

## PERSONALITIES DISCOVERED THROUGH STRESS

Many of these personalities are there to help the core personality live some kind of near-normal life. Other personalities, however, are only discovered when something causes major stress resulting in the **group panicking** and causing emotional or mental road blocks. This confusion causes the core personality to lose **it emotionally or mentally**. When this happens, the person often suffers major time loss (time they cannot account for) or memory loss. Their friends and family will start asking them things such as, "Don't you remember discussing that with me?" or "I told you all about that yesterday. Weren't you listening?"

I have also found that when a fragmented person has a **major lifestyle change**, such as moving, changing jobs, or even getting married, stress increases and personalities can start acting up. For example, the person's suffering a divorce can cause personalities to act up. The core personality may then realize that something is wrong with him. Divorce definitely causes an enormous amount of stress that will cause personalities that fear rejection or being alone to act up. This is not to say that a person without fragmented personalities will not feel the extreme hurt and stress from such a situation, but the person with fragmented personalities will **fly out of control**.

Repeatedly, I have found that the greatest pressure experienced by the lost, fragmented person comes when he gets saved and determines to have a closer walk with the Lord and to walk in His Spirit. Understandably so, all hell seems to break loose. If the pastor, loved one, or counselor of such a person is on their toes, he will see depression set in, and quickly offer help. The Bible says in Proverbs 12:25, "Anxiety in the heart of man causes depression, but a good word makes it glad" **(The Christian Life Bible New King James Version)**.[6] I believe that anxiety is worry, doubt, fear, and guilt. These are not to be in a Christian's life. When we see anxiety in someone's life, it is **a red flag** drawing attention to something being wrong. When a Christian keeps telling a pastor or counselor that he is reading his Bible and praying, but can't get free from interference such as hearing voices of accusation and condemnation, I recommend that the pastor or counselor make sure that all known sins are confessed, and then look for an ancestral demon or fragmented personality. I believe that any dedicated lay person or pastor can successfully lead such as person to victory.

## PART III

## INFORMATION ABOUT COUNSELING TECHNIQUES (ANCESTRAL DEMONS AND FRAGMENTED PERSONALITIES)

### COUNSELING TECHNIQUES

Most of my counselees come from three sources: By referral from other counselees with the same type of problems; by referral from pastors and Christians who know of my ministry; and by referral from a counselee's therapist. Sometimes, the pastor, leader, or therapist comes with them. When the counselee comes, he already, to some degree, has been schooled on who I am and why he needs to

come, as well as what we will be doing. Most of my people are not new in the counseling arena, so most of the preparatory work has already been done. This is especially true with those who come from other counselors. Due to this, the diagnosis of multiple personality disorder has usually already been made. It is my job to help make the counselee feel comfortable and safe so that we can go right to work. Sometimes making a person realize that he is safe is the most time-consuming part. Making him feel safe sometimes requires just letting him talk and ask questions. If the counselee has a good relationship with the pastor or counselor who referred him and that person will come with him, much time and effort will be saved.

I believe it is essential for the counselor to listen to enough of the counselee's story to gain the information necessary to expose the ground demons have in the person's life. There is, however, no goodly purpose in gathering all the gory details. To the contrary, I must stress that the counselor can be in danger of demonic entrapment by a demon luring him with curiosity to listen to excessive, vulgar details! I caution even the most godly counselor to gather only what is <u>absolutely</u> <u>essential</u> to get the job done and to oust the demons!

I cannot stress enough the necessity of the counselor's <u>not</u> embarking upon such counseling unless he is certain that his life is clean before the Lord! I believe that one of the biggest mistakes a counselor can make is to think that he can flippantly live a double-standard life. If the counselor is to successfully and safely deal with the demonic, he must sincerely repent of any known sins in his life. For instance, he must be free from any lying or deceitfulness. There is no place for any type of impure thoughts or immoral acts if he expects to thoroughly help his counselee. He must be careful not to harbor any unforgiveness, bitterness, or anger. He must not be resentful or jealous of others. It is imperative that he has a close walk with the Lord, spending time with Him in prayer and reading His Word. He must also remember neither to be afraid nor arrogant, for it is the Lord Jesus who is the victor over the powers of darkness.

**Before I begin the counseling session, I make certain that the counselee sincerely wants help, wants to be free, and is willing to work toward accomplishing that goal**. No matter how confusing Satan might make one think the session will be, it is important to remember that God is a God of order, and if one stays in tune with Him and obeys Him, He will unravel all the confusion with His wisdom, and the counseling session will go very well.

### HYPNOSIS IS NOT NEEDED

God taught me how to find the demons and personalities without using hypnosis. I believe hypnosis is sorcery--part of the occult. When I asked God how I could help free people from demonic strongholds and fragmented personalities, He showed me James 1:5: **"If any of you lack wisdom, let him ask of God, who giveth to all men liberally, and upbraideth not, and it shall be given him."** As I sought His wisdom, He was faithful to teach me how to accomplish this.

### THE CORE PERSONALITY PARTICIPATES

To begin a counseling session I first make certain that the counselee is sincere and serious about wanting help. I then pray, asking God to do these things:

Sweet Father, I want Satan and all his demonic powers bound, gagged and rendered totally inoperative so that they cannot cause any confusion or misunderstanding, nor misappropriate and block any truths being shared. If there is an ancestral demon and his network, I want him bound and gagged and rendered inoperative. Lord Jesus, if there are any fragmented personalities or a flip-side, I want them in a safe place with Jesus. I want to talk to and deal with the core personality that you thought up from the foundation of the world and that you love so very much. I want a shield of your blood separating the core personality from all the rest. And Lord, I want to see with your eyes, hear with your ears, and comprehend with your mind. Lord, I want to speak with your mouth and love this precious person with your heart. I want them healed by your loving hand. Papa, we want your precious Son's blood surrounding us and protecting us from all evil while we work. It is in the name of Jesus that I pray.

After I have answered any questions the counselee has about my counseling procedures, I check as thoroughly as possible to make sure the counselee is saved, for the Lord Jesus is the only solution. Then, I pray:

Lord, I want the **core personality of June Lea Doe, who is 35 years old and was saved at age 15**, not to be allowed to interfere, yet permitted to hear all that goes on. Place her with You with a shield of your blood separating everything else from her so that we can find and meet whomever we need to work with today.

Sometimes the ancestral demon will actually talk to me but most of the time he just relays the answers to my questions directly to the core personality's mind. Because of this, it is essential to instruct the core personality to be a reporter, accurately reporting everything he is hearing in his mind, no matter how frightening, offensive, or embarrassing.

## CONTACTING THE ANCESTRAL DEMON

The **ancestral demon** carrying the formal name of the core personality is **the power demon in charge**. I usually always deal with him first, because he <u>is</u> the one in charge. **I command the ancestral demon to tell me what he does in the counselee's life. I ask the demon how many demons there are in his personal network, how many types of demons there are, what their names are, and what work they do in the counselee's life. I also make the demon tell me the flip-side's name, and whether or not there are any fragmented personalities. The ancestral demon is the only demon you have to talk to in order to get all the information needed.** I have found that even though demons are liars and are untrustworthy, I still get a lot of information from them that shortens my counseling time. **The ancestral demon will tell you the flip-side's name, the number of fragmented personalities, and their names and ages. Sometimes, he thinks he knows the names of all the personalities, but sometimes he does not**. However, I have found that he generally gives their correct ages. I have found this to be true because each fragmented personality often claims to be the age that the demon has given.

As you can surmise, the demons will lie to you--**the Devil <u>is</u> the father of all lies. It is essential to check out their answers** by asking, "By the blood of the Lord Jesus, does that answer stand as truth before the eternal throne of Jesus Christ?" Even then I sometimes have to ask them several times until I have a peace that they answered me honestly. Then I ask God to bind, gag, and render inoperative all the demons until I need to address them again.

## MAKING CONTACT WITH THE FLIP-SIDE

**This is when I ask God to show me if there is a flip-side personality**. When there is a flip-side, I handle it before dealing with any fragmented personalities. This makes the rest of the work go much smoother. When the flip-side personality from the ancestral demon surfaces, I ask God to make it cooperate with me. I make certain that it is the flip-side by getting it to tell me **how old it is and what name it carries.** It will be the **same age as the core personality**; but, as I've said, most of the time it does not carry the formal name, since the ancestral demon is claiming that name. You recall that **the flip-side usually takes a name like** "I Don't Know," "I Don't Have A Name," or "My Name Is Nobody," "Anger," "Bitterness," etc.

Let's say that I have established that I am actually talking to **a woman's flip-side**. I then ask her **to tell me about herself, what she thinks about the core personality, and what she does in the core personality's life.** Perhaps the flip-side identifies herself as "I Don't Know," tells me that she is thirty-five years old, and doesn't want to talk with me. I then ask, "Why?" (They usually readily answer me.) I then ask what she does in June Lea Doe's life and gather information. I get her to tell me about herself and **what major emotions motivate her life**. Sometimes the personality will be very angry, mean, vulgar, and resistant. I use the Word of God to answer her every time she argues. If the core personality is saved, the flip-side personality eventually gives in. I ask her why she, the flip-side, didn't get saved (which is typically the case). It would amaze you to hear some of the excuses I have been given. Most of the time it will tell me, "I just didn't want to," "I didn't want to let go of control," or "I didn't need Jesus and don't believe all that stuff." When she finally submits to conviction, I ask her if she would like to enjoy having the Jesus that June has. If she says yes and seems sincere, I guide her to pray a prayer that will include confessing all the things that she feels have been done to hurt her and include all her sins as well. Here is an example of such a prayer:

> I, **flip-side** thirty-five year old **I Don't Know**, confess that Jesus Christ is the Son of God. He is the God that became flesh and dwelled among His people. He never did anything wrong but the people all did a lot of wrong things to Him. They rejected Him and treated Him as evil. They stripped Him naked, beat Him with a whip, shamed Him, tormented Him, and nailed Him to the tree. Jesus became all of mankind's and flip-side **I Don't Know's** evil and sin, so they would have an opportunity and choice to become His goodness. And, Lord Jesus, you became all my sin and the sin of those who hurt me. (At this point, I get her to name each sin that she and others committed pertaining to her.)

> Lord, those sins killed you. My sin put you in the ground three days and three nights, and God raised you from the grave and you are the Living Lord and Savior. You have victory over the grave, death, and all the sin that was done to me or by me. So, Lord Jesus, I, thirty-five year old **I Don't Know**, confess that You are man's only way to be saved, free, and secure. I repent of all the sins that you became and I ask you to come into my heart and save and forgive me. Heal me, cleanse me, and deliver me from all that I have been. (Get her to name her sins again.) Thank you, Jesus.

## FUSING AND INTEGRATING THE CORE PERSONALITY AND THE FLIP-SIDE

**After leading the flip-side personality to the Lord**, then it is essential to **fuse and integrate it with the core personality.** This is done by having both the flip-side and core personality receive each other. While they must recognize they are one, it is also necessary that they understand and agree that **the core personality is boss**. I guide the flip-side to pray:

> Lord Jesus, please deliver me from being separated from thirty-five year old June Lea Doe who was saved at age fifteen. Deliver me from my name I Don't Know. I want a new name. (I have learned to let the fragmented personality pick a new name. Most of the time they will want to join in sharing the formal name. However, if the major emotion was anger, they sometimes pick a nickname, such as a name of an emotion, like **Joy**.) Lord Jesus, I want to be a part of June Lea Doe if she will have me. June, now that Jesus lives in my life and I am no longer I Don't Know filled with anger but now **June Lea Doe filled with joy**, I want to be a part of your life if you will have me. Lord Jesus, if June will have me, make us one. And, Lord, by the power of your blood I claim back the ground that the ancestral demon and all his network has stood on. They no longer have a right to be here, and Lord, when you are ready, I want them to go to the pit.

At this point, **I ask God to keep her in a safe place with His blood hedging about her**. Then I ask God to let me speak with the core personality, June Lea Doe, who is thirty-five years old and got saved at age fifteen. When I have her back, knowing that she has heard and been a part of the whole session, I ask her if she would be willing to ask Joy to come and be one with her. If she agrees, which is usually the case, I guide her to pray in the following manner:

> Lord Jesus, thank you for showing me **I Don't Know** who now has my Jesus, shares my name, and has a new name of Joy. Thank you that she will no longer live out her lifestyle sin of anger (etc.) through my life. Lord Jesus, please **fuse and integrate Joy that used to be I Don't Know with thirty-five-year-old June Lea Doe, saved at age fifteen, and make us one.** Lord Jesus, by your powerful blood, I command the demons that have stood on **I Don't Know's ground** to give it up and when you are ready, I want them in the pit. I break all ties and claim back all ground given to the ancestral demon.

## FUSING AND INTEGRATING AS YOU GO ALONG BECOMES ENCOURAGEMENT

I have found that if it is possible, as a whole, it is very beneficial to fuse and integrate as you proceed. The results of this process is a great encouragement because the counselee begins to notice marked improvement in their behavior from one session to the next. This helps strengthen their hope and faith. An exception to the process of fusing and integrating as you go, only lies in the case of a caretaker.

## LOOKING FOR A CARETAKER

**After I have dealt with the flip-side, I proceed to look for other personalities**. During this process, I carefully watch the expression and body movements of the person. Expressions and body movements often reflect the role the personality plays, helping the counselor more easily recognize the type of personality. If the data that I gather indicates that there are a number of personalities, I first search to see if there is a personality in charge of other personalities. I pray, doing the same thing as I did with the flip-side, but ask the Lord Jesus to only bring out the **one in charge of the other personalities.**

At this point, I pray, asking God to **bind the ancestral demon and any other demons** so that they cannot pretend to be any of the personalities I am looking for. Then I begin addressing and dealing with the fragmented personalities:

> If there is a caretaker such as a teacher, mother, or a delegator, please come out and talk to me. (I also check to see if there is a baby-sitter who is in charge of the children.)

If there is a personality that does this, I will first guide him to deal with all the issues and sins that led to his coming into existence, then I lead him to the Lord. However, at this point, I will **wait to fuse and integrate him** with the core personality unless he is anxious to do so. I then ask the personality to tell me about all the **other fragmented personalities** that are **under his charge**, including their **names, ages, and duties**.

After I have gained this information, I then ask the one in charge to help me to meet each fragmented personality. As I meet each one, I will go through the same procedure. I allow them to tell God all their hurts and emotions, to confess their sins, and to take those sins to the cross. Each time I lead one to the Lord, I ask God to put it in a safe place with Jesus, the caretaker, and the other personalities until I meet all the personalities under the control of the caretaker. After I have found and dealt with them all, I have the caretaker bring back all the others so that I can give the core personality the opportunity to receive them all at the same time. However, I will address each one by his old and new name, making it a personal experience for each fragment. This individual attention to each fragment allows the core to acknowledge each one's existence and work in the core's life, and help the core to **receive** him.

After I have found, dealt with, and **fused and integrated all the fragments, and the core personality is whole again, then I call up--by the power of the blood of Jesus--the ancestral demon and all other demons**. I command him to call in all his demon network, along with all demon-produced personalities, and have them attach themselves to him. Then, I command him by the authority and blood of Jesus Christ to **tell me if they hold any other ground** that would keep me from sending them to the pit. If his answer **is no and stands as truth before the eternal throne of Jesus Christ**, then I ask Jesus to send them to the pit.

There are times when they **refuse to leave** because **they have ground to remain**--some kind of unconfessed sin in the core personality's life. If this is the case, I command them to tell me what ground they are holding. If there is ground, I ask the core personality to repent of it and deal with it.

After the core has dealt with that sin, but ground is still being held, there may be yet another personality or demon to deal with. There are also times when the demons simply lie about having more ground in order to stall their departure.

**As a precaution**, before sending the ancestral demon and his network to the pit, **I check** to see whether or not there are any more **fragments** by asking the Lord Jesus to bring any **stragglers** out to meet me. I pray:

> Lord Jesus, if there are any other fragments that will keep this person from being whole, I want to meet them. Lord, is there anyone between the ages of zero to five? (Deal with them as each comes forth.) Lord, is there anyone from ages 6 through 12; 13 through 19; 20 through 29; 30 through 35? (Move forward until you reach the age of the person.)

**Once this step is taken and you have a peace, it's time to set the captive free and liberate the bruised.**

## CASTING OUT THE ANCESTRAL DEMON AND HIS NETWORK

Then, I guide the core to pray to claim back all the ground that Satan has held on all the personalities. **Let me make it clear that the counselor cannot command the demons to leave without the core personality's taking responsibility for all his sins and sincerely repenting**. I don't care how much faith I have and how much I declare in the name of Jesus, that **core personality** must, by his faith in the Lord Jesus, repent of his sins and claim back the ground given to Satan. The counselee must also desire to be free. Only then does the pastor, counselor, or Christian lay person have the right to command the demons to go to the pit.

After such a session, particularly if we have dealt with personalities, the person will be **exhausted**. If the session is a very heavy, intense one, you may have to stop the session and continue in a following session when the counselee is more rested. Sometimes you may have a counselee who **stubbornly lounges in denial rather than facing the reality of their condition--so you must postpone counseling until they are desperate and determined enough to fully cooperate and deal with everything**. I refer to such a period of waiting as "letting a counselee cook-up." During the waiting period I ask them to get a notebook and daily write down their thoughts and feelings pertaining to their issues. **Journaling** is a very helpful tool, particularly with S.R.A. victims, due to their layers of programming.

It is essential for you, the reader, to understand that God has a solution to all counselee's problems. If the counselee lets Him, God can help him work out all his problems, and if he does need further counseling, He can lead him to a counselor who can help him. When a counselee is set free, he must, in Jesus Christ, have a total and honest desire to remain healthy and whole when that goal is accomplished. I have found that counselees, except for S.R.A. victims, are usually set free by the end of five three-hour counseling sessions. S.R.A. victims usually take no more than twenty three-hour sessions. This confirms that **even the most severely-wounded counselees do not have to become professional counselees and lose hope of getting well**.

**I believe that the Church and the Christian are responsible to help these precious souls to get free and to enjoy the abundant life**. This responsibility of God's people is not to be shirked by sending these precious souls out to non-Christian professionals to receive ungodly counsel. The Word of God says in II Timothy 3:16, 17, "All scripture is given by inspiration of God, and is profitable for doctrine, for reproof, for correction, for instruction in righteousness. That the man of God may be perfect (thoroughly) furnished unto all good works." **God clearly gives His people all they need to help liberate the bruised.**

# SUMMARY OF STEP-BY-STEP COUNSELING PROCEDURES

As you can surely understand, it would be **impossible** to give accurate step-by-step counseling procedures that would apply to **all situations** due to the fact that every counseling case differs in one way or another. Also, as you can well appreciate, I cannot come close to ever having enough time to counsel the vast number of hurting souls that know and continue to learn about my counseling ministry. However, I hope that as you precious ministers, missionaries and counselors review the following summarized outline that works so well for my ministry will be of great help to you as you seek God's will for your ministry as you serve Him in this field where the laborers are all too few.

A.  Upon scheduling a person for counseling, before I wrote this book in 1997, I required them to fill out my lengthy counseling form and asked them to read **The Bondage Breaker** by Neil T. Anderson, which was a very informative tool and encouragement to them. Then after **Liberating the Bruised** was published, I required them to read it before their first session. And now that our second book, **More Tools for Liberating the Bruised** is in print, our ministry's requirements for counseling have changed again. **(1)** The person must sign our ministry's cover page and fill out the counseling form, which are in our second book, **Chapter V, "Required Tools of Practicality." (2)** The person **must** read **Liberating the Bruised** to become familiar with the type of counseling they will receive. **(3)** In addition to reading **Liberating the Bruised**, they may **choose** to do **one** of the following: **Either (a)** listen to the set of five **"Counseling the Bruised"** CDs of Joe talking about **additional helps** that the Lord taught him **after** writing **Liberating the Bruised** while reviewing the small syllabus containing materials and illustrations discussed on the CDs, **or (b)** read **More Tools for Liberating the Bruised**.

B.  Begin all your sessions with the following sample core personality prayer:

> Lord Jesus, I ask you to allow me to speak to the core personality that you thought up from the foundation of the world, that is soft and pliable, reachable and teachable, repentable and savable. If there is a flip-side, I ask you to take it and any fragmented personalities and put them in a safe place where they cannot interfere with us, nor can they be interfered with.
>
> Lord, if there is an ancestral demon, I ask you to take the ancestral demon that carries this person's formal name (first, middle, and last; include maiden name if married woman) and bind, gag, and render the ancestral demon inoperative, including all his personal network; any other ancestral demons and their networks, lifestyle demons, demon-produced personalities, and any demons that masquerade as personalities. Lord, I want only the core personality interacting with me, and I want the core personality under the Lordship of Christ governing this person's life. I want to thank you and praise you for doing this in order for me to be able to minister to this person.

C.  Make certain that the counselee, the core personality, sincerely wants help, wants to be free, and is willing to work with determination toward accomplishing that goal. If they do not want help, cancel the remainder of their appointments until they call again and are in desperation. Be alert for professional counselees. Once you have determined that the person sincerely wants help, proceed to the next step.

D.  Briefly review about your counseling procedures and the meaning of demonic and fragmented personality terms, and answer any necessary questions the counselee may have about the counseling procedures (if you haven't already). Do not let them waste time with trivial or off-the-subject questions. Assure them that those matters can be discussed at another time, proceed with the counseling issues and begin with the following prayer:

> Sweet Father, I want Satan and all his demonic powers to continue to be bound, gagged, and rendered totally inoperative so that they cannot cause any confusion or misunderstanding, nor misappropriate and block any truths being shared. If there is an ancestral demon, I want him and his network bound and gagged and rendered inoperative. Lord Jesus, if there is a flip-side and any fragmented personalities, I want them in a safe place with Jesus. I want to talk to and deal with the core personality that you thought up from the foundation of the world, the one you love so very much. I want a shield of your blood separating the core personality from all the rest. And Lord, I want to see with your eyes, hear with your ears, and comprehend with your mind. Lord, I want to speak with your mouth and love this precious person with your heart. I want them healed by your loving hand. Papa, we want your precious Son's blood surrounding us and protecting us from all evil while we work. It is in the name of Jesus that I pray.

> **Note: Once you have learned that the demons and/or personalities are a reality in the counselee's life, drop the word "if".**

E.  Question the counselee thoroughly concerning whether or not they are saved. It is important that they know the one-and-only, correct time that they acknowledged they were a sinner and accepted the Lord Jesus as their Savior. Their knowledge of when they got saved is where their power lies in defeating Satan and conquering their problems. They do not need to know exact dates, but they should be able to remember the occasion, tell where they were, and about how old they were. (If they are not saved, witness to them. If they are not receptive to salvation, further counseling would be in vain.) Having determined that the person is saved, pray the following prayer:

> Lord, I want the core personality of _____ _____ _____, who is _____ years old and was saved at age _____, not to be allowed to interfere, yet permitted to hear all that goes on. Place him/her with You with a shield of your blood separating everything else from him/her so that we can find and meet whomever we need to work with today.

F.    Lead the core personality to confess any known sins in their life. If they stubbornly cling to one and do not deal with it, this can prevent total freedom from being achieved. In such cases, this gives demons ground on which to justly remain.

G.    Search for an ancestral demon:

> Check first, through praying for God to expose an ancestral demon if there is one, for it is through the ancestral demon you find the flip-side and fragmented personalities, and demons. Begin searching, not in your own power but only through the authority you have in Christ, to see if there is an ancestral demon carrying the person's formal name by praying:
>
>> Lord Jesus, if there is an ancestral demon carrying the full formal name of _____ _____ _____ make him come up and do business with me.

H.    Gather information from the ancestral demon:

1.    Address the ancestral demon by stating: Ancestral Demon _____ _____ _____, by the blood of Jesus, by the finger of God, I command you to come up and talk to me. By your authority in Christ, press him to answer you. And, because demons lie, it is critical that each time he gives you an answer, ask him, By the blood of the Lord Jesus, does that answer stand as truth before the eternal throne of Jesus Christ? It may be necessary to repeat the question several times until you have a peace that he was telling the truth.

> Sometimes an ancestral demon doesn't speak audibly but will speak to the counselee's mind, affect their emotions, or even give them a vision of something in their mind. So, as you ask the ancestral demon questions, get the counselee to relay any messages heard, emotions felt, and visions seen in their mind. Urge them to share everything with you, no matter how bad it is or how crazy it may seem.

2.    Command, through the Lord Jesus, that the ancestral demon tell you what his name is. If there is an ancestral demon, he will confess who he is and admit to carrying the person's full formal name.

3.    Make the ancestral demon tell you what he does--his work--in the core personality's life.

4.    Make him give you a list of all the demons in his personal network, each of their names and the work each is responsible to carry out. Ask the Lord to bind them all up until you are ready to deal with them.

5.    Make the ancestral demon tell you the flip-side personality's name. Most of the time, it will not carry any part of the formal name, but will often use names like I Don't Know, Nobody, Anger, a nickname, etc. It doesn't matter if you gather the

information from the ancestral demon or the flip-side as long as you gather accurate information.

> Flip-side personalities can range from aggressively mean and verbal or frightened and withdrawn. If the flip-side is of a frightened, withdrawn personality, the ancestral demon can hide behind it, making it more difficult to readily gather information. In this case, look for a caretaker over fragmented personalities or the youngest fragmented personality because they are easier to find and more readily give information. Keep going back and checking for the ancestral demon and flip-side personalty, for eventually they will talk to you.

6.   Ask the age of the flip-side. (It will always be the same age as the core personality.)

7.   Ask what the flip-side thinks of the core personality. (This helps in gathering information of its sins and work against the core.)

8.   Ask what the flip-side does in the core personality's life. (Ask him/her to tell you the major emotions that motivate him/her.)

9.   Ask the flip-side why they didn't accept Christ when the core personality, _____ did. Then, minister and witness to him/her as you would anyone else. Get him/her to name and deal with each sin individually that he/she committed and sins others committed against him/her. When he/she repents and accepts the Lord as his/her Savior, lead them in the following prayer:

> I, flip-side, (name), age _____, confess that Jesus Christ is the Son of God. He is God who became flesh and dwelled among His people. He never did anything wrong but the people all did a lot of wrong things to Him. They rejected Him and treated Him as if He were evil. They stripped Him naked, beat Him with a whip, shamed him, tormented Him, and nailed Him to the tree. Jesus became all of mankind's and flip-side (name)'s evil and sin, so they would have the opportunity and choice to become His goodness.
>
> And, Lord Jesus, you became all my sin and the sin of those who hurt me. Lord, I'm sorry for my sin/s of _____. Lord, my sin killed you. My sin put you in the ground three days and three nights, and God raised you from the grave and you are the Living Lord and Savior. You have victory over the grave, death, and all the sin that was done to me or by me.
>
> So, Lord Jesus, I (name), age _____, confess that you are man's only way to be saved, free, and secure. I repent of all the sins that you became and I ask you to come into my heart and save and forgive me. Heal me, cleanse me, and deliver me from all that I have been. Thank you, Jesus. I thank you, Lord, for saving me.

10.   After leading the flip-side personality to the Lord, while the core and flip-side are actually one, it is essential that they receive each other, recognize the core as the boss

personality, and agree to be in unity under the authority of the Lord and against Satan. thus, the next step is to fuse and integrate the flip-side with the core personality. Guide the flip-side to pray:

> Lord Jesus, please deliver me from being separated from core personality _____ _____ _____, age _____, who was saved at age _____. Deliver me from my negative name, _____. I want a new name. (Offer to let them pick a new name. Most of the time they will choose to share the core's name, otherwise they will select an opposite name from their old, negative name.) Lord Jesus, I want to be a part of (core personality) if he/she will have me. Now that Jesus lives in my life and I am no longer (old name) filled with (sins such as anger, etc.) but I am now (new name) filled with (new emotions such as joy, etc.), I want to be a part of his/her life if he/she will have me. Also, I want the demons on my ground removed.

11. Pray, asking the Lord to put the flip-side in a safe place with His blood hedging about him/her. Then, ask the Lord to allow the core personality, _____ _____ _____, age _____, who got saved at age _____, to speak with you. Knowing that the core has heard and been a part of the whole session lead him/her to pray this prayer:

> Lord Jesus, thank you for showing me (flip-side's old name) who now has my Jesus, shares my name, and has a new name of _____. Thank you that he/she will no longer live out his/her lifestyle sin/s of _____ through my life. Lord Jesus, please fuse and integrate (flip-side's new name) that used to be (flip-side's old name) with (core personality), age _____, saved at age _____, and make us one. Lord Jesus, by your powerful blood, I command the demons that have stood on (flip-side's old name) ground to give it up, and when you are ready, I want them in the pit. I break all ties and claim back all ground given to the ancestral demon. I thank you, Lord, for this victory.

12. Pray, asking the Lord to put the core personality in a safe place with His blood hedging about him/her before searching for fragmented personalities. Also ask the Lord to keep the ancestral demon and any other demons bound so they cannot pretend to be any of the personalities that you are looking for.

I. If there was no ancestral demon, thus, no flip-side, pray, asking the Lord to reveal the power demon/lifestyle demon controlling the person's life:

> Dear Lord, please allow us to speak with the power demon that is controlling (full name of core personality)'s life. Have that power demon/lifestyle demon speak to me that I might gather the information needed to help _____. I thank you, Lord that through your power, this will be done.

1. Command, by the power of the Lord Jesus Christ and His blood, that the power demon/lifestyle demons give you the following information:

      a.       What his name is, which often reflects his work and his ground.

      b.       A list of the names of all the demons in his network and the work each is responsible to carry out in the person's life.

      c.       How the demons were able to gain ground in the person's life.

2.      Get the core personality to confess and deal with each of the sins that gave ground to Satan and his demons.

3.      Ask the Lord to put the core in a safe place.

J.      Search for a possible fragmented personality who is a type of caretaker over a group of fragmented personalities by praying:

> Lord Jesus, please allow us to speak with and gather information from any fragmented personalities that may be an overseer or delegator of sorts such as a caretaker, a teacher, mother, or even a baby sitter.

1.      Ask the caretaker to state their name and age. (Watch all personalities throughout for facial expressions and body language, which can be helpful in determining the type of fragmented personality.)

2.      Ask the caretaker what occasion (sin as a result of trauma, etc.) brought them into existence.

3.      Lead the fragmented, caretaker personality to confess each sin to the Lord and to receive Him as their Savior. [See flip-side's example prayer.] (Wait to fuse and integrate the fragments with the core until you have dealt with all the personalities under the caretaker's charge--unless the caretaker is overly anxious to do so.)

4.      Ask the caretaker to give you the names, ages, and duties of all the other fragmented personalities under his/her charge, and ask the caretaker to introduce you to them one by one. Prayerfully following this procedure helps assure that one is not missed:

> Lord Jesus, if there are any fragments that will keep this person from being whole, we want to meet them. Lord, is there anyone between the ages of 0 through 5; 6 through 12; 13 through 19; 20 through 29; 30 through 35, etc.? (Deal with each one individually as they come forth, moving forward until you reach the age of the person.)

5.      Have each fragmented personality under the caretaker tell you their works--emotions, hurts, and sins.

6.      Lead each fragmented personality under the caretaker to confess their sins and lead them to the Lord as you did with the caretaker. Each time you lead one to the Lord, pray for them to be put in a safe place.

7. When all the fragmented personalities under the caretaker are saved, bring them all back to join the caretaker so that the core personality can receive each of them--one by one by their old and new names.

8. Fuse and integrate the core, the caretaker, and those under the caretaker.

9. Pray that each of them is put in a safe place.

K. Search for fragmented personalities that are independent from a caretaker, praying:

Lord Jesus, please allow us to speak with and gather information from any fragmented personalities. Lord, please reveal any fragmented personality that ranges from age 0 through 5, 6 through 12, etc.. (Continue until you've reached the core personality's age.)

1. Ask each fragmented personality their name and age.

2. Ask the fragmented personality what they do in the core personality's life.

3. As the fragmented personality to tell you their emotions, hurts, and sins.

4. Lead them to the Lord.

5. Fuse and integrate them with the core personality.

6. Pray, thanking God for the healing.

L. Liberate the bruised--deal with the ancestral demon, his demon network, and his demon-produced personalities:

1. Having dealt with all the fragmented personalities and knowing the core personality is whole again, pray the following prayer:

Lord Jesus, by the power of your blood, I call up the ancestral demon carrying \_\_\_\_\_ \_\_\_\_\_ \_\_\_\_\_'s name.

2. Command the ancestral demon to call in all his demon network and demon-produced personalities and attach themselves to him.

3. If the counselee has any children, no matter what their age, ask the ancestral demon, "Did you place any demons in _____'s children?"

a. If he answers no, remember to affirm his answer by asking him if his answer stands as truth before the eternal throne of God until you have a peace that he's telling the truth.

184

      b.      If he answers yes and the children are not yet the age of accountability, command him to call them in and attach them to himself. Remember to affirm his answer.

      c.      If he answers yes and the children are over the age of accountability, minister to them and offer counseling when they are open to it.

4.      Ask the ancestral demon, "Do you hold any more ground in (<u>full name of core personality</u>)'s life? Remember to affirm it.

      a.      If he holds no more ground, through the power of the Lord Jesus and His blood, proceed with sending him to the pit.

      b.      If he refuses to leave:

           1)      Search for any possible unconfessed sin in the core personality's life.
           2)      He may be lying in hopes of stalling their departure.

M.      At the close of each session, always end with a prayer of gratitude for the progress and victories gained, and encourage your counselee to continually stay **snuggled up** to the Lord and stand strong in the power of His might.

## NOTES

1. Spiros Zodhiates, Th.D., <u>The Complete Word Study New Testament (Greek Dictionary of the New Testament)</u>, p. 69.
2. Dr. Warren Baker, <u>The Complete Word Study Old Testament (Hebrew and Chaldee Dictionary)</u>, p. 112.
3. <u>Ibid</u>., p. 78.
4. <u>Ibid</u>., p. 54
5. <u>Ibid</u>., p. 113
6. Porter L. Barrington, <u>The Christian Life Bible</u>, p. 607.

# PART IV

## GOD'S CHILDREN LIBERATED!

# INTRODUCTION TO CASE STUDIES

You've heard it said that "experience is the best teacher." While this surely should not always be the case, particularly if it means "learning things the hard way," we are very prone to learn more quickly by hands-on experience. Therefore, I felt that sharing excerpts from a variety of my actual sessions in which we dealt with the demonic and fragmented personalities would further help those who care enough to help hurting souls, and would give more hope to those counselees who are bruised.

In the best interest of time, I must share thumbnail sketches of only seventeen cases from hundreds in my files. As you would expect, I have changed names, ages, places, and various other things to protect my counselees.

As I share about these precious people, you will read some realities that came forth during the sessions that are surely not pleasantries to hear or to deal with. Demons are evil, vile, vulgar beings. Their speech can reflect their nature. The works they produce in the lives of individuals can be repulsive, disgusting and ugly. I do not wish to offend any reader by the use of explicit language and descriptions. However, I have chosen to accurately record these counseling sessions as they occurred, with very little censoring. To ignore all the unpleasantries would candy-coat the sessions as well as some root issues that had to be dealt with to set the captives free. These examples, kept within brief, proper limitations, are to be used as teaching tools. Reading about them will, I pray, help prepare and cushion the counselor against some potentially-shocking realities they may encounter in cases such as these.

On the other hand, while it is very essential to share <u>some</u> details as teaching tools, to do so beyond necessity would serve only to glorify the Devil. God's Word warns us in Ephesians 5:11-12, "...have no fellowship with the unfruitful works of the darkness but, rather, reprove them for it is a shame even to speak of those things which are done of them in secret."

Now, allow me to introduce to you some of my precious counselees, and let you glean from their counseling sessions and rejoice in their victories.

# CHAPTER TEN
# ARE ONES IN CHURCH LEADERSHIP EXEMPT FROM THE DEMONIC?

## THE DOUBTING PREACHER, CASE #1

You've heard the old saying, "I'll believe it when I see it!" Sadly enough, like our biblical brother Thomas (better known as Doubting Thomas), many present-day fellow brethren follow in his footsteps when it comes to taking God at His word in all aspects. I counseled such a doubting brother--a thirty-five-year-old Baptist preacher--who was dogmatic in his belief that Christians could not have demons.

He was referred to me by a fellow minister who knew of my ministry and experience in dealing with fragmented personalities and demons. I will call the counselee **John Dean Blake**. When this young pastor arrived, he proceeded to tell me that he had come for counseling at the urging of a fellow minister, who had observed a lot of pride and anger in John's life. The pastor admitted that he had hurt his wife and family due to all this pride and anger. After gathering all the basic data from my new counselee and checking out his salvation, I proceeded to ask him if he had confessed and dealt completely with all the **known sins** in his life. (I prefaced that question with the statement that **I don't believe God will show us the unknown sins in our life if we have not already dealt with the known sins**--sins we are quite aware that we are guilty of and have stubbornly continued in without remorse. He answered, "No, I haven't," and indicated he was ready and willing to pray and repent of all the known sins in his life. As he prayed, John started calling off known sins as God convicted his heart about them. I listed them. There were nine. Then, I led John to pray:

> Lord Jesus, by the power of your blood, I confess that I, John Dean Blake, thirty-five years old, met you as my Savior at age seven. I confess that I know you've saved me and that I am secure in my salvation. Lord Jesus, I want to confess what you have shown me in my life. You have shown me the sin of **pride, anger, temper, lust, laziness, gluttony, stubbornness, prayerlessness, faithlessness (unbelief), and condemnation**. Lord Jesus, I confess that you became all of those sins on the Cross. All of them are mine, but you became them out of your love for me. My sins killed you, put you in the ground three days and three nights, but the power of God raised you up, giving you victory over the grave and death and over all of mankind's sins. You won the victory over my pride, anger, temper, lust, laziness, gluttony, stubbornness, prayerlessness, faithlessness, and condemnation. I call them sin and ask you to forgive me. Lord Jesus, I want to put them all on the Cross with all of the emotional fallout that came from them--all the pain, shame, and condemnation that Satan has used against me, as well as my wife, my children, and my church. Lord Jesus, I want all of the fallout on the cross. Satan, I command you by the authority of Jesus Christ, to give back the ground you gained in my life because of my sins (named each one again). You no longer have any right to it. Lord Jesus, by your powerful

blood by which you cleansed me from my sins, I claim back that ground. I want you to permeate that ground with your precious blood. Heal it, cleanse it, and totally restore it. Please heal my body, my mind, my soul, my spirit. Heal my memories and all the negative effects from the memories that have come from my sins (name each one again). I want no negative effects of that affecting my life, my ability to respond to my wife, my children, my church, and any other relationships, present or future. Any demon spirits that have been able to stand on this ground to mentally harass me or emotionally manipulate me, I want them in the pit by the authority of the Lord Jesus Christ. Lord Jesus, please take your powerful blood and seal the doorway to that part of my mind and heal my memories and damaged emotions. Restore those torn parts of my soul. I want to praise you and thank you that you have and that you will work all these things together for my good. By faith, I let go of them. Lord Jesus, I release them to you and confess that I no longer have to carry about all the negative fallout. They belong to you and I am free from them. With a childlike faith, I thank you for doing it.

## TESTING FOR AN ANCESTRAL DEMON IN THE PASTOR

After Pastor John had dealt with the knowns, I took time to explain to him about **ancestral demons, demons, the flip-side and fragmented personalities**. For the first time, he opened the door to consider these as truths. He had come to the point of desperation. I asked if he objected to my searching out and testing to see if there were any of these in his life, and assured him that he would be fully aware of everything that was going on. He answered that he wouldn't mind and gave me permission to proceed. I asked him to pray in his heart in agreement with me:

> Lord Jesus, by your powerful blood, I want you to take thirty-five-year-old **John Dean Blake** who got saved at age seven and put him in a safe place with you. Put a shield of your blood between him and all unwanted interference with his personality. Lord Jesus, if there is a **flip-side** or who are **fragmented personalities**, please take them to a safe place and do not allow them to interfere or confuse the issues. **Keep them safe until we call for them**. Lord Jesus, I want all ancestral demons, demon-produced personalities, demons that masquerade as personalities, and lifestyle demons bound, gagged, and rendered totally inoperative until we call for them.

> Lord Jesus, by your powerful blood, I want the **ancestral demon by the name of John Dean Blake**, if he's there, to come up from his hiding place and talk to me. I want to know by the authority of the Lord Jesus Christ what he does in John Dean Blake's life.

Immediately I heard a voice saying, "I control him." I asked him, "How?" and he said, "I won't tell you!" I said, "By the authority of the Lord Jesus, I command you to tell me how you control him." The ancestral demon answered, "Any way I want to! I do it through lust! Leave me alone! Leave me alone you b_____! Leave me alone!"

I commanded him to tell me what else he did in John's life and he answered that he produced the stubbornness, anger, fear, and worry in his life. I then commanded him to tell me how many demons

190

were in his personal network. After stalling some, he finally told me there were seventeen demons. I commanded him to name each one of them and to tell me what each one did in John's life. (I always do this so that the counselee can see that all the bizarre things in his life have not come about simply of his own doing, though the <u>counselee</u> must take responsibility to stop them. As you recall, the ancestral demon that carries the formal name is a territorial power demon--the one in charge--I don't need to talk to any of the other demons. I make him come up from his hiding place and tell me everything that he and his network are responsible for.)

## DEALING WITH THE PREACHER'S ANCESTRAL DEMON AND HIS NETWORK

The first demon that **Ancestral Demon John Dean Blake** told me about was a **demon called Anger**. **Anger** was the one who caused John to carry a chip on his shoulder and so readily lose his temper. When I learned the ancestral demon's name, I then commanded him by the blood of the Lord Jesus to call up the demon and say, "Demon Anger come up and attach to me, Ancestral Demon John Dean Blake. You're going where I'm going" **(meaning wherever Jesus sends him)**. I follow this procedure with each demon. The **second demon was Lust**, who caused John to look for opportunities to lounge in pornography and fantasize about other women. **Lust** caused him to be a flirt and have vile, perverted, wicked thoughts. As with Demon Anger, after learning of Demon Lust, I commanded the ancestral demon to call up Demon Lust and have him attach the demon to himself and inform him that he too was going where I sent him. **Stubbornness was the third demon**, causing John to always refuse to admit when he was wrong about anything. He caused him to demand his own way, refusing to give in to anyone. When I commanded the ancestral demon to call up Stubbornness to attach to him, he cried, "No! No! No! He's been there a long time!" I commanded him again and again to call up Stubbornness. After much resentment and resistance, he obeyed.

There was a **fourth demon, Demon Weakness**, who was responsible for John's lack of discipline and courage. He was called up from his hiding place and attached to the ancestral demon who then called up the **fifth demon, Demon Pain**. Pain caused John to carry around hurt feelings from his childhood, family, and pastorate. After the ancestral demon called up Pain and attached him to himself, he brought up **Demon Cruelty, the sixth one**, who caused John to have a very mean spirit and to be hateful to his wife and children. He called up and attached Cruelty to himself and then called up the **seventh demon, Demon Strife**, who caused an attitude of "always looking for a fight," daring someone to even look at him the wrong way or to say something wrong.

Demon Strife was called up and attached to the ancestral demon who then called up the **eighth demon, Demon Jealousy**, who caused dissention between John and his wife. He made John believe that his wife was running around on him and made accusations of her being a whore and a b_____. When I commanded the ancestral demon to call up Demon Jealousy, he declared, "Damn you! I won't!" After persistence with the name of the Lord Jesus and His precious blood, he called him up, attached him to himself and ordered him to go where he was sent.

Demon number **nine** was then called to him--**Demon Doubt**. This one was responsible for casting doubt on John's salvation, among other things. It caused him to doubt that others, especially his wife, loved him. After Demon Doubt was attached, the **tenth** demon was called from his **hiding place. Demon Worry** held the job of filling John with anxiety. With Demon Worry attached, **Demon**

191

**Vulgarity, the eleventh**, arrived on the scene. His work was sexual perversion and homosexuality. He lured John as a preteen to have sex with his sister and to fantasize about having sex with his mother. After Vulgarity was attached, **Demon Hatred, number twelve**, came forth. Hatred caused him to hate his wife and his dad any time he wasn't given his way. His attitude was fixed on being extremely defensive and self-centered. Hatred was attached and **number thirteen came forward-- Demon Laziness**. This one caused John to be slothful in studying, dieting, and exercising. When Laziness was attached, number **fourteen** was called--**Demon Procrastination**--who caused John to do unimportant things at the expense of important things, to the point that he got so far behind that it was impossible for him to catch up.

With Demon Procrastination attached, **number fifteen was called up from his hiding place-- Demon Gluttony**. The ancestral demon said, "Gluttony is there to kill him. Heart problems run in his family and his overeating will contribute to that risk. **On fasting days at the church, you ought to see him!** He can't fast! He sneaks around and eats while his people are fasting." The ancestral demon was made to call Gluttony to attach to him, and then I made him call demon number **sixteen** who was **Demon Faithlessness**. He caused John to doubt that God would ever give him a big church; however, because he was driven to have the best and to win, he caused John to wonder why God would not do so. Faithlessness was attached, and then **demon number seventeen was called-- Demon Ambition.** This one caused him to compare himself to others--to always look at the past and put himself down. Ambition was attached. I then commanded the ancestral demon to tell me if there were any other demons in his network. He answered, "No." When asked if that answer would stand as truth before the eternal throne of Jesus Christ, he said, "Yes," but to be sure I quizzed him several times. He continued to insist, "Yes."

## ADDITIONAL ANCESTRAL DEMONS IN THE PASTOR

I then asked him if there were any other ancestral demons with their own networks that answered to him. He answered that there were. When I commanded him to tell me the number, he replied, "Three." I asked him if that stood as truth before the eternal throne of Christ, and he replied that it would. Upon being commanded to give the names of the three ancestral demons under him, he first gave me the name--**Greed**. Greed had come from both his father's and mother's sides of the family. I asked what his work was, and Greed answered, "To make John want more. Want more! Want more! Break things so they fall apart. Make him be dissatisfied if he doesn't get it."

I commanded by the authority of the Lord Jesus Christ that the Ancestral Demon John Dean Blake tell me how many demons were in the network of Ancestral Demon Greed. **There were five**. The first called up from his hiding place was **Demon Discontentment**, causing an unsatisfiable need to gain blessings from God and a huge resentment of others being blessed by God. He couldn't rejoice with others over blessings they received. With Demon Discontentment attached, the second demon, **Demon Stingy** was called up. He caused John to be stingy with anyone other than himself, and caused John to be a joyless giver. Stingy was attached and demon number three was called--**The Best**--his job being to entice John to desire expensive things. The Best was attached and the fourth demon was called--**Demon Dissatisfaction**. His job was to keep John totally dissatisfied. After he was attached to the ancestral demon, the fifth and final demon was called. He was **Demon Debt**, holding a job of keeping John and his family in debt, never allowing them to be free of debt. The

Ancestral Demon John Dean Blake was commanded by the blood of the Lord Jesus to attach Demon Debt to himself and inform him that he was going wherever he was sent.

Having dealt with Greed, I commanded through the Lord Jesus that Ancestral Demon John Dean Blake call up the second of the three ancestral demons under his authority. His name was **Ancestral Demon Adultery**, who came from his father's side. I asked what Demon Adultery's work was in John's life. He answered, "We try to get him to commit adultery because his grandfather and uncle did it. We want him to do it!" I commanded Ancestral Demon John Dean Blake to call up Ancestral Demon Adultery and attach him to himself and for him to tell me how many demons were in Adultery's network. **There was a two-demon network**. The first was **Demon Perversion** with the job of diverting John's thoughts from his wife to other women. After Perversion was attached, the second demon was called up. His name was **Demon Voyeurism**, causing him to fantasize and "look where he shouldn't be looking." Voyeurism was called up and attached.

The **third ancestral demon** was called up from his hiding place--**Ancestral Demon Selfishness**. Selfishness had come from the father's side and his job was to cause John to desire to be the center of all attention, to have everything revolve around him. It caused him to perform--doing for others in the pretense of being humble--to have a false humility. Performing for those other than his family caused hurt to his wife and children. **Selfishness had two demons in his network**. One was called **Demon Me-First**, causing John to always see to it that his needs were met first. Demon Me-First was attached. The second was **Demon Left-Out**, who pushed everyone away, including his wife, and caused John to think he didn't need help and could make it on his own.

## ANCESTRAL DEMONS PASSED TO THE PASTOR'S CHILDREN

While we were still in contact with Ancestral Demon John Dean Blake, we commanded him to tell us by the authority of Christ if there were any ancestral demons placed in John's three children. There were. We made him call in the ancestral demons, each one by the formal name he carried, then call in and their networks and attach them all to himself.

## SHARED DEMONS

John also had a **Demon Anger that was shared between him and his wife**. Demon Anger went back and forth at the ancestral demon's command to cause turmoil between the couple. By the authority of Christ, we had the ancestral demon call it in (from where it was then in his wife). Since we were finished with the major part of uncovering the ancestral demon holding the formal name, along with all the ancestral demons and networks under him, we began inquiring to see if there were a flip-side.

## DISTINGUISHING BETWEEN A FLIP-SIDE PERSONALITY, A FRAGMENTED PERSONALITY, AND A DEMON MASQUERADING AS A PERSONALITY

This case illustrates the dire importance of always keeping in mind that Satan and his demons are liars, and that as we continually seek God's wisdom and discernment, we must aggressively question the demons as to whether or not their answers will stand as truth before the eternal throne of God. While demons are cleverly deceptive to some degree, they are not full of wisdom! The Bible says in

Psalm 64 that God will cause demons to stumble over their own tongues. Here we find this taking place. When I asked to speak to the flip-side, one came forth claiming to be the flip-side. I commanded him to tell me the name of the core personality's flip-side (who would be thirty-five years old--the same age as the core, the person originally created by God). He said his name was **Darius**, volunteering that it meant **Mighty One**, and claimed there were four fragmented personalities. I asked **Flip-side Darius** to tell me his age and something about himself. He said, "I see myself as strong and young." I asked why he had selected the name Darius; he answered that it had been given to him by Lucifer. I asked how he knew that, and he responded, "I was there when he gave it to me." I asked when and where it had happened; he replied, "on earth in Palestine." I asked him to whom he answered, and he said, "The Mighty One!" We were soon to learn that he had lied about to whom he answered.

Remember, the flip-side is always the same age as the core. Therefore, Darius revealed that he wasn't the flip-side when I questioned him as to when and where he had acquired his name, and he insinuated he had gotten it long ago in Palestine. He never mentioned the age of thirty-five. He was a demon masquerading as a flip-side personality; he confessed that he had lied about the four fragmented personalities--that what he said wouldn't stand as truth. We learned that Demon Darius actually answered to Ancestral Demon John, who was made to call him up from hiding and attach him to himself.

With thirty-five year old John Dean Blake who got saved at age seven still set aside but observing, I asked God to prevent the demons from masquerading and lying to us and to bind, gag, and render all demon networks inoperative. I then proceeded to search for the real flip-side.

**GETTING TO KNOW THE FLIP-SIDE**

I asked the Lord to bring out the flip-side to meet me. Quickly someone was up, and upon being asked his name and age, he said he was thirty-five and that **his name was I Don't Know**. Asked what he did in John's life, he said, "I fill him with doubt." I continued to ask what else he did, and he answered, "I cause him to dwell in the past...I cause him to deny everything."

I then asked him why he had missed getting saved when John did at age seven. He said, "I didn't want to. I don't want anyone telling me how to do anything, how to run my life." I told him that he wasn't doing a very good job of running John's life and asked what else he did in John's life. He replied, "Nothing." When asked to identify who was prideful and selfish, he responded, "I am! I am the ambitious one!"

While talking further with Flip-side I Don't Know concerning what a mess he had made of John's life, and while reading God's Word to him, he began to cry. I showed him that God is our sufficiency--that we can do all things through Christ--and that He wants us to have an abundant life. Then, I asked Flip-side I Don't Know if he would like to give up all the doubt and confusion. He said he would. When I asked if he would like to accept Christ as his Savior as John had done, he readily said "Yes" and I led him to pray:

I, Flip-side I Don't Know, confess that Jesus Christ is the Son of God. I confess that He's God made flesh and He never did anything wrong but men did a lot of wrong things to Him. They stripped him naked and beat him with a cat-of-nine-tails and nailed him to a tree. He became all of mankind's evil. He became all of Flip-side I Don't Know's confusion. It killed him and put him in the ground for three days and three nights and the power of God raised him up, gave him victory over the grave, death, and all of mankind's evil. He had victory over all of Flip-side I Don't Know's sins. I, Flip-side I Don't Know, confess that Jesus Christ is man's only way to get saved. I repent of being an I Don't Know and repent of my pride of wanting to do my own thing and wanting no one to control my life. I repent of all the sabotage that I've done in thirty-five year old John's life. Lord Jesus, I want you in my life like you are in John's life. I repent and ask you to come into my heart and save me. Forgive me, heal me, cleanse me, and deliver me from all my unrighteousness. Thank you for delivering me from all the I Don't Know, the confusion, selfishness and pride. Lord Jesus, deliver me from the name I Don't Know. I want a new name. I want to share John's name, John Dean Blake. Lord Jesus, if John will have me, by the power of your blood, please make us one. Concerning every demon spirit that has stood on the ground of Flip-side I Don't Know, I cancel out all that iniquity and ground. Lord Jesus, take that ground away from the demons and in the fullness of your time, send them to the pit. With a childlike faith, I thank you.

## FUSING AND INTEGRATING THE CORE AND FLIP-SIDE PERSONALITIES

After I led the flip-side to the Lord, I got the core personality to accept the flip-side by saying:

> Flip-side thirty-five-year-old I Don't Know, now that Jesus Christ lives in your life and you are no longer going to cause pride, confusion and selfishness in my life, I invite you to come be a part of my life, with your new name of John Dean Blake. Lord Jesus, by your powerful blood, I want you to fuse and integrate the thirty-five-year-old flip-side, who used to be I Don't Know, to the thirty-five-year-old core personality John Dean Blake, saved at age seven, and make us one. Any demon spirits that have stood on I Don't Know's ground no longer have a right to be there and I want them sent to the pit by the authority of Jesus Christ.

I then asked the Lord to set aside my thirty-five-year-old John Dean Blake, saved at age seven, and bind up, as before, the ancestral demon and his network--keeping them bound and from masquerading and interfering. Then I asked to meet any other personalities that may have fragmented from John.

## MEETING THE PASTOR'S FRAGMENTED PERSONALITIES

I met a fragmented personality named Sam, age seven. I asked why he had chosen the name Sam and he said that he didn't know. I asked what had brought him about. Seemingly ashamed, he answered, "I do nasty things to my sister and my brother." I asked if he felt guilty and sorry from doing sexual things to them and he began to cry. He said, "I make him feel dirty. I knew better. I hate myself for doing that. I asked my sister to forgive me but my brother is dead. I am afraid someone will find out.

195

I wish I could live it over. I fear for John's children. I don't want them to go through it. I want to be forgiven."

I asked him what he did in adult John's life. He said that he made him feel unworthy and dirty and that he kept him from having a relationship with his sister. He added, "I don't want to be around her, she's out of church, and I feel badly." I asked him what major emotions governed his life; he answered, "Fear and unlovableness." I asked if he'd like to give it all to Jesus Christ, and he prayed to do so as the flip-side had done.

The next fragmented personality I met told me he was young, was twelve or thirteen years of age, and was called **I Don't Know**. He reported that a male friend had come over and had performed anal sex on him, and said that he couldn't remember if he had also done so. I asked him how he felt about that, and he answered, "It seemed like a nightmare. It just couldn't have happened to me. I get angry at him and at myself."

I asked him what he did in the adult John's life. He said that he appealed to the perversion in his thoughts, seeking to bring forth sex as the main force in his life. He said he instigated confusion and guilt, and made him think he's a homosexual because he had committed the act. I asked what the major emotions were in his life, a question to which he replied, "Denial, guilt, condemnation, and not wanting to admit that it happened." I asked if he'd like to give all of this to the Lord Jesus, accept Him as His Savior and be one with John, and he said that he would. I led him to pray in the same manner as described earlier, and fused and integrated him with the core personality.

The third personality appeared--**I'll Show You**, age eight. When asked to tell me about himself, he said:

> When I was in the first grade, I brought home a report card with a bad grade and my dad told me to get it back like it should be, perfect. The next time, I had not brought up the grade, so I hid until Daddy left, then went in and showed it to Mother. I said that it would never happen again. I made straight A's because I must be perfect. I work in John's life and he must be perfect. John is doing the same things to his children. I am so afraid of making mistakes. I must be perfect. I must make all A's. I hold everything in. I see now that I can explode.

I asked him if he were the one governing John's temper, and he replied, "Yes." I asked what his major emotions were and he said, "Ambition. No one will ever see mistakes in my life. I don't want anyone to see them. I don't want my wife or my children or anyone to see them. I want to have a relationship with my dad." He expressed that he wanted to take all this to the cross and let the Lord handle it, and to cease being John's fragment, and I led him through the prayers as I had done with the other fragments.

My prayer has an additional step only when I have a fragmented personality such as this one that is carrying a lot of hurt. I have him pray that Jesus became man's frailty on the cross, man's perfection that would never be good enough. Jesus became all of mankind's weakness on the cross; that's what killed Him. In the prayer, I always include all the frailties and hurts held by the fragmented personality.

The fourth and final fragmented personality that I found in John's life was a little three-year-old boy named **Bad Boy**. I asked him why he was called **Bad Boy**. He said, "Because of Grandfather." I asked what Grandfather did. He said, "He touched me. I'm a bad boy." I asked him why he was a bad boy and why his Grandfather had done that. He answered, "He's my grandpa. He touched me." I asked, "Did he do that more than once?" He answered "Yes, a couple of times." I asked him why he didn't tell his mom and dad. Bad Boy replied, "He told me not to tell. It would be our secret." I asked, "What do you do in adult John's life?" He said, "I tell him not to trust people and that his wife is dirty like he is. Everybody's dirty like he is." I asked, "Do you do anything else?" He replied, "No, yes. I don't let him get too close to people because he will hurt them like Grandpa hurt me."

I found the major emotions in his life to be shame, guilt, and mistrust. He said, "I just want to be clean." I asked if he were the one who governed eating in John's life. (John, you remember, had a problem with gluttony.) He answered, "Yes." I asked him how he turned John to eating and he said that eating helped him to forget. He said, "When there are problems and stress, I just go and eat because food can't hurt me." I also found that the little boy was very jealous of others.

While dealing with Bad Boy, we discovered a **demon named Bill**, carrying his grandfather's name, who came into his life at the age of three due to the sexual abuse from his grandfather. I asked what works he did in John's life. They were masturbation and homosexuality. This demon belonged to the ancestral demon named John, and I made him call Bill up and attach him to himself. After fusing and integrating all the personalities and claiming back all the ground, I called up Ancestral Demon John Dean Blake and commanded him by the authority of the Lord Jesus Christ to tell me if all the demonic networks that I had had him call up and attach were still attached. When he answered "Yes," I commanded him to tell me if there were any ground that would allow him to remain in John's life. Again he answered "Yes"; however, when I asked him if that would stand as truth before the eternal throne of Christ, he answered, "No." I drilled him, and the answer remained, "No." By the authority of Christ we put out the ancestral demon carrying John's formal name--along with all his network--and sent them to the pit. I am happy to tell you that John is a very successful pastor doing a great job with his flock and his family. I get updates from him from time to time about how well he is doing. To the Lord be the glory!

## ANOTHER PASTOR ENSNARED, CASE #2

Another pastor who had been sexually involved with a prostitute came for counsel. Even after he had broken off the relationship with the woman, had confessed it as sin, and had asked God to forgive him, he still could not get over the overwhelming guilt. Distraught, he confessed his sin to his wife and to the church and resigned from his pastorate.

The pastor, whom I will call **George William Blank**, had been very active in counseling others in his church, and had been using highly acclaimed Christian counseling literature with his counselees. However, because many of his counselees had major demonic problems in their lives, and because he had deep-rooted problems and strongholds of his own, he easily fell prey to being sucked into Satan's traps. Here is a thumbnail sketch of what we found in his life by using the previously mentioned methods:

## ANCESTRAL DEMON GEORGE WILLIAM BLANK

Finding an ancestral demon by **George William Blank's** formal name, I asked what he did in George's life. He replied, "I torment him." When asked how, he answered, "By making him f\_\_\_\_\_ and causing him depression." I asked what else he caused, and he said, "I make him mess up and fail." I asked him how he did this; he answered, "He believes that he has to do what his father did." When asked what his father had done, he answered, "Porno--sex with other women. This makes him feel distanced from God and causes him to live a double-standard life." I asked him if there were anything else; he replied, "I cause him to be selfish and look out for self." Asking if there were anything else, he answered, "No." He balked when I asked how many demons were in his personal network, but he finally confessed to having a network of fifteen demons. They were, (1) **Nobody F\_\_\_\_\_**, who made him feel that he needed to have sex, and made him believe that he could gain love that way; (2) **Fritz**, who caused him to feel inadequate; (3) **Kretchmor**, who tried to mislead him and caused condemnation and false belief; (4) **Henry**, who sowed doubt and insecurity and made him fear failure; (5) **Afterglow**, who caused him to **glow (beam with pride)** after having sex, caused him to fear getting sucked into sex, and caused him to masturbate; (6) **Pinky**, who caused the pinky finger to stand out (When asked what this represented, he explained, "his sexual organ."); (7) **Spanky**, who caused George's father to spank and to beat him for pulling down his sister's panties. He caused George to pull down her panties, and also caused George to whip his own son **Georgy**; (8) **Failure**, who caused him to fail in relationships, to put up a guard in relationships, and to believe he couldn't be himself because he would be rejected; (9) **Hierarchy**, who attracted other demons and sowed confusion, doubt, fear, and f\_\_\_\_\_; (10) **Toto**, god f\_\_\_\_\_, who intimidated; (11) **Horror**, who brought about homosexual thoughts and tried to make him believe he was a homosexual; (12) **Pia**, who inflicted emotional pain and protected him from God. (Asked why, he said, "So he can't believe God's lie." As to what lie, he responded, "God's truths.") (13) **Pimp**, who led George to go to prostitutes' houses; (14) **Ester**, who represented witchcraft and drew him to the occult; (15) **Honaba**, who talked to the Devil about George's activities.

## A TERRITORIAL DEMON OVER SMALLVILLE

We found a territorial demon named **Trumbola** operating in the area in which George lived. Upon confronting the **Territorial Demon over Smallville**, we learned of his network. There was (1) **Betizor**, who fought against George through his mind and used people--even deacons at the church; (2) **Somberes**, who attacked little girls trying to get him to f\_\_\_\_\_, f\_\_\_\_\_, f\_\_\_\_\_, f\_\_\_\_\_ more and more; (3) **Camilot**, who hindered the Word in all the churches in **Smallville** to keep them from being effective for God; (4) **Corman**, who was a demon picked up during a relationship from a prostitute. He caused a stronghold of sexual sins, and lured him back to the prostitutes.

Through the power of Jesus, I was able to make the demon tell me about the flip-side personality, fragmented personalities, and demon-produced personalities. I found **a flip-side 40-year-old Nobody** and a **five-year-old fragmented personality named Introvert**. I also found demon-produced personalities of an aunt, his father, a grandfather on his father's side and a grandfather on his mother's side. Observe what took place.

## FLIP-SIDE PERSONALITY NOBODY

I asked Nobody, age forty, what he did in George's life; he said, "I hide." When asked why, he answered, "I can't bear the truth." I asked what he considered the truth. He said, "experience"; when asked what kind of experience, he replied, "sexual." I asked him to explain: he told of his father's taking him, at the age of five, to a cabin in the woods. When I asked him how he felt about himself, he said, "I'm no good because I'm a nobody." I asked who had told him that. He said, "My father." When I asked why his daddy had called him that, he said his father didn't tell him why. (We would later learn of an incestuous experience taking place at the cabin.)

Asked what else Nobody did in Pastor George's life, he said that he stabbed him with criticism and lied to him about the past. I asked him what he told George about the past and he said, "That he's a no-good son-of-a-b_____." I asked what else he did and he responded, "I tell him that all this is a bunch of junk. I hate him because he can't doing anything right--he gets in my way!" I asked if he were the one that went to the prostitute and attracted him to the occult, he answered "Yes."

When I asked him to identify the major emotions in his life, Nobody said, "Fear, unworthiness, and pain." I asked him whether he or the five-year-old held the guilt. He said the five-year-old held rejection. Concerning anger, he said, "I have hidden it." He also admitted that the anger was toward "...my father, mother, and God for letting all of this happen." I asked him why he didn't receive the Lord Jesus Christ as Savior when George did at the age of thirty and he said, "I didn't believe He would love me." I invited him to receive Christ as George had, and he did so. Nobody also chose to be called George, and the core and he were fused and integrated.

## FRAGMENTED PERSONALITY GEORGY

In continuing to look for fragmented personalities, I asked, "Is there a little five-year-old there?" He answered, "Yes." His name was **Georgy**, age five. I asked what brought him about; he said, "A sexual experience." When I asked him to tell me about it, he said that he didn't remember. I insisted that he <u>did</u> remember and urged him to tell me about it. I began by asking him to tell me with whom he had the sexual experience; he confessed, "My father." I asked him what he had done to him, and **Georgy** just cried. I asked him if he felt guilty--which he did--and asked again what had been done to him. He responded, "I don't know if it's true but I see the picture he wants to put his penis in my mouth." I asked if this were done to him only once, and he replied, "Yes."

When I asked him to tell me how he felt about it, he answered, "I feel dirty, guilty, rejected--and I hate him."

Then I asked him what he did in adult George's life now. He reported, "I keep him from being himself." When asked how, he responded, "By not allowing anyone to get too close to him. I am always keeping a wall up. I'm always seeking acceptance by trying to please everyone. I keep him from growing." I asked if he were the one causing him to be an introvert at times, and he said, "Yes."

When I asked him to name his major emotions, he answered, "Guilt, unworthiness, rejection, disappointment, confusion, hurt, fear of being exposed and hurt." I asked if he would like to give it all away to Jesus and to receive the same Jesus that George has. He said, "Yes, if He will have me."

While working with **Georgy**, the Lord Jesus allowed us to get information from the ancestral demon concerning the pastor's two sons. Each son had an ancestral demon carrying his formal name, as well as a territorial demon carrying the name **Trumbola**. There were also demon-produced personalities in both boys from their grandfathers and great-grandfathers. We made the ancestral demon in George call them in from the boys. (We could do this because the ancestral demon carrying George's name had put them there and the sons had not yet reached the age of accountability.) We sent them, along with the ancestral demon carrying George's name, to the pit with all the connected networks.

To God be the glory--George was free for the first time in his life. This pastor had been in the ministry for a long time; deep down in his heart he knew that something was very wrong, but he was afraid to share it for fear of what people might think of him and of how the things revealed might affect his ministry. Quite the contrary, since he didn't seek help, the secrets <u>cost</u> him his ministry. To some degree his ministry will never be the same, because his scarred testimony follows him.

It is time for Christians to be able to share about feelings and voices they hear that come from deep within--to be unafraid of being drummed out of the church, the ministry, or other professions. It is time for the Church to understand and become a place of refuge, healing, and restoration. If churches were like this, people would more readily come forward with their problems, instead of letting them stay hidden and allowing them to grow to the point of destruction.

## <u>WIFE OF A PASTOR, HINDERED BY DEMONS, CASE #3</u>

A pastor's wife, whom I will call **Sue Rae Grant**, came to me for counseling because she also knew that something was wrong. She was being a good pastor's wife, but she knew that she was just going through the motions. There was no real joy of being in the ministry or in living the Christian life. After the preliminaries, I asked God to set aside my forty-year-old (saved at the age of twenty-seven) **Sue Rae Porter Grant** by the blood of the Lord Jesus Christ, and to separate out all other influence. When I asked to speak to the ancestral demon carrying her formal name, I discovered five ancestral demons in her life.

## ANCESTRAL DEMON SUE RAE PORTER

What, I asked, do you do in Sue's life? "I make her mean" came the answer. When asked what else he did, he answered, "I make her h_____. I make her mad." "What else do you do" I asked? "I make her gripe, and be angry and loose. I make her evil. I make her hot with anger. I make her two-faced." After some resistance, I discovered six demons working in his personal network. They were: (1) **Sluggard**, who made her slow and caused her to put things off--to procrastinate; (2) **Penis**, who made her loose and h_____--made her scum; (3) **Filth**, who kept her from being a clean housekeeper and made her lazy; Filth worked together with Sluggard to amplify his work of procrastination; (4) **Crazy**, who made her crazy with anger; (5) **Cunt**, who made her promiscuous, h_____, mean and evil; made her nice in a fake way, and made her blab and talk too much about people; (6) **Dirt**, who made her dream--he scared her with old dreams (satanic) and played mind games; he caused hate and was evil, loud and obnoxious.

## ANCESTRAL DEMON BOGOD

**Ancestral Demon Bogod**, from her father's side, worked to deceive, lie, and trick her; he represented total deception and had no demons in his network.

## ANCESTRAL DEMON S_____ FACE

This demon came from her mother's side, and his job was to make her angry, give her false happiness and false peace. It also made her feel ugly, insecure, and hopeless.

## ANCESTRAL DEMON DOLDRUMS

Some of his works were to cause listlessness, carelessness, and complacency. He also sowed doubt, made her sorry she was living, and made her feel selfish. He made her overly cautious, mistrusting, and mean. Three demons were in his network and their names and works were: (1) **Eager**, who made her eager for anything and made her trust in herself; (2) **Plain**, who made her feel boring, insecure, hateful, and doubtful; (3) **Sweat**, who made her mean and hateful; made her hypocritical and two-faced; caused her to **eat uncontrollably and gluttonously** ("because she is a pig"); made her **verbally eat people and consume them by meanness** ("eats flesh").

## ANCESTRAL DEMON FEAR

Coming from her mother's side, this ancestral demon's work was to make her feel afraid, particularly of being alone with men. He made her afraid of being hurt by people and afraid of being attacked. He caused irrational fear. He had no network of demons, but confessed there was a flip-side personality whose name was **Sexy**.

## FLIP-SIDE PERSONALITY SEXY

**Sexy** said she was forty, and felt lonely and isolated. When asked what she thought about her husband Bob, she answered, "He's nice." I asked her what she thought about Sue and she said, "She's stupid and never finishes anything. She's slow in thinking." I asked Sexy why she didn't get saved when Sue did and she said, "I didn't want to". When I asked why, she replied, "I've always been smarter than her and I didn't want to."

I quizzed her on what she did in forty-year-old Sue's life; she answered, "I give her bursts of anger. I make her think and be logical. I like things done my way. She gives in to Bob so much of the time--catering to him--and I hate her for that."

"Who had the sexual affair at age twenty-seven?" I asked. "Me," she replied. When asked why she had done so, she answered, "I just wanted to." I asked her if she realized that demons had influenced and programmed her, and she said, "Yes." I said, "That's not fun, is it?" She said, "You're right." I asked if she did anything else in Sue's life. She said, "Not anymore." I asked her if she realized how she is ruining Sue's life and she said, "Yes, but I don't want to." I asked her if she'd like to give all this to Jesus and let Him become her Savior like Sue had done. She said that she would and followed through. She chose the new name of Sue, and was fused and integrated.

This precious lady is free from bondage today, enjoying victory and peace in her life. "To God be the glory, great things He hath done!"

## THE CHURCH PIANIST, CASE #4

This case is another case that would seem unbelievable if one weren't aware of the cunning deceits of Satan, the fallen prince and power of the air. This dear Christian lady was referred to me by her husband, who was a church choir director, and by her pastor. I will call her **Jessie**. She was the church pianist. The former pianist had been disciplined by the church due to some sinful behavior. Despite the church's attempt to restore her, the former pianist had refused to repent and to get her life right with the Lord. Whenever Jessie would begin to play the church piano, she would become overwhelmed with fear and begin trembling. Her body temperature would even rise and actually run a fever.

Jessie had approached one of my dear brothers in the Lord--who is a minister and who had come to their church to preach a warfare conference--for guidance and prayer. He had prayed for God to break all her ancestral ties, plus any curses that may have been placed against her or the church by the former pianist. As she shared her story, she explained that even though this had been done, the problem continued to plague her. She then began to share with me that she was a pastor's daughter, that their family had moved around a lot, and that she had always felt a great amount of insecurity and fear in her life.

After gathering essential data during the first three-hour session, we began the next session asking the Lord Jesus to help us to bring Jessie to victory. I asked the Lord to take thirty-eight-year-old, saved at age seven, **Jessie Gray Albertson**, to a safe place where she could not interfere but could observe. I asked Him to bind up all the demons where they could not hinder, and I began looking for Jessie's flip-side, age thirty-eight. Instead of getting <u>her</u>, I met a five-year-old who told me she was going to kindergarten and she was afraid. She also told me that her name was **I Don't Know**. Her major emotion was **fear of change and new things**. After we had given her a new name and fused and integrated her with the core personality, we began to search, asking the Lord to bring forth any fragmented personalities from age zero to five. To Jessie's and my surprise, we ended up meeting fourteen personalities that had come into existence before the age of five! They began telling me their names and ages. They were (1) **I Don't Know**, age five; (2) **Resentment**, age five; (3) **Unloved**, age five; (4) **Depression**, age five; (5) **Critical Spirit**, age five; (6) **Rebellion**, age four; (7) **Fear**, age five; (8) **Anger**, age four or five; (9) **Selfish**, age five; (10) **Selfish**, age four; (11) **Self Pity**, age four; (12) **Rebellion**, age five; (13) **Fearful Restraint**, age five; (14) **Harshness**, age five. All were fused and integrated.

The Lord then exposed sixteen older personalities. As with the previous ones, their weaknesses and strengths were usually reflected by their names. I met (15) **Rebellion**, age sixteen; (16) **Lies and Harassment**, age six; (17) **Lies**, age twelve; (18) **Miss Foster**, (the name of her second grade teacher) age seven; (19) **Trouble at the Church**, age nine; (20) **Worry**, age eight; (21) **Flip-side Silence**, age thirty-eight, who actually stood for rebellion; (22) **Astrology**, age sixteen; (23) **Stefanie**, age twenty-six; (24) **Sherri Elch**, age twenty-seven; (25) **Fear of People**, age twenty-nine; (26) **Prideful**, age twenty-nine; (27) **Lies**, age thirty; (28) **Pride**, age thirty-six; (29) **Fear**, age seven; (30)

**Labor**, age twenty-six. All were fused and integrated. Over a period of eight three-hour sessions, the Lord had revealed these thirty fragmented personalities.

While I have neither the time nor the space to relate what each personality had to say, I wanted to cite this particular case for a very important reason. This dear lady had never been physically abused. When she was five years old, a man touched her sexually, one time, at church. What made her fragment into thirty personalities to cope with life? The question was answered when we learned that the key to all the fragmented personalities was the involvement of the ancestral demons and their networks, along with a lifestyle demon that had come with a curse from the former church pianist.

We then began searching for ancestral demons and other demons in Jessie's life.

## ANCESTRAL DEMON JESSIE GRAY ALBERTSON

The Lord was faithful to reveal the demons and the ground they had in Jessie's life. I dealt with **Ancestral Demon Jessie Gray Albertson** who was the demon in charge, and he declared that he was there to ruin Jessie's life. He admitted that he did it through **fear, satanic--evil--emotions, weakness, hopelessness, pride, and rebellion**. He told me that he caused fear in her life, in order for him to be able to control her life. She was afraid of almost everything. He caused her to fear her dad and to believe that she was being abused by him. The demon's indoctrination caused her to be rebellious and defiant.

## THE INIQUITY OF THE FATHERS IN JESSIE'S FAMILY

We found that the iniquity of the fathers in Jessie's family came through her great-grandmother, grandmother, and mother. They all feared men and rebelled against their authority. From the time of Jessie's birth, a demon had been there strictly to make Jessie afraid of her daddy. Every time her dad would pick her up to lovingly hold her, the demon would make Jessie cry. This hurt and frustrated her dad. After a time, he no longer picked her up. This same demon told Jessie that she was unloved. Most of the fragmented personalities came into being as a result of what the demons were telling Jessie from the inside. They abused and tormented her with imaginations--destroying her relationship with her dad to the point that she and her dad had no fellowship with one another. Only after having gained victory through the Lord has Jessie, now in her thirties, been free to begin building a relationship with her dad. It is clear to see that the Devil intended not only to hurt the relationship between a daughter and her father, but also to hamper God's ministry through His preacher, her father.

## FOURTEEN DEMONS IN THE ANCESTRAL DEMON'S NETWORK

The Lord exposed these fourteen demons: (1) **Fear**, who made her afraid of everything; (2) **Anger**, who made her angry all the time; (3) **Hopelessness**, who made mountains out of molehills and told her that situations were impossible to handle; (4) **Stoic**, who caused her to always be the same emotionally--detached emotionally--almost without expression; (5) **Bitterness**, who brought deeply-rooted bitterness--iniquity ancestrally passed down from her father's side; (6) **Resentment**, who used her dad's resentment of her resisting him to make Jessie, in turn, resent her dad; (7) **Unloved**, who caused anger, resentment, and fear of Dad and God; (8) **Distrust**, who caused her not to trust people;

(9) **Mockery**, who caused her to believe that all this was not happening and that she was a fool; (10) **Prim and Proper**, who filled her with pride and created the detached emotional behavior; (11) **Unbelief**, who filled her with unbelief in Christ and the cross. (She submitted to Unbelief's doctrine and chose not to let anyone have any authority over her. She also believed the demon's lie that God wouldn't take care of her); (12) **Rebellion**, who caused anger at God because "He wouldn't take care of her"; (13) **Fighting**, who caused her to fight against God's will; (14) **Cursing**, who tormented her with thoughts--harmful imaginations.

## DEMON-PRODUCED PERSONALTIES

The Lord showed us fifteen demon-produced personalities in Jessie. They were (1) **Grandmother Clara;** (2) **Dad**; (3) **Mother**; (4) **Great-great-great-grandmother** who was a full-blood Indian, steeped in superstitions; (5) **Great-grandmother Bea**; (6) **Great-grandmother Amey**; (7) **Fear**, age four; (8) **Jessie**, age four; (9) **Jessie**, age thirty-eight; (10) **Anger**, hooked to Dad; (11) **Jessie**, age thirty-five; (12) **Jessie**, age thirty-six; (13) **Jessie in Labor**, age twenty-six; (14) **Jessie**, age thirty; (15) **La Maze**, age twenty-six.

## ANCESTRAL DEMON LIAR

**Ancestral Demon Liar** was from her dad's side. His job was to lie to Jessie and tell her that all men are bad and not to be trusted or obeyed. He had no network and answered to Ancestral Demon Jessie.

## LIFESTYLE DEMON FAYE PAYNE

**Lifestyle Demon Faye Payne**, (carrying the name of the former church pianist), came into Jessie's life by way of a curse from the previous church pianist. His job was to cause fear of playing the piano and also to place a curse of illness on Jessie when she played. There were three demons in Lifestyle Demon Faye Payne's network. They were (1) **Fever**, who brought fever when she played for the church and who made her miserable and tired; (2**) Fear of Playing**, who made her tremble and become fearful; and (3) **Liar**, who lied and confused the issue, causing her to be afraid that she would be incapable of playing the piano.

## DEMON-PRODUCED PERSONALITY FAYE PAYNE

This **Demon-Produced Personality Faye Payne** acted out her rebellious attitude toward the pastor and his authority. The demon curse was invited in by the Ancestral Demon Jessie, and it answered to him.

## ANCESTRAL DEMON UNLOVED

From Jessie's dad and mother's sides came **Ancestral Demon Unloved**. His job was to make Jessie feel unloved and unacceptable. He made her uncomfortable with any kindness that was shown to her, and filled her with self-pity. This ancestral demon had six demons in his network. They were (1) **Doubt**, who inflicted her with doubt and caused her to have to be shown to believe anything. He caused her to doubt God and the truth that He cared for her, and also caused her to fear being

vulnerable; (2) **Shyness**, who kept her from getting close to people in relationships; (3) **Unbelief**, who caused her to feel vulnerable, to doubt, and to mistrust everyone; (4) **Callousness**, who caused hardness of heart and stoicism--shutting down her emotions--causing her to be unkind and uncompassionate; (5) **Nothing**, who caused a void and a restlessness in her life; (6) **Silence**, who caused her to want to be silent and told her that her daddy liked her to be that way. He made her want her children to be silent, also.

## ANCESTRAL DEMON MOCKERY

From Jessie's grandmother on her daddy's side came **Ancestral Demon Mockery**. His job was to make her mock people and their beliefs. This ancestral demon had no network. He also answered to Ancestral Demon Jessie.

## ANCESTRAL DEMON PRIDE

Jessie's **Ancestral Demon Pride** came through her dad's side and caused her life to be crippled with pride.

## ANCESTRAL DEMONS IN JESSIE'S CHILDREN

By the authority of Jesus Christ, Ancestral Demon Jessie gave me information about Jessie's children. There were ancestral demons in both her son and her daughter, carrying their formal names. Because the ancestral demon had been placed there through Ancestral Demon Jessie and because the children had not yet reached the age of accountability, I was able to make him call all his network in from them. The Lord also healed damage done to Jessie's children's flip-side personalities. Through Jesus' power, the ancestral demon and his network were sent to the pit.

The last time I heard from Jessie, her husband, children, and she were all doing great. So, once again, to God be the glory, great things He hath done!

## MISSIONARIES' GRANDDAUGHTER ABUSED IN DAY-CARE CENTER, CASE #5

There was a dear missionary couple who came to me. I will call them Jill and John. They brought their three-year-old granddaughter, whom I will call **Beth**, to me for counseling. They were greatly troubled over Beth's drastic change in behavior. Their daughter and son-in-law had moved back from another city and were living with them temporarily. All of them had done all they knew how to do to help little Beth. They were desperate to attain help for her. Jill and John had been referred to me by one of their Christian friends who had been to me for counseling. Considering Beth's age, I requested that they not bring her to the first session to avoid my possibly upsetting her while I gathered background information and their opinion as to what might be troubling little Beth.

Jill and John shared that Beth had been acting very strangely. Previously she had been a very friendly child, but now she had become withdrawn and had ceased letting anyone other than her parents and grandparents hold her on his lap. They had questioned Beth about what was wrong; they had begun by asking about how others had treated her. Little Beth opened her heart to them and the horror story from her day-care center in the other city unfolded.

As the parents and grandparents carefully gathered data from Beth, they soon learned that some of the workers had taken a select group, all the blue-eyed, blond-haired girls and boys, from the day-care center to another place. They eventually learned that the children had been locked in rabbit cages and were made to watch rabbits being killed and skinned right before their eyes. The children had been instructed that if they told anyone, the same thing would be done to them and to their parents.

After the rabbits had been killed and skinned, the children were then stripped of their clothes, placed on the workers' laps, and made to handle the blood and internal organs of the rabbits while the workers sexually abused them. Apparently, this had been going on intermittently for about three months, before the parents realized that Beth's problem was so critical. During this time, besides being sexually abused by the adults, the boys and girls were made to play with each other sexually and perform sexual acts with the adults as well.

Little Beth was brought to see me. She was wide-eyed and overly cautious. I spoke softly and kindly to her, but understanding her background, I kept a safe distance. God instructed my heart to keep things very simple with Beth. I began to pray, simply asking the Lord to bind up any demons that had transferred to Beth from the abusers. I expressed to the Lord our desire and need for Him to heal any personalities in Beth that may have fragmented as a result of all the horrible abuse she had been made to endure. After praying--before I asked Beth to share her story--the Lord instructed my heart again. He told me to invite Beth to come sit on my lap and to tell Jesus her story about what those mean people did to her. When I asked her if she wanted to do that, she immediately answered, "Yes," and quickly crawled up and sat on my lap. She began praying and pouring her little heart out to Jesus. Her grandparents looked on in amazement and joy. When she finished praying, including forgiving her abusers, she smiled, hugged, and kissed my cheek! Little Beth is, indeed, healed and whole again.

The reason I felt led to share this case is because many people are struck with feelings of helplessness when it comes to counseling such young children. This case illustrates that God will give you His great wisdom to help heal such fragile little ones. The Lord Jesus Himself said, "...Suffer (allow) little children, and forbid them not, to come unto me; for of such is the kingdom of heaven. And he laid his hands on them..." (Matt. 19:14, 15b). I thank the Lord for healing little three-year-old Beth, and give Him all the praise and honor!

# CHAPTER ELEVEN
## MORE SESSIONS IN GOD'S COUNSELING ROOM

### ADOPTED CHILDREN AND ANCESTRAL DEMONS, CASE #6

**Benny** was a man who came to me before I knew the importance of the ancestral demon carrying the formal name. Benny was a staff member in a Baptist church located in another city. He and his pastor later contacted me to let me know that Benny was still having some trouble, and in some ways more than before counseling.

As I began working with him and asked for his full formal name, he reminded me that he had been adopted by his grandmother, and didn't carry the surname given him at birth. We proceeded to look for the ancestral demon carrying both surnames--the one given him at birth and the one given him at adoption. We found **Ancestral Demon Benny Ray Maulden (birth) Manness (adopted).**

I must inject here in behalf of many people who do not know their birth name, that even if the ancestral demon refuses to give that name, God knows their name and He will make the demon do business with you no matter what that formal name is. You can guide them to pray, through the power of the blood of the Lord Jesus--regardless of their not knowing their formal birth name--that the Lord will show them any inherited sins of their father's and mother's that need to be dealt with. After dealing with those, guide them to pray to sever all ties to the iniquities of their real parents, and to claim back all ground given to Satan. After you have done this, you have the right to deal with the ancestral demon and send him out. Then guide the counselee to pray by faith, thanking God that everything is handled. I have learned in my years of counseling that whatever is needed in a counseling session to get the solution to the problem, God is our ultimate source. He loves us so much that He will make known everything that we need.

Knowing Benny's full formal name, we proceeded to find out information from **Ancestral Demon Benny Ray Maulden Manness**. We learned that all of our first work, indeed, was incomplete--we had been lied to, and the personalities had not fused.

### ANCESTRAL DEMON BENNY RAY MAULDEN MANNESS

We learned that his work was rage, confusion, and tiredness. He kept insisting he didn't know anything, repeatedly saying, "I don't know." We prayed for Jesus to remove the block of confusion, which He did. We found out that there were two demons in the ancestral demon's network. Their names and works were: (1) **Fear**, who caused fear in Benny's life to the point of his not being able to have relationships with others, and (2) **No-sleep**, who didn't allow him to sleep and made him tired. No-sleep was not discovered, however, until much later in the session.

### ANCESTRAL DEMON LYNN

The Lord revealed another ancestral demon, **Ancestral Demon Lynn**, who had coequal power. Even though Ancestral Demon Benny Ray Maulden Manness **was the boss**, or territorial demon,

Ancestral Demon Lynn frequently usurped his authority and was the spokesman. Lynn was Benny's grandmother's name. I asked, "What do you do in Benny's life?" The answer came, "Well, I destroy him through people. They hurt him and he's tender. I hurt him and I hurt him. I cause confusion sometimes. I give Beth (his wife) a hard time. I never let him forget his mistakes or her affair. It hurts him and I like that!"

When I asked who was in his network, he announced, "They're gone!" I asked where they were, and he said, "I left it at home." I asked where home was, and he retorted, "Lynn, stupid!" I then commanded through the name and blood of the Lord Jesus that he call them in from Benny's grandmother Lynn, and he obeyed. He told me that three demons were in his network, and he declared that that stood as truth before the eternal throne of Christ. The demons were: (1) **Hurt**, who hurt him and magnified the hurt, and said, "He's tender"; (2) **Confusion**, who confused his thinking, twisted things he heard, and prevented his hearing accurately, making it difficult for him to communicate properly; (3) **Silly**, who assisted Confusion and removed the power of the Gospel pertaining to his life.

Upon asking Ancestral Demon Lynn if he had prevented the fusing and integrating of four-year-old Benny and the forty-one- year-old flip-side, he replied, "Yes!" I asked him what had prevented our fusing the little four-year-old and he said, "The fear-demon blocks you." That demon (previously mentioned) belonged to Ancestral Demon Benny Ray Maulden Manness. I then sought the flip-side.

## FLIP-SIDE PERSONALITY I DON'T KNOW

When someone began speaking, I asked if I were talking to **Flip-side I Don't Know**. "Yes," came the answer, and he said that he was forty-one years old. Further questioning revealed that he was afraid of both men and women. I asked if he were afraid of us (his pastor and me). "Yes," he replied. "What are you afraid of besides men and women?" I asked. He declared, "Everything!"

I questioned him as to why he didn't get saved when Benny did at age twenty-seven. He answered, "I didn't hear." I told him that perhaps I had only <u>thought</u> I had been talking to him earlier, when actually I had been talking to the ancestral demon. When I questioned him again about the matter, he confirmed it and shared, "I could hear him talking about me to you."

Asked what he did in adult Benny's life, he said, "I make him afraid of everything." He admitted that the major emotions governing his life were "Fear and confusion." When asked if he would like to give all of that to Jesus, and to let Him be his Savior as Benny had done, he said that he would. **I Don't Know** chose the new name of **Joy** and was fused and integrated with Benny.

## FRAGMENTED PERSONALITY LITTLE BENNY

**Little Benny**, age four, appeared withdrawn and reflected the expression of a little child. "Where are you?" I asked. He softly replied, "I'm in the closet." "Why are you in the closet?" I asked. "I'm hiding from Grandmother Lynn." "Why?" I asked. He answered, "She hurts me." I asked how she hurt him. "She does bad things to me." When asked what kind of bad things she did, he said, "I can't tell." I asked him if he would tell Jesus so that he could "get rid of them," and he said, "It's not my fault. I didn't want to do it. It's bad. She touches me and makes me touch her. It's bad!"

I then asked fragmented personality Little Benny, what he did in Big Benny's life. He answered, "I hide! I make him afraid of women. I make him afraid of any people in authority. I make him afraid of people who know more than he does." I asked, "What else?" He said, "I eat! I like to eat. It makes me feel good." Questioning what his main emotions were, he answered, "Shame. I'm so bad--fear and confusion."

I asked if he affected Benny's marriage. He said, "I remind him of her unfaithfulness. He fights me about it, but I make him remember everything. I never let him forget." I then asked him if he wouldn't like to give all this junk to Jesus and let Him save him from his sins like adult Benny had done. He said that he would and followed through. When we then prayed to see if there were a peace in adult Benny's life, there was none. In asking the Lord Jesus to show me why, at this time the Lord Jesus brought up the demon by the name of "No-sleep" (mentioned earlier), who belonged to Ancestral Demon Benny Ray Maulden Manness. His job was to make Benny tired and prevent him from sleeping. I asked Little Benny if he would like to quit being so tired. He said that he would really enjoy some sleep. When I asked him if he would like to give his tiredness to Jesus, he declared, "Yes!" We had already fused and integrated the flip-side to the core, and now the four-year-old fragmented personality Little Benny (who chose the name **Big Benny**) joined them. All the fusing and integrating done, we then sent all the demon networks to the pit.

Today, Benny's life has changed completely and the Lord is accomplishing a great work through his life. Again, I must say, "To God be the glory, great things He hath done!"

## A TROUBLED AIRLINE PILOT, CASE #7

A counselor brought a troubled airline pilot to me for help concerning his failing marriage. I'll call him **Jack Rick Smith**. He was thirty-nine years old, had been saved at the age of six, and was active in a good, solid church. Jack's troubles, however, extended far beyond marital problems.

### LIFESTYLE DEMON RAMA

We found no ancestral demon by Jack's formal name, but the Lord revealed a **lifestyle demon** by the name of **Rama**. Rama had come into his life at the age of thirteen while Jack was seeking information from an Ouija board. "When did you enter Jack's life?" I asked. "At age thirteen," he answered. I asked for his origin and he said, "Through his sister's Ouija board." Asking what work he did in Jack's life, he replied, "I make him think he's God's gift to everyone!"

I asked **Lifestyle Demon Rama** what else he did, and he said, "I don't do anything else--but my demons do!" "How many do you have in your network?" I asked. After delaying some, he finally confessed to having seven. They were: (1) **Carlos**, who claimed to be like a fox, with bright eyes and big teeth, drawing and attracting women to Jack; (2) **Cyhote**, who said he was like unto jail bars including the pain in being held behind the jail bars. He claimed to hold fast to all Jack's emotions to make Jack feel in control and tough; (3) **Pelo** the Lion, who made him tough and got other pilots to bring in porno movies to make Jack fall; (4) **Cyclone**, who caused Jack to burn out in his marriage and to want to give up; (5) **Barney**, who gave him a vision of a big velvet tent with a sword in front of it. We learned he caused Jack to fantasize in the areas of sex, wealth and power; (6) **Black Crow**, who caused Jack to waste and devour time, procrastinate; (7) **Book**, who said he set him up to draw

209

people of the occult to him. He drew his mind to things involving the demonic and witches being burned at the stake.

By the authority of Christ we made **Rama** call up all his demon network including the ancestral demons he had placed in Jack's children. These were ancestral demons by their formal names and there were also demons by the names **Rama, Salem, and Snake**. These ancestral demons came into Jack's children at conception through **Rama** because of the ground Jack gave through the Ouija board and his pride. After we had claimed back the ground lost by the use of the Ouija board and by his sin of pride, we were able to send the demons to the pit. By the grace of God and His awesome love, Jack is free and working on his relationship with his wife.

## A FATHER ACCUSED OF INCEST, CASE #8

A wonderful Christian we will call **Roy Howard Hall** came to me for counseling. He came for two reasons: first, his daughter Amey had told her mother that she had been made to touch him sexually when he was drunk (This had happened a number of years back when the daughter was only eight-- she was in college when she confessed the matter to her mother); second, his wife **Rhonda's** coming for counseling had made such a positive change in her life. The tremendous anger she had once held toward him for what he had done was now gone. Seeing such a major change in her life gave him hope that he could be helped also.

Roy was weary of the guilt, and desperate enough to wait the seven months until I could see him. We prayed, asking God to set fifty-four-year-old Roy Howard Hall, saved at age forty-six, aside, and not to allow him to interfere. We prayed for God to show us if there were an ancestral demon by his formal name, and if so, to allow us to meet him. We found none, but because Roy had been involved in pornography, I looked for a lifestyle demon.

## LIFESTYLE DEMON ALEXANDER

The Lord exposed **Lifestyle Demon Alexander**. I asked when he had come into Roy's life and how he had gained access. He replied, "I came in ten years ago through his watching dirty movies." I asked him if that stood as truth and he insisted it did. I asked what his work was in Roy's life and he declared, "I can make him do anything. I can make him masturbate and think things that he shouldn't." "What else do you do in his life?" I asked. "I make him look at other women with lustful thoughts." I asked whether or not he did anything else. "I make him watch dirty movies," he answered. (I asked Roy if he still did that and he said, "Sometimes.") I asked what connection he had with Roy's daughter, Amey, and he said that he had none--that he just had control over Roy. I asked him if he were the one who caused Roy to do those things to Amey and he said, "Yes, and I want to do more!"

The Lord made Lifestyle Demon Alexander tell me how many demons were in his network. There were four and they were: (1) **Charles**, who caused conflict between Roy and his wife Rhonda; (2) **Billy**, who lured Roy to women; (3) **Ralph**, who caused havoc in Roy's life--causing him to go to too many places, continually, to spread him too thin and fatigue him; (4) **William**, who sought to control Roy and induce him to go to prostitutes.

When Roy was growing up, he would play under the bridge near his house. A boy with whom he would play molded the shape of a woman in the sand and made him have sex with it. The boy would make him masturbate him and then the boy would do the same to him.

I asked God to set fifty-four-year-old Roy, saved at age forty-six, aside. I looked for a fragmented personality, and found a seven-year-old personality carrying the name **Bradley**, the name of the ten-year-old boy that had sexually abused him beneath the bridge.

## FRAGMENTED PERSONALITY BRADLEY

I met **Fragmented Personality Bradley**, age seven, and asked him why he had chosen the name Bradley. He replied, "That's my name." Tell me about yourself, I said. "Well, I don't wear a shirt and I wear cut-off jeans and I'm barefoot. I like to play in the woods. I like to go craw fishing." I asked him what else he did. "I play with my dog and we go in the woods and look for rabbits," he replied.

I asked him if he could tell me about anything that had happened to him. He answered, "Bradley and I went craw fishing under the bridge but they weren't biting, so we started talking about girls. We drew this form of a woman in the sand and gave her boobs and female parts. We had sex with it. I didn't like it because the sand hurt me." What else happened, I asked? "We masturbated each other. I didn't want to do it. I was scared because I had never done that before. Then we heard someone coming, and we had to hurry and get our clothes on and I didn't like it. Bradley said we would do it the next day, but I didn't want to because I didn't like it."

I asked him what he did in adult Roy's life, and he said that he made him masturbate. I asked if he'd had anything to do with Amey and he answered, "I wanted to touch her." I asked if he had touched her and he said, "No, but she touched me." I questioned whether there were anything else, to which he replied, "No."

"What emotions do you feel?" I asked. "Lust, masturbation, and fear of getting caught." I asked him if he were the one who shuts everything down so that Roy can't remember. He confirmed that he was. I asked him if he would like to give all this to Jesus and let Jesus save him as He had Ray, to which he replied, "Yes."

Please notice that Roy fragmented because he feared getting caught naked under the bridge. This sin and resulting fear would make him more accessible to the demons when he began at the age of forty-four to watch porno movies with his next-door neighbor. Satan is so subtle. He began working on Roy while he was still a small boy, using another boy to abuse him. The little boy's imaginations were demonically influenced, and he became obsessed with women's bodies--wanting to touch them--and with masturbation. He fell easy prey to the demons attached to the pornography, and they readily took opportunity to enter him. I dealt with the fragmented personality in the usual manner and he was **fused and integrated** with the core and **chose to share the same name, Roy**.

## ALL THINGS DO WORK TOGETHER FOR GOOD, CASE #9

This case pertains to the last one, and through it, I want us to see how Romans 8:28 proved true through Roy and his wife Rhonda's situation. You recall that I mentioned that Rhonda had come to me before Roy did. She had done all she had been told to do concerning her anger toward Roy and claiming back the ground, yet the anger still lurked, hidden within. When I had counseled Rhonda, I had not yet learned about the ancestral demon's carrying the formal name. By the time Roy had come, however, God had unveiled that truth. Roy had made such rapid progress that I was able to give Rhonda the last of his five appointments.

Watch what I am about to show you concerning both before and after I learned of the ancestral demon carrying the formal name. We had asked God to take thirty-eight-year-old Rhonda Hall who got saved at age nine, set her aside, and bring out anything that was causing the anger within.

### FRAGMENTED PERSONALITY I DON'T HAVE A NAME, AGE FOUR OR FIVE

The Lord revealed **I Don't Have a Name**, age four or five, who said, "I live at Mother's and I don't have a name because I'm not supposed to be here." I asked why and she replied, "I'm not wanted. I don't belong. I'm only trouble." "Who said that about you?" I asked. "My sister Nancy." "Why did she say that?" I asked. "I'm taking her mother. Nancy believes I'm taking all of Mother's time."

"What do you do in adult Rhonda's life?" I asked. "I control." "Why?" I asked. "To keep her under control because she doesn't know what to do. She's never been able to get it right." I asked what else she did in her life. "Nothing," she replied. I asked, what she thought about Amey. She answered, "I think she's a hurt little girl." I questioned what she thought about Rhonda's ex-husband and she said, "I don't think about him." I then asked what she thought about Roy, and she said, "He's a phony. He wants everyone to think good things about him that aren't true." "Are you the one having a hard time forgiving Roy?" I asked. "Yes."

I asked for her major emotions and she replied, "I have a need to control and I'm scared. I'm so scared, so very scared that if I don't do it right now they won't love me anymore. I feel insecure and rejected." I invited her to give it all to Jesus and allow Him to be her Savior and also make her one with Rhonda. She readily accepted the invitation, was fused and integrated with Rhonda and chose to share her name.

### FRAGMENTED PERSONALITY I DON'T HAVE A NAME, AGE SIXTEEN

The Lord then showed us fragmented personality **I Don't Have a Name**, age sixteen, who said, "They want to commit me because I am not perfect. I was going to kill my mother by making her unhappy and it would be my fault." I asked, "Why did they say this?" She replied, "I never understood why they said I would be the cause of my mother's death." I asked what she did in adult Rhonda's life. She said, "I hide and make her run and hide. I don't let her be herself." "Why?" I asked. "Because they will send her away. She must be what people think she must be." When I asked what her major emotions were she answered, "Fear of being found--if they can't find me then they can't send me away." I asked her why she didn't know the Lord Jesus as Rhonda did, and she answered, "I don't know. I believe I felt betrayed. Mom said Jesus would take care of me. Both

Jesus and Mom let me down. I'm disappointed and angry and betrayed." However, I was able to help her understand that Jesus <u>could</u> help her. She received Christ as her Savior and was fused and integrated with the core personality, choosing to share her name, Rhonda. The Lord helped Rhonda further by exposing the ancestral demon causing other hurts in her life.

### ANCESTRAL DEMON I DON'T KNOW

I asked **Ancestral Demon I Don't Know** how long he had been in Rhonda's life. He said that he had always been there and that he had come from her dad's side. He confessed the iniquities to be jealousy and hate. When I asked of the work he did in her life he said, "I fight her conscience. I keep her from totally giving her life over to the Lord. I put doubt in her mind and I scare her a lot and cause confusion." There was no demon network, but he admitted that there was a flip-side of Rhonda.

### FLIP-SIDE PERSONALITY NO-NAME

When the Lord brought forth **Flip-side No-name**, she said, "I don't want anyone to know I'm here." I asked why she didn't get saved when Rhonda did and she said, "I was hiding." When I asked what her work was in Rhonda's life, she confessed, "I give her doubt, anger, and jealousy." Then another ancestral demon was exposed.

### ANCESTRAL DEMON I DON'T HAVE A NAME

I asked **Ancestral Demon I Don't Have A Name** where he had been when I had looked for him earlier. He answered, "Hiding. I came from her dad's side." When I asked what he was doing in Rhonda's life he said, "Jealousy--I'm the one that made Rhonda give all the material things to Amey to cause jealousy in the family." When asked if he were the one causing confusion, he answered, "Yes! Any kind I can!"

In previous counseling sessions, we had thought that we had finished dealing with Rhonda's issues. When Rhonda came back, however, using the appointment her husband didn't need, I checked to see if there were an ancestral demon carrying her formal name. He was there.

### ANCESTRAL DEMON RHONDA LEA RATHER (MAIDEN NAME) HALL

I questioned **Ancestral Demon Rhonda Lea Rather Hall**, inquiring as to what he was doing there, and he responded, "Confuse her." I asked how he accomplished that, and he answered, "I make her very insecure and put thoughts in her mind. She doesn't even know where they come from because she doesn't believe in them." I asked what else he did and he said, "I cause her total abuse by giving her doubt and making her question her belief in God." The Lord exposed two demons in his network and they were, (1) **Bitterness**, who haunted her with thoughts of incest between her husband and daughter, gave her night sweats, and made her question why the incest had happened and had caused so much pain; (2) **Grudge**, who kept visually portraying the act in her mind. He caused unforgiveness, telling her that there were some acts that didn't merit forgiveness. He put obstacles in her way; every time she began to get things under control he caused her to doubt and question if she was doing anything right.

213

In addition, the Lord exposed other demons that had prevented the flip-side from fusing and integrating. He also revealed **Demon Hate**, **a sharing demon** between her daughter and her, belonging to the ancestral demon bearing her name. We made the ancestral demon call it in, along with an **ancestral demon Amey** that was in the daughter's life. We dealt with everything in the usual manner and, by the power of Jesus, sent all the demons to the pit.

Roy and Rhonda, are doing wonderfully well, and the daughter is beginning to work on her anger, though she is prone to think I've sided with her parents. When she chooses to let God help her, she too will have her emotional bruises healed.

## NOBODY CARES, CASE #10

I had previously counseled a man in his forties, who had had an ancestral demon and a flip-side. At that time, he was divorced and had a son who was living with his mother (the counselee's ex-wife) and his step-dad. Later the son had come back to live with his dad, and brought numerous problems with him. I'll call the son **James William Bryant**. James' father brought him to me for counseling. James, age sixteen, had been saved at age nine. He was angry, sad, and lonely and believed that nobody cared about him. I found that anger was his major emotion. When I asked him who he was angry with, he told me he might be angry at Don, his step-dad. He felt his step-dad hated him. His step-dad had told him that he couldn't do anything right, including his schoolwork. James' mother and Don had sent James to live with his dad because a pistol had been found under James' bed at their house, and they were afraid that James might kill his step-dad.

In the process of counseling, James told me that he had sought to know the future from an Ouija board at a next door neighbor's house. He stated that about a year ago, while playing the game, a **demon named Rex** had spoken--telling James to shut-up and that he didn't like him. I led James to take to the cross the sin of his playing with the Ouija board and of his anger against Don and his real mom and dad. He did this and claimed back the ground that he had given to Satan through these sins. After James had done this, we checked to see if there were an ancestral demon, keeping in mind what we already knew about his dad.

## ANCESTRAL DEMON JAMES WILLIAM BRYANT

During three three-hour counseling sessions we located **Ancestral Demon James William Bryant** and his network of eight demons. The ancestral demon told me that his job was to torment James. I asked the ancestral demon how he was able to accomplish all this and he said through James' yielding to drugs, alcohol, lust, and depression. The Lord then enabled me to deal with the demons who were, (1) **Lust**, who caused James to masturbate; (2) **Rage**, who caused him to lose his temper, to knock holes in the walls of the house, and to fight a lot; (3) **Energy**, who caused him to be controlled by self-worth and caused him to desire power with which to control his life, the world and the earth; (4) **Rex**, the demon acquired from using the Ouija board, who controlled his well-being and made him neglect himself; (5) **Confusion**, who caused confusion with regard to his schoolwork; (6) **Destruction**, who made him want to kill and murder people, especially his step-dad Don; (7) **Lying**, who lied, deceived, and concealed; and (8) **Anger**, who attempted to destroy him through his temper.

214

## DEMON-PRODUCED PERSONALITIES

I looked further for demons, and found three demon-produced personalities in this network: **Mom, Dad, and James**. I asked the Lord to reveal any other demons.

## ANCESTRAL DEMON REX

We found an ancestral demon from his dad's side that first said that his name was **Murder** but later admitted that his real name was **Ancestral Demon Rex**. This was not the same Rex acquired from playing with the Ouija board, but was the ancestral demon who had given the name Rex to that demon. His job in James' life was to murder, kill, and destroy. There were four demons in his network: **Kill, Rage, Lying, and Luther Who Connives**.

## FLIP-SIDE PERSONALITY JAMES, SHARING THE SAME NAME WITH JAMES

When I met **Flip-side James**, he said that he was there to destroy the core personality James' life with drugs, alcohol, bad friends, and lust. When I asked what he thought about James, he said, "I like him." "Then why," I asked, "are you trying to destroy him?" He said, "I don't know. I guess because he's a Christian." I then asked why he hadn't received Jesus as the core James had. He replied, "I don't like Him (Jesus)." Being asked why, he said, "I follow Satan." I inquired further as to why. "I don't know," he answered. I asked him why he would want to follow a loser and he replied, "Because he's king." I informed him that Satan is not king, only Jesus is the King.

I asked him if he got depressed; he said, "No, the little boy that's three years old does." I asked, "Then what do you do?" He said, "I ruin life." When I asked him why, he answered, "Because I have to." I asked him who told him that he had to, and he answered, "Luther". I asked him who Luther was and he answered, "the Devil."

I invited him to accept Jesus so that he didn't have to live that way anymore, but he declined. He would only say "Because" when asked why he declined. He said he didn't know why he had followed the Devil. I said, "You like James, so why don't you want Jesus?" He answered, "Because of Luther." His major emotions were: "Sorrow for my mom and her life" and "hatred for Don." Again, I invited him to be free from all the mess and to accept Jesus, but again he refused.

Please take note: I was able to find out that Luther was the demon from the Karate instructor with whom James was studying, and that Rex was the one who had called him in. Luther was the one trying to keep James from getting saved and fused and integrated with the core personality. So, I continued to work with Flip-side James. I asked him how he really felt about the step-dad. He said, "I feel bad, mad, and I want to kill him." When I asked him if he were the one who had hidden the pistol under James' bed, he admitted that he was.

I told him: "I know when I was talking to you earlier that Demon Luther was breaking in and causing problems. So, would you like to ask Jesus into your heart now?" Again he answered in the negative. When I asked him why, he said he didn't know. I asked if it were because he was angry and bitter and wanted to protect James. He said, "No," but said he didn't know why he refused to receive Jesus Christ. I told him that I believed that he <u>did</u> know why he was rejecting Jesus. I pressed him to tell me; he answered, "I don't want to forgive Don and I want to hurt him!" I asked if he were the one who got James to join the gang. He denied it, and said that the demons did. I asked him if he wanted the demons to ruin James' and his life, and he said, "No!" Eventually he invited Jesus into his heart and gave Him all the hurt, anger, and desire to kill. The flip-side and core were fused and integrated; then we searched for fragmented personalities.

## FRAGMENTED PERSONALITY NOBODY, AGE 13

When I asked **Nobody** to talk with me, he at first refused, but then chose to tell me, "I hate living in Kansas." I asked him if he were the one causing James to cry himself to sleep. He said, "Yes, and I hate this place that I've been made to move to! It's depressing! I'm all alone and I miss my dad." I asked him what he thought about his grandmother. He said that he didn't like her and didn't know why. I asked if she were mean to him and he answered, "Yes and no."

I asked how people at school were treating him, and he responded, "Bad." When asked why, he replied, "I guess because they don't know me." "What do you do in sixteen-year-old James' life?" I asked. "I make him depressed and mad." I learned that Nobody's major emotions were anger and depression, and that he was "...angry at everybody." After my reading God's Word to him, he chose to invite Jesus into his heart and to become one with James. I continued to search for fragmented personalities.

## FRAGMENTED PERSONALITY NO-NAME

The Lord revealed a fragmented personality **No-name**, age eleven. I inquired, "Do you live in Kansas?" He answered, "Yes." I asked him to tell me about himself, but he refused to talk. I asked him why he wouldn't tell me about himself--he still refused to talk. When I told him that he was surely uncooperative, he stormed, "No, I'm not!" When I asked him about what he thought about living in Kansas at the farm house, he said, "I hate it! I'm lonely there!" I asked where his dad was; he said he was at home. When I asked if he were glad to be away from Don, he said, "Yes." I asked what he thought of Don and he said that he hated him. I inquired as to why: "I just do." I asked if Don had done something bad to him, and he said, "Yes. He kicked me real hard." He reported that that was the only bad thing Don had done.

I questioned him as to what he did in sixteen-year-old James' life, and he reported, "Nothing." I asked if that were the truth and he said, "No." "What do you do?" I asked. He said, "I fish and hunt and make him lonely." I asked him if he thought anyone loved him. He said, "Yes. Mom and Dad." His major emotions were loneliness, confusion, and hatred toward Don. I asked him if he hated anyone besides Don, and he answered, "Yes. My mom." When I asked him why, he answered, "For taking me to Kansas." I was able to lead **No-name** to the Lord and fuse him with the core personality, at which time he said he wanted to be called James also. The demons were sent to the pit.

Only a few days ago I received a phone call from James' dad giving me an update on him. He thanked me for helping James and gave a testimony that great things had been happening in James' life since his counseling sessions. He gratefully shared that he and his wife were now seeing and enjoying the core personality of James which had previously been hidden by the demons. He reported that James readily reflects his love for the Lord and that he has indeed been set free, delivered from his bondage.

He is doing well in school, has a part-time job, and is involved in church activities. James' dad rejoiced over how readily James expresses his love for the Lord. What a joy to receive an update of continuing victory over the evil one in a precious soul's life! I am so grateful when souls choose to believe and apply God's truths that set the captives free!

## MEDICATIONS AREN'T THE ANSWER!  CASE #11

A sweet Christian lady we'll call **Jane Renee Wilson**, age twenty-seven, saved at age twenty, came to me for counseling. She held a master's degree and worked for a major company offering mental health care. She was a counselee at another well-known clinic. Here, they told her that she had a chemical imbalance, and put her on four different drugs, assuring her that the medication would solve her emotional problems. However, she kept getting worse.

Jane belonged to a very conservative church, well-respected for its biblical stance--but they didn't believe Christians could have demons. There was a Christian counseling ministry in her church with a full-time paid staff member who was a professional counselor. He said he couldn't help her, and sent her away with instructions to "Just trust God and everything will be all right."

In our two four-hour sessions, the Lord revealed many problems in her life. She related to me that she had come from a good background and that all her family were Christians, but that her dad and some other relatives were Masons. Jane also shared that at the age of five she was divisive and rebellious and had begun to masturbate.

After explaining my counseling procedures we began looking for the ancestral demon carrying her formal name. A voice in her mind started to talk to her. When I told Jane to repeat what she was hearing, she reported, "He's not going to find anything. The best thing that you can give your husband is your virginity." Jane had previously shared that one of her biggest guilt trips involved the fact that when she had married her husband, she had not been a virgin.

I commanded the **Ancestral Demon Jane Renee Wilson** to come up and talk to me. As I asked the questions, he answered in Jane's mind, and she quoted what he said. This is what we learned:

## ANCESTRAL DEMON JANE RENEE WILSON (MAIDEN NAME) FRANKLIN

I asked what he did in Jane's life; he said, "I want to kill her. I want to torment her. "Why?" I asked. "I hate her. I hate who she is." I asked if he were there to destroy her Christian life, and he answered, "Yes." I asked from which side of her family he had come; he answered, "I come from a long way back on her mother's side, and there's witchcraft." We found eight demons in his network. They were, (1) **Death**, who wanted to destroy her, wanted her dead, and gave her fear of everything; (2) **Fear**, who sought to destroy her through unbelief and made her doubt her salvation; (3) **Anger**, who condemned her and sought to destroy her through hatefulness, and hated Jesus; (4) **Destruction**, who sought to destroy her through sin; (5) **Torment**, who caused torment; (6) **Sickness**, who caused mental anguish and fatigue; (7) **Unbelief**, who made her doubt God and her salvation; and (8) **Confusion**, who tried to confuse her with confusion.

## FLIP-SIDE PERSONALITY SAMANTHA

I then met **Flip-side Samantha**, age 27, and asked what she did in Jane's life. She answered, "I listen to the evil spirits." When I questioned if she were the one who started masturbating at the age of five, she answered, "Yes." I then asked if she were the sexual personality in Jane and she confirmed that she was. I inquired if she were also the drinker; she answered, "Yes. I do anything immoral!" Asked what she thought of Jane's husband, she said, "Oh, he's okay." When I asked what else she did in Jane's life besides the immoral things, she answered, "I get her to drink." She also admitted that she was the one who caused Jane's eating disorders. I invited her to receive Christ, break the bondage with witchcraft, and be fused and integrated with Jane. She readily did these things, and chose to share Jane's name with her.

## ANCESTRAL DEMON SAMANTHA

We also discovered **Ancestral Demon Samantha**. When I asked what he did in Jane's life, he responded, "I do several things. I lead her away from Christ. I make her feel guilty. I ruin her mental stability and lure her to get involved with witchcraft." I asked his purpose and he said, "I set out to destroy her." "Through what means?" I asked. He responded: "Through unbelief, fear, and insanity. And I tell her bad things about God. We (he and his network) work together to use God's Word against her." Four demons were in his network and they were, (1) **Sex**, who sought to destroy her relationship with God and caused confusion through lies and distortion; (2) **Fear**, who caused her not to believe God and caused bondage through fear and many other things; (3) **Deception**, who made her believe everything the demonic network said about God. They made her doubt God's love and believe that she was guilty and God could not forgive her; (4) **Temptation**, who drew her to sin and away from God and wanted to destroy her like the other demons did. All of these demons had one common goal--their purpose was to destroy Jane's relationship with God.

## DEMON-PRODUCED PERSONALITY SAMANTHA

**Demon-Produced Personality Samantha** was responsible for distorting truth and making her believe lies. He had two demons working under him: (1) **Deception**, who caused deception and had **six demons in his network, all called Deception** and performing the same work of deception; and (2) **Fear**, who caused her not to believe the work of God or his goodness. **He had twelve demons in his network**, all carrying the same name--Fear--and all performing the same work--that of instigating fear. When I questioned **Fear** as to whether or not there were any more demons in his network, he at first said, "No." He later confessed to having four more, and that he (**Fear**) answered to all the demons.

## A SHARING DEMON

A demon named **Destruction** was a sharing demon between Jane and her husband. Demon Destruction worked for Ancestral Demon Samantha. He was dealt with in the usual manner.

## JANE'S SON'S UNWANTED INHERITANCE

We learned that Jane's son **Kenneth Warren Franklin** had a flip-side and an ancestral demon. Four demons, **Unbelief, Fear, Deception, and Rebellion**, were in his network, plus two demon-produced personalities by the names of Samantha and Devon. Through the Lord Jesus, her son's flip-side was healed and fused. The ancestral demon and his network were called in, attached to Ancestral Demon Jane Renee Wilson, and sent to the pit.

After this was accomplished, my next session was due to begin. Time had run out to make certain the flip-side and core were fused and integrated, to check for any fragmented personalities, and to make certain the demons had left. We met for a second session, which I began by asking the Lord to bring up **Ancestral Demon Jane Renee Wilson** if he were still there; and if he were, to make him reveal the remaining ground in Jane's life. He answered, "I'm not going to answer you!" I rebuked him in the name of the Lord Jesus and demanded him to answer me. I asked him if he were hiding any fragmented personalities and he said, "Yes." I asked him if that would stand as truth before the eternal throne of Christ, and he still said, "Yes!" However, when I told him to give me the names of the fragmented personalities, he cried, "No! We don't know!" I told him that I knew he was lying. I then asked him if he had prevented the flip-side and core from fusing and integrating. He said that they had not fused. I pressed him and asked if that stood as truth before the Lord and he said, "Yes." I asked how he had prevented their fusing; he said, "I lied! Flip-side Samantha is a part of witchcraft and I kept her from praying to give it to Christ and receive him!"

I asked what ground he held to be able to prevent this, and he replied, "It's been passed down." When I asked him how, he said, "By the family." I pressed him further, demanding he tell me what had been passed down through the family. He said, "I've already told you! By witchcraft! I sent up a lying demon to pray when you asked Flip-side Samantha to pray and break all ties with witchcraft. We fooled you!"

I asked the Lord to restrain the demons and to allow Flip-side Samantha to talk with me. She said that she was hindered in praying, but that she really wanted to. At that point, I led her to pray, inviting the Lord Jesus into her life and breaking all ancestral ties with witchcraft. For her new name, flip-side Samantha chose to share the name Jane with the core, and they were fused and integrated. This completed, I asked the Lord to bring forth the next personality.

## FRAGMENTED PERSONALITY NO-NAME, AGE FOUR

Upon asking **No-Name, age four**, to tell me about herself, she answered, "I'm afraid." When I asked what she was afraid of, she replied, "I don't know." "What brought you into existence?" I asked. "I don't know," came the answer. Asked what she knew about adult Jane's life, she said, "She's fearful." When asked if she were responsible for doing that to Jane's life, however, she denied it. I pressed her to tell me what she <u>did</u> do in adult Jane's life, and she insisted, "I don't know." I asked her what the word **confusion** meant to her; she admitted, "I'm confused and scared." "Is that what you do in Jane's life?" I asked. "Yes, but I don't want to be this way--this is just the way I am. I just want to feel loved," she answered.

Jane had told me earlier about always feeling afraid of a certain picture on a wall. I asked this personality if she knew anything about the picture; she said, "Yes, it scares me." She took responsibility for scaring Jane concerning the picture. Her major emotions were **fear, confusion, loneliness, and a desire to feel loved**. When I invited her to give all of this to Jesus and accept him as her Savior, she readily did so. She also was readily made one with Jane--was fused and integrated and shared her name.

## FRAGMENTED PERSONALITY NO-NAME, AGE SEVENTEEN

When fragmented personality **No-name**, age seventeen, was asked to talk about herself and what brought her into existence, she replied, "Sin--sexual immorality brought me about." When asked what she did in adult Jane's life, she admitted, "I make her feel guilty and I frighten her." I asked how she managed to frighten her. She said, "I frighten her with sex." I asked if she did that within her marriage, and she replied, "Yes. I make it seem dirty and disgusting." I asked her if she did anything else in Jane's life, she said, "Just guilt and fear of punishment."

I continued to question her, asking if she were the one who made Jane believe that she were going to lose her salvation. She replied, "No, I just make her feel guilty and fear punishment." I asked if she were the one trying to make her believe that she's going to get AIDS (a fear mentioned earlier). "Yes! I was raped by a Mormon at the age of seventeen! He may have had AIDS!" came the reply. I asked if this is when she, No-name, came into existence, and she said, "Yes."

I asked No-name if she would like to receive Christ and give all her problems to Him, and she answered, "Yes, but will He forgive me?" After assuring her that He would, she prayed to receive Christ and took on the core's name and was fused and integrated with her.

I proceeded to look for more personalities by asking if there were anyone else between the ages of thirteen and nineteen. There were none. Then I asked if there were any between twenty and twenty-seven. I heard a soft, "Yes," and found a twenty-three-year-old fragmented personality.

## FRAGMENTED PERSONALITY NO-NAME, AGE TWENTY-THREE

The Lord revealed a fragmented personality named **No-name**, age twenty-three. I asked what had brought her into existence and she answered, "Sin." when asked what kind of sin, she responded, "Sexual immorality." When I asked her to tell me about herself, she balked. I asked her what she did in twenty-seven-year-old Jane's life, and she replied, "I try to draw her away from the Lord through sin." When I asked what kind of sins, she replied, "All kinds of sins!"

I learned that the major emotion ruling in No-name's life was **rebellion**. When I asked why she didn't know the Lord as her Savior, she said, "I don't know." I asked if Jane's salvation meant anything to her and she replied, "Yes, it does. It means to spend an eternity with God, but I'm bad and I never wanted to be that way. It all started with sexual immorality with Ed" (who is now her husband). "Is this when you were created?" I asked. "Yes" came her answer. When asked whether she made Jane feel guilty about that, she admitted that she did. However, when asked whether she made Jane doubt her salvation, she said that she didn't.

She readily repented, and said she wanted to give all her sins of sexual immorality, as well as the guilt and the shame, to Jesus and to accept Him. She assumed Jane's name and was fused and integrated with her. We searched for other fragmented personalities between the ages of thirteen and nineteen. There were none. I asked if there were any from the ages of twenty through twenty-seven; a twenty-six-year-old personality spoke.

## FRAGMENTED PERSONALITY UNBELIEF AND FEAR

Like the others, **Unbelief and Fear**, age twenty-six, said that sin brought her into existence. As her name reflects, however, her sins were unbelief and fear. When asked what she did in Jane's life, she said, "I cause her to doubt the Word of God and His goodness. I cause her to have fear because of those things." I asked if she were also the one causing her to doubt her salvation. She said, "Yes. I don't ever let her enjoy peace."

I asked her if she were miserable and would like to enjoy the peace of knowing that Jesus loves her and will never leave her. She answered, "Yes". She confessed her sins, gave them to Jesus and received Him as her Savior. Then, she was fused and integrated with Jane the core and shared her name. All ground was reclaimed from the demons who stood on that ground. Then, I questioned the **Ancestral Demon Jane Renee Wilson** as to whether or not he had any more ground. After pressing him to make certain his "No" was truth, we sent all the demons to the pit and had a free lady, rejoicing over her victories through our dear Lord Jesus Christ!

## NO DEMONS, NO FLIP-SIDE--JUST A FRAGMENTED PERSONALITY, CASE #12

While it is a joy to be a part in helping set souls free from the demonic, demons are surely no pleasure to deal with. So I must admit it is refreshing when I find a counselee with none. Such was the case when a charming, fifty-three-year-old Christian lady, whom I will call Anna, came to me for counseling. She had gotten saved at age eleven and really loved the Lord, but knew down deep inside that something was wrong. During her second year of college she had married a man whom I'll call Pete, and they had two children. Anna and Pete were married only three years. Pete was a drunk and a wife beater. Anna was deeply hurt in this marriage, very much stepped-on--not only by Pete, but also by her own mother, who was a very jealous person. Anna's mother was jealous of Anna and of her own husband, Anna's dad. When Anna had been inducted into her school's honor society, her mom and dad hadn't come. Anna longed for her mother's acceptance and love, and had not dealt well at all with the rejection. No matter what Anna would achieve, it would never please her mother.

Time passed; Anna married again. While her second husband didn't physically abuse her, he rejected her with verbal abuse, indicating that she didn't measure up to his expectations. Anna also suffered some great hurts from her first two children. I must inject, however, that she was blessed with loving children from her second marriage.

At this point in our session, she took all her known sins and hurts to Jesus and left them on the cross. She claimed back the ground she had given Satan by hanging onto the hurts, unforgiveness, etc. As Anna told her story, she was a very soft, loving, caring, but very hurt lady. The tears just poured while she told her story. One thing I learned about Anna was that at the age of twenty-one, she had stopped going by the name of Anna and took on the name Annie. After I had explained the procedure

in dealing with the ancestral demon and flip-side, I asked God to set aside fifty-three year old Anna Jean Gray Smith. After searching diligently for the ancestral demon carrying her formal name and for the flip-side, I was confident that there were none. Then, I asked the Lord to reveal any fragmented personalities. One called Annie began to speak.

## FRAGMENTED PERSONALITY ANNIE

I asked **Annie**, age twenty-one through fifty-three, to tell me about herself and she exclaimed, "I get all the junk! She lets people hurt her. I'm her safety net because she cares too much about people." I asked what she held most against Anna and she replied, "She lets her mother hurt her, and she doesn't make demands. I guess she's afraid people won't love and care for her. Anna never makes demands on people. She just takes what everybody hands out to her, and I won't! I come up; I get in their face and make demands. Nobody is going to unjustly step on me!"

Annie revealed to me that she knew the Lord Jesus just like Anna did, but that she was not going to take anyone's junk. I found that Anna had created Annie to take over when people hurt her. If people put undue pressure on Anna, Annie would come up and protect her. Annie would prevent anyone from being rude or from stepping on Anna. Annie became the rude, tough one. She wasn't going to put up with anything!

Because Anna had allowed Annie to come about and both were saved, I had to get both of them to go to the Cross and ask Jesus to forgive them. Both had to claim back ground and ask one another's forgiveness. They were fused and integrated and readily asked the Lord to make them one, sharing the name Anna.

Today, when I have the opportunity to see Anna, she is literally a different lady! She is beautifully balanced in her personality. While she is very soft, loving, and caring, she has a quiet strength and boldness that comes from God. Anna labors faithfully in serving the Lord and speaks boldly of His truths, and she no longer lets people intimidate her or take advantage of her. Anna, indeed, is a very neat Christian lady to be around. Rita and I love her dearly, as well as her husband and children. I have worked with the entire family and they are a joy and pleasure to be around.

## ANNA'S HUSBAND, RANDALL LEE SMITH, CASE #13

Anna's husband, **Randall Lee Smith**, is now a very tender-hearted man who loves Jesus a great deal. The love of Christ is evident in how he treats his wife, his children, and his fellow brethren. He is a very strong, faithful worker for the Lord.

When he came to me, he also knew that something wasn't right deep down inside his being. He was well aware that he had deeply hurt Anna, and that he was frequently very hard, prideful, insensitive, and hurtful toward other people as well. Randall took all his known sins to the cross and claimed back the ground from Satan. Prior to Randall's session with me, I had asked him to journal to help save time in our session. He recorded things that God had shown him that were contrary to God's will for his life.

Among his other problems, Randall had a major problem with lust--no matter how much he called it sin and confessed it, he was bombarded with it. He had done everything I had suggested and had claimed back the ground, but he was still tormented by lust. This is an example of having a desire to change, but continuing to struggle with a stronghold, finding it seemingly impossible to control. In such cases, someone else may have a tighter grip on the controls.

I prayed, asking God to set aside our fifty-eight-year-old Randall Lee Smith who got saved at age nineteen, but to let him be aware of all that was going on. I asked God to place a hedge of Christ's blood between him and all that was opposed to God. Then I called for **Ancestral Demon Randall Lee Smith.**

## ANCESTRAL DEMON RANDALL LEE SMITH

"What do you do in Randall's life?" I asked. "I control him," he replied. I asked, "How?" "Any way I want to," he boasted. "What else do you do?" I asked. "I make it hard for him to remember scripture passages, and I make him hurt other people. I make him hurt Anna." Upon further questioning, he replied, "I make him have lustful thoughts." I asked what other purposes he had in Randall's life; he said, "I want to destroy his witness!" Asked how many demons were in his personal network, he said there were three. They were: (1) Lust, who made him have lustful thoughts; (2) Confusion, who kept him from understanding and remembering scripture and other things he read, and made him impatient and angry if things weren't going well with business; (3) Randall L. Smith, who declared he was the one in the front--not only the businessman meeting the public, but also the man getting angry and ruining his testimony for Christ.

## SHARED DEMONS BETWEEN RANDALL, ANNA, AND THEIR CHILDREN

Upon discovering shared demons between Randall, Anna, and their children, we made the ancestral demon Randall Lee Smith tell us what was in each one and made him call in all the demons and attach them to himself. Every time we had looked for demons in Anna and his children, we found none; the shared demons would hide in Randall. We learned that they would come and go as they pleased, going back to Randall because that was their original, **real** home.

All the shared demons belonged to Randall. Through the name of the Lord Jesus, I made **Ancestral Demon Randall** call them in and they were sent to the pit. I thank the Lord over and over again for the victory we have through Him over the powers of darkness! What a joy it is to know that this dear family is doing so well through our Lord Jesus!

## A CHRISTIAN MOTHER HELPS SET HER SON FREE FROM AN ANCESTRAL DEMON, CASE #14

Some time back, I had counseled a delightful Christian woman who dearly loves the Lord. She had stayed in contact with me and became very interested when she learned I was writing a book in hopes of passing on the things I had learned to those who would counsel others. She volunteered to help proof-read the book, so I sent her a copy of what I had written thus far. After only proofing the first few chapters, she wrote a letter with the following excerpt:

As a result of the information that is written in this book and a personal witness to this form of counseling, I began seeing and realizing that my oldest son Chase, who is now sixteen, was in bondage and controlled by something other than Jesus Christ. Chase was not a bad child but just seemed to not have joy in his life. He could not gain victory in some areas of his walk, which caused him to just give up. He couldn't explain why he would lie to me, knowing he would get caught, or why he would rebel in a deceptive sort of way, but sooner or later would be caught in this as well. I knew he needed help but he must be willing to receive this help. I began sharing the truths of this book with friends and family. Chase, listening to this, came, asking me to see if there could be an ancestral demon in his life. I knew if we did not act upon this information, he would live a defeated life which could even cause him to turn away from Christ altogether.

I took Chase and prayed, asking God to help us see if there could be an ancestral demon by taking the ancestral demon and his network of demons, along with the flip-side and any fragmented personalities, bind them, gag them, make them inoperative and place them in the heavenlies for a period of one week. What Chase felt and I saw was proof enough that there was indeed an ancestral demon. During that week, Chase had joy, excitement to read God's Word and understand it. There was no block to keep him away from this. After the week was up, they did come back and it was obvious. We both knew that we had to follow up with this. We did find an ancestral demon carrying his formal name with a flip-side and eight demons in his network. I was surprised to see the hold they had on him. Masturbation, Pride, Lies, Rebellion, Deception, Lust, Stubbornness, and Selfishness. The flip-side who was sixteen had so much hate for Chase because of his love for the Lord. He wanted Chase to hate as well and to feel sorry for himself. After leading the flip-side to Jesus and bringing the two together like Ephesians 2:14-16 says, and also by attaching all the network of demons to the ancestral demon and sending them to the pit, Chase was freed. There has been such a change in his life and attitude. He must stop some of the habits that were formed, but they no longer control him and the trials are there only for his growth now. 'To him who is free, he is free indeed.' John 8:36.

Chase's mother went on to share the following testimony of what God had been doing in her own life:

As a result of a lot of things, God has been teaching me about the heart. In Jeremiah 17:9-10, He writes, 'The heart is more deceitful than all else, and is desperately sick. Who can understand it? I, the Lord, search the heart, I test the mind. Even to give to each man according to his ways. According to the results of his deeds.' I realized He says the heart is deceitful above all else, only God knew it, I don't even know my own heart, it was deceiving me. The Word of God says 'Blessed are the pure in heart for they shall see God', Matthew 5:8. I knew I wanted to see God in all His glory as Moses saw God in Exodus 33:17-23, but only God knew my heart, only He could make it pure. So, I asked God to reveal to me the deception in my own heart. He did immediately.

I have an illness, and I've made remarks to friends, 'I'm honored God finds me worthy enough to bear this disease.' The Lord showed me the deception in this. He said, 'You are not worthy in such a statement. You have exalted yourself above others.' My heart had deceived me thinking myself to be humble. I was full of pride. Only God and God alone is worthy. I've repented and am truly aware of how very easily the enemy can deceive our hearts. God desires for us to know truth. He longs to show Himself to us. I am learning daily to allow God to show me the deception in my heart as He exposes the lies of our adversary the Devil. Truly I can do nothing apart from God, not even be ill. To God be glory, honor, and praise forevermore.

What a blessing it is to receive such wonderful updates on how people are applying God's truths to bring victory, peace and joy to their lives! **Again, to God be the glory!**

# CHAPTER TWELVE
## CONQUERING CONFUSION

### THE CONFUSED KARATE MAN, CASE #15

I met a fine couple, David and his wife Jan, while preaching a revival in a church where they were members. David continued to contact me from time to time; the subject matter always concerned his doubting his salvation. I had led him to the Lord over the phone and thought his salvation was settled. He called me again, however, telling me that his pastor had led him to pray and he had gotten saved.

David became very active in his church and everything seemed to be going great for his family and him. A couple of years later, however, David again was doubting his salvation. As he told me of his struggles pertaining to his salvation, I responded by telling him that if he were still having trouble after all this time, it was quite possible the problem was demonic. We scheduled some appointments to get to the bottom of it. David had originally thought he was saved at the age of thirteen or fourteen.

What started off being a simple problem turned into a huge problem stemming from S.R.A. and Karate. While I cannot give you a detail-by-detail account of the sessions, I will attempt to summarize David's case as briefly as possible. When I first started working with David, I had yet to learn of the ancestral demon carrying the victim's formal name. I first discovered a demon named **Lucifer**, and he bragged of the ground he held in David's life.

### DEMON LUCIFER

**Demon Lucifer's ground** was David's **lust** and **anger at God** for not helping him, and there were seven demons in his network. They were, (1) **John I,** who caused pain; (2) **Fred**, who was mean and caused David to be mean; (3) **Melissa**, who caused perverted sex and bestiality; (4) **Chuck**, who performed the Karate; (5) **Ed**, who caused David to hit people; (6) **John II**, who caused David to whimper and whine; and (7) **Edward**, who cheated and stole.

### DEMON-PRODUCED PERSONALITIES

I found two demon-produced personalities and both of them were connected with David's involvement with Karate and its meditation. They were, (1) **John**, age five, who said, "I'm visiting. I fly here and there. I fly to hell and other places through meditation"; and (2) **Chuck**, age thirty-five, who said, "I'm a thirty-five-year-old Chuck and I came flying in through meditation."

### DEMON ED

Then, we met and dealt with **Demon Ed**, who caused David to mock people and make fun of them.

## DEMON MOLLY

We met **Demon Molly** who reported: "I came into David's life at age fourteen when he had sex with his cousin Molly. I tempt him to have sex and to lust."

## FLIP-SIDE PERSONALITY DAVID

The Lord enabled us to meet **Flip-side Personality David**, age thirty-two, who boasted, "I'm the Karate expert. I like to kill people." I asked Flip-side David what he thought about the other core personality David and he replied, "He's weak." Then he proceeded to tell me, "I hate my dad and I'm mad and depressed." I inquired about his salvation and he said he didn't get saved when the core David did at age thirteen or fourteen because, "Dad's mean and he said I didn't get saved. This is **a bunch of bull**" (was laughing very hard). I asked him again what he thought about David; he replied, "He's dumb and he does stupid things!" "Why?" I asked. "He just does." Flip-side David said, in describing his major emotions: "I'm angry with Dad because he slaps me, chokes me, and he beats up on me with words." He was fused and integrated with David and continued to share his name.

## DAVID'S ANCESTRAL DEMON (NOT BY HIS FORMAL NAME)

Sometimes the ancestral demon would permit demons to give their names and the works they performed and we were able to do away with them, however, upon learning of ones who seemed to have stronger holds on David, confusion abound. Despite our not yet knowing about the ancestral demon carrying the formal name, the Lord caused the ancestral demon to give us a great deal of information that allowed us to continue to make headway with David.

## DEMON FRED

We dealt with **Demon Fred**, who bragged, "I tell him what to do. I tell him he's lost. I came into his life at the age of thirty, when he thought he got saved, so he wouldn't grow in the Lord."

## DEMON JOHN

It was **Demon John** who confessed to bringing confusion into David's life. He said, "I came through David's hating a friend of his dad's. Demon John had two demons in his network and they were: (1) **Profanity** and (2) **Vulgarity**.

## DEMON DON

**Demon Don** said he was connected with Karate vows and was a trans-talker. We learned that when David was in meditation **Demon Don** was free to influence him concerning the **Karate vows**.

## AN ANCESTRAL DEMON MASQUERADING AS A FLIP-SIDE PERSONALITY

Due to the ancestral demon's stronghold and my not yet knowing about the formal name, he was able to masquerade as the flip-side of David. Because of this, until I learned of the ancestral demon carrying the formal name--Ancestral Demon David Wayne Flack--it was three sessions later before I was able to deal with the real flip-side and it was finally fused and integrated. (We can see why it is so important that the ancestral demon called by the formal name has been bound and gagged so that he cannot lie and masquerade as a personality.) We prayed and claimed back all the ground that was connected with sexual perversion and with Karate, then commanded the demons to leave. David was back in my office, however, in less than a month. I had asked David to journal for me. The session began with David's sharing this information from his journal: (1) I'm not sleeping well; (2) I'm drawn away to places where I don't intend to go; (3) I watched two movies with martial arts and sex in them. I changed the channel when the sex scenes appeared, but I wanted to switch back to it; (4) I am full of depression; (5) I feel attacked concerning salvation; (6) I feel low self-esteem and unworthiness; (7) I think lustful thoughts along with accusing and condemning thoughts; (8) I feel like there is a lot of deception; and (9) I still feel like Chuck's inside. I then began looking for any fragmented personalities that truly belonged to David, and the Lord showed us four.

## FRAGMENTED PERSONALITY JOHN I

**John I**, age five, spoke, saying, "I keep him awake and afraid of the darkness. A monster will come in the door and I will jump out of my bed and fight him." The usual procedure took place and he chose to share David's name.

## FRAGMENTED PERSONALITY RON

Then we met **Ron**, age fifteen. His works were fear and confusion, and he said, "I fear God because He's holy." He was confused about salvation, and added, "I doubt. I don't understand why He would save me, so I don't believe He did." The usual procedure took place and he, too, shared David's name.

## FRAGMENTED PERSONALITY CHUCK

We then met **Chuck**, age 30 or 32, who announced, "I'm the Karate expert. I'm mean and cocky. But I have doubts about salvation because I'm unworthy." He, too, made things right between the Lord, David, and himself, and shared David's name. I then began searching for any demon-produced personalities.

## DEMON-PRODUCED PERSONALITY KARATE CHING

**Demon-produced Karate Ching** represented the **silent death touch, a fatal curse that kills**. This demon-produced personality stood on the ground of the fragmented personality named Chuck. On the ground of Ching stood four demons. They were, (1) **Demon Zen**, who reported that he was there because of Karate and the belief in earth, wind, and fire. Zen had the power to kill without use of the physical hand; (2) **Demon Kai**, who came through Karate and held the power of Karate from the center of the body. He also claimed the power of meditation to look through an object; (3) **Dumb**

229

**Spirit,** who claimed he had ground and cursed the body. He reported that he came from a Masonic Lodge in another city to curse him with dumbness; and (4) **Demon Affliction**, who caused pain and headaches so he couldn't think clearly.

At this point in counseling, we broke all ties with Karate, commanded the demons to the pit, and thought we were through. However, David called, telling me he was still troubled. I had already ceased taking counseling sessions and had begun writing this book, so he had a long wait before him. He began suffering increasingly heavy thoughts that something within him was trying to kill him. When driving, he felt as though something were going to drive him off a bridge. I could make him wait no longer. I had him come over and was excited about his coming, for since I had last seen him, I had learned of the ancestral demon's carrying the formal name. I also learned that if there is an ancestral demon, he can sit in the shadows and disrupt the counseling session, causing all kinds of lies and confusion. I sought the ancestral demon.

## ANCESTRAL DEMON DAVID WAYNE FLACK

The Lord revealed **Ancestral Demon David Wayne Flack**; then the Lord also showed us **Ancestral Demon Jack Wayne Flack**. This second ancestral demon carried the name of David's dad and had coequal power with Ancestral Demon David, and all the other demonic network worked for both of them. The Lord began uncovering a major demonic programming in David associated with Karate. We began learning some significant key names of demons: **Chicken**, who claimed to make David fight, **White Sheet**, which stood for blanking out David's mind, and **Flame**, a picture appearing in David's mind of flame by which stood a Kung Fu priest named **Chung Ling** with demons working directly for him. David's confusion was on its way to being dissolved.

## FRAGMENTED PERSONALITY CAPTAIN FROGGER I

We met **Captain Frogger I.** When I asked him what he did in David's life, he responded, "I go diving." "What else do you do?" I inquired. "I swim." "What else?" I asked. "Be the Captain! I help him!" Asked how he helped him he responded, "He needs me for support and strength. I'm the feisty one." Upon asking what his major emotions were he declared, "I have all of his emotions and I stuff them. I spear them like a great fish!"

After gathering the information, I invited him to meet the Lord Jesus; he stated, "David doesn't show me what it's like." I asked him what he meant, and he said, "David loves Jesus, but I am the Captain of his life. He used to go diving a bunch, and he prayed, asking God whether or not He wanted to use him in a diving ministry. If He didn't, to show him and get him out. We came face to face with a shark and we have not been back. I was scared because he asked Jesus to show him if he was to stop diving or not. Diving was like a god to him because that's what I like to do in his life." Having God's salvation offered to him, he readily received Him, confessed his sins--**including having diving as his god**--and claimed back all the ground. He gave it all to Jesus and invited Him to be the Lord of his life. He very appropriately chose the new name of **Victory I**. There was also a demon named **Captain Frogger**, working for **Ancestral Demon David**, stationed to this ground.

## FRAGMENTED PERSONALITY JOHN II

The Lord then revealed another fragmented personality. **John II** came forward crying. I asked him if someone had hurt him, and he said, "Yes." I asked who and he replied, "My daddy." I asked him his name again and he answered, "John II," while still crying. I questioned him again as to who had hurt him; he sobbed, "I can't see. I don't want to tell." I asked what his daddy did to hurt him and he said, "I don't want to tell." When I asked if he had hurt him sexually, he replied, "I'm blindfolded. He put his thing in my mouth. He raped me." His major emotions were shame and hurt. Upon inviting him to receive the Lord Jesus as his Savior and give all his hurts and memories to Him, with much crying, he asked, "Will He take away the pain?" I assured him that Jesus would, and he followed through, receiving Christ and being fused and integrated with David. He had chosen the wonderful new name of **Triumph**.

## FRAGMENTED PERSONALITY MR. GRIND

We then met a fragmented personality named **Mr. Grind**, age twenty-five. Upon my asking what he did in David's life, he answered, "I deal with it." What do you mean, I asked? "I get things done." I questioned, what else do you do? "I grind--I'm a cool dude." When he told me that his major emotion was anger, I asked what he was angry about. He answered, "Jan." I asked, why are you angry with Jan? He declared, "She doesn't do anything!" Knowing David was sometimes verbally cruel to his wife, I asked him if he were the one who was so mean to her. He said, "Sometimes." I asked if he were also the prideful one; he replied, "I get things done and I can be boastful and cocky sometimes." After confessing that his pride was surely messing up his marriage and his entire life, he confessed his sins to the Lord and received Him as his Savior. He expressed that he really wanted the Lord to change his lifestyle, and took on the very appropriate new name of **Abundant Life**.

## FRAGMENTED PERSONALITY MR. GADGET

"What is your work in David's life, **Mr. Gadget**, age twenty-seven?" I asked? "I make him sleepy." "Why?" I questioned. "Because I'm tired of everybody putting everything off on me!" "Why do you think they do that?" I asked. "Because when they tell me to make something, I do it." Mr. Gadget's major emotion was **hate**. He declared, "I hate people pushing me. They always push things off on me. I feel insecure and doubtful about things I do." Mr. Gadget readily confessed his sins--including his hatred--and turned his life over to the Lord and received Him as his Savior. The usual procedure was followed and he chose the new name of **Conqueror**.

## FRAGMENTED PERSONALITY CAPTAIN FROGGER II

After I met **Captain Frogger**, age twenty-three, I asked what he did in David's life. He stated, "I play frogger games. We jump over logs and when cars go by we try to jump between them. I go diving." "What else do you do?" I asked. "I used to go with the diving one, but he is now fused, so I just play games." I asked him what kind of games he played. He retorted, "I play with people's emotions!" I asked if he were able to manipulate their emotions. He answered, "Yes. I make Jan feel bad about herself because she spends too much money. I make the boys feel bad about themselves when I'm correcting them." Captain Frogger repented also and said he would stop playing hurtful games with people's emotions. He accepted Jesus and chose the new name of **Victory II**.

**FRAGMENTED PERSONALITY G.I. JOE**

We then met a fragmented personality named **G.I. Joe**, age seven, who admitted that his work in David's life was to play games. When I asked what kind of games he played, he answered, "People fighting." When I inquired as to what type of fighting, he said, "The good guys and the enemy!" I asked if he did anything else and he replied, "No." I asked if there were more than one G.I. Joe and he said, "Yes. G.I. Joe II." When I asked G.I. Joe II's age, he replied, "He's eight years old and he's better than I am! He's a Commando!"

I inquired further as to what he did in adult David's life and he said, "I play." What do you play, I asked? "I play with my dog. I play ball. I play Chess. I am programmed to do perverted things." I asked what type of perverted things he did, and he replied, "Sexual things with animals and I'm the one who looks at sexy billboards. My left eye hurts and so does my head." Soon, he did as the others, confessing his sins, receiving the Lord and turning his life over to Him. He chose a great new name, **Warrior in Christ**.

**FRAGMENTED PERSONALITY G.I. JOE II**

The Lord showed us **G.I. Joe II**, age eight. He reported, "I'm G.I. Joe the Commando! I set bombs and play tricks. I play tricks on people." I asked what type of tricks he played? "All kinds. I used to do that all the time and I'm sneaky, kinda like a Ninja fighter," he answered. When I asked him what he did in adult David's life, he admitted, "I do sneaky things, but David doesn't let me act like a Ninja fighter. He doesn't allow it but we tried." He also confessed, "I find things out. Like when David was almost in a divorce, we tapped into the phone lines to hear Jan talking. I try to control things, people, and circumstances. I even get him to play church games. I play like he's a respectable Christian. And I give him eye and head pain too." G.I. Joe II said that he would like to stop the games, give it all to Jesus and receive Him as Savior. He picked the wonderful new name of **Ambassador for Christ.**

**FRAGMENTED PERSONALITY JACK**

Upon meeting the next fragmented personality, **Jack**, age seventeen, in asking what he did in David's life he responded, "I stutter and copy people. My name came from another Jack, somebody at David's work who stutters," he answered. Do you do anything else in David's life, I asked? "I stutter and confuse his thoughts, break his thoughts. I play games. I used to play jokes by throwing dirt clods at people. I make fun of people by stuttering. I mimic those who stutter. They (the demons) tell me to block. They push me in front of a lot of people and I cause David to stutter. When he faces making a decision or dealing with authority, the demons push me there and cause the bosses to misunderstand David because he stutters." Jack repented, gave all the stuttering games to the Lord and received Him as Savior. He chose the new name of **Peace** and was fused and integrated.

**FRAGMENTED PERSONALITY JOHN III**

We met fragmented personality **John III**, age five. I asked what his work was; he said, "I name people." How, I asked? He replied, "I play cards." I asked what kind of names he gave people. He answered, "Funny names." I asked what he did in adult David's life and he replied, "I smile a lot and

get him into trouble." I asked what he meant and he said, "When he's supposed to be serious, I just smile." I inquired as to what else he did. "I yawn a lot and do funny things that are cute. I'm a game player. My eyes hurt. They travel around the cards. They travel in Kung Fu and Karate. They travel from one player to the next. They send a curse through me. I am used by the Mercenary and he's real mean!" I asked him if he were willing to repent of his sins, receive Christ as Savior, and ask Jesus to throw **Demon Mercenary** out. He indicated that he would and followed through. He chose the new name of Joy, and was fused and integrated.

## FRAGMENTED PERSONALITY THE DUDE

Then, we met a fragmented personality who called himself **The Dude**, age twenty. "Tell me about yourself and what you do in David's life," I asked. He answered, "I keep it straight. I'm legalism. I make David get it right. I make sure he does it right. I make him feel bad. I depress him because he can't do it right." I asked him if he thought he knew everything, and he boasted, "I've held back-- saved the best for the last! **I am The Dude!** I make him think legalistically. I'm Kung Fu connected and I do the Karate moves right. I drive him and the Commando. I used to make him do speed and other drugs." Upon sharing God's salvation plan for him, The Dude confessed that he was tired of trying to be perfect and having to be the best. He confessed all the junk in his life as sin, and received the saving grace of the Lord Jesus. He chose his new name--**Grace**.

## FRAGMENTED PERSONALITY HOOK-AND-CABLE

We then met a fragmented personality named **Hook-and-cable**, age twenty-five. When asked what he did in David's life, he said, "I cause problems in his mind. I like to swim and run." I questioned him as to what he did in his mind and he answered, "I confuse his mind. I swim in his mind and cause his thoughts to leave. I opened up a space for a curse to be put on him." I said, "Well, Hook-and-cable, you're really messing up his mind. You're not helping him at all, are you?" He admitted he wasn't. Based on information I had read in David's journal, I asked him if he kept David fastened like a hook and cable to the demons. He admitted that he did, but repented, received Christ as Savior, and allowed the Lord to unhook him from the demonic so that he and David could be free and fused. He chose the name **Peace-and-joy**.

## FRAGMENTED PERSONALITY SLEEPY

Sleepy, age eight, was the next fragmented personality we met. He bragged that he kept David tired and sleepy. He added, "I cause him not to be able to think straight. I block his thoughts. I have the curse on his mind and the curse on his eyes. I'm the one who used pot. I'm the one who keeps his mind in a fog and darkness." When I witnessed to Sleepy of God's plan of salvation, he asked, "Would He do that for me?" I told him that Jesus would love to do that for him; in fact, He <u>had</u> already done that for him. He readily confessed his sins and placed his trust in Him. The new name he chose was **Light-of-Truth**.

## FRAGMENTED PERSONALITY EDDIE

The next fragmented personality was named **Eddie**, age nine. Will you come out and talk with me, Eddie, I asked? He said, "No. You're mean." I asked why he thought I was mean and he responded,

"You yell." Even though he had said that he wouldn't talk to me, he opened up and spilled his emotions. I asked for him to please tell me about Jamie and her family. David had mentioned them in his journaling. He responded, "She's a blond, her mom's a brunette with long hair, and her dad has long hair too. They gave me a peace sign." They had given Eddie an article bearing a peace symbol-- an article of paraphernalia used by satanists. They had put a curse on David's mind to block his memory from having had sex with Jamie in front of her parents. As I shared God's grace through salvation to him, he repented and received Christ as his personal Savior. The new name he chose was **Love**.

## FRAGMENTED PERSONALITY JOHN

**John**, age eight, was the next one we met. I asked John to tell me about himself. He softly replied, "I'm the little boy left in the deer stand after dark." "Who left you there?" I asked. "Daddy," he replied. When I asked him why he thought his daddy left him there, he answered, "I don't know." I asked how he felt and he answered, "I feel hopeless." I questioned him as to what he did in David's life, and he said, "I make him afraid and I make him cry. I make him pity himself and make him pout. I make him complain and feel hopeless." When I asked him if he wanted to get rid of all that pity, fear, and hopelessness, he replied, "Yes! I want to get rid of all of it!" He confessed his sins and received Christ. The name he chose was **Hope**.

## FRAGMENTED PERSONALITY BULLY

The Lord allowed us to meet another fragmented personality. His name was **Bully**, age nine. Knowing of a particular incident, I asked **Bully** if he were the one involved with the lawn mowing incident, and with beating a boy up with a hammer. "Yes," he confessed. I asked, "Why?" He answered, "Daddy told me if I didn't beat him up, he was going to whip me. I hit the boy seven times in the head and he cried and left."

I asked **Bully** if he were also the one who smirks in David's life when he hears something bad. He smirked and admitted that he was. Asked what else he did in David's life, he replied: "I'm the one who whips his sons too hard." "Why do you do that?" I asked. "They deserve it!" Bully's major emotions turned out to be revenge, hate, unforgiveness, bitterness, and fear. His fear stemmed from the dread of his daddy's whipping him if he didn't defend himself. He readily chose to turn all of his bully behavior over to the Lord, confess his sins and receive Christ as His Lord and Savior. He chose the new name of **Love**.

## FRAGMENTED PERSONALITY RONNIE I

Then, we met **Ronnie I**, age four, who admitted, "I have the memory and I can't see because it's dark. It's dark here." "Why is it dark?" I asked. "Because they have put something over my eyes." "What do you do in adult David's life?" I asked. "I give him fear." Asked what he was afraid of, he said, "Them guys--the meanies--the demons. They pass me around. There's a star in a circle and there are five places there." I questioned who was there. "The little ones. Daddy took me to that room and they covered up my eyes and they whipped me. There's one little boy and he's Ronnie II," he answered. "What do you do in adult David's life?" I asked. "I fear. They control." "Who are they?" I asked. "They are Free Masons where Daddy belongs." Ronnie expressed his desire to be free from

the fears and other hurts. He gave them to Jesus, confessed his sins and accepted the Lord as his Savior. Ronnie I also chose the name of **Hope**.

## FRAGMENTED PERSONALITY SPIKE

The next fragmented personality was **Spike**, age thirteen. "Can you tell me how old you are, **Spike**?" I asked. "No," he answered. I asked why he couldn't. "I don't know." I inquired as to what he did in David's life. "I lie and tell jokes." I asked what else he did; he answered, "I accuse people. I sneak out of the room at home. I ride a motorcycle and I smoke. I dip tobacco. I'm the one who threw oranges at the old lady too." Tell me your age, please," I said. "You know", he replied. "But, I want you to tell me," I appealed. "I'm thirteen," he answered.

When I asked him what else he did in David's life, he responded: "I cause David to look at the billboards that have sexy women on them. I do the masturbation, the pornography, and lust. I fought with Mike Diaz in the sixth grade, and I also fondled a young girl." As I offered God's plan of salvation, he said, "I want God to clean up my life if I'm not too dirty." I assured him that he was not too dirty, and that God loved him and died for him. He told me he wanted to repent and accept Christ; but asked me if I would help lead him in the prayer. He chose the name of **Long-suffering.**

## FRAGMENTED PERSONALITY RONNIE II

"Who are you?" I asked the next fragmented personality. He responded, "I'm **Ronnie II,** age five, that sits on the stand in the circle." He yawned and I said, "I see you yawning. Are you the sleepy one?" "Yes, and they hit me for not paying attention. I don't mind them and I don't listen." I asked what they wanted him to do and he replied, "Sit," he answered. "What else?" I asked. He said, "I don't know." I then questioned what he did in David's life. He responded, "I do like I did the people in the room. I don't hear and I ignore." I asked who the people were in the room. "They are Daddy's friends--the Free Masons and Satanists." Soon, he gave all his hurts to Jesus, confessed his sins, and received the Lord Jesus as Savior. Ronnie II also chose the name **Light-of-Truth** and was fused and integrated with David.

## DEMONS MASQUERADING AS PERSONALITIES

While counseling David and looking for fragmented personalities, I discovered a number of demons masquerading as personalities. They went by the names of **Baby I, Baby II, and Baby III**, all nine months old; **John, Jr.**, two years old; **No-name**, three years old; **Ronnie, five years old**; another **Ronnie, 6 months old**.

## FRAGMENTED PERSONALITY BABY

Then I met a fragmented personality named **Baby**, age six months. What do you do in David's life, I inquired? "I'm fearful and I'm lazy. I just sit here. I just sit. I was dedicated to Satan by my daddy." I asked who his daddy was, and he answered, "He's Jack Wayne Flack. I'm full of confusion of what to do. I keep David from dealing with the known sins in his life." Eventually, Baby righted everything with the Lord and with David and chose to use David's name and be fused and integrated.

I found that this fragmented personality was considered the **ancestral demon's first fru**it. Ancestral demons strive to protect the flip-side and the first fragmented personality, for he considers this his **formal ground on which he claims power**.

## FRAGMENTED PERSONALITY RAYMOND

I asked the next fragmented personality, age four, where he got his name, **Raymond**. He answered, "I'm not sure. I don't know." "What brought you into existence, Raymond?" I asked. "I had to shoot something," he answered. "What?" I asked. "I can't see," he replied. I asked the Lord Jesus to help him see what he had shot, and he then said, "I had to shoot a body with long hair." I asked him why he shot it; he answered, "My Daddy Jack made me shoot the body."

I then asked him to tell me about the girl with the long hair. He began crying hard and answered, "I don't know who she is. I just know I had to shoot her body with the rifle that was given to me. I didn't want to shoot her but my daddy made me do it. I didn't want to shoot her" (still weeping hard).

"What do you do in David's life?" I asked. "I cause him guilt and shame. I try to protect him from rejection and cause him to do anything to be accepted," he answered. I invited him to give all the fear, shame, guilt, and rejection to the Lord, and he immediately did so. I asked him if he wanted to give Jesus the hurt of the memory of shooting the girl with the long hair and he cried, "Oh, yes! I didn't want to shoot her! Daddy made me do it!" He confessed his sins and received the Lord. He chose the new name of **Accepted**, and was fused and integrated with David.

## FRAGMENTED PERSONALITY DAVE

Upon meeting the next fragmented personality, **Dave**, age eight, I asked him why he had chosen the name Dave for himself. He answered, "From Dave Harding--he's my dad's friend." I asked what brought him about. "I ran away from home," he answered. "Why?" I asked. "I can't remember," he responded. "What do you do in adult David's life?" I questioned. "I run, run from dealing with things. There is pain in my head." I asked, "Why do you think there is pain in your head?" "I don't remember. I cause David not to remember. The pain in my head just comes," he replied. "What are your major emotions, Dave?" I asked. "I'm afraid of whippings. Jack slaps me on the side of my head and it hurts. I hate Jack." "Do you think that's why you ran away from home?" I asked. "Yes. I hate Jack," he replied. I asked if his dad treated Dave Harding all right, and he said, "Yes. He likes him." I asked if he had selected the name Dave in hopes that his dad would like him. He said, "Maybe. I just want dad to like me and accept me." I ministered to him concerning Jesus' liking him, even loving him enough to die for him. He quickly received him as his Savior and repented of his sins. He chose the new name of **Accepted**, and was fused and integrated with David.

## FRAGMENTED PERSONALITY RONNIE III

When I met the next fragmented personality, **Ronnie III**, age five, I asked for him to please tell me when he got his name. "You're not supposed to know," he responded. "Was it given to you in the circle?" I asked. "Yes," he answered. "Who gave it to you?" I asked. "Jack," he replied. When I asked **Ronnie III** what he did in David's life, he said, "I make him nervous and make him run from doing what he's supposed to do. I can't decide what is right. I have a hard time making decisions."

Asked what he ran from, he answered, "Commitment." Then he asked, "Why is it so dark?" My office was well-lighted, and I asked him why he thought it was so dark. He replied, "They keep it dark and they give me something and I don't understand." I asked what they gave him, and he answered, "Some kind of drug or medicine and it makes me tired, so I can't think. They put a blindfold on me and they hit me." "Who hits you?" I inquired. "I don't know. I can't see." He said that his major emotions were **fear, darkness, anxiety, and nervousness**. I asked him if those in the circle made him do anything else and he responded, "They make me light a candle." "Anything else?" I asked. "I can't remember," he replied. When I asked him if he would like for Jesus to come and take him out of the darkness and put him into the light, he replied, "Yes! I don't like the darkness, and I don't like to be tired." He, too, received Christ; he chose the new name of Patient and was fused and integrated with David.

## FRAGMENTED PERSONALITY STUPID

We met the next fragmented personality. Right away, **Stupid**, age six, spoke while holding his head, "Jack causes it!" Asked what he caused, he responded, "My head!" "What's wrong with your head?" I inquired. "It hurts!" "What do you think makes your head hurt?" I asked. "Somebody is slapping me with the palms of his hands." I asked whom he thought was doing so, and he answered, "Jack." "Why is he hitting you?" I asked. "Because I'm stupid. I can't do anything right. That's why Jack hits me." "What are your major emotions?" I asked. "I'm just **nervous** and **shaky**. I'm **tired** and **sleepy**. My head hurts," he answered. As I invited him to meet Jesus as his Savior and let Him take away all the stupidity, hurt, and so on, he readily did so. He chose the new name of **Wisdom**, and was fused and integrated with David.

## FRAGMENTED PERSONALITY DUMMY

Upon meeting the next fragmented personality, **Dummy**, age six, I learned that Jack used Dummy to cause confusion. "Who called you **Dummy**?" I asked. "Daddy", he said. "Why did he called you that?" "I don't remember." "Is it your job to make David not remember and to be confused?" I questioned. He answered, "Yes." When I asked what he did in adult David's life, he replied, "Yes, I can't remember and I do dumb things!" Asked what kind of dumb things, he answered, "I keep his mind thinking about other things. I don't let him think on the things he needs to think about," he answered. He said his major emotions were **nervousness, fear, and confusion**. He soon received the Lord, chose the new name of **Knowledge**, and was fused and integrated with David.

## TWO ANCESTRAL DEMONS AND THEIR HELPERS

David said, "Something is making my body feel different." It was at this point that I discovered ground that brought about **Demon Stupor and a mind-controlling demon named Blank**. Both worked for **Ancestral Demon Jack Wayne Flack** to keep David in a state much like that of hypnosis under their direction. This was the ancestral demon that had taken on David's daddy's name and was in coequal power with **Ancestral Demon David Wayne Flack**.

After we had found all the fragmented personalities, we dealt with the demons. Before reporting on this, let me give you a little background on David's dad. You recall that we learned that at the age of six months David had been dedicated to Satan by his dad. An aunt, acting as a high priestess, also

assisted in his dedication, along with a number of his father's fellow Masons. David's dad, a Mason and a Vietnam War Veteran, suffers from memory lapses and can't remember many things in the past. He told David that he coped with tough situations in life and in the Vietnam War by just going away in his mind. David and I are in hopes that in the near future we can help set his dad free from his own bondage.

I hope that in learning something about David's background and about his dad's background, you can better understand why David was a prime target for demonic entrapment in Kung Fu and Karate meditation. When David discontinued his Karate classes, he was only one test away from earning his Black Belt. The martial arts, steeped with eastern religion and culture, provided a fertile field for David's becoming programmed with demons. David is not an isolated case. I have worked with quite a number of people who have become demonic through the realm of martial arts. I believe that because of the days we're living in, filled with so much crime and violence, many fearful people have turned to martial arts to learn self-defense. As a result, many have fallen into traps of the demonic. There are others who enter such classes with a need to edify themselves--to build themselves up in their own eyes and, perhaps, in the eyes of others. I have been saddened when I have warned some people entering the martial arts of the dangers, but they have insisted they won't pick up demons because they don't participate in the meditation. While they may not intend to venture beyond **what they deem learning innocent self-defense**, Satan is cunning and will attempt to lure them beyond. A fact some fail to consider is that the instructor holding a Black Belt had to move into the dark world of meditation, giving his pain away to someone beyond and seeking power beyond himself and his normal physical abilities. While many stubbornly choose not to believe it, it is possible that they can even pick up demons and curses from the instructor.

## DECEPTION BEHIND FREE MASONRY

With regard to Free Masonry, my intent is to help free men from the deceptive grasps of such organizations. All too many Christian men are involved in this. I believe that by the time a member passes the level of a thirty-second degree Mason, he is deep into satanism. He may not recognize it but this is truth. Here again is another subject that I cannot cover as thoroughly as I would like to due to the lack of time and space. However, it is a very critical issue, therefore, I want to recommend that you read a Bible-based book entitled **Scarlet and the Beast** which comes in three volumes. This is an awesome reference researching Free Masonry written by **John Daniel**. This work can be purchased through **Jon Kregel, Inc.**, Box 131480, Tyler, Texas 75713. I would especially encourage pastors and counselors to have all three volumes in their library. I say this mainly because of the numerous ancestral demons that I have found connected with those involved in Free Masonry. I firmly believe that it truly has no rightful place in a Christian's life!

## MORE DEMONS IN DAVID'S LIFE

Continuing with David's story, you can see that it was taking an unusually long time to uncover all the demons in his life. Please keep in mind that the ancestral demon carrying the victim's formal name is always the one in charge of the others. There are times, however, when he will have a demon that works alongside him that has coequal power. If you counsel someone having such a system, don't be intimidated. Always force the ancestral demon with the formal name to give you the needed answers,

unless, of course, he actually doesn't <u>know</u> the answers. If that's the case, make the demon with the coequal power answer. We had such a situation in David's case.

## ANCESTRAL DEMON DAVID WAYNE FLACK

When I got **Ancestral Demon David Wayne Flack** up by the victim's formal name in our next session, I was able to find out that **Demon Lucifer (along with his thirteen-demon network) and Ancestral Demon David Wayne Flack were one and the same.** The network of **Demon Lucifer** had included: (1) **John I,** who caused pain; (2) **Fred**, who was mean, caused David to be mean, and told David he was lost; (3) **Melissa**, who caused perverted sex and bestiality; (4) **Chuck**, who performed the Karate; (5) **Ed**, who caused David to hit people; (6) **John II,** who caused David to whimper and whine; and (7) **Edward**, who caused cheating and stealing. Now we could see others: (8) **Ed II**, who caused David to mock and make fun of people; (9) **Molly**, who came at age fourteen when David had sex with his cousin, and who tempts David to lust and have sex; (10) **Hook-and-cable**, who kept him hooked and in bondage; (11) **Sleepy**, who kept David sleepy and tired; (12) **AC-DC**, who came through rock music concerts; and (13) **Captain Frogger**, who made diving David's god.

## DEMON-PRODUCED PERSONALITIES, HOOK-AND-CABLE, AND SLEEPY

We found demon-produced personalities: **Hook-and-cable** kept David hooked and in bondage, and worked with **Sleepy** to make David think he couldn't be free.

## ANCESTRAL DEMON JACK WAYNE FLACK

We found that the **ancestral demon** coming from David's dad's side and **carrying his father's name**, represented the **Masons and the satanists**. He said that he had gained ever-increasing ground through **shame** while David's dad was sexually abusing him. The six demons in his network were, (1) **Stupid**, who made him appear stupid; (2) **Shamed**, who belonged to the high priestess; (3) **Ronnie**, who caused homosexual desires; (4) **John**, who caused confusion and had two demons in his network, (a) **Profanity** and (b) **Vulgarity**; (5) **Stupor**, who controlled the mind through Demon Blank; and (6) **Rafo**, who caused the pain in David's head.

## DEMONS MASQUERADING AS PERSONALITIES

As we began searching for any **demons** that were **masquerading as personalities**, we found there were **eight** and that they were there to confuse David's work--stop it or at least slow it down. The masquerading demons were: (1) A seven-month-old calling itself, **Baby**; (2) an eight-month-old calling itself, **Baby II;** (3) a nine-month-old calling itself, **Baby III;** (4) **a two-year-old**; (5) **a three-year-old**; (6) **a six-month-old; dedicated to Satan during ritual worship to him**; (7) **a six-month-old claiming to be a twin**; and (8) **Ronnie**, who said he was ancestral born.

## DEMON CHUNG LING

**Demon Chung Ling** was the Kung Fu Monk Priest standing by the flame that David kept seeing in his mind. The ancestral demon confessed that Demon Chung Ling had thirteen demons in his network. Their names and works were, (1) **Leroy**, who was the Ninja fighter; (2) **Bruce**, also a fighter; (3) **Buddha**, who had power; (4) **White Sheet,** who had mind control; (5) **Chicken**, who performed the trigger or control work; (6) **Kai**, who had mind control, claiming power from the center of the body to look through objects; (7) **Don**, who was a trans-talker and was connected with a vow; (8) **Zen**, who claimed power with earth, wind, and fire, and power to kill; (9) **Ronny**, who traveled, transcending. He goes down, down, and performs hypnosis; (10) **Shadar**, who kills and is a mercenary; (11) **Ratatagh**, who was a gate keeper with the job of keeping a door open for the demons; (12) **Johhje**, who sent curses through the eye and had the death touch; and (13) **Doyopchagi**, who came from the Karate instructor.

## DEMON-PRODUCED PERSONALITIES

The Lord then revealed **five** demon-produced personalities. They were, (1) **John**, age five, who came through meditation; (2) **Chuck**, age thirty-five, who came through meditation; (3) **Ching**, who had the Karate silent death touch; (4) **Hara-Cara**, who controlled suicidal thoughts; and (5) **Dumb One**, who caused him not to be able to discern. The Lord enabled us to call in and deal with the demons from David's wife and two sons. The curses that had been placed on them and on me, were cancelled. (The demon had placed a curse of tiredness and weight gain on me.) We are so thankful that through our Lord Jesus Christ, the demons are rendered inoperative, their works cancelled out!

As you can well see, what started out to be a very simple case turned out to be a very lengthy, complicated one. I hope that you see, however, that the Lord Jesus was David's Counselor (using me as His vessel). Today, David and his family are free and productive for the Lord, and are in a Bible-centered church, solid in the Word. **God has truly done great things. To Him be the glory!**

# CHAPTER THIRTEEN
## DEFEATING DENIAL

### LADY DENIAL, CASE #16

**Susan Lynn Denial** is the name I have chosen to protect the identity of this delightful Christian lady I counseled. Susan was referred to me by a Christian therapist several years ago. After ten years of counseling--the last five with a Christian psychologist--Susan was still in a pitiful state. The referring therapist and I had worked before with one of her S.R.A. counselees, and she was very comfortable working with me. We were in total agreement concerning doctrine, including the issue of demons. Susan's psychologist, however, was opposed to Susan's coming to me, despite observing very little consistent improvement in Susan. The psychologist knew that in my counseling I dealt with demons, an area with which she struggled. She was afraid that I might destroy what had been accomplished in Susan's life. Considering Susan's critical state, however, and the possibility that I could help her, she allowed Susan to come. We scheduled five three-hour sessions in hopes that they would be sufficient, since some groundwork had already been laid.

The therapist had told me that Susan was an M.P.D. patient, but that she didn't believe there were many fragmented personalities. She also told me that Susan's psychologist, whom I'll call Dr. Amber, was talking to the personalities, but did not know how to fuse and integrate them. The therapist said that she believed that once **Dr. Amber** saw positive results from my work, she would not be opposed to my working with Susan. I am so grateful this turned out to be true.

### PITIFUL LITTLE SUSAN LYNN DENIAL

When **Susan** showed up for her first session, she was very frightened and withdrawn. She came to my office (which you recall is in our home). When Rita and I met her at the front door, her countenance was obviously that of an extreme introvert. She had a large bag hanging from her shoulder. As she sat down in my office, she opened her bag and took out a doll and a wadded up T-shirt. She curled up in the chair and hugged them tightly, withdrawn like a frightened, whipped puppy. The first three-hour session was spent mostly in just getting to know each other and in dispelling her fears. I shared what she could expect from my counseling, my plans for our next four sessions, and the high hopes I had for her full and speedy recovery.

I must say that even though this forty-year-old lady was so pitifully withdrawn, she **was so desperate that I saw glimpses of bravery beneath her cowering**. Susan expressed her sincere desire to be free. Susan shared that even though Dr. Amber hadn't really wanted her to come to me, she had felt in her heart that God had wanted her to come. Her trust in God--this almost-hidden spiritual stamina, would keep her coming back until she was totally free. Being diagnosed previously with M.P.D. (but believed to be having only a few fragmented personalities), neither she nor I had begun the session considering that she could be an **S.R.A. victim with fifty-three personalities** (including her core), **and a vast number of demons and their networks.** As you would guess, this case required more than the typical five three-hour sessions.

## MEETING TWELVE OF SUSAN'S FRAGMENTED PERSONALITIES

During those first five three-hour sessions, we found the **first group of fragmented personalities totaling twelve.** The old names and ages of the fragmented personalities were: (1) **Nobody**, age unknown; (2) **Mary**, age four; (3) **Julie**, age two or three; (4) **Katie**, age unknown; and (5) **Christian**, age nine or ten who was a boy who protected Susan. (He once tore up Dr. Amber's office and hit her.) (6) **Peggy**, age twelve; (7) **Susan**, age 20, who did the writing, liked sex, and helped the forty-year-old carry out the sex in her marriage. There was (8) **Debra**, age seven; and (9) **Donna**, age thirteen, who was very negative and said, "Susan is a pain in the b_____ to everybody, to the people that love her--she's just a b_____." She reported that she saw a baby on an altar and someone doing something gently to the baby, and then becoming violent with it. She believed the baby was dead. She also said there was a Claudia who was a b_____ to Casey (a neighbor and Satan worshipper). We were told by (10) **Claudia**, age five, "I do what Casey makes me do and I have sex with her, her husband, Mom, Dad, and two other neighbors. I take all the pain from adult Susan." Then, we learned that (11) **Cindy**, age eight, took the tears so the adults wouldn't hurt Susan. They hurt her more if she cried. I then met (12) **Susan Full of Doubt**. After dealing with her, I dealt with the twelve fragmented personalities as usual; all were fused and integrated and took on the same new name, Susan Lynn Denial.

## MEETING FLIP-SIDE PERSONALITY SUSAN

We then met **Flip-side Susan** who was angry and believed the core personality to be a wimp who could do nothing right. I then dealt with her and fused and integrated her with the core personality.

## S.R.A. VICTIM SUSAN'S DEMON DENIAL AND HIS HELPERS

The first demon we found was **Demon Denial** with ten demons in his network. Please keep in mind that most of the time that I worked with Susan, I didn't know about the ancestral demon with the victim's formal name. I learned that Demon Denial's ground was satanism and sexual abuse from Susan's dad, mom, and four neighbors. The names of the ten demons in his network were: (1) **Depression**; (2) **Alcohol addiction**; (3) **Fear**, (4) **Control**; (5) **Cigarettes**; (6) **Masturbation**; (7) **Rejection**; (8) **Anxiety**; (9) **Confusion**; and (10) **Anger**.

The Lord **confirmed** my growing suspicions that **Susan was an S.R.A. victim**, and, with Susan's permission, I contacted her pastor and Dr. Amber to inform them of what we had found. Dr. Amber then shared that she had over two hundred pictures that Susan had drawn, as well as numerous writings. She said she would allow Susan to bring them with her to our next session.

As soon as I began looking through the drawings and reading some of the writings, **any doubt** that Susan had been an S.R.A. victim **vanished**. Susan knew down deeply in her heart that it was true, yet having a natural love for her parents in spite of their abuse, she tried with all her might to deny and bury the horrible truth. What made her case even harder was the fact that her parents were professing Christians, active in leadership. This was not the first heartbreaking case I have had, with the parents professing to be Christians by day, yet being satanists by night. One case actually involved a pastor and his family using church facilities for satanic purposes in the wee hours of night.

From the beginning, Susan's parents had been opposed to her seeking counsel. However, when Dr. Amber appealed to them to come work with her to help Susan, they came to one session in order to save face. They were not at all cooperative, and were particularly upset when she asked them if they knew whether or not Susan had ever been sexually abused. Of course they denied the possibility. Susan's parents were active members of a very large Baptist church; when they learned that I had begun working with Susan, they sold their home and moved to another state.

## SUSAN'S MOMMY PERSONS AND TWO MORE FRAGMENTED PERSONALITIES

In Susan's next session, I met two more personalities. When I met fragmented personality (13) **Becky**, under the age of one, she said, "I don't like being a person or being away from the **mommy person. Dr. Amber is my mommy because I don't like my real mommy**. My real mommy makes me have **mommy sex**." When she spoke of the mommy person, I learned that from time to time, the children amidst the satanists were tended to by a woman other than their real mother, and that they referred to her as the **mommy person**.

Then I spoke with fragmented personality (14) **Ann**, who said, "I'm sad, confused, angry and frustrated." When I asked why, she said, "I had to have sex with daddy at the lake house. He fooled around with my brother sexually in front of me. We did sexual things together and he would masturbate." Following the usual procedure, we fused and integrated Becky and Ann during the session and they both assumed Susan's formal name.

You recall that I mentioned earlier that I have found that it is best, if possible, to fuse and integrate as you proceed. Susan said that doing this proved to enlarge her hope and faith, for she was beginning to see marked improvement in herself.

## THREE MORE FRAGMENTED PERSONALITIES

Susan's next session with me revealed three more fragmented personalities. There was (15) **Boo**, a boy age eight who liked to play while teasing and scaring people. He just liked to have fun. Then, there was (16) **Jenny**, age five, who would only allow Susan to cry if the mommy person were far away. She caused Susan to remember the **cave stuff** (which will be described later) and people putting rags in her mouth and sometimes **daddy sex** in her mouth. And then there was (17) **Sarah**, age four, who wanted to sleep all the time because she was so tired. She was tired because they kept her awake almost all night. These personalities were fused and integrated and assumed Susan's name as the others did.

## A DEMON NAMED SATAN

At this time, we found a **demon named Satan** who performed the sacrifices and had four demons in his network: (1) **Murder**; (2) **Perversion**; (3) **Fornication**; and (4) **Bestiality**. The demons on that ground were sent to the pit.

## ANOTHER FRAGMENTED PERSONALITY, WENDY

I had been looking for a **caretaker, baby sitter, or mother figure** within Susan, but thus far my efforts had been in vain. At Susan's next session I found an important fragmented personality, but not one who was a caretaker. Her name was (18) **Wendy**, age two, who held the emotions involved during the satanic sacrifices. I led Wendy to the Lord and fused and integrated her with Susan. She also took Susan's name.

## ALICE, THE CARETAKER

As I continued to search, I met (19) **Alice**. She was twenty-eight years old; she told me that she read a lot and needed to be in control. I asked her if she were a **caretaker**, and she answered, **"I'm in charge of Jennifer**, age four; **Pam**, age fifteen; **Lynn**, age ten; **Cathy**, age 2; **Suzanna**, age seven; and **Melody**, age sixteen." I led Alice to the Lord and she agreed to help me in our next session by introducing me to the ones under her care.

## DEMON BAAL PEOR AND HIS WORKERS

I had almost finished talking to Alice when **a demon suddenly came up--rudely interrupting**. His name was **Baal Peor,** and he had ten demons in his network. They were all connected to the ground in two-year-old Wendy. The ten demons were called, (1) **Inferiority**; (2) **Agnosticism**; (3) **Magic**; (4) **Promiscuity**; (5) **Cowardice**; (6) **Phallus** (means symbol of the penis); (7) **Goddess of sex;** (8) **Breast**; (9) **Blood**; and (10) **Waste**. I dealt with each as usual and asked the Lord to send them to the pit.

## EIGHT MORE FRAGMENTED PERSONALITIES

Over the next two sessions, I **met, through Alice's help, the six fragmented personalities of whom she was in charge**. As I met each one, I dealt with them as usual and led them to the Lord. I asked the Lord to place each one with Alice and to build with His blood a hedge of protection around them until we were able to fuse and integrate them all at the same time. From the six personalities under the care of Alice, I learned that (20) **Jennifer**, age four, liked to paint pictures of the sun with watercolors, and (21) **Lynn**, age ten, was an outside person, a tomboy who liked to play Dare Devil. Then I was introduced to (22) **Cathy**, age two, who was afraid and felt lost. She liked babies. She wandered around a lot and was very lonely. She also liked to read. Then I met (23) **Melody**, age sixteen, who said, "I build a fantasy world for Susan. I give her a place of escape and a way to cope. Good things in life are not real and they can't last."

**Alice** then introduced me to fragmented personality (24) **Pam**, age fifteen, who liked the outdoors. She said, "I like to take care of animals that need a mother. I like babies and I like keeping my sister. I like to put feeling and energy into taking care of animals. It keeps me from thinking about my need of a mommy or someone to take care of me. It hurts when no one cares. Somebody ran over my cat and it hurts."

Then, **Alice** introduced me to the next fragmented personality (25) **Suzanna**, age seven. Sucking her thumb between speaking, she said, "I suck my thumb so they can't put things in my mouth. I'm afraid

244

of the cave--they will kill me. They don't have faces. They hurt people, animals, and me. I don't like our neighbor Bill. He killed a deer and cut it all up and he tells me he will do the same thing to me. He puts his penis in my mouth and makes my neck hurt. I don't like him. He's dirty and a bad man." After I had dealt with all six personalities, I led Alice to invite each of them to come with her to meet Susan. All six were then fused and integrated.

While still in that session, I met two additional fragmented personalities, (26) **Jim Bob**, age ten-- another tomboy who protected Susan, and (27) **Melody**, twenty years old, who came about when Susan was having serious problems with her husband. I also learned that while she was in college, Susan found out about secret satanic meetings involving some young men she knew.

## MORE DEMONS IN SUSAN

After fusing and integrating Melody with Susan, I sought to find a demon that was apparently bothering Susan. **Demon Sanballat the Evil Spirit** surfaced, saying, "I invoke evil and the power of darkness in her life. I give her power and control over people that hurt her, especially her husband." **Sanballat** had a demon network of four: (1) **Intimidator**; (2) **Rage**; (3) **Sabotage**; and (4) **Lies**. Through the power of Jesus, I sent them to the pit.

## ANOTHER FRAGMENTED PERSONALITY, SHELLY

Susan came to the next session and we found fragmented personality (28) **Shelly**, age eight, who sucks her thumb. She told me, "Mommy is gone and they killed her and put her in a box." She kept crying because of her sorrow over the mommy person's death. I learned that children like Susan would have to watch the mommy person who had tended them be hurt or killed and, sometimes would even be made to participate in her murder.

## MEETING FRAGMENTED LITTLE SUSAN

It was during that same session in which we met Shelly that we met fragmented (29) **Little Susan**, who had been saved at the age of eight or nine. She had carried all the hurt because adult Susan wouldn't believe that she had gotten saved. I fused and integrated Little Susan with adult Susan after Adult Susan asked little eight or nine-year-old Susan to forgive her for doubting that she had gotten saved. From that day forward, Susan never doubted the day of her salvation. She had previously said she thought she had been saved at the age of fifteen or sixteen but was not confident of that fact.

## DR. AMBER HELPS US MEET TWO MORE FRAGMENTED PERSONALITIES

The next session would prove to be a tough but fruitful one. Dr. Amber came with Susan that day, because there were two personalities that showed up only when Susan was with Dr. Amber. As I began looking for the personalities, Susan laid across Dr. Amber's lap. Soon I met the two fragmented personalities, (30) **Marilyn**, age three, and (31) **Rose**, age three to six months. Both had been sexually abused on the altar when the **mommy person** was murdered. Both of these personalities desired **a mommy person, breast, and mommy sex**. Dr. Amber always did a great job at keeping proper boundaries with Susan and her other counselees, refusing to submit to their desires

to become involved physically. We got Marilyn's and Rose's stories and allowed them to give everything to Jesus, then fused and integrated the personalities.

## DEMON BEN-HADAD ARRIVES ON THE SCENE WITH HIS CREW

That same day, we found **Demon Ben-hadad. His ground was the worship of Satan**. He had stood on the ground of the now-fused Rose, age three to six months. He told me that Susan had been born with the **religious name, Isis**, and that she had been made **Satan's daughter at the age of two, and his wife at the age of five.** He had an eight-demon network: (1) **Abandonment**; (2) **Murder**; (3) **Fear**; (4) **Anxiety**; (5) **Helplessness**; (6) **Intimidation**; (7) **Harassment**; and (8) **Inferiority**.

## ANOTHER FRAGMENTED PERSONALITY PLUS THREE DEMONS ARE MET

At the next session we were able to meet (32) **Julie Anna** who was seven years old. She had been made to play the piano during some of the satanic rituals. She had made Susan feel guilty when she played the piano at church.

That day I also dealt with three major demons that stood on Julie Anna's ground. (1) **Gildad** who mocked Susan's God and said, "I'm told what to do to her by the lord Satan. I'm part of the sexual acts that were done on the altar to little Rose." (2) **Destroyer of Peace** who reported, "I'm a part of three-year-old Marilyn's ground. I make sure the murder of the mommy person destroys the peace in Susan's life. I hold her addiction to cigarettes and drinking." Then I dealt with (3) **Shinkar** who bragged, "I'm the Master Musician. I play for lord Satan. When Susan plays at church, I try to make Julie Anna play for lord Satan." Having dealt with them, I sent them to the pit.

## NIGHTMARES, NIGHTMARES, NIGHTMARES!

Susan called me about a week later and said that every night at two o'clock in the morning she would suddenly wake up, having had a nightmare. Each night the nightmare was the same. She began describing it, saying, "I saw three people in robes and I was upon the altar. I saw a shallow pit and a child was there. It was me. An iron grate was over the pit. I also saw a woman cut open and a baby being pushed into her stomach so it could be born again. I saw women in black, see-through robes and I could see their breasts in my face."

## ANOTHER FRAGMENTED PERSONALITY TO HELP

When Susan came back for her next session, I found (32) **Salinda**, age three, a fragmented personality who had suffered through agonizing experiences. We learned that she had been waking Susan up every night, further exposing the reality of what Susan had been through. This proved beneficial in helping confirm to Susan what she knew in her heart was truth. She was, indeed, an S.R.A. victim. Despite the pain, admitting this reality to herself drew her closer to freedom and peace of mind. Little Salinda met Jesus and gave all her pain to Him.

## DEALING WITH BEELZEBUB, THE MASTER DEMON

With Salinda fused with Susan, I went looking for the **ground of Salinda**. A demon spoke, identifying himself as, **Beelzebub, the Master Demon,** and he bragged of having twenty-seven demons in his network. Their names were, (1) **Murder**; (2) **Mockery**; (3) **Blood**; (4) **Captive**; (5) **Death**; (6) **Fear**; (7) **Loneliness**; (8) **Isolation**; (9) **Hunger**; (10) **Thirst**; (11) **Nightmare**; (12) **Depression**; (13) **Lust**; (14) **Shadow**; (15) **Sleeplessness**; (16) **Harassment**; (17) **Distortion**; (18) **Denial**; (19) **Hate**; (20) **Mistrust**; (21) **Confusion**; (22) **Suicide**; (23) **Destroyer of Peace**; (24) **Destroyer of Joy**; (25) **Worthlessness**; (26) **Exhaustion**; and (27) **Discomfort**. I asked the Lord to send Beelzebub and his twenty-seven demon network to the pit. (Remember, this was before I knew of the ancestral demon carrying the formal name.)

## ANOTHER FRAGMENTED PERSONALITY, SATAN'S DAUGHTER AND WIFE

Time for Susan's next appointment came. This was the day we came to meet and deal with fragmented personality (34) **Candy**. We learned that she was the one that Demon Ben-hadad said had been given the religious name of **Isis**--the one that was made Satan's daughter at age two and his wife at the age of five during satanic rituals. Candy told me, "I don't have any feelings. I just don't feel anything. I'm afraid and I'm scared I will die. I'm lying down and this face is over me and it's telling me that I'm his wife and I will see his face everywhere I go until the day I die."

Satan himself showed up and declared that I would not get his wife. I rebuked him by saying, "The Lord Jesus Christ rebuke you. Let Candy and Susan go, and tell me your demon network that stands on Candy's ground!" There was an **ancestral demon named Gana** that had a personal network of eleven demons. Their names were, (1) **Hostility**; (2) **Perversity**; (3) **Fear**; (4) **Guilt**; (5) **Shame**; (6) **Vindication**; (7) **Narcissism**; (8) **Mysticism**; (9) **Vanity**; (10) **Timidity**; and (11) **Salinda**.

There were also demons placed there by lord Satan himself called, **Hoz and Galiel**. **Demon Hoz** held the job of mental confusion, while **Demon Galiel** worked to cause faces in Susan's mind. Galiel had five demons in his network, (1) **Distortion**; (2) **Confusion**; (3) **Fear**; (4) **Mockery**; and (5) **Doubt**. We asked the Lord Jesus to overrule Satan's commands, and send them to the pit, and thanked Him for the power He gives to overcome Satan.

## ANOTHER FRAGMENTED PERSONALITY IS FUSED AND INTEGRATED

After this victory over Satan, we moved to the next group of fragmented personalities. Many surfaced who shared a great deal of information. I met pitiful little (35) **Becky**, age eight. She told me, "Holding and sucking a breast is love. Mommy taught me that while she held me and rocked me. She touched my breasts and in the part where my panties are. She took me to the cave. Daddy put something there where Mommy touches me--things you are supposed to eat--something that looks like Daddy's penis but it was off of a dog. It was a dog's part. They wanted the breast to be my god. I'm the one that drew the picture. They put a knife in her stomach and they put a knife in her breast. They put a penis in her mouth with the knife. They put a crown on her head and she was wearing a mask. Someone had the baby and held it upside down. They threw the baby in a big place. There were red eyes and they looked at me and there was a long black breast with eyes and it got on me and

then, that's all I could see." Becky readily allowed the Lord Jesus to take all this horrible mess to the cross. She received Him as Savior, welcomed His peace and joy, and became whole with Susan.

## MORE VICTORIES ARE WON OVER THE DEMONIC

On the **ground** of Becky, the Lord Jesus uncovered a **major network of demons**. All of a sudden a voice said, ***"I'm Satan, the most powerful, and I will not give up this network!"*** I responded to him by saying, "The Lord Jesus Christ rebuke you! Give up the ground and give me the names of the demons in your network!" He proceeded to tell me that the demon in charge was **Demon Lust** who had twenty-five demons in his network. They were: (1) **Sex**; (2) **Breast**; (3) **Death**; (4) **Alcohol**; (5) **Negative**; (6) **Bitch**; (7) **Suffering**; (8) **Enticement**; (9) **Blasphemy**; (10) **Manipulation**; (11) **Atheism**; (12) **Confusion**; (13) **Deceit**; (14) **Delirium**; (15) **Sucking**; (16) **Immaturity**; (17) **Infantile Spirit**; (18) **Cross-fire who fires hateful, negative thoughts and is malicious**; (19) **Cannibal**; (20) **Incantation**; (21) **Breast-Cut-Off**; (22) **Slumber**; (23) **Killer**; (24) **Gangrene-Barrier** who claimed to be like a wall; cuts off whatever he chooses from her; covers her face with blood; keeps out healthy love; keeps out truth; causes deafness and numbness; (25) **Self-Destruction.**

## SIX DEMON-PRODUCED PERSONALITIES DEFEATED

Then, we discovered six demon-produced personalities in **Susan**. There were demon produced personalities of (1) **Dad**, (2) **Mom**, (3) **Brenda** (a cousin on her dad's side); (4) **Marge**; (5) **Jenny**; and (6) **Nanna**. They were dealt with as usual.

## SEVEN MORE TRAGICALLY FRAGMENTED PERSONALITIES

In our next counseling session, I met two personalities. The first was (36) **Wanda**, a three-year-old, who came up crying. Between whimpers she said, "I cry and I make Christmas bad for Susan. I had to watch them hurt baby Jesus. The manger scene is not like it's supposed to be. They mock the birth of Jesus. I talk to the dogs that belong to the people in the cave. The dogs are yellow. They make me see where they wet and they make me look at their poop. I cry because I am sad and scared. Christmas makes me think of all the people that were dancing naked and all the sex." As with the others, I led Wanda to give all this to Jesus.

Then I met the other fragmented personality, (37) **Loucis**. She said, "My name Loucis stands for Lucifer and Halloween." Then she shared, "I talk in rhymes. I feel fear when you (Joe) are near and I don't like it here. I want Dr. Amber soon. I want to see her soon." I encouraged her not to be afraid of me--that I loved her and wanted to help her. She then shared, "On Halloween things are seen, and they are mean on Halloween. They hurt me too. They s_____ and p_____ and make me eat it. The grate's on top and I cannot get out of it or they will s_____ on me and make me drink their p_____. Tick-tock, tick-tock goes the clock, throw the block, and lock the lock. When it's time for them to dine, the blood and the flesh and all the rest, they make a mess, they hurt me less. But if I pout they lock me out within the grate, where I am hid they lock the lock and close the lid. They sit on top, they p_____ and s_____ and I can't do anything about it. They touch me bad and it makes me mad, and I feel sad. Much touch, touch much. Touch much means love much. Amber is a safety touch and Amber loves me much. With Jesus will I be safe just to be me? 'Cause Jesus is the Light and there's no more defeat at night because I'm in His Light.  My Jesus is my Light.  In the day, will He light the way, and in Him all is right because the darkness, He turns to light."

In our next session, we met five more fragmented personalities, **Amey, Debbie, Push-Button, Big Girl, and Charleen.**  As I met strong little (38) **Amey, five years old**, she said, "I ain't gonna run no more but I ain't gonna talk.  They put diapers on me and they like to do things to me.  I pretend that it's not really me.  They put their penises out and p_____ all over the babies in the baskets.  I ain't gonna cry about it.  He (the demon) makes me act like a baby."

We then met poor little (39) **Debbie**, age one, who said, "They take me away from my mommy and make mommy stay with another baby and watch me hurt.  I want to be the only baby."  After dealing with Debbie, I spoke with (40) **Push-Button**, fifteen years old, who shared, "I push all the buttons on the phone and I tell her what to do.  I push all the buttons on the phone that gets her help.  I push the buttons that get you (Joe).  I push the buttons that keep her going."

It was (41) **Big Girl**, age twelve, who spoke next.  She shared, "I feel crazy.  I punish myself when I'm jealous of the babies.  I must punish myself.  I'm angry and I can't cry.  The baby, the baby.  If the baby dies, it's not my fault!"  Then, I met (42) **Charleen**, age two, who said, "I'm there for Amber to love.  They put me in the grate and the dogs walk on the grate and they p_____ when it's late."

## DEMONS HIDING BEHIND THE NAME OF JESUS

After I dealt with the five personalities, I then dealt with a large demon network, some uniquely different from those usually dealt with.  I must say at this point that the counselor dealing with demons must **be wisely discerning concerning some demons that actually take on names such as Jesus, Baby Jesus, and God the Father.  This discernment, of course, must come from the Lord, for the demons can fool the counselor if he is not right with the Lord and depending strictly upon Him for wisdom.**  A demon may cause the counselee to pray in mockery to another demon rather than to the Lord Jesus.  This is particularly true in S.R.A. cases.  This is why I stress the importance of thoroughly questioning **"Will this stand as truth before the eternal throne of Jesus?"** until you have a confidence and peace.  When you ask if this is truth, the demon may answer, "Yes" because he is thinking of it standing as truth before the <u>demon</u> carrying the name Jesus.  As you persist, the Lord will aid you in exposing the truth.  When the Lord reveals to me that we have contacted such a demon, I begin having the counselee pray to the "Lord Jehovah or Yahweh who threw Lucifer out of heaven and will soon throw him into the lake of fire."  When you clarify exactly which Jesus you are talking about, the demon cannot say that it will stand as truth before the real Jesus Christ.  Now, let's take a look at the next demon network we found in Susan's life.

## DEMON TORMENT AND HIS NETWORK

We found **Demon Torment**, who caused her to hate; **he had twenty-seven demons in his network**.  They were, (1) **Unforgiveness**, who was opposed to one of her counselors; (2) **Sleepless**; (3) **Greed**, who caused Susan to want all the love; (4) **Terrify**; (5) **Fear**; (6) **Slumber**; (7) **Gangrene**, who claimed to cause the disease (destruction) of the mind; (8) **Termite**, who ate away at all good; (9) **"Jesus"**, who confused, deceived, and lied; (10) **Lord Baal**, who called himself lord, lord; (11) **Pig**, who was gluttonous; (12) **Alcohol**; (13) **Nicotine**; (14) **I See**, who saw inside her and told her that she was bad; (15) **Death**, who put self-destructive thoughts in her mind; (16) **Nasty**, who put nasty (vulgar) thoughts into her mind; (17) **Fang**, who gave her nightmares; (18) **Cradle**, who kept the babies so they couldn't grow up; (19) **Flower**, who kept beauty in the dark so it couldn't be seen; (20) **Light**, who made her see dark; (21) **Benadad**, who put her in the circle with the candle; (22) **Wizard**, who did magical spells to make her act crazy; (23) **Pierce with Knife**, who pierced babies with the knife; (24) **Gorilla**, who was on top of the babies, raping them; (25) **Champion**, who fantasized and bragged about having the biggest penis; (26) **Hate**, who hated the babies; and (27) **Jealous**, who felt jealous of the babies.

I commanded Torment to tell me if there were any more networks besides his and he said, "Yes," and reported Demon Savilinel, a demon who stood on Amey's ground and had only one demon in his network--Passive. Torment also reported Demon Flesh Eater whose ground was in Susan, and Demon Eternal Black Hole who was in charge of the mockery and telling Susan that she will never get better.

## FRAGMENTED PERSONALITY AMEY

In Susan's next session with me, I met her next fragmented personality: (43) **Amey, age two**. When I began questioning **Amey**, she said, "I'm too sleepy. I've been up all night and I can't sleep. I have to go with them to the dark place. They make me drink something--Coke in a bottle--and it makes me sleepy. I get hungry and my stomach hurts." I asked if they kept her from eating and she answered, "Yes--no--maybe sometimes. I don't want the **mommy person** to go away. They hurt the **mommy person**. I have to eat birds. I dreamed about two birds that we had to eat. They say if the baby dies it's my fault. I did not want the **mommy person** to have another baby. There will be no room for me. I don't want to grow up."

## DEMON RITUALISTIC ABUSE AND HIS NETWORK

The demons I found on Amey's ground were (1) **Demon Ritualistic Abuse** who reported, "I harass, confuse, and distort the truth. I promote helplessness, hopelessness, and insecurity in spiritual things." There were thirteen demons in his network, (1) Dogma, who indoctrinated false teachings; (2) **Sanheim**, who sucked away the truth; (3) **Criss-cross**, who defiled the cross and perverted the story of what was done there; (4) **Damage**, who promoted destruction and decay in Susan's relationships and fellowship; (5) **Thumb Sucker**, who promoted immature behavior that interfered with her growing up; (6) **Jim Bob,** who caused hopelessness and discouragement. He sent messages of despair that nothing positive would work. He made it difficult for Susan to work and grow in the Lord. The remainder of the thirteen demons were (7) **Finiel**, who fought truth; (8) **Gloom**, who brought dark clouds and fog and made it hard for Susan to understand things, to play, to work, or to feel alive; (9) **Breast Baby**, who maintained a mental attachment to Dr. Amber's breasts and baby nurturing; (10) **Rejection**, who caused Susan to reject the genuine love of Jesus; (11) **The Shield**, who kept out the truth and said that it couldn't be penetrated--even with God's love--and also claimed to keep out healing and maturity from the victim; and protected other demons; (12) **Penetration**, who penetrated Susan's heart with lies, numbness, and confusion. He also penetrated her heart with selfishness, fear, insecurity, anxiety, panic, and all manner of darkness; and (13) **The Eye**, who watched for friends and people like himself. He had the right to draw them in to affect Susan's life with evil and discouragement, and he had one demon--**Clincher**--working for him.

## CLINCHER, THE SHARED DEMON

**Clincher**, working for **Demon The Eye, was a shared demon between Susan and another woman**. **We'll call her Vicky**. Vicky was a new member in Susan's church and she was demonic. **Clincher** caused Susan to want to grasp Vicky and cling to her. While counseling Susan, **Clincher** reported that he was a sharing demon from Vicky and he said, "I'm here to suck her into my power and clinch her in my fist. I'm here to cause her to hate God, to hate life, to hate truth, and to bring questions of doubt about her counselor, Joe Allbright!" Because **Clincher** was actually Vicky's demon standing on ground in her life, **I had no other choice but to send it back to Vicky and seal, by Susan's choice, the doorway against his being able to re-enter Susan's life.** Susan's and my hope was that Vicky would eventually consent to being counseled and to let God free her also.

## ANOTHER FRAGMENTED PERSONALITY

In my next session with Susan, we met another pitiful, fragmented personality--(44) **Julie**, age three. She sadly told me, "When I hurt myself, I get a bottle to suck on. So, I hurt myself on purpose so I can have a bottle, but sometimes I hurt myself accidentally. Sometimes I hurt myself out of anger. When other people hurt me, I get a bottle too." I asked Julie how they hurt her and she replied, "They touch me." I questioned to learn if they had hurt her sexually and she shared, "They let me touch myself and they watch and it makes them feel good. Also, they show me their bodies. The mommy gets on me and the daddy gets on me and they do things to me."

## DEMON SELF AND HIS HELPERS

The demon that I found on three-year-old Julie's ground was named **Demon Self**, and he had eleven demons in his network. They were: (1) **Self Pleasure**; (2) **Split Self**, who split Susan in two; (3) **Self Focus**; (4) **Sex**, who did mommy and daddy sex; (5) **Depression**; (6) **Control**; (7) **Fear**; (8) **Terror**; (9) **Abandonment**; (10) **Insecurity**; and (11) **Yanni**, who lied, deceived, and planted seeds of doubt, and plotted confusion and vain imaginations.

## FRAGMENTED PERSONALITIES ANDRA AND BABY CHARLIE

As we would **deal with the final nine fragmented personalities** and the demons that were standing on their ground, **we were at the lowest level**. Please understand if I were to give some of the information I received, reading about this and other S.R.A. cases would be extremely unpleasant. Therefore, I have shared only enough material that I have deemed necessary to help counselors know what to expect from S.R.A. counselees in general. Even leaving out the more horrifying, morbid, and vulgar details, this continues to be a sad but true story.

The next fragmented personality was sorrowful little (45) **Andra**, age four, who proceeded to tell me, "I have to watch the yucky stuff in the cave. One time when Susan's stomach was hurting, I told her to cut the woman's stomach open with a cross. I had to watch the yucky stuff. All the men stood around on each side of the woman with her stomach cut open. They put things inside where she was cut and they drank out of it." Andra continued, "Sometimes I want mommy sex. I put my head under my shirt so I can see my breasts. When I touch my breasts, I don't have to cry. I like to do sexual things with myself."

I questioned Andra as to what she thought about adult Susan and she said, "I like her." I then asked Andra if she would like to get well and she said, "Yes, but I still want to hold the mommy person's breast. I'm afraid of Susan's husband. I'm not safe with anyone but the mommy person." Andra finally released her attachment to the mommy person and received the Lord Jesus as her safe place, her refuge. She gave all the yucky stuff to Jesus. She also gave away her need for mommy sex and to hold onto a mommy. She prayed to be free of her fear of Susan's husband also. Then Andra prayed, asking Jesus to give her a new name. She wanted to share Susan's name.

Next, I met fragmented personality (46) **Baby Charlie**, age one. He proceeded to tell me, "I'm too tired and I like to stay with Dr. Amber and I like to sleep. It feels so good when Dr. Amber holds me and just lets me sleep. The people will not let me sleep. They put stuff in the bottle and it keeps me awake. It tastes sweet." I asked Charlie what they did with him when he was awake and he replied, "They make my eyes stay open and they want to see my thing (penis). They say Susan wants a thing because her brother and all the men have one. I cause her to put things on herself so she will think that she has a thing. I like to suck my thumb."

"What else do you do in Susan's life?" I asked. Charlie replied, "I make her stay awake at night and think." I then asked if he were the one who makes her so tired during the day so that she can't get her work done. He said, "I don't mean to make Susan tired. I want Dr. Amber to hold me even though she has her own grandbaby."

## DEMON GOLIATH AND HIS CREW, MET AND DEALT WITH

The demon that stood on Andra's ground was **Demon Goliath**. He reported, "I make her afraid because I'm a giant and my job is to make her feel little." Demon Goliath had ten demons in his network. They were, (1) **Joe-Blow**, who did sexual things; (2) **F_____-head**, who kept foul language in Susan's life; (3) **G.D.,** who put words in her head; (4) **Jimmy G.,** who made Susan like and want to feel Dr. Amber's skirts and legs; (5) **Bottleneck**, who made her keep liking baby bottles and made her put things in herself; (6) **Fool**, who told her she was a fool and made her feel like a fool; (7) **Piddler**, who made it hard for Susan to stay focused on one thing and to finish it, and he found many ways to sap her energy and destroy her attention; (8) **Black**, who kept a lot of darkness in both her husband's and her lives. He kept Susan, her husband, and children blinded from truth they needed to see; (9) **Spiral**, who kept things going around in a cycle to cause confusion and hopelessness. It ruined Susan's relationship with her husband, who hated the cycle. Susan improved slightly, only to get worse again. Both feared the cycle would never end. Then there was demon (10) **Midnight**, who woke Susan at midnight, bringing thoughts of horror, keeping her awake, and interfering with her rest.

## DEMON WORLDLY AND HIS NETWORK

On one-year-old fragmented personality Charlie's ground, I found **Demon Worldly**, who declared that his job was to keep Susan in a worldly walk so that she wouldn't have a godly walk as a Christian. **Demon Worldly** had four demons in his network. They were (1) **Counterfeit**, who caused Susan to seek after love from everyone except Christ, the Truth. He caused her to hear things that weren't truth; (2) **Exhaustion**, whose job was to keep her so tired that she felt depressed, helpless and hopeless; and (3) **Lust of the Flesh**, whose job was to cause her to desire many things of

the world that were contrary to God's plan for her life. He filled Susan's life with feelings of loneliness, lust, and discontentment, and kept her from getting her flesh under control. Then, I dealt with (4) **Infant**, who kept Susan focused on staying little and believing it's better to stay little. He worked to keep her from receiving things as an adult, insisting she must receive things as a little person, or that it wouldn't be any good.

## MEET THREE MORE FRAGMENTED PERSONALITIES AND THEIR DEMONS

In our next counseling session, we met fragmented personalities, **Anna, Jan, and Elizabeth**. As I spoke with sad little (47) **Anna**, age two, she shared, "I stay in bed, and I don't move. I have to stay in bed because I can't get out. They tie my hands and feet to the bars on the bed. Nobody will come and I don't like the dark. Mommy won't come. Nobody comes and they leave me in the dark and I can't see. I want my mommy. Nobody will cover me and nobody will touch me. Nobody will give me a drink and I can't see."

I asked Anna what she did in adult Susan's life; she replied, "I come when she doesn't feel good or she's very tired and hungry. I come when she's hurt and doesn't feel like going on. That's when I want to be with Dr. Amber or phone her. When Susan feels tired, I feel all those things again in her head and emotions. I make her phone Dr. Amber and if she's not there I cry." I asked, "Anna, are you the one who tells me you must be touched so that you will be assured that you are really there?" She answered, "Yes. Nobody would come. Nobody would touch me."

## DEMON FEAR AND HIS NETWORK IS DEALT WITH

After dealing with Anna as I had the others, I discovered **Demon Fear and his network** that stood on two-year-old Anna's ground. Demon Fear bragged, "I cause fear and loss of control in Susan's life, giving her a loss of security over her feelings when she's in situations. I keep her from feeling up to par." I learned that he had nine demons in his network, and they were: (1) **Loneliness**, who magnified her feelings of emptiness and caused despair and loneliness; (2) **Helplessness**, who prevented her from taking charge; (3) **Insecurity**, who prevented her from being secure in knowing who she was in Jesus Christ; (4) **Immaturity**, who caused her to handle matters immaturely; (5) **Sadness**, who stole away her joy; (6) **Coldness**, who made her put her needs first and to be uncompassionate toward the needs of others; (7) **Carelessness**, who hardened her heart toward God and her husband; (8) **Darkness**, who caused her days to be dark and depressing; (9) **Blindness**, who blinded her from seeing what God wanted her to see and know.

Upon talking with the next pitiful little fragmented personality, I met (48) **Jan**, age three-years-old, who sadly reported, "They stick things in my mouth. They take off my clothes and do things to me. They tie me down so I can't do anything about it."

I asked Jan what she did in adult Susan's life; she said, "I tell her about all they did to her and I make her think bad things." I asked her if the bad things were about sex, and she answered, "Well, a little. I tell her that her body is not pretty and it is nasty to let her husband touch her body. But, I like to snuggle with the mommy person. I wish the mommy person would snuggle me. I don't like her (Susan's) husband to touch me. I don't want the mommy person to see me because she will see what they did to me and think I'm dirty."

## DEMON SHANTU AND HIS NETWORK OF FRIENDS

**Demon Shantu** was the demon that stood on three-year-old Jan's ground. He declared, "I am the godhead, and I interfere with her sex with her husband. I cut off all her feelings when she is with him. These feelings belong to Satan and his friends. I bring back feelings that she's not safe and I make her feel little. I bring up the desire for her to have sex with herself because she thinks that's safe." Demon Shantu had five demons in his network and they were: (1) **Incest**; (2) **Homosexuality**; (3) **Masturbation**; (4) **Fear**; and (5) **Numbness**. All were defeated!

## FRAGMENTED PERSONALITY ELIZABETH

It was time to meet fragmented personality (49) **Elizabeth**, age five, who makes Susan sleep. She shared, "When I'm in Dr. Amber's office, I make Susan turn her back away from Dr. Amber and act like she's asleep." I asked her why she would do that, and she admitted, "I don't want Dr. Amber to look at me. I hide behind things but I want to be close enough to touch. I want her to rock me and hold me. She makes me mad because she won't let me touch her breasts. Sometimes I cry and hide behind the pillow and I feel very sad."

I asked her what else she did in adult Susan's life and she shared, "I don't let her tell the secret about Ann Frances (Susan's mother) and what she did to me. She did a number of sexual things to her. Why did she and Daddy go around me without any clothes on?"

## LUCIFER, SINGING PRAISES TO HIMSELF

Just as we were finishing up fusing and integrating the personalities, **an evil voice started singing**, "Drink, drink from the cup. Drink, drink it all up. Praise me, lord Lucifer!" I commanded him to stop singing and tell me the ground that he stood on. He confessed that he stood on Elizabeth's ground, and swore repeatedly, as truth before the eternal throne of Jesus Christ, that he was Lucifer who was thrown out of heaven. He reported that he placed **Demon Golson with a network of six demons** in Susan's life. Through the power of the Lord Jesus Christ, he was sent out from Susan's life and I dealt with Demon Golson and his network. Lucifer had said about Demon Golson, "He's my friend! He's my brother! He's my right-hand man! He reduces productivity and causes exhaustion. He causes Susan to drink and go to sleep and not to take care of her family the way she should."

**Within Demon Golson's network**, I dealt with the six demons, (1) **Denial**, who boasted of being the gate keeper and of holding the job of making Susan stay in a state of denial; (2) **Alcohol**; (3) **Mute**, who kept Susan and Elizabeth from telling the secret; (4) **Mommy Sex**; (5) **Black Robe Sex**; and (6) **Bondage**.

## DEMON-PRODUCED PERSONALITIES, SUSAN AND ANN FRANCES

I also dealt with two demon-produced personalities named **Demon Susan** and **Demon Ann Frances**, with which I dealt. They were there to lure Susan to entertain memories of the sexual abuse and satanic rituals and consider getting involved in such acts.

## ANOTHER FRAGMENTED PERSONALITY, LURI

During the next counseling session, I met (50) **Luri**, age five, who said, "The woods are aflame. That's where we play the game. The game and the flame are always the same. I like to dance in the circle and they are going around in the circle. As they go around in the circle, they open their robes to show their bodies because they have no clothes on. They drop their robes."

When I asked Luri what she did in adult Susan's life, she said, "I keep her quiet! She has a big mouth and tells too much. I also pull her to the woods and get her to drink to forget. I, Luri, am here to keep secrets." Having dealt with these personalities as usual, I moved on to deal with the demons.

## SEVEN MORE DEMONS DEFEATED

I learned that **Demon Self** held the ground on five-year-old Luri, and that there were seven demons in his network. They were: (1) **Destruction**; (2) **Pleasure**; (3) **Self Medication**; (4) **Destroyer**; (5) **Anxiety**; (6) **Self Loathing**; and (7) **Critical Spirit**.

## MOMMY PERSON, MOMMY PERSON! I NEED YOU, MOMMY PERSON!

In our next session, Susan and Dr. Amber knew that we were very close to being through--at least with my part of the counseling. Two more sessions would follow this one. Dr. Amber and I learned that we still had **some little ones who stubbornly refused to let go of the mommy person**.

I feel led to inject a critical truth here. As a counselor, it is of the utmost importance not to let your counselee lure you into letting them remain in a baby stage because you sympathize with their having been deprived of having a good mother or father. Many truly sympathetic counselors fall into the trap of trying to give a deprived counselee the parent they longed for and never had. Dr. Amber, out of her love and sympathy for Susan, did make the mistake of letting Susan stay in the baby stage through five years of counseling. In doing so, Susan was allowed--through her personalities--to become addicted to her counselor, substituting her for the sweet and kind mother she never had. I must add that there are even some counselors who easily fall into **Satan's parent-trap** out of their own personal need--their need to feel needed. **This wasn't the case with Dr. Amber**. A counselor having godly compassion and mercy upon such counselees, will lovingly but <u>firmly</u> share God's truths that will set the counselee free to let Him become their Father. He is the only one who can bring them to ultimate freedom and maturity!

## ONLY A FEW MORE FRAGMENTED PERSONALITIES TO GO

In this session, I met **Too Tired and Frances**. When I met (51) **Too Tired**, eight years old, she pled, "I just want to be held and I don't want to talk anymore. I just want to go to sleep so I won't have to feel anything and I can be safe. I don't want people to see that I'm ugly and undressed. I want to play games and be silly and when the bad stuff comes, I just want to hide and go to sleep on the mommy person. I get angry when my mommy person (Dr. Amber) doesn't understand what I need. I feel too ashamed and embarrassed. I feel very attached to her. I don't want to let her go because there won't be anyone else there to love me. I don't want to share her with others. I'll just get pushed down in the dirt." She was so insistent about clinging to Dr. Amber, that time ran out in our session and I had to deal with Too Tired again in our next session. She did then release her mental grasp on Dr. Amber, turned to the Lord for her comfort and security, and was fused and integrated with Susan. She also received Dr. Amber for whom she was supposed to be for her--a Christian counselor who would help her to grow into the mature adult God intended her to be.

Fragmented personality (52) **Frances**, age two, was, with the exception of her age, almost a carbon copy of Too Tired. She, too, didn't want to turn loose of her mommy person, Dr. Amber. Shortly, she also confessed her unhealthy dependence, however, and became one with Susan.

## THE ANCESTRAL DEMON CAUGHT STUMBLING OVER HIS OWN TONGUE!

By this time I had learned of the ancestral demon carrying the formal name of the victim. As you have no doubt noticed, many of the demons--those that stood on the ground of various personalities-- had names that were identical or similar to those of the personalities. As I've said earlier in the book, the ancestral demon carrying the formal name stays in the shadows and can feed a lot of lies to you. Even before I learned this, God was very merciful in helping me expose and deal with scores of personalities and demons in many people's lives. I'm so grateful that He finally got my attention concerning the demon in charge--who still had the power to call in more demons even after the previous ones had been made to leave and we had thought that we were finished.

## A MASQUERADING CLONE OF SUSAN

During this session **I commanded by the authority of Christ that Ancestral Demon Susan Lynn Denial come up and talk with me.** All of a sudden a voice shouted, "She's a G.D. B_____ and that God of hers, I hate! I want her dead!" I asked why he hated Jesus and he declared, "Because He's the victory!" He told me that the **iniquity he had was passed down through satanism.**

I then asked him if he had been masquerading as a clone of Susan, as a flip-side, alongside her core from age zero to present. He bragged, "That's what I do!" I asked him if he made Susan believe that he were actually Susan--that his thoughts and feelings were hers. He answered, "Yes! She's a sorry, weak little worm that can't do anything!" I asked him if he were the one making the two personalities **Too Tired and Frances** hold onto the **mommy person.** He boasted, "I lock them and their emotions up and I have the key. You can't get them! I didn't let them fuse and integrate because I have the key--**not only to them but there is another you will not find because she's the button to it all!"**

You will recall from reading the beautiful Psalm 64--applying it to the counselee in demonic bondage, that God can make the demons stumble over their own tongues. Prayerfully read from **The Christian Life Bible in the New King James Version** this principle that can bring victory to the most tightly bound of counselees:

> *Hear my voice, O God, my meditation; preserve my life from fear of the enemy. Hide me from the secret plots of the wicked, from the rebellion of the workers of iniquity, who sharpen their tongue like a sword, and bend their bows to shoot their arrows--bitter words, that they may shoot in secret at the blameless; suddenly they shoot at him and do not fear. They encourage themselves in an evil matter; they talk of laying snares secretly; they say, 'Who will see them?' They devise iniquities: 'We*

*have perfected a shrewd scheme.' Both the inward thought and the heart of man are deep. <u>But God shall shoot at them with an arrow; Suddenly they shall be wounded. So He will make them stumble over their own tongue.</u> All who see them shall flee away. All men shall fear, and shall declare the work of God; for they shall wisely consider His doing. The righteous shall be glad in the Lord, and trust in Him. And all the upright in heart shall glory.*

As you read this Psalm, mindful of applying it to the demonic and spiritual warfare, you can see a powerful statement and promise as you look at verses seven and eight (underlined). You can see that God even promised those as tightly bound as Susan to shoot their demons with an arrow, so that they would be wounded and **stumble over their own tongue**. We can see this promise being fulfilled in Susan's life.

Turning our focus back to Susan's ancestral demon carrying her formal name, you will recall that he had told me that he had the two personalities plus the flip-side locked up, preventing the three personalities from fusing and integrating. When the ancestral demon told me that there was another that was the button to it all, he tripped over his own tongue and revealed the existence of another personality. This again verifies that as we trust in the Lord to help us counsel, He will always provide His wisdom necessary for each situation (Phil. 4:19). I asked the Lord to break the lock of which the ancestral demon spoke, and to bring up the personalities, which He did immediately. The Lord fused and integrated two-year-old **Frances** and eight-year-old **Too Tired**, along with the forty-three-year-old **Flip-side**.

## MEET BUTTONS, THE FRAGMENTED PERSONALITY

While the demons were still bound away, I sought to find the undiscovered personality of which the ancestral demon had spoken. I felt certain that he may have tripped over his own tongue and given a **clue** when he boasted, **"There's another you will not find because she's the button to it all."** As you will see, often their **stumblings** come in very clear, simplistic forms. **I asked to speak to the personality called Buttons**. The personality named (53) **Buttons**, age nine, declared, "I fold things and make things out of nothing. I can be very creative. I never get to do anything. Susan doesn't let me do anything. Susan thinks she can do it better. I'm the one who draws in Dr. Amber's office."

I asked Buttons what she did in adult Susan's life. She answered, "Sometimes I don't do her any favors. I hate it when her husband screams or the children act up. I create problems with my mouth!" I asked her why she wouldn't come out and talk with me when I had been looking for personalities earlier. She replied, "They wouldn't let me talk to you. They kept telling me I wasn't worth anything unless Dr. Amber loved me and held me. I can't do anything without calling Dr. Amber. I'm the one who used to push all the buttons and they made me act like I shouldn't. I wonder if one of my buttons makes me feel far away from God even though He says He loves everybody. I don't feel like He loves me. I have a smart mouth because it keeps the hurt away." After nine-year-old Buttons was fused and integrated, and I was unable to find any more personalities, I went after the ancestral demon and his network.

**ANCESTRAL DEMON SUSAN LYNN DENIAL**

When I got Ancestral Demon Susan back by the power of the Lord Jesus, I made him tell me about all his network. His personal network was made up of ten demons. I asked him if he did anything else in Susan's life. He replied, "I make her hate who she is--her name means **lame and crippled**. I gave her a blue shirt." I asked what the blue shirt meant, and he said, "Sadness, depression, and darkness--doom and gloom." (This was the T-shirt she clung to.) I asked him if he were the one responsible for her attachment to the **mommy person**. He admitted that he was. I then asked if all the demons that we thought we had dealt with actually existed. He said, "Yes and no. Some of them were real, and I let you have them so I could stay covered, and some of them were just me--lying so I could waste your time!"

The Lord revealed ten demons in his network. They were (1) **Passion**, who gave her passion for ungodly thoughts and things; (2) **Jupiter**, who sent into her mind unidentified flying objects to make her think she was crazy, and to waste her time by her trying to determine what the objects were and whether or not they were real; (3) **Nonsense Language**, who caused her to speak in rhymes; (4) **Slinky**, who prevented all her memories--from the age of zero to the age of forty-two--from going away; (5) **Loss**, who caused the loss of joy, happiness, motivation, love, mercy, existence, humanness, humility, security, and maturity; (6) **Ranu**, who caused her to focus on other gods--Satan and the idol of idleness; (7) **Blue Shirt**, who caused sadness, depression, darkness, doom and gloom; (8) **Gossip**, who reported whispering lies into her head about her not being worth anything. He told her lies about what she could and couldn't do. He acted out and told lies about God. He told her that her worth was wrapped up in how Dr. Amber treated her--whether or not she touched her, and how she touched her when she did. He intimidated her by telling her that if she grew and matured, she couldn't have a relationship with Dr. Amber and that <u>Susan</u> would be a loser. If she made a mistake, she was bad. He was there to magnify every fault and to whisper in pictures, words and feelings; (9) **Deceit**, who kept a wall between Susan and her husband and children. He worked in subtle ways: the wall kept others from really seeing Susan as she was; and (10) **Denial**, who caused her to deny truth and Scripture. He also caused the emotional, physical, sexual, spiritual, and satanic abuse. He made her deny the positives that people really felt and thought about her.

**DEMON-PRODUCED PERSONALITIES IN SUSAN**

There were demon-produced personalities in Susan that went by the names of **Mom, Dad, Richard Lane, Grandmother Proof, Dr. Amber, and her husband Roy**. These demon-produced personalities represented all the evil, negatives, and weaknesses in each person. As you have noticed, in all demon-produced personalities, you will only see negatives, never any positive attributes.

**SUSAN'S VICTORY IS COMPLETE! THANK YOU, LORD!**

I made Ancestral Demon Susan tell me about all the satanic demons--demons performing rituals in satanic worship--for whom he was responsible, including the ones that were yet to be dealt with. Through the power of the Lord Jesus, he was made to call the remaining ones up. This ancestral demon--being the demon in charge, as a territorial demon is--was made to call in every demon under his command and attach them to himself. I then asked the Lord Jesus to send them all to the pit.

I have written this on December 3, 1994. I just talked with Susan this week and she is really doing well. She and Dr. Amber are working on her being responsible for her life as an adult. As I spoke with her on the phone, she sounded as if she were really growing in the Lord by leaps and bounds. **For a lady who was at one time such a grievous mess, such a sad little person, it was delightful to hear happiness as well as maturity in her voice. Once again, to God be all the glory, for He hath done great things!**

# CHAPTER FOURTEEN
## A DESPERATE YOUNG MAN WITH A GLIMMER OF HOPE, CASE #17

I received a long distance phone call from a lady, whom I'll refer to as **Amy**. She was seeking help for her nephew. I'll refer to him as **Jack**. He had been in a number of lock-ups in different types of mental hospitals. Amy was desperate for Jack to get help and felt that his condition was not due to mental illness but rather to the demonic. In spite of it being about six months before I could see Jack, Amy set up appointments.

Shortly before Jack's appointment time came, Amy called and cancelled them. Jack was back in mental lock-up and the hospital refused to allow her to bring him to Houston for his appointments. Amy rescheduled appointments for three months down the line. She was convinced if she could get Jack here for counseling, God would heal and set him free.

At last, Jack was out of the hospital and Amy could bring him. They were standing at my door thirty minutes early, desperate and anxious to begin the counseling. When Rita and I greeted them at the door and invited them in, Amy was bright-eyed and smiling beautifully with eyes full of hope. Jack, handsome as he was, looked pathetic. Perspiration was running down his face, he was trembling all over and stammering in speech. Clearly, he was deeply depressed, troubled, and heavily medicated. We could see that he was desperate and only weakly held to a glimmer of hope.

As we began work that day, I found that Jack's family had experienced problems with him most of his twenty-two years. He had almost died of food poisoning somewhere between three to six months of age. Jack told me that he had been hospitalized most of his life because of his anger and rage. At one time, he had even been placed in a home for retarded children.

He shared that the doctors had diagnosed him as A.D.D. (Attention Deficit Disorder), manic depressive, bi-polar-manic, and paranoid-schizophrenic. He was on nine medications. One medication was to reduce his blood pressure because some of the other medications caused it to rise to a dangerously high level. These medications made him literally drip with perspiration to the extent that Rita brought him a towel to keep draped around his neck to wipe with.

Jack told me how he would become angry and go into raging fits. When I asked him what triggered the raging, he told me that the noises in his head drove him so mad that they sent him into fierce raging. I asked if he had ever heard voices. He responded that he had heard voices and drums beating in his head all his life, and that the beating of the drums would grow so loud that he was afraid he would lose his mind. Jack added that when he got saved at age seven, the sounds of the drums grew worse. His raging only increased with the years. Sometimes he would rage to the point of even wanting to kill his parents, but he was able to refrain from it and instead destroy personal properties in his parents' home.

Over the several days that we worked, God showed us an ancestral demon carrying Jack's full formal name, plus a number of demon networks. God also revealed a flip-side of Jack and a number of fragmented personalities. Some came about during his sickness with food poisoning as a young child. Others came about during the hospitalizations, his stay in the home for the retarded children, and when he was rejected by his parents and others involved in his life. God allowed us to fuse and integrate the personalities including the flip-side, and to cast out all the demons and send them to the pit. Jack was free at last.

Our counseling sessions were completed and Jack and his Aunt Amy were leaving for home. Jack turned to me and smiled a beautiful smile and said, "I'm not hearing the drums and voices. For the first time in my life, I feel peaceful."

I had advised Jack and Amy to consult with his doctors about tapering off the medications, and asked them to please keep me posted on his progress. A few weeks later, Amy called and assured us that Jack had only a few very minor struggles. She also reported that he was off of all his medications except a mild sedative and a blood pressure medication, which they felt he could quit taking soon. She said that he was really growing in the Lord.

A number of months later, we received handsome pictures of Jack, clearly reflecting the peace and joy of Jesus, along with the following letters:

**Excerpts from Aunt Amy's letter:**

> Dear Rita and Joe,
>
> Do you recognize the young man in the picture? He doesn't look like the Jack Jones you all first met, does he?
> I just wanted to let you both know how much I appreciate what you did for Jack through our Lord and Savior, Jesus Christ. Sometimes when I think back, it all seems pretty hard to believe.
> As a word of testimony: Jack was in a state school to the tune of $10,000 a month. He was heavily medicated, compulsive, violent, and most likely going to spend the rest of his life in a state mental institution. After prayer and counseling with you, Joe, his life has changed dramatically. He has lost 50 pounds, is living independently in an apartment, owns and drives his own car, goes to church regularly, and recently became friends with some fine Christian university students in our church. He went from smoking three packs of cigarettes a day, compulsively, to none at all the last three months. He had a job at his apartment complex this summer and we are working with the state's rehabilitation commission to find him a full-time job. The medication he takes at night is a

mild sedative. That certainly sounds like a miracle, doesn't it? He has no bad dreams at night and sleeps peacefully. He also sees his parents several times a week and seems to have a good relationship with them now. He has had no violent or explosive behavior since we came home. Now, I'm not going to say that the moment we came back, it was a bed of roses. It wasn't. There were a few frustrating days, but God was faithful and true to His Word....

Jack's letter:

Dear Joe and Rita,

Thank you for saving my life through Christ. It Makes me want to cry for joy when I think about the past, the way I was before. Me and my family are so close--it is so cool. I met this really nice, good, and fine Christian girl, and we go to luncheons, Bible studies on college campus, and church together.

Thanks so much for the help you have given me. I finally have the heavenly peace that Christ gives.

Letter from Jack's mother:

Dear Joe,

Words cannot express how thankful we are that God has brought you and your wife, Rita, into Jack's life and into our lives. We see our Lord working in Jack's life every minute of every day.

Thank you for helping Jack find freedom through our Lord Jesus Christ. Jack has a wonderful testimony of how he has found freedom through Jesus Christ.

Please continue to keep Jack and all of us in your prayers.

As you can see from the above letters, Jack and his family are enjoying the spiritual healing and freedom that God wants His children to enjoy. **To God be the glory, great things He hath done, indeed!**

# Glossary

# PART I
## THE DEMONIC

1. **Lucifer**: The anointed cherub before his fall from heaven. (Isaiah 14:12-14; Ezekiel 28:11-17)

2. **Day Star**: Another name for Lucifer or Satan (Isaiah 14:12-14; see note in New Scofield Study Bible, page 725)

3. **Satan**: The name given to Lucifer after his fall; the name Satan means adversary, accuser. (I Peter 5:8; Revelation 12:10)

4. **Demons**: Evil spirits, unclean spirits, fallen angels working for Satan. They tempt, lie, and deceive.

5. **Demonic influence/attack**: Temptation, lies, and deception coming at a person from the outside.

6. **Demonization**: Control by one or more demons from within a person.

7. **Power Demon**: The head demon controlling a person's life. If a person has an ancestral demon carrying his or her formal name, and perhaps other demons as well, the ancestral demon is the power demon--the boss. Like a General in the military, he is the demon in authority over any other demons the person may have. If a person is demonized but there are no ancestral demons from any relatives, there will still be a power demon positioned higher--like unto a Captain or Lieutenant--in authority over all other demons operating in that person's life.

8. **Demon networks**: A group of demons following orders of the power demon and/or another demon leader over them. There can be many networks with leaders like unto Sergeants, Lieutenants, and Captains, but all the leaders answer to the power demon.

9. **Ancestral Demon carrying a person's formal name**: The ancestral demon is one acquired at conception, inheriting iniquity passed down from a parent. (Numbers 14:18; Deut. 5:9) The ancestral demon always arrogantly carries the full formal name of the person he holds captive. If a person has this type of demon, it is <u>always</u> the top demon--like unto a General-- over all other demons that person may have. That ancestral demon has the ability to pass down to the next generation.

10. **Ancestral Demon carrying another relative's name or work**: This type of demon is passed down from ancestors other than the parents. While it is ancestral, it still operates like unto a Colonel under the authority of the General, the ancestral demon carrying the person's formal name. Frequently, they admit from whom they came but go by names describing the work they do or did in a person's life, such as Rage, Lust, Bitterness, Greed, Jealousy, etc.

11. **Lifestyle demon**: A demon picked up through a person's consistently sinful lifestyle. Involvement in pornography, homosexuality, prostitution, rock music, Ouija board, occult activities, etc, welcomes demons. If the person does not repent and reclaim the ground, they can pass this demon down as an ancestral demon to the next generations.

12. **Demons masquerading as personalities**: These demons masquerade--or mimic--the person's core, flip-side, or fragmented personalities, in an effort to prevent the real core, flip-side, or fragmented personalities from being dealt with. However, they sometimes profess to be a fragmented personality that does not really exist--again, to side-track the counselor.

13. **Demon-produced personality**: A demon that carries the name and age of another, real person. They are like a clone of a person and answer by that person's name. They reflect all evil, negativeness, and weakness in that person's life. It may be a demon-produced personality like unto a relative, abuser, or sexual partner. They enact that person's abusive lifestyle in the person they are indwelling.

14. **Demon Satan**; Demon Lucifer; Demon Destroyer; Demon Jesus; Demon Heavenly Father, etc: Demons sometimes use such names to intimidate and confuse the person and his counselor. They all answer to the power demon.

15. **Demon of false tongue**: An act of gibberish language performed either by an ancestral demon or a demon that was acquired while begging for the gift of tongues and/or submitting to improper laying on of hands. The demon deceives the person into believing they are exercising God's gift of tongues.

16. **Demon of clairvoyance**, sorcery, or special knowledge: Demons passed down ancestrally or through seeking supernatural powers contrary to God.

# PART II
## PERSONALITIES

1.  **Core personality**: The individual's personality that God thought up from the foundation of the world. This personality should be the one in charge of their life. The core is always soft and pliable, and holds the ability to be teachable, repentant, and open to salvation.

2.  **Flip-side**: The flip-side is the opposite, negative side of the core personality. As a second-soul, split-soul, or duplex, it manipulates and controls the core personality. At conception, the ancestral demon brings the flip-side into being and programs the flip-side with the iniquity of the fathers and his own personality as well.

3.  **Fragmented personality**: A personality that fragmented off from the core or the flip-side during a traumatic experience such as verbal abuse, emotional abuse, sexual abuse/rape, loneliness, abandonment, rejection, etc.

4.  **Administrative personalities**: A type of fragmented personality that keeps the other fragmented personalities organized to some degree so that the core personality can still function in the everyday world. Often, they operate under names such as Mom, Caretaker, Controller, Teacher, Organizer, Delegator, or Baby Sitter.

5.  **Helper personalities**: Fragmented personalities that perform certain duties that the core personality feels incapable of handling. The fragmented personalities frequently do house and/or office work, cook, handle parental obligations, submit to sexual obligations in the marriage, etc.

6.  **Suicidal or destroyer personalities**: Fragmented personalities acquired through the core personality suffering rejection or abuse. The suicidal or destroyer personality torments the core with lies of his/her being so bad that they don't deserve to live, or that life is so unbearable that they would be better off dead or at least punished with self-inflicted pain.

# ANSWERS TO QUESTIONS MOST COMMONLY ASKED

1.  **Can Christians have demons?** Yes. They are acquired ancestrally as a result of the iniquity of the former generations and/or through one's own personal iniquity.

2.  **Can a Christian have a flip-side personality and fragmented personalities?** Yes.

3.  **If a person hears voices or has fragmented personalities, are they crazy and incurable?** No to both! It is not normal to hear voices that constantly chatter, curse, or condemn you. God says that He wants us to have an abundant life, which one can't have if they have all that confusion going on within. (John 10:10) Also, He wants us to have a sound mind and a renewed mind. (II Timothy 1:7; Hebrews 12:1,2)

4.  All **Christians, including those set free of demons, are subject to demonic attack (or influence). How does this differ from demonization in its effects and in its remedy?** Demonic attack or temptation comes in forms of temptation from the outside with hopes of gaining ground, thus control. The Christian under demonic attack must choose to either yield to the temptation or resist by biblically standing in their authority in Christ and commanding Satan and his demons to flee. James 4:7 says, "Submit yourselves therefore to God. Resist the devil, and he will flee from you". Demonization differs from demonic attack or influence in that the demons have already acquired ground, thus control the person by issuing orders from the inside. The demonized person has the choice to either yield to the controlling demons or resist by turning to Christ, repenting, reclaiming the ground, and commanding the demons to leave.

5.  **Is a person evil if they have a demon?** Yes and no. Yes if they are aware of living a sinful lifestyle, enjoy it, and choose to keep it. They have willingly allowed themselves to be saturated with evil. No if they sincerely want to cease living a sinful lifestyle, detest it, and want to be released from the stronghold. In that case, only the demon is evil.

6.  **Does a counselee have to have a good understanding of the demonic (belief in capabilities of demons, understanding of how personalities are produced, etc.) in order to be freed?** I believe the more informed the counselee is about the demonic and personalities, the more apt they are to relax, agree with and help the counselor. Trust and unity are great weapons of spiritual warfare for the counselee and counselor. The Bible says, "Can two walk together, except they be agreed?" (Amos 3:3). Therefore, the more unity in understanding and applying the information, the more readily the counselee and counselor can accomplish their goals.

7.  **Though the counselee sincerely desires to be helped and is open to the techniques of the counselor, will skepticism about demonization hinder their liberation?** Yes! I have found that this type of person will either never enjoy freedom or will take much longer to attain freedom than someone who is more confident in God's teachings on the matter. Skepticism stands in opposition to faith in God's truths that assure the captive freedom. As

Jesus told the woman who reached out and touched the hem of his garment, "...thy faith hath made thee whole. Go in peace..." (Mark 5:34).

8.  **Can a person with demons and fragmented personalities be healed without being a Christian?** No. The lost individual must first recognize their lost, sinful state and repent and receive Christ as their personal Savior. It is through their belief in Him as their Redeemer that they are made whole and have the Holy Spirit living within as their power to defeat Satan and his demons.

9.  **Can the demons within a person be removed and sent to the pit without the personalities being fused and integrated with the core personality?** No, because the unhealed, still-fragmented personalities are the ground, the sin or iniquity, that the demons still stand on in that person's life. They can only be sent to the pit when they have no more ground on which to stand.

10. **When a flip-side is fused and integrated can a person acquire another flip-side?** No, the ancestral demon creates a flip-side only at conception or birth.

11. **If a person confesses all sin and reclaims all ground, would all demons (except ancestral demons) leave without further action being taken?** While this is not impossible, I have not found this to be typical, particularly with acutely demonized persons. The demons usually stubbornly stand, awaiting an opportunity to reclaim the ground taken from them, until they are confronted and challenged by the name and presence of the Lord Jesus Christ. The Lord encourages those who are spiritually stronger to "...encourage the fainthearted, support the weak..." (I Thess. 5:14) and two in unity with God are assured in God's Word, "...where two or three are gathered together in my name, there am I in the midst of them" (Matthew 18:20). Often a stronger Christian backing the person brings quicker and more lasting results.

12. **Can a Christian individual, through the Lord Jesus, free himself from demons?** Yes, but it is usually done a lot easier and in a shorter period of time by someone who knows how to help them.

13. **Can a person live a godly, fruitful, obedient life despite demonization?** Yes. However, while they appear to others to be strong, godly people, on the inside they are tormented and void of God's intended abundant life--true peace and joy. Often, the person even joins forces with the demons by condemning and beating-up on themselves.

14. **Can one acquire a demon or demons from a Ouija board if they nonchalantly play with it?** Yes. The demon doesn't care about the measure of your openness to seeking knowledge against God's will. All the devil needs is for the door to be left ajar. "Give him an inch and he will take a mile."

15. Can **a person pick up demons from rock concerts and listening to hard-rock tapes?** Yes. I have dealt with people who have picked up demons both ways.

16. **Can one pick up a demon from having their palm read or having their fortune told?** Yes. God forbids seeking fortune tellers. Demons can be transferred while you hold hands with the fortune teller and when you open your mind and heart up to seek and know the future that is not yours to know.

17. **Can one pick up demons while having sex with a demonic person?** Yes. If the person having sex with a demonic person has sin in their life, the demon has a right to transfer.

18. **Do prostitutes, male or female, have demons?** Yes. I have never worked with a prostitute or a homosexual person who did not have demons. If a person has sex with them, because such an act of submitting to their lifestyle is a sin, the demon has an open invitation to enter that person also.

19. After a demonic person is liberated, are demons likely to attack them from without with the same type of deceit, lies and temptations as those that formerly came from within? Yes. Satan and his demons always hit first where a person is most vulnerable. They attempt to regain control of the liberated person by discouraging them in any way possible. They typically lie, trying to make them doubt that they are really free. When a victim is freed from satanic ritualistic abuse, it is not uncommon for the satanic brotherhood to send demons out in an attempt to get the person back. The demons typically bombard the person with lies, trying to make them believe that God does not really love or want them and that He is not powerful enough to set them free or keep them free.

20. **Can ancestral demons be passed down from sides of both father and mother?** Yes. It is because God holds the male responsible for his family--accountable as the authority figure-- that God addresses the issue as "...iniquity of the fathers...".

21. **Since the probability of iniquity somewhere within three or four generations of ancestry is very great, isn't it likely that there is a far less percentage of people who do not have an ancestral demon?** The longer I have dealt with ancestral demons linked with the iniquity of the fathers, I have come to believe there are far more people affected by ancestral demons than I ever thought possible.

22. **Can ancestral demons pass down from a person to their children and/or grandchildren?** Yes.

23. **If someone has an ancestral demon and they have five children, will all of them have ancestral demons in their lives?** Not necessarily. I have seen all, none, or only a few of a family's offspring have ancestral demons. I have also seen the ancestral demon in either all the boys or all the girls in a family. I've also observed in some families that only the first-born, girl or boy, has the ancestral demon.

24. **Through personal counseling, can a father/mother set their children free from the ancestral demon without the children going to counseling?** Yes and no. Yes if the children are not yet of the age of accountability. The demons can be called in from them

through the ancestral demon carrying the father's formal name. And, no if the children are of the age of accountability, since they are then responsible for their own actions.

25. **If a demonized Christian dies, will he go to heaven?** Yes. The demon leaves the deceased's body and will also leave the body of a demonic, raptured Christian, for they can't go to heaven with the Christian. Also, there is nothing that can keep a Christian from going to heaven. But, as long as he or she is in their earthly body, they will be tormented until they are set free.

26. **Can a Christian with fragmented personalities go to heaven?** Yes. The moment the Christian dies or is raptured, his soul is healed and restored. But, as long as they are in their earthly body, they will be tormented unless they are healed and whole.

27. **If a person has a flip-side or fragmented personalities that reject Christ and need to accept Him and be fused and integrated that they might be a spiritually whole person, will only a part of that person go to heaven if they die before they are healed?** No! Jesus Christ saves the whole person positionally but while they are in their earthly bodies they need to be healed like unto a fragmented, splintered bone. When they die, they are immediately liberated and whole.

28. **Can demons come back in a person after they have been freed?** Yes, if they don't stay **snuggled up** to the Lord and keep their life clean they will be in worse shape than in the beginning. (Matthew 12:43; Luke 11:24)

# BIBLIOGRAPHY

Alexander William M., Demonic Possession in the New Testament. Michigan: Baker Book House, 1980.

Anderson, Neil T., The Bondage Breaker. Eugene, Oregon 97402: Harvest House Publishers, 1990.

Atkinson, Basil, Commentary on Leviticus Pocker Commentary on the Bible. Chicago: Moody 1957

Baker Warren, Ed., The Complete Word Study Old Testament. Chattanooga, Tn. 37422: AMG Publishers, 1994.

Bubeck, Mark I., The Adversary. Chicago: Moody Press, 1975.

Criswell, W. A., The Criswell Study Bible. Nashville: Thomas-Nelson Publishers, 1979.

DeHaan, Richard W., Satan, Satanism and Witchcraft. Grand Rapids: Zondervan Publishing House, 1972.

Dickason, Fred C., Demon Possession and the Christian. Westchester, Illinois: Crossway Books - A division of Good News Publishers, 1989.

Edersheim, Alfred, The Life and Times of Jesus the Messiah, Vol. 2. Grand Rapids, Michigan: W$^m$. B. Eerdmans Publishing Co., Reprinted, March 1980.

Ensign, Grayson H. and Edward Howe, Counseling and Demonization. Amarillo, Texas 79114: Recovery Publications, 1989.

Frangipane, Francis, The Divine Antidote. Cedar Rapids, IA 52410: Arrow Publications, 1944.

Freeman, Irwin Rocky, D.Min., Th.D., Ph.D., Victory Flight Over Powers of Darkness. Fort Worth, Texas: Patroc Publishing, _____.

Frieson, James G., Ph.D., Uncovering the Mystery of M.P.D. San Bernardino, Ca. 92402: Here's Life Publishers, Inc., 1991.

Gilmore, George W., Demon, Demoniac, New Schaff-Herzog Encyclopedia of Religious Knowledge, Vol. III, Grand Rapids: Baker Book House, _____.

Gothard, Bill, The Life Purpose Journal, Vol. #4. Oak Brook, Il: IBLP Publication, _____.

Guinness, Alma E., Ed., <u>ABC's of the Human Body</u>. Pleasantville, New York, Montreal: The Reader's Digest Association, Inc., 1987.

Heim, Karl, <u>Jesus Der Weltvollender</u>. Verlag, Berlin, 1937.

Hester, H. I., <u>The Heart of the New Testament</u>. Twenty-third Printing, Liberty, Missouri: The Quality Press, Inc., 1963.

Hodge, Charles, <u>Systematic Theology II</u>, reprint, Grand Rapids, Mich.: W. B. Eerdmans, N.d.

Koch, Kurt, <u>Between Christ and Satan</u>. Grand Rapids: Kregal Publications, 1961. _____.

<u>Christian Counseling and Occultism</u>. Grand Rapids: Kregel Publications, 1972. _____.

<u>Demonology Past and Present</u>. Grand Rapids: Kregel Publications, 1973. _____.

<u>Occult ABC</u>. Germany: Literature Mission Aglasterhausen, Inc., 1978. _____.

<u>Occult Bondage and Deliverance</u>. Grand Rapids: Kregal Publications, _____.

Langton, Edward, <u>Satan, A Portrait</u>. London: Sheffington and Son, Ltd., 1945.

Meade, Russell, <u>Victory Over Demonism Today</u>. Chicago: Christian Life, 1962.

Morris, Henry M., <u>The Genesis Record</u>. Michigan: Baker Book House, 1976.

Nevius, John L., <u>Demon Possession</u>. Grand Rapids: Kregal Publications, 1968.

Newport, John P., <u>Demons, Demons, Demons</u>. Nashville: Broadman Press, 1972.

Oesterreich, T. K., <u>Possession, Demonical and Other Among Primitive Races in Antiquity, Middle Ages, and Modern Times</u>. New York: R. Long and R. Smith, Inc., 1930.

Peck, M. Scott, M.D., <u>The Road Less Traveled</u>, New York: A Touchstone Book Published Simon and Schuster, 1978.

Pember, G. H., M.A., <u>Earth's Earliest Ages and Their Connection with Modern Spiritualism and Theosophy</u>, revised and enlarged edition of Earth's Earliest Ages and Their Lessons for us, 1876. Westwood, N.J.: Fleming H. Revell Co., Ca. 1900.

Penn-Lewis, Jessie, <u>War on the Saints</u>, New York: Thomas E. Lowe, Ltd., 1979.

Rockstad, Ernest B., <u>Symptoms of Demonic Invasion</u>. Andover: Faith and Life Publications, __.

Scofield, C. I., The New Scofield Study Bible. New York: Oxford University Press, 1967.

Spence, H. D., Very Rev. M.A., D.D., Pulpit Commentary, Vol. 5. Grand Rapids, Michigan: W^m. B. Eerdmans Publishing Company.

Spurgeon, C. H., Treasury of David, Vol. II, Grand Rapids, Mich.: Guardian Press, 3 printing, 1981.

Stanley, Charles, Forgiveness. Nashville: Oliver Nelson - A Division of Thomas Nelson Publishers, 1987.

Strong, Augustus H., Systematic Theology. Valley Forge: Judson Press, 1907.

Sumrall, Lester, Demons the Answer Book, Nashville: Thomas-Nelson Publishers, 1979.

Taylor, Jack R., Victory Over the Devil. Nashville: Broadman Press, 1973.

Tenney, Merrill C., Ed., The Zondervan Pictorial Encyclopedia of the Bible, Vol. I, II, III, IV. Grand Rapids: Zondervan Corporation, 1980.

The Christian Life Bible, The New King James Version. Nashville. Camden. New York: Thomas Nelson Publishers, 1985.

The Holy Bible. King James Version, New York: The World Publishing Company.

The New American Standard Bible. California: The Foundation Press Publications, 1971.

The New Testament and Wycliffe Bible Commentary. New York: The Iversen-Norman Associates, 1973.

Unger, Merrill F., Biblical Demonology. Wheaton, Ill.: Scripture Press, 1975._____.

Demons in the World Today. Illinois: Tyndale House Publishers, 1971. _____.

What Demons Can Do To Saints. Chicago: Moody Press, 1977.

Vine, W. E., An Expository Dictionary of New Testament Words. Westwood, N.J.: Fleming H. Revell Co., 1966.

Webster's Dictionary, The New Lexicon of the English Language. New York: Lexicon Publications, Inc., 1989.

Webster's New Twentieth Century Dictionary, Second Edition, William Collins and World Publishing Co., Inc.

Wright, J. Stafford, <u>Christianity and the Occult</u>. Chicago: Press, 1971.

Wuest, Kenneth S., <u>Word Studies from the Greek New Testament</u>. Grand Rapids: Eerdmans Publishing Co., 1973.

Zodhiates, Spiros, Th.D., <u>The Complete Word Study Dictionary New Testament</u>. Chattanooga, Tn. 37422: AMG Publishers, 1992.